DIVIDED SOCIETY

DIVIDED SOCIETY

The Ethnic Experience
in America

EDITED BY

Colin Greer

BASIC BOOKS, INC., PUBLISHERS

NEW YORK

CONTENTS

APPENDIX I

APPENDIX II

APPENDIX III

Contents

PREFACE

TO some extent this book opposes what I have called the "Handlin School" of ethnic studies. I use that phrase because I believe that the perspective represented by Oscar Handlin, and by many students of ethnicity and immigration who followed him, has been detrimental to our real understanding of American society. At the same time, I would not minimize Handlin's achievement: he presented a marvelously human—though grandiose—vision of the American ethnic experience in *The Uprooted* and in his succeeding work, which reinforced the American Dream after years of war, disunity, and terrible domestic persecution. Furthermore, he has not been —by any means—as narrowly tied to his own early formulations and perspective as have his disciples. Indeed, many a young revisionist historian has acknowledged his debt to Handlin. And as the reader may see in "The Goals of Integration" (in Appendix II, p. 334), Handlin has recognized, with foresight, the real ethnic issues at stake in platforms for "racial integration."

My challenge to Handlin and his School is that I do not see evidence for believing in the continuing progress of America's historic democratic destiny, nor am I able to justify the human costs that the School is willing to pay for such progress. This book is an attempt to reinterpret, and thereby clarify, what has become a conventional misunderstanding.

The anthology is organized thematically. "Assimilation and Mobility" suggests the complexity of the accommodation process, the inclusion of blacks within it, the standards which have dominated, and the personal agonies involved.

It also looks at the economic experience of millions of immigrants. "Most (Un)Favored Peoples" addresses various aspects of the culture and national origins of different groups which may have determined the specific experience of that group in America. Finally, "Ethnicity and Class" suggests the complicated overlapping and interaction of class and ethnic issues in America and is the theme of my introductory essay. Appendixes of shorter selections are intended to provide more detail.

PART I

REMEMBERING
CLASS:
AN INTERPRETATION

THE new emphasis on ethnic identity in the early 1970s shows that our views on immigration and ethnicity have changed little since Oscar Handlin's work in the 1950s. Handlin still provides the framework for understanding the absorption of immigrants in expanding American cities, and our public policy, as well as the education of those who make it, adheres to the myths of the Handlin School—which actually bear so little relation to the misery of the lower classes in the cities. Since, however, these myths celebrate the democratic structure of American society, constantly including more and more in its prosperity, those who are perennially left behind are blamed for their immobility; it is the miserable victim who is blamed for his own condition.

Thus, the individual's ethnic consciousness becomes the impetus for scaling the socioeconomic ladder. Ethnic solidarity then (or the lack of it) explains success and failure. So one of the ironic contradictions in capitalism, that it perennially throws up the expectation of improvement among those it needs to exploit, leads to unfortunate situations in which urban white workers, for example, disdain "black welfare" or "Jewish capital" or "Appalachian ignorance" to an extent that seems to undercut the commonality of their work experience and the frightening insecurities which very often go with it.

Social position, as defined by one group's hegemony over another, reflects a picture of America in which various factions resolve conflicts between their respective ambitions and hostilities through a detente predicated on the respective strength and status of their grouping; this armed truce is supposed, because of the alleged ability of the democratic, egalitarian socioeconomy, to be at once a benefit to the individuals involved and to the nation as a whole.

3

As in the 1950s, scholars and pollsters are monitoring these groups, their cultural characteristics, their political preferences, and their voting potential—thereby confirming the assumptions underlying the ideology of ethnicity in America. Ethnicity is becoming the keystone of a contemporary facade designed to obscure the fragility of America's egalitarian self-image. It seems to be growing in an effort to provide an excuse or rationale for the inability of this nation to honor its promises of the 1960s, promises which had to do with recognizing—for a brief moment in history—the vast gap between wealth and poverty in this nation (and the relative poverty of conventional notions of adequate income) and trying to do something about it.

Ethnicity has been used in this way before. In the 1950s the dual faith in those myths—in ethnic diversity (Pluralism, as it was called) and in economic mobility—was so powerful that it was in fact only when that faith was brought into serious question, if only temporarily, that even the tentative egalitarians in the sixties could begin to flourish. Now we witness a self-styled New Pluralism being constructed, a new drive in political and intellectual conservative circles to encourage our resignation to these old myths once again—to the old promises and to the old social paralysis. Contemporary spokesmen for a conservative social stance dispense with what they consider to be naïve and utopian images of an improved society and look back to a time when people with the strength of character and strength of will to make it did so— and others were not expected to. Given the restrictive and restraining conditions of the social order, they claim, social security and mobility was never easy for anybody. There is social stability in this direction, unpleasant though it might be for some; indeed, it is important to recognize that society is comforted from social disequilibrium with the aid of this illusory conservative history and sociology, particularly the kind of violent social upheavals that we became accustomed to in the 1960s. In this context ethnic diversity serves as a focus in a new attempt to convince ourselves of the "making-it" story in America.

What we are talking about, then, is not a vision of America which posits a different method by which the improved society may be achieved, nor even a view of America which posits an excusatory rationale by claiming an historic trend in which gradual steps toward the improvement of society have been taken. Rather we are looking at a long-standing viewpoint in American social criticism (in decline in the 1960s) which views the particular vision of the improved society of the 1960s as naïve and unattainable. This is a viewpoint in which, as Irving Kristol expressed it, certain kinds of costs are paid and justified by the standards of excellence we achieve as a culture—standards of excellence, incidentally, which are enjoyed and experienced by a small minority of individuals in that culture.[1]

I'm not talking about a view which denies failure and the cost of failure, but rather a view which minimizes it even though it is here at high cost for vast numbers. Two things are operating: one, the world is improving for some people, for parts of groups; two, democracy is working—given the limitations of culture and preparation with which people came to this country, how could one expect more? We are on a slowly progressing continuum to the future. As Oscar Handlin, following years of study of immigrant acculturation and a new application of his historical work to contemporary problems,[2] wrote in the early 1960s: "Certainly tragedy was an intimate part of the life of all immigrants, from those who came to Jamestown to those who only yesterday fled from

[1] "About Equality," *Commentary*, Vol. 54 (November 1972), pp. 41–47.

[2] Handlin wrote *The Newcomers* in 1959, in which he examined current nonwhite urban poverty against the backdrop of his historical analyses of white urban poverty fifty years earlier.

5

Hungary. Even those who earned all the exterior measures of success nonetheless carried forever the marks of the losses they suffered from migration." [3]

People moved then because they had to, because their homeland could no longer support them, because they looked for more in America. And so, Handlin continues:

In this perspective such American achievements as the absorption of the immigrants and the settlement of the frontier have the quality of greatness precisely because these were not simply success stories. To recall that these immense accomplishments were rooted in tragic origins or were accompanied by the disruption of traditional communities and were paid for in heavy human costs, is to add the dimension of grandeur to American history. [4]

Grandeur! I see very little. I see only a huge, preposterous, and one-dimensional presumption about the costs it is unavoidable to pay for particular outcomes. I see a facile refusal to question either the route or the outcomes. But this kind of optimistic rationalizing of existing sociocultural norms is intrinsic to the miserable conditions in which so many Americans continue to endure generation after generation. Such lyrical history writing is ideology; it serves to confuse social conscience by a romantic involvement with the magnificent triumph of some individuals over great adversity. It does not necessarily follow, however, that the spectacle of that triumph exonerates our system from responsibility for the less fortunate or for the everydayness of adversity itself.

What must be remembered is that the labor of millions of poverty-striken immigrants was necessary for the industrial expansion of the United States. This is the reason that America's doors opened to indentured servants, slaves, serfs, and their descendants. This is what has determined the character

[3] Oscar Handlin, "Immigration in American Life: A Reappraisal," in *Immigration and American History,* edited by Henry Steele Commager (Minneapolis: University of Minnesota Press, 1961).

[4] Handlin, "Immigration in American Life."

of ethnic pluralism in this nation. And so, despite the absence of an overtly structured status system on the model of post-feudal societies, issues of ethnicity, race, and culture have been superimposed on economic and occupational differences to provide a recognizable historical and sociological basis for discrimination, prejudice, and inequality.

Further, beyond this optimistic conservatism of the Handlin consensus school are problems in a methodology which purports to speak of immigrants but in effect does not.

The years following publication of *The Uprooted* in 1951 have not altered the validity of the review by the distinguished Norwegian-American scholar Karen Larsen, who wrote in 1952:

Nevertheless, Professor Handlin has not fulfilled his promise. Instead of showing the effects of immigration on the 35 million people who came to our shores in the nineteenth century, his book is actually a study of those immigrants only who came from the village background of central and southern Europe and were stranded in our eastern cities, notably New York. It is questionable how far the sweeping generalities of the book have a universal application, even to this group.[5]

The point is documented further by Rudolph Vecoli with respect to Italians: "The historian of immigrants must study the distinctive character of each ethnic group [and not do as Handlin who] overemphasizes the power of environment and underestimates the toughness of cultural heritage."

The term *immigrant* is misleading; it requires specific definition before any intelligent questions about poverty and assimilation can be asked. Failure to do this has permitted sophisticated social scientists like Oscar Handlin to toe the line of earlier filiopietist students of immigration; in effect, many conservative social scientists come to their study of the past convinced of the efficacy of America's socioeconomy to pro-

[5] See Appendix I.

vide opportunity and they confirm that conviction with the apparent force of social scientific rigor and sophistication.[6] Tradition, the urban immigrant ghetto origins of social historians and social analysts like Handlin himself, and the naturally experienced need for internal unity and harmony in the late 1950s and early 1960s made immigration at once a cause and effect of American democracy.

Handlin sees blacks moving in the same positive direction, too. Professing great sensitivity to the suffering of the poor—white or black—Handlin manages to miss the contradiction between sympathy and assumptions about the social structure which maintains it. He misreads black history, missing the terms of its horrifying constancy by insisting on a dimension of suffering that is only a function of being the "last of the immigrants"—which, of course, they were not. Furthermore, he misrepresents what blacks would in fact become if indeed they were only the contemporary successors of immigrants. This is the nub of the problem because in strictly institutional terms—in schools, in hospitals, in unskilled labor, in inner cities—blacks have inherited the urban lot of earlier groups, of black as well as white newcomers to the Northern cities [7] (though achieving the special poignance of the record for low status on the socioeconomic ladder), while greatly underestimated numbers of earlier immigrant groups continue to occupy them, too.[8] While the fact of black dominance in these areas can be considered an aspect of American racism, the

[6] When I use the term *filiopietist* I have in mind the previous generation of immigrant historians before Marcus Lee Hansen, Carl Wittke, and Oscar Handlin—rarely social scientists—who collected large amounts of fact (and fiction) about specific groups, often the group from which they themselves came.

[7] See: Seth M. Scheiner, *Negro Mecca: A History of the Negro in New York City 1865–1920* (New York: New York University Press, 1965); Gilbert Osofsky, *Harlem: The Making of a Ghetto, Negro New York 1890–1930* (New York: Harper and Row, 1965); Allen H. Spear, *Black Chicago: The Making of a Negro Ghetto 1890–1920* (Chicago: University of Chicago Press, 1967) for well-documented evidence of the conditions of blacks in Northern cities at the turn of the century.

[8] See Appendix III.

condition itself must be understood as an intrinsic feature of American social organization.

Despite almost a half century in which almost no immigration from Europe or Asia has taken place, social mobility as well as assimilation among the foreign born and their American children has been highly selective, though no longer the pressing problem it once was. Our traditional image of certain mobility and assimilation must be replaced by an image of a moderately restrictive and fundamentally segregationist society.[9]

By ignoring the constancy of economic immobility and subsequent poverty for white Americans, immigrant historians have been able to view blacks as though they alone suffer from the scarcity of room to breathe in a modern world—as though the prognosis, based on the experience of all other minority groups as newcomers to the city, was unequivocally optimistic.

The comparative approach I'm criticizing here has been powerful and generally reinforced by our acceptance of the so-called Great Migration Thesis, which posits that unprecedented numbers of Southern blacks came North to meet World War I industry manpower demands following shrinking European immigration. This movement has been viewed as the beginning of significant Negro exposure to urban life (ignoring the sizable increases in urban black population in New York and Chicago following the Civil War) and the origin of the condition of black ghetto life (despite the existence of such ghettos in the early 1900s). Indeed, at the turn of the century, urban blacks had already fought for, and lost, the chance for decent living conditions in Northern cities. The discrete temporal delineation on which the Great Migration Thesis depends takes no account of the increasing numbers of blacks who came to New York after reconstruction to compete for industrial opportunities with foreign immigrants. But

[9] See Appendix V.

thanks to the place of the Great Migration Thesis in the narrative of United States history, we all know that the black population was redistributed in the 1920s, thus making the American Negro a more characteristically urban than rural part of the population.[10]

Building on Myrdal's conclusion that the movement of Negroes North before 1917 was not great, students have sought qualitative amplification of the apparently assured quantitative evidence. Oscar Handlin points out that urban blacks cannot be expected to avoid the fate in patterns of mobility which applied to early ethnic newcomers to the city.[11] Less optimistic observers conclude that because so many black migrants streamed into the city over a short period of time, the Negro immigratory stream was relatively unassimilated economically, socially, and politically. On occasion, pessimistic observers of the contemporary scene try to correlate the disintegrative family structures and social organization of the ghetto slum with the poor preparation for indigenous security and family solidarity caused by slavery. It has been forgotten, regardless of the date chosen to pinpoint heavy Negro northward migration, that the black movement to the North never equalled the size of the European migration, which numbered one million immigrants per year for several years in succession. It has been forgotten too that many an immigrant family exhibited the familiar shortcomings commonly attributed to the conditions of slavery. And it has also been forgotten that conditions among urban lower classes, generally, produced a pattern of social adaptation appropriate for survival among dependent classes in any setting.

What has happened is that a subtly different set of stan-

[10] Gunnar Myrdal, *An American Dilemma: The Negro Problem and Modern Democracy* (New York: Harper, 1944); Oscar Handlin, "The Goals of Integration," in "The Negro American—2," *Daedalus* (Winter 1966); Nathan Glazer and Daniel P. Moynihan, *Beyond the Melting Pot: The Negroes, Puerto Ricans, Jews, Italians and Irish of New York City* (Cambridge, Mass.: M.I.T. Press, 1963).
[11] Handlin, "Goals of Integration."

dards for addressing the problems of blacks has developed, and the difference can always be justified by the more extreme deprivation they endured, whether in 1900 or 1970. To be sure, urban blacks in 1900 confronted racist conditions that immigrants did not. The gap between Negro and European migrants as groups has steadily widened, and the difference in their respective rates of social and economic progress has been intensified by changing economic demands and by their different abilities to meet those demands.

But the remarkable thing about assessments of black deprivation is that they have not become appreciably different over the years. Furthermore, and perhaps even more striking, is the fact that these assessments replicated almost exactly what were then—and for several decades—observations of white lower-class problems in cities. Unfortunately, the close similarity of conditions among urban poor people—black and white—at any time has not really influenced our examination of poverty and those who live it. Indeed, the most poignant inaccuracy of urban social science has been the continuing use of the special methodology for perceiving black problems; and inherent in this method, for blacks and whites alike, is the inaccurate image of white mobility together with the belief that solutions are possible neither for the poor black nor for the implicitly ignored poor white. So by separating blacks as a matter of concern and concentration, the democratic mythography about American mobility is sustained on the basis of implicit comparison, and not on analysis at all.

The truth is that even under the best of circumstances, immigration and in-migration involved enormous social and psychological difficulties, whether in the movement from rural to urban areas or from one country to another. Where immigrant tradition coincided with American needs, assimilation, as defined by mobility, took place; where matching was less sure, so too was progress; where there was no matching, there was severe deprivation—or, in some cases, immigrants

either gave up and went home or were sent home by dissatis-
fied employers who arranged and paid for their passage.[12]

As Marc Fried has described it, the foreign immigrant's success was more the result of a "slow, arduous, intra-genera-
tional and inter-generational change in status" than of any
well-assured pattern of assimilation. The truth is that the mobility of white lower classes was never as rapid nor as sure as
we have traditionally believed. The 1920 Census, for example,
showed large numbers of even the favored English and Welsh
migrants tied to the insecurity of unskilled labor; 40 percent
of their number worked in coal mines and cotton factories.

Once intra-ethnic comparisons begin, the concept of "making it" becomes tenuous indeed. Blau and Duncan's [13]

[12] Theodore Saloutos, "Exodus U.S.A.," in *In The Trek of the Immigrant*, edited by O. F. Ander (Rock Island, Ill.: Augustana College Library, 1964).

[13] Peter M. Blau and Otis Dudley Duncan, *The American Occupational Structure* (New York: Wiley, 1967) yielded the first definitive
measurements of occupational mobility among U.S. males showing the
systematic rigidity of occupational stratification in the U.S. between
men and their fathers; recruitment to economic privilege in this society
from various classes remains, as evidence suggests that it functioned in
earlier periods, proportionately and hierarchically constant—so, too,
therefore inequality of opportunity and outcome in the socioeconomy.
(For example: only 10 percent of the sons of manual workers move into
professional and kindred occupations as opposed to more than 20 percent of the sons of the nonprofessional middle class and around 40 percent of the sons of professionals.) Arguments for recently increased and
long-standing equality of opportunity in American society are generally
made possible only by diverting attention from the quite contrary reality through the homogenization of immigrant experience on the one
hand, and by the exclusion and the separate and comparative study of
blacks and women as minorities and exceptions to "the general rule of
equal opportunity" on the other. See Daniel Bell, "On Meritocracy and
Equality," *The Public Interest*, Vol. 29 (Fall 1972), pp. 29–68; Irving
Kristol, "About Equality," *Commentary*, Vol. 54 (November 1972), pp.
41–47; Seymour Martin Lipset, "Social Mobility and Equal Opportunity," *The Public Interest*, Vol. 29 (Fall 1972), pp. 90–108; Ben J. Wat-
tenberg and Richard M. Scammon, "Black Progress and Liberal Rhetoric," *Commentary*, Vol. 55 (April 1973), pp. 35–44; for the distortion
just described. For my view of the reality of social mobility and equal
opportunity, see the remainder of this essay; also, Stephan Thernstrom,
Poverty and Progress: Social Mobility in a Nineteenth Century City
(Cambridge, Mass.: Harvard University Press, 1964); S. M. Miller and
Pamela Roby, *The Future of Inequality* (New York: Basic Books, 1970);

comparison of the mobility patterns of nonwhites and whites, divided into ethnic generations—foreign-born, second-generation Americans, and native-born Americans of native parentage—suggests that it is quite inaccurate to draw images of American society using the broad category "the immigrant experience" as an interpretative tool. Different groups had different experiences, though all made some progress of the sort depicted in popular folklore. Some groups progressed more than others over comparable periods while significant parts of all groups made hardly any progress at all. Whereas Jews were dramatically mobile, the Irish experienced a great deal of short-term upward mobility, but unusually high downward mobility as well; they were among the slowest to rise as a group. Remember too the recent work of Paul Cowan on today's Jewish poverty in New York City,[14] the demographic data coming out of local community mental health centers about white urban poverty today,[15] and the general awakening of lower-class and working-class ethnic consciousness among Poles, Italians, and Irishmen in New York, Detroit, and Chicago expressed in terms of a realization of unfulfilled promises instilled through tradition.

But Oscar Handlin's presentation of an "ideal type" immigrant in *The Uprooted,* having been established as the conventional wisdom, has proved difficult to dislodge. The belief that the vast majority of immigrants after the late 1800s has successfully been included in the nation's dominant middle-class affluence has, as I have said, meant that the existing problem of black poverty in inner cities is explained by the

---

Richard Parker, *The Myth of the Middle Class* (New York: Liveright, 1972); Glazer and Moynihan, *Beyond the Melting Pot,* Tables 1–8, pp. 317–324; Marc Fried, "Deprivation and Migration: Dilemmas of Causal Interpretation," in *On Understanding Poverty,* edited by Daniel P. Moynihan (New York: Basic Books, 1969), p. 195.

[14] Paul Cowan, "Jews Without Money" and "Jews Without Money, Revisited," *The Village Voice* (1972).

[15] See, for example: Maimonides Medical Center Program Evaluation Section, "Demographic Information by Health Area" (September 1967), mimeographed.

experience of slavery or the deprivations of urban poverty it-self. If blacks have not made it (and it isn't their fault ex-actly), it is—in the optimism of our most enlightened policy makers and the social scientists who serve them—the fault of something in Negro history.

As Nathan Glazer and Daniel Patrick Moynihan put it in *Beyond the Melting Pot:*

There is little question where the major part of the answer must be found: in the home and family and community—not in its overt values, which, as we have seen, are positive in relation to educa-tion, but in its conditions and circumstances. It is there that the heritage of two hundred years of slavery and a hundred years of discrimination is concentrated; and it is there that we find the seri-ous obstacles to the ability to make use of a free educational sys-tem to advance into higher occupations and to eliminate the mas-sive social problems that afflict colored Americans and the City.

The big lie as normative reality! With the public school historic and strong, city problems and problems in city schools are black problems now not because blacks have them but because blacks, alone, fail to conquer them.

But the story of "immigrant" success is a legend, too.[16] We have been bemused by the successes—the Jews in particular—and the easy location of failure—among blacks, for exam-ple. But millions in all ethnic groupings have suffered misera-bly in America and continue to do so.

The high degree of academic achievement, preceding dis-proportionate economic success among Jews, did not mean success for all Jews. Otherwise, why the remedial classes and dropout panic in several of the schools on New York's Lower East Side with as much as 99 percent "Hebrew" registration? Where the family was poor enough to take in boarders to cover rental costs, and desperate enough to join the city's welfare rolls, delinquency and criminality were then, as they

[16] Fried, "Deprivation and Migration." See Appendixes IV and V.

are now in some urban neighborhoods, the burden of Jewish families, too.[17]

There is a hard core of reality behind the story depicting the entry of the Eastern European Jewish immigrant into the small business enterprise and then of his son into the university and the professions. The "business" quality of the ethnic community has not itself been the vital ingredient; the key factor is the indigenous grounding of the unit within the ethnic boundary; that is, the establishment of an ethnic middle class before scaling the walls of the dominant society.

Economic stability for the group preceded its entry onto the broader middle-class stage via education. The correlation between academic achievement and economic status was so high that, in school surveys carried out in the Midwest during the 1920s, it became necessary to separate Scandinavian-Americans from other "ethnic" Americans because the school performance of their children so outdistanced other foreign Midwest groups. Census figures reveal that the degree of economic security among farm-holding Scandinavians and storekeeping Jews (surprisingly high even in 1920) was much greater than among more characteristically wage-laboring groups. As Theodore Saloutos points out, the Greeks, too, were among the first to make this transition. Similarly, in 1940 in San Francisco, the recently arrived Japanese community—tightly organized around its own business enterprise—ranked high on school achievement measures.

Once we consider the heterogeneity of immigrant experience in this way, it also becomes necessary to consider the heterogeneity of immigrants' experience before America as a variable in the respective achievements of different groups. This relationship with homeland preparation is frequently ignored and superseded by a preference for a discussion of ei-

[17] Colin Greer, *The Great School Legend: A Revisionist Interpretation of American Public Education* (New York: Basic Books, 1972), Chap. 5.

ther cultural or genetic heritage. Rudolph Vecoli, for example, showed for Italians, as did Thomas and Znaniecki for Poles, that the occupational experience of the homeland was a significant ingredient in the pattern of adaptation in the United States, and therefore immigrant experiences were both turbulent and varied. Moses Rischin recently made it clear that the outstanding rate of Jewish mobility in the cities of the Northern United States depended in large measure on their urban and small-township entrepreneurial experience in Eastern Europe.[18]

Each of these works also pictures the living conditions of lower-class workers in New York, and other major cities, in the early decades of the twentieth century. Also, a large body of contemporary observations has made the miseries of factory life staggeringly clear. Isaac Hourwich showed in 1912 that even the more favored "old" immigrant from Western and Northern Europe progressed at much slower rates and in much lower proportions than those who opposed "new" immigration from Southern and Eastern Europe argued was the case. Robert E. Park, Herbert A. Miller, Jacob Riis, Jane Addams, Lillian Wald, and many others confirmed the picture with moving descriptions of what they saw among the urban

[18] Walter Laidlaw, *Statistical Sources for Demographic Studies, Greater New York, 1910* (New York: New York Federation of Churches, 1912), p. 183; and *1920* (New York: New York Federation of Churches, 1922), pp. 45, 52; Niles Carpenter, "Immigrants and Their Children," Census Monograph No. 7 (Washington, D.C.: Government Printing Office, 1927), Vol. 1, Table 16, p. 32; Masakazo Iwata, "The Japanese Immigrants in California Agriculture," *Agricultural History* (January 1962); Saloutos, "Exodus—U.S.A.," pp. 199–201; Oscar Handlin, *The Uprooted* (New York: Grosset and Dunlap, 1951); W. I. Thomas and Florian Znaniecki, *The Polish Peasant in Europe and America* (Chicago: University of Chicago Press, 1918; New York: Knopf, 1928, Dover, 1958); Tora Bøhn, "A Quest for Norwegian Folk Art in America," *Norwegian-American Studies and Records*, Vol. 19 (1956); Rose Hum Lee, *The Chinese in the United States of America* (Cambridge: Oxford University Press, 1960); Alex Simirenko, *Pilgrims, Colonists, and Frontiersmen: An Ethnic Community in Transition* (New York: Free Press, 1964); Rudolph J. Vecoli, "Contadini in Chicago: A Critique of *The Uprooted*," *Journal of American History* (December 1965).

lower classes.[19] United States census data for 1910, 1920, and 1930 reveal that assumptions of academic success preceding social progress, where it occurred, are as ill-informed as most popular assumptions about the inevitability of mobility itself. Actually, things worked in quite the reverse order, with cultural background and economic status being reflected and reinforced in the school, not caused by it.

From very early on, schools seem to have had quite different effects among the ethnic groups. In 1911, Immigration Commission research workers found that even controlling for exposure to America—length of residence—ethnic differences still predominated, with Irish and Italians considerably less advanced than Russian Jews. These results were confirmed between 1911 and 1920 in big cities such as New York and in smaller ones such as St. Paul and Minneapolis. Smaller studies of expanding towns such as Hartford, Connecticut, also confirmed these findings. Census data in 1920 and succeeding decades up through 1960 make it clear that, even when immigrants became Americans, neither schools nor society offered the mobility imagined.[20]

In 1950, in New York and New Jersey more than 80 percent of working men of Italian, Irish, and Slavic extraction were employed in unskilled or semiskilled occupations. Twenty years later the same phenomenon persisted nationwide. What have now become known as "white ethnic groups" continue to drop out of school early in large numbers and continue to work in increasingly less available blue-collar jobs. Indeed, analyses of census data from 1920 to 1969 show that, in comparison to the sons of college-educated fathers, the sons of fathers with fewer than eight years of education have had little effective access to college, and thus even less access to upper-level jobs. It should be noted that this persistence of social and economic immobility among the descendants of the "new immigrants" who flocked to America at the turn of the

[19] Greer, *Great School Legend.*
[20] Greer, *Great School Legend.*

17

century has been a serious factor encouraging the current re-discovery of ethnicity by white working-class groups, particularly by the Italians and Slavs in Boston, New York, Baltimore, Cleveland, Pittsburgh, and Detroit.[21]

Yet we forget that the United States, by virtue of its simultaneous youth and rapid expansion, turned to aliens for labor. Different periods brought different immigrant groups to America, and very soon the industrial class structure reflected—and reinforced—all those differences. But we do not generally judge Americanization nor the continuing phenomenon of diverse ethnic consciousness by the underlying division of labor and class fabric of which it was an expression.

A group's position in the social order rested on its ability to meet particular conditions with appropriate skills to draw on. It is the ethnic cultural base as a setting for the continuing socialization of that readiness which keeps the ethnic structure strong—indeed, essential to the class level of behavioral conformity permitted it by the dominant culture. An ethnic group's local stability preceded its entry into the more prosperous reaches of society.

Once Old-World links are broken, the indigenous ethnic culture becomes increasingly characterized by modifications to the American culture and by the ongoing encounter of that modified ethnic culture with the social fabric as a whole. Gradually the ethnic groups, especially once immigration is stopped through restrictive legislation and newcomers are cut off, become aspects of an American cultural pattern—dominated by class hierarchy—not the product of a surviving projection of the Old World. When we say that the extent to which children of particular origins do well or badly in school

---

[21] Miller and Roby, *Future of Inequality*, p. 133; Glazer and Moynihan, *Beyond the Melting Pot*, pp. 322, 324; U.S. Bureau of the Census, Current Population Reports, Series P-20, No. 207, "Educational Attainment, March 1970" (1971), p. 7.

can be explained in large part by the cultural patterns of their ethnic group, we are not simply saying that Poland prepared people better than Italy. What we are saying is that the cultural adaptation of ethnic patterns, which developed from the first meeting with America, emphasized some characteristics and discouraged others. Cultural patterns in a land of origin were basic to the potential success experienced by specific groups in America, but what the child brings with him to the public school classroom is not a pure or direct product of an historic homeland but the combined product of some of those patterns established by the group in order to survive in its assigned place in America. These are the factors which contribute to ethnic self-image and to varying degrees of preparedness for "making it."

Meanwhile, notwithstanding the fact of ethnic diversity in America, the melting pot did melt: most groups in American society have been successfully integrated into an urban, hierarchical class structure which expresses itself in ethnic categories. The cues of felt ethnicity turn out to be the recognizable characteristics of class position in this society. When we refer to ethnic groups we are, more often than not, communicating quite specific implications about income and status in this society. To feel black, Irish, Italian, or Jewish has meant emphasizing aspects of culture which become synonymous with hierarchical markings in an hierarchically stratified production system.

William Shannon, speaking about the American Irish, finds Ortega y Gasset's principle of community intactness appropriate in this context: "Groups which form a state come together and stay together for definite reasons. They do not live together in order merely to be together. They live together in order to do something together." Clearly, doing things as a group increases the desire to remain a group and so indigenous culture is reaffirmed out of common experience. But what it is important to understand is that it was the appropriateness of the skills and cultural background of specific groups which reinforced those traditions in a strong "hyphenated" American identity.[22]

Rudolph Vecoli has shown how the small-town laboring background colored the activities of Italian immigrants from southern Italy. He has also made it clear that Italian criminal organization, not to be ignored as a vehicle for Italian security in America (whatever its dubious morality), did not emerge as a response to the American city by desperate peasants, but rather was the continuation of the organized depredations of the "Black Hand," which terrorized Sicily after 1900.

Out of the experience of political dependence on England, most Irish immigrants who settled in American cities brought with them political sensitivity and technique for organizing political associations. Even the Molly Maguire unrest among Irish workers in Pennsylvania anthracite fields in the latter half of the nineteenth century represents a transference of homeland activism against English or pro-English landlords.[23]

The Scandinavians, largely small owner-farmers in Sweden and Norway, took advantage of America's free soil in order to start farms. The Germans, who came during the mid-nineteenth-century Scandinavian immigration, did not for the

[22] See also William Shannon, *The American Irish* (New York: Collier-Macmillan, 1963), p. 19. Bøhn, "Quest for Norwegian Folk Art in America"; Lee, *Chinese in the United States of America;* Glazer and Moynihan, *Beyond the Melting Pot;* Moses Rischin, *The Promised City: New York's Jews, 1870–1914* (Cambridge, Mass.: Harvard University Press, 1962); Simirenko, *Pilgrims, Colonists, and Frontiersmen;* Thomas and Znaniecki, *Polish Peasant in Europe and America;* Vecoli, "Contadini in Chicago"; Theodore Saloutos, *The Greeks in the United States* (New York: Teachers College Press, Columbia University, 1967).

[23] Karen Larsen, "Review of Oscar Handlin's *The Uprooted,*" *American Historical Review* (April 1952); Vecoli, "Contadini in Chicago"; Alan Conway, *The Welsh in America: Letters from the Immigrants* (Minneapolis: University of Minnesota Press, 1961); Wayne G. Broehl, Jr., *The Molly Maguires* (Cambridge, Mass.: Harvard University Press, 1964).

most part benefit from free land; more frequently they settled in cities, following their largely urban habits. And yet the Finns, coming to America at the turn of the twentieth century, when free soil was no longer generally available, accepted, because they were farmers, deserted agricultural regions in New York and New England—abandoned farms at low prices—or "cutover" areas in Wisconsin, Michigan, and Minnesota. Only a fortunate few secured good homesteads in the Dakotas and northern Minnesota.[24]

Moses Rischin has shown that Southern- and Eastern-European Jews, like the Germans, were for the most part people with urban experience. They frequently became small businessmen in America, living primarily in cities. Rischin suggests convincingly that many Jewish men and women had experienced the life of the sweatshop well before they emigrated. Over 66 percent of those gainfully employed in America at the turn of the century had had "industrial" experience in Europe; no other immigrants approached such a percentage. Rischin describes how these immigrants played a major part in reshaping the structure of New York industry, and makes especially clear the strong unions' contribution to psychological as well as economic welfare among urban Jews.[25]

Similarly, Robert Cross argues that if the Greeks were peasants, "they must have been peasants with a difference." Their transition in America resembles that of Eastern-European Jews much more than it resembles that of peasant Italians, Poles, and southern Slavs. It has been suggested, although it is hard to substantiate, that they came with prior

[24] Nathan Glazer, "Ethnic Groups in America: From National Culture to Ideology," in *Freedom and Control in Modern Society*, edited by M. Berger, T. Abel, and C. H. Page (New York: Octagon, 1964); A. William Haglund, "Finnish Immigrant Farmers in New York, 1910–1960," in *In The Trek of the Immigrant*, edited by O. F. Ander (Rock Island, Ill.: Augustana College Library, 1964); John A. Hawgood, *The Tragedy of German America* (New York: Putnam, 1940).

[25] Rischin, *Promised City*, pp. 51–75; Rudolph Glanz, *Jew and Irish: Historic Group Relations and Immigration* (New York: Waldon, 1966).

commercial experience similar to that of Jewish immigrants, which facilitated their entrance into urban American society; it is possible that those from the countryside were neither so attached to the soil nor so involved in an extended family system as other peasant groups seem to have been. Furthermore, the Greeks appear to have come with a uniquely vivid ethnic pride. Theodore Saloutos notes, though he does not fully endorse, the theory that the most socially mobile of the Greek immigrants came from the *irridenta,* where ethnic self-consciousness was particularly acute. In any event, the Greeks prided themselves on their individualism. And the Greek child was encouraged by both his family and his community to "make a name for himself." For Greeks, and for Jews too, this meant small business and the professions. As a result, Greek life, like Jewish life, has been characterized by American middle-class values.[26]

There was a large difference in the experience of various ethnic groups after they reached America. The 1950 Census revealed, for example, that the occupation levels of ethnic groups of the "old" immigration from Northern and Western Europe (England, Wales, Germany, Norway, Sweden, and Ireland) are generally higher than those of the "new" immigration from Eastern and Southern Europe (Austria, Russia, Poland, Czechoslovakia, and Italy). There are exceptions, of course. For example, regarding the "new immigration," the Jews in particular are at the higher end of the success continuum and the Irish of the "old immigration" are at the lower. Nevertheless, success or failure could still be plotted in ethnic terms and the constancy of each group's relative place in the social hierarchy continues to suggest the essentially class nature of American ethnic designations.

Not only has definition by ethnicity and its corollary sense of ethnic identity been an important base for whatever mobility did exist, but it has also been an Americanized clue to so-

[26] Saloutos, *Greeks in the United States.*

cial status; it was, as Andrew Greeley put it, a "totemic clan" system around which the social order was organized.

Ironically, the traditional depiction of an urban experience unique to blacks confirms the significance of group characterizations just described. And yet, it is only in the case of blacks that ethnic characteristics supersede American institutional strength in conventional views of minority group progress. It is important to be aware of two things in this context: one, that American institutions—like the school in particular—were no more efficacious for white poor than black poor people; all groups were consigned to transpose their historic experience on the style and quality of their urban life. Two, for ever so long—and still to a considerable degree—white poverty and black poverty are closely similar phenomena. The black experience differs in the extreme degree to which blacks inherit that condition—not in the condition itself. Whites and blacks of all ethnic origins continue to be poor in America today.

For too long it has been customary to ask for patience on the grounds that American blacks were doing very nicely for slow starters. Successive reports of improved economic data, for example—a little less behind the white statistic as a total figure than when they were more behind—suffer less from a credibility gap than a reality gap.[27]

This view of blacks has been indispensable to the myth of immigrant assimilation and mobility in the United States. One crucial result has been that "integration," so crucial to the recent history of American blacks, remains badly misunderstood as a dynamic of American history.

For blacks, "integration" following the experience of slavery symbolized the undoing of the overt segregation and separation of slave status. As such it represented a truly ethnic

[27] This kind of popular wish fulfillment, as D. H. Lawrence perceived Americans with respect to James Fenimore Cooper's Indian, makes it so hard for the real thing to come through later.

23

focus for group organization and identity, and not, as many had feared, the extermination of black ethnicity in America. The demand for integration provided a powerful rhetorical force for achieving specific goals, such as economic security and legal equality. Both the rhetoric and concrete goals expressed real needs of the black community and, in expressing them, have been a catalyst for the forceful black separateness which followed it.

Booker T. Washington, notorious among blacks for compromise, was actually responding to the fact that immigrant groups were to "make it" in America by indigenous ethnic solidarity. This was what he anticipated when he spoke, in his now infamous Atlanta address, of blacks as one of "five fingers of the hand"—separate from other groups in things social, together with other groups in things national. While this was not the sentimental desegregation faith we grew accustomed to after 1964, it was a realistic assessment of what American pluralism is all about. Washington responded at an economic level, believing that if blacks stayed in the South where they had roots and a culture defined to a great extent by their role as servers, they might achieve an industrial proletarian relationship to the expected new Southern (industrial) economy on the lines enjoyed by immigrants, to the exclusion of blacks, who occupied a slave relation to industry via menial and strikebreaking employment in the North. W. E. B. Du Bois, who agreed with Washington for several years after the Atlanta address, responded with the viewpoint of an intellectual who identified with the urban North. To make room for the "talented tenth" was more important than—but did not exclude—economic advancement for the "undifferentiated mass," as Du Bois called black poor masses in general. And so he stood firm as a keen Pan-Africanist. It was not until many years later that his conversion to Communism as well as his earlier position led him to emigrate from America. From 1890 to 1930, Du Bois' Pan-Africanism, like much of his work as editor of *Crisis,* was an effort to build a black American identity—to make the Afro-American hyphen like any other.[28]

Despite popular white models of black leadership, black leaders like Washington, Du Bois, even Marcus Garvey (who admired Washington) or Malcolm X, James Farmer, and Stokely Carmichael have reached for integration at the only level, at least since 1850, where it has meant anything for urban newcomers—namely economic integration for the few, exclusion for the many. These leaders testify to the fact that blacks, like "the sons and daughters of the immigrants" (as Oscar Handlin sees immigrants but not blacks), were soon Americans; they were, according to Handlin, one of the more exposed portions of American society, and therefore particularly sensitive to its strains. But still they became a part of it. Being "a part of it" in that exclusionary context has been the overriding characteristic of minority-group acculturation in this country.[29]

There are three major theories of assimilation; each, in its time, accurately reflected the exclusionary, highly competitive nature of American society. The first, Anglo-conformity—the belief on the part of "native Americans" that foreigners should give up their past cultural identity entirely and take on the social and cultural habits of their new homeland—is the most prevalent ideology in American history. The second theory is that of the melting pot, which presupposes a biological merger and a blending of cultures into a new American type. The third theory is that of cultural pluralism, the preservation of communal life and significant portions of the cul-

[28] Colin Greer, *Cobweb Attitudes: Essays on American Education and Culture* (New York: Teachers College Press, Columbia University, 1970); Howard Brotz, *The Black Jews* (New York: Free Press, 1964); Herbert Aptheker, ed., "Some Unpublished Writings of W. E. B. Du Bois," *Freedomways*, Vol. 5 (Winter 1965), pp. 103–110, 117–118.

[29] Handlin, "The Goals of Integration," and *The Uprooted* (New York: Grosset and Dunlap, 1951); Edmund D. Cronon, *Black Moses: The Story of Marcus Garvey and the Universal Negro Improvement Association* (Madison: University of Wisconsin Press, 1955).

ture of an ethnic group within the context of American citizenship.

By the end of the nineteenth century, and after many millions of immigrants had come to this country, both natives and immigrants realized that the process of mutual accommodation was much too complicated to permit the simple Anglo-conformist faith in making Americans. Politics wasn't everything, and ways of life were more complicated than one's political loyalty. So the notion of the melting pot became popular. Some people still meant by it that immigrants, upon arrival, ought to be melted down so that they would within a very short time resemble totally the older Americans —becoming, as it were, complete facsimiles of George Washington, Benjamin Franklin, or the passengers on the *Mayflower*. Others thought that the melting pot would produce a race of Americans different in some ways from anything that had been seen before; because different ethnic groups were entering the pot, the final product would be different. But both versions of the melting pot assumed that the final product would be homogeneous.

The trouble was that the melting pot didn't melt in the manner it was expected to. Two kinds of reaction developed. Scholars—like Yale sociologist Henry Pratt Fairchild, author of *The Melting Pot Mistake*—concluded that many immigrant groups entering the country could never integrate; at best, they would lose their foreign virtues, while retaining in virulent form their foreign evils. Others, like philosopher Horace Kallen, were more optimistic; they believed that America would be richer as the result of the diversities resulting from immigrant groups that didn't melt. Very quickly the differences in outlook became manifest in a struggle over legislative restriction of immigrants.

Cultural pluralism has become the increasingly dominant theme since World War I but, as Milton Gordon has argued, the "ideal model of the cultural pluralist society" has never really existed. In fact, the American experience approximates some elements of this model and falls short of others. "The most salient fact," Gordon believes, "is the maintenance of the structurally separate subsocieties of the three major religions and the racial and quasi-racial groups, and even vestiges of the nationality groupings, along with a massive trend toward acculturation of all groups—particularly their native-born— to American culture patterns." He finds that "a more accurate term for the American situation is structural pluralism rather than cultural pluralism, although some of the latter also remains." In other words, "structural pluralism, then, is the major key to the understanding of the ethnic makeup of American society, while cultural pluralism is the minor one." Behavioral conformity is achieved, but, in many cases, not structural integration. The great majority of newcomers and their offspring have held fast to a communal life made up of their fellow-immigrants.[30]

Cultural pluralism did not really change the melting-pot dream. Americanization took place through particular peoples adjusting to the reality of the American Dream. To date we have only judged a rhetorical acculturation by a rhetorical dream, whereas Americanization, judged on the basis of its own avowed criterion—namely equal opportunity—must be declared a charade. (So, too, must the belief that ethnic identity was worth preserving in order to provide a healthy infusion into American culture.) But judged as a practical, stratifying class framework for accommodating the multiethnic nature of labor in this country, Americanization must be seen as a powerful and successful process.

Some years ago Nathan Glazer described ethnic identities in America as "ghost-nations" deriving power from the folklore fantasy of the past handed down over generations. Al-

[30] Milton M. Gordon, *Assimilation in American Life* (London: Oxford University Press, 1964); pp. 105–117; Will Herberg, *Catholic-Protestant-Jew* (New York: Doubleday, 1955).

though he was right, he forgot to pinpoint the fact of socio-economic life which made those "ghost-nations" an *American* reality.

Ruth Elson's studies of textbooks in the nineteenth century and my own study of early twentieth-century textbooks show that all minority groups, white as well as black, with the exceptions of the English, Scots, Germans, and Scandinavians were negatively portrayed. Jews, Italians, Chinese, and blacks were mean, criminal, immoral, drunken, sly, lazy, and stupid in varying degrees. But rather than this contributing to a poor self-image among the children of these groups, these texts probably are much more a symptom of the education of the more privileged children in dominant cultural attitudes toward lower-class newcomers. After all, until World War I, most poor children were not in public school—they were on waiting lists due to overcrowding, on truant lists because the pressure was to work, or they were in parochial school. It was the unchanging nature of textbooks that finally allowed lower-class children to confirm their status in the world through a classroom experience dominated by the ethos characterized in textbooks; but only after the limits of ethnic desirability, the axis of American acculturation, had been fully established.

Even the so-called rediscovery of ethnic identity in the 1920s and after, whereby settlement programs and philanthropic reformers purported to recognize and respect the ethnic diversity and indigenous ethnic culture, rarely meant more than acknowledgment of such superficial symbols as food and holidays. The goal remained: the homogenization of family life style to the norms of the dominant culture; and native European cuisine was a window dressing for the means (e.g., schools, settlement houses). Window dressing, absent the sensitivity which accompanies respect, encouraged stereotypes derived from the same paternalistic preconceptions. The case of blacks is poignantly illustrative. Here settlement workers, bent on paying deference in some small measure to ethnic background, had men acting out Uncle Remus stories in adult education classes. A harsh, judgmental, moral attitude and an overriding sense of racial superiority merged in the White Anglo-Saxon Protestant and German-Jewish social workers with an increasing professionalism in social work. The result was a strong pressure on the new immigrants to conform to established Anglo-Puritan standards. These standards formed the inspiration for the expansion of public school services.

In this context ethnic consciousness becomes a negative, static base and, above all, an American cultural form. Just as blacks, though their African origins were absorbed into black-American culture, are an American subgroup and a phenomenon of the American class/culture system, so white ethnic identity is a phenomenon on that spectrum too. Mobility, the alleged outcome of ethnic solidarity, developed out of a negative definition of self; more groups than blacks have been led, over and over again, to define their ethnicity against dominant stereotypes and to be aware of it because of the emotional punches and physical bruises which too often made awareness inevitable. Proving the stereotype wrong is a major factor in what Leonard Covello, the first New York City school principal of Italian origin, referred to as Americanization by shame for those who surpassed the tortoiselike socioeconomic progress of the group.[31]

[31] Andrew Greeley, *Why Can't They Be Like Us? America's White Ethnic Groups* (New York: Dutton, 1971); Stanley Lieberson, *Ethnic Patterns in American Cities* (New York: Free Press, 1963); Glazer, "Ethnic Groups in America"; Ruth Miller Elson, "American Schoolbooks and Culture in the Nineteenth Century," *Mississippi Valley Historical Review,* 46 (December 1959), and "Immigrants and Schoolbooks in the Nineteenth Century" (History of Education Society Eastern Regional Meeting, April 1971); Roy Lubove, *The Professional Altruist: The Emergence of Social Work as a Career, 1880–1930* (Cambridge, Mass.: Harvard University Press, 1965); Paul Violas, "Jane Addams and Social Control" (Urbana, Ill.: University of Illinois, 1969; mimeographed). Peter Schrag, *The Decline of the WASP* (New York: Simon and Schuster, 1971); Leonard Covello and Guido D'Agostino, *The Heart Is the Teacher* (New York: McGraw-Hill, 1958); Greer, *Cobweb Attitudes.*

The New Republic (January 29, 1916) editorial typifies the progres-

So the quest for cultural pluralism, just as the quest for Anglo-conformity which it succeeded, confirms the class patterns in American society. The retention of ethnic identity is as important for its recognizability as for its being felt. After all, how can group diversity be meaningful in any other way when it has to exist in relation to a dominant culture which permits progress with adjustment only. The Old-World patterns are gone, and what is left is a group identity which makes for solidarity and—more importantly—the imprisonment of the individual in a group ego. These groups came to America at different times and the degree of adaptation and progress each group made (each group lost its Old-World ways) is now captured in an ethnic label. The cultural pluralism of which Americans have been so proud since World War II is a phenomenon of class, not the successful defense of variously indigenous people against homogenization.

The conventional view of minority group accommodation and mobility through powerful ethnic identification, so well expressed by Nathan Glazer, simply misreads and misrepresents the process: ". . . past cooperation loses its relevance as it dawns on Jews and others as well that many Negro leaders are now beginning to expect that the pattern of their advancement in American society would take quite a different form from that of the immigrant ethnic group . . . But that it is a new form, a radically new one, for the integration of a group into American society we must recognize." [32]

---

sive liberal's selective observations of the contemporary social structure and his precarious balance between immigration and restriction, until World War I provoked fear of internal disunity and those still "new" to America became a "special" instance of breakdown in the hitherto effective assimilation apparatus: "Only recently . . . we had absolute confidence in our power of assimilation. Serb, American, Lithuanian, we assured ourselves, would put off their national characters and become good Americans . . . as . . . Irish, Germans, and Scandinavians had become merged with the original English stock . . . This optimism is hard to remember."

[32] See also Nathan Glazer, "Negroes and Jews: The New Challenge to Pluralism," *Commentary* Vol. 46 (1964); Blau and Duncan, *American Occupational Structure;* Glazer and Moynihan, *Beyond the Melting Pot;* Rob-

But it is not so new a form at all. It is no more than a different style. It is radical and threatening only to the extent that the group lowest down is among the groups wanting in now; wanting in at the various institutional occupations—in public service employment in general, and education in particular—which hitherto represented progress from blue-collar to middle-class employment, but which increasingly represents the most extensively expanding sector of the economy at a time when the old, blue-collar occupations are shifting equally rapidly. The escalator is moving so fast that people are bumping into each other—or are afraid that they will. Black demands do not really challenge the right of ethnic subcommunities to exist. That right is ideology for both whites and blacks in America. The demand for integration, when that demand was flourishing, was in fact organized around a quite clear ethnic base. It is built on pluralist assumptions, despite its rhetoric to the contrary. The fact of the matter has been that integration, the issue of desegregation, as a political focus is a black statement of what Oscar Handlin saw emerging among immigrant groups at a point in time when their ethnic consciousness was becoming politically engaged: namely the exercise of power, both political and economic, through the state which before, as Handlin pointed out, ". . . embodied all the socially recognized instruments of control and coercion." Blacks, like immigrants before them, were moving from experiencing the state as exclusively a coercive, repressive instrument to experiencing it as participants in government. As Handlin maintains in *The Uprooted,* "the separateness of the immigrants was an immediate challenge to all other groups." After all, "an election had only one outcome and, once the contest was over, left only victors and vanquished." The state, and its institutions and agencies, represented a system of defensive inter-

ert Coles, *Still Hungry in America* (New York: New American Library, 1969).

ests, conventionally categorized by ethnic group around a
ladder built to take a few at a time.

Ethnic Pluralism—the New Pluralism as some call it
now [33]—stands as a fundamental national ideology. Still we
are told that ethnic consciousness is important to American
vitality.

Michael Novak rightly observed recently:

No one has yet contrived an image, let alone a political system, for
living in a genuinely pluralistic way. The difficulties are obvious.
How can each cultural minority be true to itself without infringing
on the liberties of others? How can each person belong to a given
ethnic group to the extent that he or she chooses, and be free as
well to move into other groups? [34]

Novak, however, goes on to argue that a strong ethnic identity will tend to avoid the aggressive relations existing among
so many ethnic groups in this country.

The problem is, however, that neither ethnic identity nor
ethnic solidarity has meant understanding and tolerance of
other groups in this country. It has not meant a peaceful, pluralist, international policy—quite the contrary (and with di-
sastrous consequences at home). Further, the primacy of ethnicity has generally meant an identity of defense against and
exclusion of other groups, and there is little in American family patterns—whatever the group—that seems to be based on
the kind of consensual relations that would favor individual
growth and autonomy.

This country is not new to the concept of ethnicity; its arti-
facts are well rehearsed in terms of both intragroup pressures
on the individual and intergroup hostilities. It is important to
realize the uncanny simultaneity of the "rise of the ethnics"
and America's regressive stance on issues—like busing for

[33] See, for example: "The Rediscovery of Cultural Pluralism," *The
Antioch Review*, a special issue, Vol. 31 (Fall 1971).
[34] Michael Novak, *The Rise of the Unmeltable Ethnics* (New York:
Macmillan, 1972), p. 8.

desegregation—that concern the continuing struggle to eman-cipate this nation from poverty and the cultural heritage of slavery. Indeed, in the 1950s the dual faith in ethnic diversity ("cultural pluralism") and in economic mobility was so pow-erful that it had to be transcended—albeit only temporarily —before even the tentative egalitarian and libertarian zeal of the 1960s could flourish. If schools in both North and South still cannot be integrated, it is because the image projected by desegregated schools is not the one by which this nation recognizes itself. And as long as American ambition can be stated in terms of ethnic solidarity and Horatio Alger hero-ism, our image will remain the same.

The perfect cover for the hostility which characterizes the actuality of American ethnic diversity is the illusion that the defensive fear and aggressive face so typical of it represent life in the raw on the cutting edge of survival: real people not yet contaminated by the plasticity of affluence. The illusion is that ethnics know life, their blood is rich with it. Water runs in the veins of WASPs. The picture of the "insipid" WASP drawn by Novak, for example, denies this group the defer-ence and respect he demands for other groups. Middle- and upper-class WASP culture is experienced by actual living and breathing people too; it reflects pain and joy, costs and bene-fits, albeit with the material comforts of life at the top of the pyramid. Furthermore, it would be a mistake to sound the demise of the privilege and exploitation which seem to ac-company socioeconomic power by confusing ruling classes with ethnic origins—no matter how closely the two appear to be related at any given time.

To be sure, life on the cutting edge of subsistence and vul-nerability does generate valuable and wonderful cultural forms. But the viciousness and vindictiveness of it all are real and have to be taken into account. The fact is that cultural pluralism, as the expression of progressive social life in diver-sity and unity, is a shallow concept until pressed to the level of individual differences. Otherwise we merely create polarities whenever we try to respond to a culture and a people; we sanctify it and make it a measure of general desirability against which others are negatively assessed.

And so, lost in the ethnic interstices of the American social structure, the larger question of class is never engaged, nor is even at issue. This kind of ethnic reductionism forces us to accept as predetermined what society defines as truth. Only through ethnicity can identity be securely achieved. The result is that ethnic questions which could, in fact, further our understanding of the relationship of individuals to social structures are always raised in a way that serves to reconcile us to a common heritage of miserable inequities. Instead of realizing that the lack of a well-defined stratification structure, linked to a legitimated aristocratic tradition, led Americans to employ the language of ethnic pluralism in exchange for direct divisions by social class, we continue to ignore the real factors of class in our society.

We must recognize that the heritage of white as well as black ethnic groups is, as I argued earlier, a combination of Old World and New World factors. Since America is the present, immediate past, and immediate future for most ethnic groups, the tension of Old World characteristics against American pressures must be examined in order to understand ethnic reality in this country. And in this perspective pluralism is a red herring. What we must ultimately talk about is class. The cues of felt ethnicity turn out to be the recognizable characteristics of class position in this society; to feel black, Irish, Italian, Jewish has meant to learn to live in accommodation with that part of your heritage that is compatible with the needs and opportunities in America upon arrival and soon thereafter.

In reality most groups in American society have all been successfully integrated into a hierarchical class structure that expresses itself in ethnic categories. The dichotomy we establish between "integration" and "pluralism" to permit our decennial swings from one social emphasis to another is far too simplistic to provide an adequate basis for the analysis of American social problems. Although the terms *integration* and *pluralism* might well have the potential for immense social and philosophical subtlety, they are employed in analyses of this culture to define the parameters within which ambition and frustration can be safely asserted.

As a result, ethnic-centered analyses serve to perpetuate the illusion of classlessness and the legend of equal opportunity and mobility. It is a pernicious syndrome. In large measure these myths account for the rationalization of poverty in this country through the promise that everybody who is willing and able can eventually make it. In other words, a secular state of grace is instituted that legitimates the existing pyramid of power, encourages competitive and oppressive relationships along the various "ethnic" horizontals on the pyramid, and diverts attention from the parallel oppression and exploitation of the larger class system.

To be sure, those groups and those parts of groups who today suffer from the shallowness of the American promise must be given access to the middle-class affluence and security so long denied them; no higher principles should stand in the way. And ethnic consciousness may be a step along that way. But if ethnicity continues to rationalize the ferocity of the rat race, then most of those who suffer now—however nobly—can expect to continue that way; those who can will make the most of it, while, as Paul Goodman observed, the less fortunate "are mesmerized by the symbols and culture of the rat race."

PART II

DIVIDED SOCIETY:
AN ANTHOLOGICAL
PERSPECTIVE

CHAPTER 1

*Assimilation and Mobility: Nature and Extent**

THE NATURE OF ASSIMILATION

MILTON GORDON

LET us, first of all, imagine a hypothetical situation in which a host country, to which we shall give the fictitious name of "Sylvania," is made up of a population all members of which are of the same race, religion, and previous national extraction. Cultural behavior is relatively uniform except for social class divisions. Similarly, the groups and institutions, i.e., the "social structure," of Sylvanian society are divided and differentiated only on a social class basis. Into this country, through immigration, comes a group of people who differ in previous national background and in religion and who thus have different cultural patterns from those of the host society. We shall call them the Mundovians. Let us further imagine that within the span of another generation, this population group of Mundovian national origin (now composed largely of the second generation, born in Sylvania) has taken on com-

FROM: *Assimilation in American Life: The Role of Race, Religion, and National Origins* by Milton M. Gordon, pp. 68–81. Copyright © 1964 by Oxford University Press, Inc. Reprinted by permission.
    ° See also Appendix I and Appendix II.

pletely the cultural patterns of the Sylvanians, has thrown off any sense of peoplehood based on Mundovian nationality, has changed its religion to that of the Sylvanians, has eschewed the formation of any communal organizations made up principally or exclusively of Mundovians, has entered and been hospitably accepted into the social cliques, clubs, and institutions of the Sylvanians at various class levels, has intermarried freely and frequently with the Sylvanians, encounters no prejudice or discrimination (one reason being that they are no longer distinguishable culturally or structurally from the rest of the Sylvanian population), and raises no value conflict issues in Sylvanian public life. Such a situation would represent the ultimate form of assimilation—complete assimilation to the culture and society of the host country. Note that we are making no judgment here of either the sociological desirability, feasibility, or moral rightness of such a goal. We are simply setting it up as a convenient abstraction—an "ideal type"—ideal not in the value sense of being most desirable but in the sense of representing the various elements of the concept and their interrelationships in "pure," or unqualified, fashion (the methodological device of the "ideal type" was developed and named by the German sociologist, Max Weber).

Looking at this example, we may discern that seven major variables are involved in the process discussed—in other words, seven basic subprocesses have taken place in the assimilation of the Mundovians to Sylvanian society. These may be listed in the following manner. We may say that the Mundovians have

1   changed their cultural patterns (including religious belief and observance) to those of the Sylvanians;
2   taken on large-scale primary group relationships with the Sylvanians, i.e., have entered fully into the societal network of groups and institutions, or societal structure, of the Sylvanians;
3   have intermarried and interbred fully with the Sylvanians;

4 have developed a Sylvanian, in place of a Mundovian, sense of peoplehood, or ethnicity;

5 have reached a point where they encounter no discriminatory behavior;

6 have reached a point where they encounter no prejudiced attitudes;

7 do not raise by their demands concerning the nature of Sylvanian public or civic life any issues involving value and power conflict with the original Sylvanians (for example, the issue of birth control).

Each of these steps or subprocesses may be thought of as constituting a particular stage or aspect of the assimilation process. Thus we may, in shorthand fashion, consider them as types of assimilation and characterize them accordingly. We may, then, speak, for instance, of "structural assimilation" to refer to the entrance of Mundovians into primary group relationships with the Sylvanians, or "identificational assimilation" to describe the taking on of a sense of Sylvanian peoplehood. For some of the particular assimilation subprocesses there are existing special terms. . . . The full list of assimilation subprocesses or variables with their general names, and special names, if any, is given in Table 1.

Not only is the assimilation process mainly a matter of degree, but, obviously, each of the stages or subprocesses distinguished above may take place in varying degrees.

In the example just used there has been assimilation in all respects to the society and culture which had exclusively occupied the nation up to the time of the immigrants' arrival. In other instances there may be other subsocieties and subcultures already on the scene when the new group arrives but one of these subsocieties and its way of life is dominant by virtue of original settlement, the preemption of power, or overwhelming predominance in numbers. In both cases we need a term to stand for the dominant subsociety which provides the standard to which other groups adjust or measure their relative degree of adjustment. We have tentatively used the term "host society"; however, a more neutral designation

TABLE 1
The Assimilation Variables

SUBPROCESS OR CONDITION	TYPE OR STAGE OF ASSIMILATION	SPECIAL TERM
Change of cultural patterns to those of host society	Cultural or behavioral assimilation	Acculturation
Large-scale entrance into cliques, clubs, and institutions of host society, on primary group level	Structural assimilation	None
Large-scale intermarriage	Marital assimilation	Amalgamation *
Development of sense of peoplehood based exclusively on host society	Identificational assimilation	None
Absence of prejudice	Attitude receptional assimilation	None
Absence of discrimination	Behavior receptional assimilation	None
Absence of value and power conflict	Civic assimilation	None

* My use of the term here is not predicated on the diversity in race of the two population groups which are intermarrying and interbreeding. With increasing understanding of the meaning of "race" and its thoroughly relative and arbitrary nature as a scientific term, this criterion becomes progressively less important. We may speak of the "amalgamation" or intermixture of the two "gene pools" which the two populations represent, regardless of how similar or divergent these two gene pools may be.

would be desirable. A. B. Hollingshead, in describing the class structure of New Haven, has used the term "core group" to refer to the Old Yankee families of colonial, largely Anglo-Saxon ancestry who have traditionally dominated the power and status system of the community, and who provide the "master cultural mould" for the class system of the other groups in the city.[1] Joshua Fishman has referred to the "core

[1] See August B. Hollingshead, "Trend in Social Stratification: A Case Study," *American Sociological Review*, 17 (December 1952), p. 686; and August B. Hollingshead and Frederick C. Redlich, *Social Class and Mental Illness*, New York, John Wiley and Sons, 1959, Chapters 3 and 4. It is not entirely clear to me whether Hollingshead reserves the term "core group" for "old family" Yankees in the upper class and upper-middle class only, or for Yankees throughout the class structure.

society" and the "core culture" in American life, this core being "made up essentially of White Protestant, middle-class clay, to which all other particles are attracted." [2] If there is anything in American life which can be described as an over-all American culture which serves as a reference point for immigrants and their children, it can best be described, it seems to us, as the middle-class cultural patterns of, largely, white Protestant, Anglo-Saxon origins, leaving aside for the moment the question of minor reciprocal influences on this culture exercised by the cultures of later entry into the United States, and ignoring also, for this purpose, the distinction between the upper-middle-class and the lower-middle-class cultural worlds.

There is a point on which I particularly do not wish to be misunderstood. I am not for one moment implying that the contribution of the non-Anglo-Saxon stock to the nature of American civilization has been minimal or slight. Quite the contrary. The qualitative record of achievement in industry, business, the professions, and the arts by Americans whose ancestors came from countries and traditions which are not British, or in many cases not even closely similar to British, is an overwhelmingly favorable one, and with reference to many individuals, a thoroughly brilliant one. Taken together with the substantial quantitative impact of these non-Anglo-Saxon groups on American industrial and agricultural development and on the demographic dimensions of the society, this record reveals an America in mid-twentieth century whose greatness rests on the contributions of many races, reli-

[2] Joshua A. Fishman, "Childhood Indoctrination for Minority-Group Membership and the Quest for Minority-Group Biculturism in America," (mimeo); a revised version of this paper was published under the title "Childhood Indoctrination for Minority-Group Membership," in "Ethnic Groups in American Life," *Daedalus: The Journal of the American Academy of Arts and Sciences,* Spring, 1961. See also, Jurgen Ruesch, "Social Technique, Social Status, and Social Change in Illness," in Clyde Kluckhohn and Henry A. Murray (eds.), *Personality in Nature, Society, and Culture,* New York, Alfred A. Knopf, 1948, for a use of the term "core culture" to refer to lower-middle-class culture in America.

gions, and national backgrounds.[3] My point, however, is that, with some exceptions, as the immigrants and their children have become Americans, their contributions, as laborers, farmers, doctors, lawyers, scientists, artists, etc., have been made *by way* of cultural patterns that have taken their major impress from the mould of the overwhelmingly English character of the dominant Anglo-Saxon culture or subculture in America, whose dominion dates from colonial times and whose *cultural* domination in the United States has never been seriously threatened. One must make a distinction between influencing the cultural patterns themselves and contributing to the progress and development of the society. It is in the latter area that the influence of the immigrants and their children in the United States has been decisive.

Accordingly, I shall follow Fishman's usage in referring to middle-class white Protestant Americans as constituting the "core society," or in my terms, the "core subsociety," and the cultural patterns of this group as the "core culture" or "core subculture." I shall use Hollingshead's term "core group" to refer to the white Protestant element at any social class level.

Let us now, for a moment, return to our fictitious land of Sylvania and imagine an immigration of Mundovians with a decidedly different outcome. In this case the Sylvanians accept many new behavior patterns and values from the Mundovians, just as the Mundovians change many of their ways in conformance with Sylvanian customs, this interchange taking place with appropriate modifications and compromises, and in this process a new cultural system evolves which is neither exclusively Sylvanian nor Mundovian but a mixture of both. This is a cultural blend, the result of the "melting pot," which has melted down the cultures of the two groups in the same societal container, as it were, and formed a new cultural product with standard consistency. This process has, of course, also involved thorough social mixing in primary as

[3] See Oscar and Mary F. Handlin, Chapter 1, "The United States," in *The Positive Contribution by Immigrants*, Paris, Unesco, 1955.

well as secondary groups and a large-scale process of inter-marriage. The melting pot has melted the two groups into one, societally and culturally.

Whether such a process as just described is feasible or likely of occurrence is beside the point here. It, too, is an "ideal type," an abstraction against which we can measure the realities of what actually happens. Our point is that the seven variables of the assimilation process which we have isolated can be measured against the "melting pot" goal as well as against the "adaptation to the core society and culture" goal. That is, assuming the "melting pot" goal, we can then inquire how much acculturation of both groups has taken place to form such a blended culture, how much social structural mixture has taken place, and so on.[4] We now have a model of assimilation with seven variables which can be used to analyze the assimilation process with reference to either of two variant goal-systems: 1) "adaptation to the core society and culture," and 2) the "melting pot." Theoretically, it would be possible to apply the analysis model of variables with reference to carrying out the goal-system of "cultural pluralism" as well. However, this would be rather premature at this point since the concept of cultural pluralism is itself so meagerly understood. . . .

Let us now apply this model of assimilation analysis in tentative fashion to selected "minority" ethnic groups on the American scene. The applied paradigm presented in Table 2 allows us to record and summarize a great deal of information compactly and comparatively. We shall deal here, for illustrative purposes, with four groups: Negroes, Jews, Catholics (excluding Negro and Spanish-speaking Catholics), and Puerto Ricans. The basic goal-referent will be "adaptation to core society and culture." The entries in the table cells may

[4] I am indebted to Professor Richard D. Lambert of the University of Pennsylvania for pointing out to me that my array of assimilation variables must be applied with reference to the basic assimilation goals. In my original scheme of presentation I had implicitly applied it only to the goal-system of "adaptation to the core society and culture."

be regarded, at this point, as hypotheses. Qualifying comments will be made in the footnotes to the table.

One of the tasks of sociological theory is not only to identify the factors or variables present in any given social process or situation, but also to hypothesize how these variables may be related to each other. Let us look at the seven assimilation variables from this point of view. We note that in Table 2, of the four ethnic groups listed, only one, the Puerto Ricans, are designated as being substantially unassimilated culturally. The Puerto Ricans are the United States' newest immigrant group of major size. If we now examine the entries for the Negro, one of America's oldest minorities, we find that assimilation has not taken place in most of the other variables, but with allowance for social class factors, *has* taken place culturally. These two facts in juxtaposition should give us a clue to the relation of the cultural assimilation variable to all the others. This relationship may be stated as follows: 1) *cultural assimilation, or acculturation, is likely to be the first of the types of assimilation to occur when a minority group arrives on the scene; and* 2) *cultural assimilation, or acculturation, of the minority group may take place even when none of the other types of assimilation occurs simultaneously or later, and this condition of "acculturation only" may continue indefinitely.*

If we examine the history of immigration into the United States, both of these propositions are seen to be borne out. After the birth of the republic, as each succeeding wave of immigration, first from Northern and Western Europe, later from Southern and Eastern Europe and the Orient, has spread over America, the first process that has occurred has been the taking on of the English language and American behavior patterns, even while the creation of the immigrant colonies sealed off their members from extensive primary contacts with "core society" Americans and even when prejudice and discrimination against the minority have been at a high point. While this process is only partially completed in the

TABLE 2

Paradigm of Assimilation
Applied to Selected Groups in the United States—
Basic Goal Referent: Adaptation to Core Society and Culture

GROUP	TYPE OF ASSIMILATION						
	CULTURAL *	STRUCTURAL	MARITAL	IDENTIFICATIONAL ‡	ATTITUDE RECEPTIONAL	BEHAVIOR RECEPTIONAL	CIVIC
Negroes	Variation by class †	No	No	No	No	No	Yes
Jews	Substantially Yes	No	Substantially No	No	No	Partly	Mostly
Catholics (excluding Negro and Spanish-speaking)	Substantially Yes	Partly (variation by area)	Partly	No	Partly	Mostly	Partly §
Puerto Ricans	Mostly No	No	No	No	No	No	Partly

* Some reciprocal cultural influences have, of course, taken place. American language, diet, recreational patterns, art forms, and economic techniques have been modestly influenced by the cultures of non-Anglo-Saxon resident groups since the first contacts with the American Indians, and the American culture is definitely the richer for these influences. However, the reciprocal influences have not been great. See George R. Stewart, *American Ways of Life*, New York, Doubleday and Co., 1954. . . . Furthermore, the minority ethnic groups have not given up all their pre-immigration cultural patterns. Particularly, they have preserved their non-Protestant religions. I have thus used the phrase "Substantially Yes" to indicate this degree of adaptation.

† Although few, if any, African cultural survivals are to be found among American Negroes, lower-class Negro life with its derivations from slavery, post-Civil War discrimination, both rural and urban poverty, and enforced isolation from the middle-class white world, is still at a considerable distance from the American cultural norm. Middle and upper-class Negroes, on the other hand, are acculturated to American core culture.

‡ As I pointed out earlier, ethnic identification in a modern complex society may contain several "layers." My point is not that Negroes, Jews, and Catholics in the United States do not think of themselves as Americans. They do. It is that they also have an "inner layer" sense of peoplehood which is Negro, Jewish, or Catholic, as the case may be, and not "white Protestant" or "white Anglo-Saxon Protestant," which is the corresponding inner layer of ethnic identity of the core society.

§ Value and power conflicts of Catholics with a large portion of the rest of the American population over such issues as birth control, divorce, therapeutic abortion and church-state relationships constitute the reason for the entry of "Partly" here.

immigrant generation itself, with the second and succeeding generations, exposed to the American public school system and speaking English as their native tongue, the impact of the American acculturation process has been overwhelming; the rest becomes a matter of social class mobility and the kind of acculturation that such mobility demands. On the other hand, the success of the acculturation process has by no means guaranteed entry of each minority into the primary groups and institutions—that is, the subsociety—of the white Protestant group. With the exception of white Protestant immigrant stock from Northern and Western Europe—I am thinking here particularly of the Scandinavians, Dutch, and Germans—by and large such structural mixture on the primary level has not taken place. Nor has such acculturation success eliminated prejudice and discrimination or in many cases led to large-scale intermarriage with the core society.

The only qualifications of my generalizations about the rapidity and success of the acculturation process that the American experience suggests are these: 1) if a minority group is spatially isolated and segregated (whether voluntarily or not) in a rural area, as is the case with the American Indians still on reservations, even the acculturation process will be very slow; and 2) unusually marked discrimination, such as that which has been faced by the American Negro, if it succeeds in keeping vast numbers of the minority group deprived of educational and occupational opportunities and thus predestined to remain in a lower-class setting, may indefinitely retard the acculturation process for the group. Even in the case of the American Negro, however, from the long view or perspective of American history, this effect of discrimination will be seen to have been a delaying action only; the quantitatively significant emergence of the middle-class Negro is already well on its way.

Before we leave specific examination of the acculturation variable and its relationships, it would be well to distinguish between two types of cultural patterns and traits which may characterize any ethnic group. Some, like its religious beliefs and practices, its ethical values, its musical tastes, folk recreational patterns, literature, historical language, and sense of a common past, are essential and vital ingredients of the group's cultural heritage, and derive exactly from that heritage. We shall refer to these as *intrinsic* cultural traits or patterns. Others, such as dress, manner, patterns of emotional expression, and minor oddities in pronouncing and inflecting English, tend to be products of the historical vicissitudes of a group's adjustment to its local environment, including the present one (and also reflect social class experiences and values), and are in a real sense external to the core of the group's ethnic cultural heritage. These may conveniently be referred to as *extrinsic* cultural traits or patterns.[5] To illustrate, the Catholicism or Judaism of the immigrant from Southern or Eastern Europe represent a difference in *intrinsic culture* from the American core society and its Protestant religious affiliation. However, the greater volatility of emotional expression of the Southern and Eastern European peasant or villager in comparison with the characteristically greater reserve of the upper-middle-class American of the core society constitutes a difference in *extrinsic culture*. To take another example, the variant speech pattern, or argot, of the lower-class Negro of recent southern background, which is so widespread both in the South and in northern cities, is a product of external circumstances and is not something vital to Negro culture. It is thus an *extrinsic* cultural trait. Were this argot, which constitutes such a powerful handicap to social mobility and adjustment to the core culture, to disappear, nothing significant for Negro self-regard as a group or the Negro's sense of ethnic history and identity would be violated. While this distinction between intrinsic and extrinsic culture is a tenta-

[5] Compare with the distinction in types of cultural traits made by William E. Vickery and Stewart G. Cole in *Intercultural Education in American Schools,* New York and London, Harper and Brothers, 1943, pp. 43–4.

tive one, and cannot be uniformly applied to all cultural traits, it is still a useful one and may help cast further light on the acculturation process, particularly in its relationship to prejudice and discrimination.

As we examine the array of assimilation variables again, several other relationships suggest themselves. One is the indissoluble connection, in the time order indicated, between structural assimilation and marital assimilation. That is, entrance of the minority group into the social cliques, clubs, and institutions of the core society at the primary group level inevitably will lead to a substantial amount of intermarriage. If children of different ethnic backgrounds belong to the same play-group, later the same adolescent cliques, and at college the same fraternities and sororities; if the parents belong to the same country club and invite each other to their homes for dinner; it is completely unrealistic not to expect these children, now grown, to love and to marry each other, blithely oblivious to previous ethnic extraction. Communal leaders of religious and nationality groups that desire to maintain their ethnic identity are aware of this connection, which is one reason for the proliferation of youth groups, adult clubs, and communal institutions which tend to confine their members in their primary relationships safely within the ethnic fold.

If marital assimilation, an inevitable by-product of structural assimilation, takes place fully, the minority group loses its ethnic identity in the larger host or core society, and identificational assimilation takes place. Prejudice and discrimination are no longer a problem, since eventually the descendants of the original minority group become indistinguishable, and since primary group relationships tend to build up an "in-group" feeling which encloses all the members of the group. If assimilation has been complete in all intrinsic as well as extrinsic cultural traits, then no value conflicts on civic issues are likely to arise between the now dispersed descendants of the ethnic minority and members of the core society. Thus the remaining types of assimilation have all taken place like a row of tenpins bowled over in rapid succession be a well placed strike. We may state the emergent generalization, then, as follows: *Once structural assimilation has occurred, either simultaneously with or subsequent to acculturation, all of the other types of assimilation will naturally follow.* It need hardly be pointed out that while acculturation, as we have emphasized above, does not necessarily lead to structural assimilation, structural assimilation inevitably produces acculturation. Structural assimilation, then, rather than acculturation, is seen to be the keystone of the arch of assimilation. The price of such assimilation, however, is the disappearance of the ethnic group as a separate entity and the evaporation of its distinctive values.

DEPRIVATION AND MIGRATION
MARC FRIED

BY the middle of the nineteenth century, many Americans became fearful of the ruinous effect of newcomers on their society. After the Civil War, the great territorial and industrial expansion led to a diminution in nativist sentiment.[1] The material need for an expanding population was great; the same national groups, predominantly German, English, and Irish, continued to be the dominant immigrant forces. By the late 1870s and 1880s, however, new patterns of nativism began their opposition to the "new immigration" only to reach a peak during and immediately following World War I.

FROM: Chapter 5, "Deprivation and Migration: Dilemmas of Causal Interpretation," by Marc Fried, in *On Understanding Poverty*, edited by Daniel P. Moynihon, with the assistance of Corinne Saposs Schelling, © 1968, 1969 by the Academy of Arts and Sciences, Basic Books, Inc., Publishers, New York.

[1] John Hingham, *Strangers in the Land: Patterns of American Nativism, 1860–1925*, rev. ed. (New York: Atheneum, 1963).

Viewed as a large, historical phenomenon, nativist sentiment with its strong source in opposition to foreign competition, foreign ideology, and foreign culture may have undergone a slow and variable progression partly modified by the pervasive sense of the United States as both haven and melting pot. Concretely, however, most foreign groups that entered the United States in large numbers and differed in striking ways from Americans were subjected to extreme difficulties. For the English, this was mitigated by the fact that, unlike most other immigrants, they came to fill relatively skilled jobs in specific industries. Cultural similarities also facilitated a rapid transition.[2] For the Germans and Scandinavians, the movement toward specific regions, generally of low-population density, permitted them to follow a path that had already been prepared and, despite low rates of assimilation, to experience little long-term antagonism.[3] But whether the extremely low social position, the cultural and religious distinctiveness, the competitive economic situation, or some larger change in the society as a whole was responsible for the difference, during the latter part of the nineteenth century and the early part of the twentieth century, the Irish, Italians, Slavs, Jews, and others who emigrated to the United States were subjected to brutal experiences of isolation, exploitation, and exclusion.[4] The more recent experiences of Negroes,

[2] Rowland Tappan Berthoff, *British Immigrants in Industrial America, 1790–1950* (Cambridge, Mass.: Harvard University Press, 1953).

[3] Hingham, *op. cit.;* Mack Walker, *Germany and the Emigration, 1816–1885* (Cambridge, Mass.: Harvard University Press, 1964).

[4] Robert Ernst, *Immigrant Life in New York City* (New York: Kings Crown Press, 1949); Oscar Handlin, *Boston's Immigrants: A Study in Acculturation* (Cambridge, Mass.: Harvard University Press, 1959); Marcus Lee Hanse, *The American Migration 1607–1860* (New York: Harper, 1940); Hingham, *op. cit.;* Samuel Joseph, *Jewish Immigration to the United States: From 1881 to 1910* (New York: Atheneum, 1963); Edward M. Levine, *The Irish and Irish Politicians* (Notre Dame, Ind.: University of Notre Dame Press, 1966); George Potter, *To the Golden Door: The Study of the Irish in Ireland and America* (Boston: Little, Brown, 1960); William C. Smith, *Americans in the Making* (New York: Appleton-Century Crofts, 1939); George M. Stephenson, *A History of American Immigration* (Boston: Ginn, 1926); William Thomas and

Deprivation and Migration

Puerto Ricans, and Mexican-Americans follow a well-trodden path of discrimination and segregation in the urban, industrial areas of the United States. . . .

While the cyclical patterns of employment and immigration were similar, the sheer volume of migration remained high through prosperity and depression and corresponded less closely to the level of employment. These patterns held not only for European immigration as a whole but also for each of the separate, large migration streams from different European countries.

The vast majority of the immigrants to the United States during the nineteenth and twentieth centuries were relatively uneducated people from rural areas: farmers, farm laborers, unskilled or semiskilled workers, and rural or semirural craftsmen.[5] The United Kingdom, of course, provided a larger proportion of skilled workers than any other region of the world; they were also distinguished by their specific occupational interest, by the eagerness with which their services were sought, and by their continuity in occupations they had held before emigrating.[6] Between 1875 and 1910, more than half the immigrants from Wales and Scotland were listed as skilled laborers and nearly as high a proportion from England. By contrast, throughout this same period, immigrants from Ireland were preponderantly common laborers or servants and rarely numbered as many as 10 per cent skilled laborers.[7] The data for Italian immigrants suggest a picture similar to that for the Irish, with agricultural labor substituting for the servant category. The German migration seemed

Florian Znaniecki, *The Polish Peasant in Europe and America* (Chicago: Chicago University Press, 1918; New York: Knopf, 1928).

[5] Niles Carpenter, *Immigrants and Their Children, 1920* (Washington, D.C.: U.S. Government Printing Office, 1927).

[6] Berthoff, *op. cit.*

[7] Brinley Thomas, *Migration and Economic Growth* (Cambridge: Cambridge University Press, 1954) (Tables 80 to 84). The amount of distortion in these data is unknown, and one may well anticipate some upgrading of occupations generally and the substitution of urban work categories for farmers in anticipation of occupational alterations in the United States.

to draw more heavily on farmers and rural craftsmen, but nonetheless included predominantly the higher categories of low-status workers.[8]

Although there have been no thorough studies, at least in English, of the occupational histories of migrants compared to nonmigrants, there is a general consensus that low-status newcomers to an area suffer serious disadvantages compared to natives of similar status.[9] These disadvantages occur through entering the lowest-status jobs and through a high degree of job insecurity. Thus, migrants have higher levels of unemployment and among the lowest incomes in urban areas. While there almost certainly are large differences depending on educational level, urban experience, and social acceptance of different ethnic or racial groups, the phenomenally low status of migrants appears to be quite general. . . . Lipset and Bendix show evidence for marked differences in occupational status and mobility depending both on migration status and size of community of origin in several American studies as well as in Sweden and in Germany.[10] Thernstrom provides data showing the marked differences in occupational mobility of immigrants compared to natives in nineteenth-century Newburyport.[11] And Blau and Duncan's analysis of more recent data, more carefully controlled than previous studies although heavily weighted by more recent and more highly

---

[8] Robert F. Foerster, *The Italian Emigration of Our Times* (Cambridge, Mass.: Harvard University Press, 1919); Walker, *op. cit.*

[9] The findings of Karl E. Taeuber and Irene B. Taeuber, *Negroes in Cities: Residential Segregation and Neighborhood Change* (Chicago: Aldine, 1965) and of Peter M. Blau and Otis Dudley Duncan, *The American Occupational Structure* (New York: Wiley, 1967) reveal that this does not hold for those migrants who are of relatively high status and predominantly migrate from one city to another. But the disadvantage of migrants does hold, in these more recent data on internal migration within the United States, for migrants from nonmetropolitan areas (Taeuber and Taeuber, *ibid.*) and for migrants from farm residence (Blau and Duncan, *ibid*).

[10] S. M. Lipset and Reinhard Bendix, *Social Mobility in Industrial Society* (Berkeley: University of California Press, 1959).

[11] Stephen Thernstrom, *Poverty and Progress* (Cambridge, Mass.: Harvard University Press, 1964).

selective migrations as well as by recent periods of economic expansion, indicates an improvement in rates of occupational mobility for immigrants with continuing disadvantages for those immigrants from the least-favored countries.[12]

THE MYTH OF SOCIAL MOBILITY
AND SOCIAL ASSIMILATION

The many millions of immigrants from European countries from the middle of the nineteenth century until relatively recent decades bore the full brunt of the low-status positions accorded the newcomer, the foreign-born, the rural peasant or worker, the uneducated, and the socially ostracized. Although few studies permit us to clarify the components of background or status most clearly implicated in the demeaning occupational conditions of the immigrant, the data are unambiguous in revealing their lowly state.[13] At the extreme, immigrants from Ireland, Italy, and Poland were at the bottom of the occupational ladder and worked under conditions of unbelievable degradation and exploitation. However, even the migrants from England, Scotland, and Wales started at levels considerably below the native population.[14, 15]

[12] Blau and Duncan, *op. cit.* While many controls were possible for this study that could not be done with earlier data, they do not take account of changes in the occupational structure that have increased the proportion of higher status occupational positions and, thus, necessarily produce a pattern of social mobility that is built into the process of social change. Moreover, even assuming that the occupational distribution approximates an interval scale and, therefore, that occupational changes at both ends of the distribution truly represent similar degrees of mobility, an assumption to be verified, the greater variance in the occupational distributions of immigrants than of natives in their sample suggests that the rates of occupational mobility for immigrants can be more seriously affected than those of natives by differentials in occupational mobility at different levels of the occupational scale.

[13] Carpenter, *op. cit.*

[14] Thomas, *op. cit.* (Table 40).

[15] Thomas's (*ibid.*) data and some of Lieberson's (Stanley Lieberson, *Ethnic Patterns in American Cities* [New York: The Free Press, 1963]) findings suggest that many migrants enter the host society at a lower

A matter of more serious concern than low initial status is the slow and difficult process of mobility and assimilation. For the British, whose occupational distributions were higher than those of the native Americans by the second generation, assimilation presented no special problems.[16] For other groups like the Germans and Scandinavians, who often lived in ethnically homogeneous enclaves, the process of social mobility occurred with moderate facility.[17] Among the Jews, who have been the proverbial representatives of rapid social mobility, the process has been uneven and reveals some of the special problems of both mobility and assimilation in the face of overwhelming discrimination and restrictions.[18] And although the Chinese and Japanese, among the non-European immigrants, have achieved extremely high levels of education and occupation, their slow and painful accomplishment is hardly testimony to the open-mobility pattern or the ease of assimilation in the United States.[19]

The most recent urban migrant groups, the Negro, the Puerto Rican, and the Mexican-American, have suffered severely, but many earlier immigrant groups have also experienced an extremely slow and precarious process of social mo-

level than that of their former occupations. This tends to confound any simple analysis of social mobility since, either for intragenerational or intergenerational mobility, the distance from the lower initial status of the immigrant will exaggerate mobility achievement compared with the distance from the prior, pre-immigration status.

[16] Thomas, *op. cit.*; E. P. Hutchinson, *Immigrants and Their Children, 1850–1950* (New York: Wiley, 1956), Table 41a.

[17] Christen Tonnes Jonassen, "Cultural Variables in the Ecology of an Ethnic Group," *American Sociological Review,* XIV (1949), 32–41.

[18] Nathan Glazer and Daniel P. Moynihan, *Beyond the Melting Pot: The Negroes, Puerto Ricans, Jews, Italians and Irish of New York City* (Cambridge, Mass.: Harvard and M.I.T. Press, 1963). See Hingham, *op. cit.*, for a description of some of the recurrent waves of anti-Semitism that led to many of the quota systems, residential restrictions, and recreational exclusions during the anti-foreign outbreaks of the 1920s and have begun to diminish only during the past few decades.

[19] Calvin F. Schmid and Charles E. Nobbe, "Socioeconomic Differentials Among Nonwhite Races," *American Sociological Review,* XXX (1965), 909–922.

bility. This has been particularly notable among the Irish.[20] In 1870, more than twenty years after their great migration and about a half century after the beginning of a substantial migration stream, 68.6 per cent of the first generation were manual workers or servants; by 1900, it had increased to 71.6 per cent of the first-generation Irish. By contrast, the entire population of the United States, including many other low-status immigrants, contained only 45.1 per cent in these occupational categories in 1900. Moreover, progress was very slow for the second generation: In 1900, 59.7 per cent of the second-generation Irish were classified in manual work or domestic service.[21] Indeed, by 1950, the foreign-born Irish, including many who had migrated shortly after the turn of the century during the era of dwindling Irish immigration, were markedly underrepresented in white-collar occupations although they had achieved some status as semiskilled and skilled workers, managers, officials, and proprietors. The second generation, however, was moving rapidly toward parity with the native white population of native parentage.[22]

The situation of the Irish was fairly extreme and was compounded by a long history of degradation and restriction, by the rush to depart that often led them to inappropriate destinations, by the severe anti-Catholicism that met them, and by the dominance of parochial education that sheltered the second generation from the impact of American values and orientations.[23] But the Italians, arriving more recently than the Irish, were also markedly underrepresented in all higher-status occupations as late as 1950, and the second generation was moving more slowly than the Irish to an occupational

[20] Glazer and Moynihan, *op. cit.;* Oscar Handlin, *The Newcomers* (New York: Doubleday, 1959).
[21] Thomas, *op. cit.* (Table 40).
[22] Lieberson, *op. cit.* (Tables 52 and 54).
[23] Glazer and Moynihan, *op. cit.;* Handlin, *Boston's Immigrants, op. cit.;* Potter, *op. cit.;* Thomas, *op. cit.;* Cecil Woodham-Smith, *The Great Hunger: Ireland 1845–1849* (New York: Harper, 1962).

distribution comparable with native whites of native parentage.[24] The Germans and the Poles had mobility rates higher than the Irish-Italian pattern but considerably lower than the English, Scotch, or Welsh. By 1910, the Germans were showing a modest level of mobility, but were still underrepresented in high-status occupations. By 1950, the first-generation Germans were close to parity with native white Americans, but the second generation was not yet equivalent to native whites of native parentage.[25] The Poles found opportunities for mobility from unskilled to skilled ranks in the major manufacturing industries. But few moved on rapidly to positions as skilled workers.[26] By 1950, however, the Poles of foreign birth had moved far and were well represented among skilled workers, managers, and officials.[27]

What these facts highlight, imperfect though they may be, is the great gap between an image of continuous and rapid mobility and the reality of slow, arduous, intragenerational and intergenerational change in status. There is no question that the process of upward mobility among immigrants has been continuous. But if, sixty to one hundred years after an ethnic group has initiated large-scale immigration into this country and much of that immigration necessarily occurred more than forty years ago, there is still such a wide discrepancy in occupational achievement from the host population, then we must alter our conceptions of the process. The rungs of the mobility ladder are wide apart for migrants to an urban, industrial society. Just as the melting pot has failed to melt and consolidate its ethnic prey, so has the mobility process failed to amalgamate its poverty-stricken, uneducated, and unskilled immigrants or their children in a vision of success. The deprived migrants of another era remain relatively disadvantaged, and their children suffer the consequences of

[24] Lieberson, *op. cit.* (Tables 52 and 54).

[25] Thomas, *op. cit.* (Table 40); Lieberson, *ibid.*

[26] David Brody, *Steelworkers in America: The Nonunion Era* (Cambridge, Mass.: Harvard University Press, 1960).

[27] Lieberson, *op. cit.*

these deprivations while slowly overcoming their effects.

At the very least, we must consider the conventional conception of mobility and assimilation of ethnic minorities in the United States a myth. Some few ethnic groups have, in fact, been highly mobile particularly if they brought scarce skills or moved into a prepared environment. Other ethnic groups, the large majority, have been slowly mobile and have had to overcome gigantic obstacles in their struggles for educational attainment, occupational status, and high income. And a few ethnic groups have struggled, virtually in vain, until a new generation, bearing fewer of the marks of ethnicity and in a different social environment, were able to confront the problem without the preformed conviction that they were doomed to failure. We must also forego any ready assumptions about the ease of social assimilation. While social mobility is often a stage in the larger assimilation of immigrants, there are large gaps in the process, and mobility achievements among immigrants, as with the Negro, Puerto Rican, and Mexican-American, have often proved necessary, but hardly sufficient, for social assimilation.

After almost a half century during which there have been no mass immigrations from Europe or Asia, the issue of the social mobility and social assimilation of the foreign-born and of their native-born children is no longer as trenchant and pressing a problem as it once was in the large cities of the United States. Although some ethnic groups have not yet reached parity with the population as a whole in education, occupation, or income, and have not yet achieved total desegregation in housing, the differences are not large. Buoyed by several periods of great prosperity that have facilitated, probably with disproportionate advantage, the mobility opportunities of immigrants, and in the context of a high standard of living in an affluent society, the problem seems academic.

However, the problem is far from academic. If these conclusions are correct, we must not only dismiss the image of rapid mobility and assimilation, but must place, in its stead, an image of a moderately restrictive and fundamentally segregationist society. Despite the absence of an overtly structured status system on the model of post feudal societies, issues of ethnicity, race, and culture have been superimposed on economic and occupational differences to provide a basis for discrimination, prejudice, and social inequality. The labor of millions of poverty-stricken immigrants was necessary for the industrial expansion of the United States, and only because of this were its doors open to indentured servants, slaves, serfs, and, as a result, to their descendants. But the people were themselves viewed as a vast and impersonal, low-status labor force to whom society owed nothing. Translations of the Elizabethan Poor Laws discouraging vagrants and the indigent and pioneering work in the development of an urban police force were our primary control mechanisms. Little attention was given to the social and personal needs of immigrants until the explosion of urban social problems made their desperate situations unavoidably evident to a few people. Even then, the society offered the immigrant with less evident needs and who was a less evident threat little or no assistance and placed great impediments in the path of establishing a meaningful and integrated life experience in the new world.

SOCIAL MOBILITY AND
ASSIMILATION AMONG NEGROES

In order to provide a meaningful comparison of the situation of the foreign-born immigrant to the United States and that of the Negro American whose migration patterns to urban industrial areas we have traced in gross fashion, we must now examine rates of social mobility and of social assimilation for Negroes. In examining the social mobility and assimilation of the Negro migrant, whose period of massive movement has occurred since approximately 1910 and shows only slight indications of diminution during the 1960s, we must rely heavily on recent data. Moreover, a consideration of social assimilation must depend almost exclusively on residential segregation. That there have been difficulties in both social mobility and residential segregation of Negroes long before the large-scale migrations of the past half century, however, is clear. Although several historians point to the fact that, prior to the increased immigration associated with World War II, the resident Negro population in northern cities had begun to achieve a modicum of occupational and economic advancement, these reports are based on isolated cases rather than systematic population or sample data.[28] Whatever minimal achievements the settled Negro population in northern cities experienced, residential segregation was pervasive and more severe than for other in-migrant populations.[29]

A wealth of data indicates that urban, industrial societies have quite high rates of social mobility and that this is true and has been true for some time in the United States.[30] But, apart from the technical difficulties of making even moderately precise estimates, evaluations of mobility rates as "high" or "low" are extremely subjective.[31] Thernstrom's compilation of ten different studies of occupational changes from fathers to sons covering periods from 1860 to 1956 illustrates a fairly

[28] Handlin, *The Newcomers, op. cit.*; Gilbert Osofsky, *Harlem: The Making of a Ghetto* (New York: Harper, 1966).

[29] St. Clair Drake and Horace R. Cayton, *Black Metropolis: A Study of Negro Life in a Northern City* (New York: Harcourt, Brace, 1945); Osofsky, *op. cit.*; Jacob A. Riis, *How the Other Half Lives* (New York: Sagamore Press, 1957).

[30] Lipset and Bendix, *op. cit.*; Lloyd W. Warner and Leo Srole, *The Social Systems of American Ethnic Groups* (New Haven, Conn.: Yale University Press, 1945); Thernstrom, *op. cit.*; S. M. Miller, "Comparative Social Mobility," *Current Sociology*, IX (1960), Chapter 1; Peter M. Blau and Otis Dudley Duncan, "Some Preliminary Findings on Social Stratification in the United States," *Acta Sociologica*, IX (1965), 2–24; Sidney Goldstein, "Migration and Occupational Mobility in Norristown, Pennsylvania," *American Sociological Review*, XX (1955), 402–448.

[31] Whether these rates are viewed as high or low is dependent on (a) subjective expectations or (b) the application of a linear model of mobility to a criterion population (for example, native white Americans). Both of these bases for evaluation are, at best, inadequate for a clear understanding of complex mobility patterns.

61

similar pattern.[32] All of these studies vary around estimates that approximately 50 to 60 per cent (ranging from 48 to 71 per cent) of the sons of unskilled laborers were themselves either unskilled or semiskilled laborers. That the occupational progress of Negroes has been slow and halting by any criterion, however, is quite evident from the gross estimates of changes in occupational position between 1910 and 1960. Tobin, quoting Hiestand's data, shows significant improvement only during the period from 1940 to 1960, although there had been some improvement relative to whites since 1910.[33] Even these changes, which bring the occupational position of Negro males to the level of 82.1 per cent of white males by 1960, may overstate the degree of change experienced. (On the other hand, most analyses of changes in education, occupation, or income of Negroes over the last few decades fail to distinguish the South from other regions of the country, which leads to another serious distortion of the results.) These differences between Negroes and foreign-born whites diminish in the light of these data not because of the very high levels of manifest achievement but because both the foreign immigrants of the earlier period and the Negro migrants of the past half century have similarly fought against great obstacles and severe inequalities only to experience slow and meager gains. We have no objective way of measuring or even estimating the differences in opportunities for educational, occupational, or economic mobility for the earlier European immigrant and the more recent Negro migrant from the South. It appears almost indubitable that Negroes have experienced the most devastating forms of prejudice and limitation of opportunity. But this emerges as a serious intensification of continuing patterns of discrimination and inequality of opportunity in our society rather than as a wholly unique phenomenon.

[32] Thernstrom, *op. cit.*

[33] James Tobin, "On Improving the Economic Status of the Negro," *Daedalus* (Fall 1965).

Deprivation and Migration

While the earlier literature about the foreign immigrants was invariably hostile and critical and, from our present vantage point, unbelievably insulting, as early as 1890 Riis noted the more severely underprivileged and degrading situation of the Negro.[34] It may, indeed, be the case that the modest degree to which the Negro American population has achieved mobility is all the more remarkable a feat. The scattered evidence of very high levels of motivation and aspiration among Negroes, of widespread and effective community leadership in either collaboration or revolt, of outstanding achievements in numerous fields, even the fact that the most striking occupational gains of the past five years have been in the most highly skilled professional and technical pursuits, suggest that we must alter our image of the Negro in the United States. In view of the serious impediments to achievement, the level of accomplishment may well be remarkably great. And in view of the evidence for extremely slow progress among the immigrants of the great European migrations, there may be far less discrepancy in social mobility between white immigrants and Negro migrants than we ordinarily imagine.

Although we do not have any adequate measure of discrimination and the significance of inequality of opportunity as a basis for evaluating mobility achievements, measures of housing segregation do provide some basis for evaluating the role of discrimination in social assimilation. In comparing residential segregation of foreign-born immigrants and their second-generation offspring for earlier periods with the early or more recent patterns of segregation of Negroes, we have only the reports of observers. That such segregation was widespread both along ethnic and social class divisions, however, is quite clear from the literature.[35] While the Irish, Poles, Italians, Jews, and other groups each tended to form its own little ethnic enclave, ethnic differences often merged on the basis of

[34] Riis, op. cit.
[35] Handlin, The Newcomers, op. cit.; Riis, op. cit.; Robert A. Woods, Americans in Process (Boston: Houghton Mifflin, 1902).

both social class similarities and time of arrival. Even in the earlier reports, this distinguished the Negro from other ethnic groups.[36] Negro residential areas tended to be ethnically distinctive and represented a wider range of social class positions as a consequence of pervasive discrimination in housing.

Lieberson's analysis of residential segregation from 1910 to 1950 highlights the continuities in these patterns.[37] First, he found high levels of residential segregation among all ethnic groups for all the cities studied, with little evident difference between the "old" immigration (those who predominated prior to 1880) and the "new" immigration (those who predominated between 1880 and 1920). They were quite uniformly high. Second, over time, there was a gradual dispersion, but as recently as 1950, patterns of residential segregation by ethnic group was still evident. Finally, depending on time of arrival, there is a gradual dispersion of ethnic groups both in diminished rates of segregation and in movement out of the central city. While there is some evidence in these and in other data of similar patterns among the urban Negro population, rates of residential segregation are consistently higher than for any of the immigrant ethnic groups, rates of change over time are less clear, and associations between residential dispersion and social class achievements are less marked.

CONCLUSIONS

It has become conventional to point out the great gap between the achievements of the European immigrants who peopled the United States during more than a century between the end of the Napoleonic wars and the first major restrictions on immigration in 1924 and the failure of achievement, on the other hand, among Negroes whose major

---

[36] Osofsky, *op. cit.;* Riis, *op. cit.*
[37] Lieberson, *op. cit.*

entrance into the urban industrial environment started around 1900 and continues apace. In the course of reviewing the extensive, albeit inadequate, data concerning social mobility and assimilation among both the European immigrants to the cities of this country and the Negro migrants from the South to the industrialized areas of the North and West, we have been forced to challenge this conclusion and to reconsider the implications of the melting pot ideology. . . .

We have tried to show that the European immigrant most often experienced the transition from rural, pre-industrial areas and largely agricultural occupations in southern, eastern, and central Europe to the cities and low-status manual occupations in the United States as an extremely painful, difficult, and threatening process. Immigrants left and continued to leave their native homes because they could look forward to nothing but misery and a deteriorating economic and social situation. . . .

The second generation experienced a less restrictive environment but it was far from the myth of unlimited opportunities for social mobility and assimilation. It is difficult to determine precisely how long it took and under what conditions it was possible to gain a reasonable approximation to equality of status. But for many ethnic groups, full residential assimilation had not yet been realized as late as 1950.[38] The relatively rapid social mobility of the English, Jewish, and Japanese immigrant must, in this view, be treated as one extreme of a continuum, although the Jewish and Japanese immigrant suffered a fairly typical history of severe discrimination, restriction, and ostracism. Educational and occupational mobility and cultural parity were not enough to insure social

[38] Schmid and Nobbe (*op. cit.*) present interesting data for several non-white ethnic groups. The Chinese situation is of particular significance because Chinese immigration was more forcibly cut off (in 1882) than that of any other nationality. For the Chinese, whose immigration occurred largely between 1830 and 1882, meaningful equivalence to white American statuses in education, occupation, and income was not established until 1930–1940, one hundred years after the beginning, and fifty years after the end, of large-scale immigration.

acceptance. And for the largest proportion of the immigrants, educational and occupational mobility were extremely difficult and unduly costly achievements. Thus, the idea of the United States as a melting pot emerges as a mythical elaboration of a fragmentary truth and gives way to an image of widespread inequality, racist attitudes, and ethnic segregation as the dominant reality.[39]

In a different era, when foreign-born immigrants and their children were often viewed as expendable, it was possible to disregard their desperate needs for support in facilitating social mobility and assimilation. Under different economic conditions, when the economy was a captive of the business cycle and its operation less subject to deliberate manipulation, it was more difficult to create jobs, educational opportunities, or other resources for encouraging rapid change. And in an environment in which demands for equality and opportunity were more impetuously violent, more fractionated along ethnic or occupational lines, less broadly goal-directed, and in which a democratic ideology was more limited in conception, it was possible to accept police suppression and the power of the national guard or of the armed forces as an effective means of eliminating a problem by eliminating its manifest expression. All of this has changed. We have an unparalleled potential to create a situation in which rates of achievement among the Negro population can more nearly approximate overt aspirations, needs, and demands.[40] Yet, we remain relatively paralyzed in our focus

[39] For a different view of the term "racism" and its utility, see Daniel P. Moynihan, "The New Racialism," *Atlantic Monthly,* CCXXII (1968), 35–40. Moynihan argues that the term "racialism" is more appropriate to the current situation which is largely a matter of one group's antagonism toward another group with conflicting interests.

[40] Stanley Lieberson and Glenn V. Fuguitt, "Negro-White Occupational Differences in the Absence of Discrimination," *American Journal of Sociology,* LXXIII (1967), 188–200, point out that, in the absence of discrimination, two generations would bring about a high level of parity in the status of Negroes and whites. In view of the high levels of aspiration and motivation among Negroes, appropriate policy might conceive this as the lowest possible limit.

on short-term goals and in our concern with such symptoms as riots rather than with those features of inequality of opportunity that lie beneath these symptoms.

It is an easy escape to define the problem as if its source lay in those who experience the problem most directly and to deal with the "Negro problem," the "poverty problem," or even the "urban problem." These, however, are simply symptomatic or localized expressions of broader problems of our society. Only by shifting from transitory conceptions to long-term change, from local or focal issues to pervasive difficulties, from an expectation of perpetual progress to an appreciation of the sporadic nature of gains and the return of periodic failures, can we hope to achieve a reasonable solution even to immediate and pressing problems. These problems, symptoms though they be, are expressed most strikingly in the poverty and inequality that Negro Americans experience despite a century of individual achievements and social change. But the realistic resolution of these specific and perhaps temporary "problems" requires that our analyses and solutions transcend them and deal with the underlying injustice and restrictions that continue to characterize our society.

THE IMMIGRANT AND
THE AMERICAN NATIONAL IDEA
WALTER O. FOSTER

IF one uses the decades from 1861 to the 1890's as a watershed, the history of both American nationalism and American immigration divides into two roughly equal periods of

FROM: O. F. Ander (ed.), *In the Trek of the Immigrant* (Rock Island, Ill.: Augustana College Library, 1964), pp. 159–175. Reprinted by permission.

seventy years, with a transitional generation of about thirty or thirty-five years between them. The very nature of the subjects involved suggests that they have some significant connection. Changes occurring in both these important aspects of national life from their first to their second phases are substantial, perhaps fundamental. Yet both the similarity of developments and their intersection have been the object of only superficial or partisan attention. With an excess of courtesy, scholars pursuing either of these themes usually seem content to leave the other to their colleagues. Consequently the concurrence of major phenomena in the history of immigration to the United States and in the morphology of American nationalism is largely overlooked in the face of an extensive parallelism that calls for serious attention.

Perhaps it would be useful to sort out what is and what is not constant in American nationalism. It is characteristic of both major periods under discussion that national unity has sought expression in political-social ideology. At neither time has America sought to base itself on the ethnic, cultural, or historical distinctiveness that is the genius of other nationalisms. Confronted by the chronic diversities of the population, no other formula has ever seemed appropriate for the United States. Yet in spite of a common mode of expression for the nationalism of both eras, profound differences have developed. The contrast must, of course, be oversimplified in order to draw the distinction with sufficient brevity; but the change is real. The earlier version of American nationalism extolled a hard core of permanent values supposedly shared by all the people; it sought to express these values primarily in political institutions, and invited support of the government on that basis; thus it hoped to construct a society that featured both consensus and voluntarism of political association, indeed to achieve the former by relying on the latter. The later version worked with similar materials, but achieved drastically different results. It assumed the permanence of political association on the part of all citizens, irrespective of their preferences or

68

commitments; it demanded support of the government, even when political institutions expressed unacceptable or shifting values, as the only practical alternative to perpetual tumult; thus it, too, hoped to construct a society that would achieve consensus, but not by voluntary association—indeed it sought to attain the former by sacrificing the latter.

. . . That any ideology, unsupported by other forces, would have been able by itself to rivet together for two or three generations the diverse groups that originally constituted the raw material of American population is highly questionable. Some degree of social tolerance and intellectual sophistication would be required, some common idioms of value, and a public forum that would be peaceful long enough to express and discuss them. This much history provided even in the formative years. Already by the last decade of the eighteenth century, the lengthening experience of living and fighting together had begun to soften some of the differences and rivalries. Unfortunately this could be reversed, and would be. More important is the fact that a saving measure of ethnic and cultural similarity reinforced the non-ethnic, non-geographical, and certainly non-historical conceptions of nationalism in the United States. Americans were sufficiently diverse that the appeal to any but a political nationalism would have been fatal. However, they were at the same time sufficiently homogeneous to save a nascent nationalism that might otherwise not have survived on the basis of appealing to the single political factor. It was almost as though Americans actually shared more than they dared admit for fear of destroying its unifying effect. For reasons indicated, the political credo could be trumpeted, while the themes of ethnic, cultural, and social community had to be muted. But this necessary system of priorities did not change the fact that both were indispensable, especially at the outset.

Naturally the durability of the emerging national commitment was tested by strains that had their origin within and outside the group. Immigration was probably the most persistent of these and, with the exception of the North-South split, the most important. Fortunately for Americans trying to establish a national society, major developments on both the European and American continents prevented additions through immigration from attaining their normal rate for the first half of the period from joint Constitution-making to making war on one another. Thus Americans were enabled to let the combination of stabilizing forces operate with full effect, and to develop a poise that would not be too severely shaken by the crescendo of immigration when its volume first began to increase thirty-five to forty years later. Under these circumstances the centripetal forces of nationalism were strong enough to launch the Union and give their name to a full generation following 1800. Thereafter nationalism carried on, more and more falteringly, for another thirty years, finally to succumb to growing social cleavage and loss of political consensus. Of course, the end was not foreseen in 1830 or 1831. On the contrary, national spirit was still so high that it could take satisfaction from Jackson's readiness to meet challenge with force, rather than to take alarm that the threat should have been necessary. But the issue was now defined, even if not yet joined. Realization would come slowly; fateful choice only at the end. Meanwhile, for most of one self-contradictory generation, Americans would vent their national feeling in the enthusiasms of external expansion, while carrying the germs of internal conflict in the body politic. This was the confused and deceptive scene as the first major contingent of immigrants put in their appearance.

The earliest immigrants arriving in sufficient volume to test the temper of American nationalism were the Germans. In many ways they provide the best basis for examining the problem. Other than the immigration from Britain, that from Germany is the most sustained, in greatest volume, over the longest span of time. In any period, German immigrants are one of the important elements. They are also the single most representative group, in so far as they, more than any other, encompassed the full, rich range of varied immigrant motives and types. It was they who encountered America from century to century, in all her shifting moods. In the sense of constituting a test, however, the Germans can hardly be described as a severe one. With the exception of the language barrier, which they shared with most of their fellow immigrants, the Germans were probably better attuned to the environment they were entering than was any other group. Whether the emphasis in American history is on religious freedom and non-conformism in colonial times, or on political liberalism in the individualist tradition of the nineteenth century; whether on the need for farmers to populate the vast reaches of an agricultural and vigorously expansionist United States, or on skilled workers and technicians in the rush toward the industrialized society, the Germans are there in force.

These broader generalizations are more specifically reinforced by a glance at the political complexion of the first small wave to create a bulge in the immigration statistics of the nineteenth century, namely the German *Dreisziger*. The majority of these people found themselves in prompt and easy rapport with Jacksonian democracy, which could with relative ease accommodate all the shades of liberalism that the refugees of abortive revolutions against Metternich's Europe afforded. In any case, most of them were moderates by America's more relaxed standards. Even the conservative elements that came in the thirties steeled themselves against the shocks of democracy and announced their readiness to subscribe to the basic conceptions on which American representative government was grounded. Soon they were volubly insisting on them.

During the 1840's and 50's, the character of German additions to the population changed less than immigration as a whole, or the American society receiving them. Volume rose sharply, but within the group there was the same spectrum of liberal to conservative, with the *Achtundvierziger* replacing the exiles of the early thirties. There were relatively few radicals at either extreme. If anything, the acceptance of American democratic principles was more pronounced than in previous decades. Their new loyalties were probably as thorough and fervent as those of any comparable segment of immigration. At some points their commitment to the inalienable rights of man was firmer than that of the country claiming these rights as its cornerstone. German immigrants of the decades before the Civil War tended to be anti-slavery and for this, as well as economic and other reasons, gravitated much more to the North than the South. Politically it became less and less a matter of course for them to join the Democratic party; first they had a choice of the Whigs, later, and more enthusiastically, the Republicans. These reminders of the general political orientation of pre-Civil War German immigrants should serve to recall the casualness of their integration. When newcomers are numbered in the hundreds of thousands and millions, they have seldom experienced less difficulty in identifying themselves with the nationalism of the community they were joining than did this element in this period.

German immigration probably did more to strengthen the American national idea and less to modify its basic values than any immigration save the English. If this is true, it was not because, as a group, they were less conscious of, concerned about, or committed to such values than others, but because their own were closer to the basic pattern into which they were being fitted. Among themselves the various components of the total would differ on whether they prized most in their new environment its religious freedom, its Jeffersonian liberalism, its representative government, or some other similar quality. But the common denominator among all these attitudes was that each demanded commitment to *something* that was a part of American nationalism and which found fulfillment here. An affirmation was involved, rather than a negation. This the German immigrant understood; this required no adjustment of him.

German villages did indeed send over some stolid peasant types that tended to withdraw, and would have had difficulty distinguishing between a ballot and a summons—even if written in German. But these are not remotely the majority. In fact, when nineteenth-century opponents of immigration sought examples to spice their alarums, they had to reach back into the seventeenth and eighteenth centuries for reference to the "Pennsylvania Dutch." At the other extreme, German universities did indeed send some passionate revolutionary misfits, with a carefully cultivated superiority complex, a genius for making trouble, and not a single practical notion of what they would do with a government if they were handed one. But these are even farther removed from the majority. The bulk of these arrivals had no incentive to change the national ideology or political institutions to accommodate themselves. The marks most characteristic of the United States and most frequently advanced as identifying it were usually those the German immigrant shared. Herein lies the valid summation, and the proper point to stress, for the immigration of the period from 1820 to 1860. Additional studies in depth from several vantage points of historical investigation may lead to modification of the conclusions. That is one reason they should be undertaken. But generalizations may be risked at the present time if they make allowances that help to reflect the historic situation instead of merely reflecting the imbalance that results from an uneven intensity of research in the subject.

Companion to German immigration before 1861 was that from Ireland. Together these two streams account for so high a percentage of pre-Civil War arrivals that they dominate the period. Actually, however, neither can be regarded as setting the tone without the other, although much of the time they are performing in different keys. The catalog of their differences is so extensive that they can only be indicated here: Variety of motivation, level of education, economic status, vocational skills, urban-rural patterns of settlement, religious distribution, and patterns and objects of revolutionary impulse. The Irishman's traditionally political Gaelic nationalism intruded much more upon full acceptance of American allegiance than the amorphous ethnic or cultural nationalism that most Germans brought out of a still predominantly particularist middle Europe. German revolutionaries were concerned with freedom for the individual and the problem of how governments can be made to honor, and perhaps even further, it. When they revolted, the target was their own repressive government. Irish revolutionaries were concerned with "freedom" for a national group and, with a classic singleness of purpose, fixed their minds on political independence, disregarding the problems with which this might endow them. So, when they revolted, the target was the British government; and their hate-filled gaze never wavered. Basically, the Irish were much less concerned with the character of government as such, than whether they controlled the particular one which was closest at hand. As a group, therefore, neither was their rapport with American political philosophy severely limited, nor were they greatly interested in the pattern of precarious institutional development that had brought forth the system they saw before them. They sensed the advantages of political power and grasped that in this society they were permitted to participate in its pursuit. That was enough. They vaulted into the fray and, with an unerring instinct for the jugular, soon were racking up more or less bloody victories over Americans, German immigrants, both, or over one in coalition with the other.

. . . Serious consideration of any nationalism demands at the very least an effort to understand its content and to evaluate the depth of the people's commitment to it. It would be helpful if at last Americans—including its scholars—could come to a recognition of the fact that the United States is no exception in these matters. And neither such content nor commitment can be assessed while trying to ignore the influence of an immigration as numerous as that to the United States by the 1840's. All responses to the fact of various immigrant strains in the American people imply some fixed point of reference from which we are moving, which now exists, or toward which we are striving. Assimilation implies the assumption of an historically dominant group whose values and patterns are essential out of the past, in the present, and for the future. Exclusion makes similar assumptions, merely taking a more protective attitude where the maintenance of such dominant group values and characteristics are concerned. The "melting pot" conception of meeting the problem of a variety of nationalisms certainly does not make a *denial* of nationalism the answer. Instead its implied formula is to destroy all previous ones, the better to create a new one, however synthetic. Even the idea of "pluralism" does not remove the necessity for dedication to something that will serve as the cohesive force in order to make possible freedom and individuality at other points. In fact, it may be cogently argued that the more diversity in the composition of a population strains the concept of unity, the greater the necessity for proportionately deeper attachment at the remaining points of similarity. This necessity may be denied, either in principle, or simply by failing ever to find *any* point on which to agree that there must be agreement. But whether this be principle, maneuver, or default, it is tantamount to a denial that a national state needs to have a focus of national commitment. The consequence of such a position is to eliminate the "national" and merely leave the state. This, too, is an option which Americans may choose. But it was not the spirit of American nationalism in the pre-Civil War era. And that age will probably have to be judged by the standards of its own conception of the national character.

Those elements of the population who advocated restriction of immigration, or more exacting requirements for citizenship, no doubt had a variety of reasons. But the present discussion centers around the effect of immigration on American nationalism. At this point the Nativist asked the question: How much of what kind of immigration can be permitted before it begins to weaken the national fabric? Obviously, this is the kind of question that cannot be answered; it can scarcely be debated. So positions were taken on the issue, but in much more specific terms. Through the policies he advocated, the Nativist said in effect: I may not know *how* much, but the present volume is too much of the kind we are getting. He was probably wrong, although this is a matter of judgment any time. But if he estimated too low, it is important to remember that this "low" figure was more by far than any country in the world was then accepting. Favorable results were not a foregone conclusion. In any case, he was recognizing the fact that more was involved than economic support for so many more bodies, merely requiring transportation with dispatch to workbench or farm. What would happen to the whole system of values for which America was coming to stand, and which in her case, more than most, constituted the core of her national commitment? Was there no longer a vital national idea? Were Americans about to shoot one another over a dead horse? Was it reasonable to assume that national commitment was not needed? That it was shared by strangers? Or automatically acquired after several years' residence? How much did many of the new arrivals actually understand of the society in which they were making their home?

It was not wholly honest to brush aside these queries in order to proceed with annihilation of the Nativist's mistaken answer to his own questions. But the temptation was irresistible. He made himself so very vulnerable. Total exclusion was too extreme to be politically practicable. Longer residence in the United States might help, but it was a dubious remedy. Those who arrived with basically different values were usually poor prospects for conversion. Others who came equipped with basic commitments to American values were some of the staunchest supporters of Jeffersonian-Jacksonian democracy. There was no single answer for all groups or all people. Plainly, it was possible to be born in the United States and nevertheless not recognize or share the fundamentals of the national community. In fact, the greatest changes in the concepts of American nationalism would be effected by native Americans, not immigrants. If he thought he could stop this, the Nativist was watching the wrong people.

Inevitably, the immigrants insisted on replying. The fundamental response, shared by many but expressed most vigorously by the political-minded German of this period, was the irrefutable one that Americanism was a thing of the spirit, hence was not necessarily bound by lines of national origin. As far as it went, this was impeccable. Unfortunately, it did not go far enough to answer the practical question: Do these prospective citizens share it? At this point, the immigrant was probably less correct in assuming that the fact of coming proved or bestowed national commitment, than the Nativist had been in assuming that different origins prevented it.

Native-born opponents of immigration restrictions were quick to refute and ready to ridicule the fallacious arguments of the Nativists. (If they saw fallacies also in the hurt rejoinder of immigrant apologists, they preferred to overlook them.) Unrestricted immigration became the dogma of the anti-Nativist, without a serious effort to test its validity. However, embedded in the doctrine of no restriction was a troublesome choice of propositions: either that all immigrants shared the values of American society, or that American society had none, or that it did not matter whether it did or they did. Seldom was this set of alternatives brought into the open. But it was no less surely present. By and large, the advocates of unrestricted immigration preferred to take refuge in the formula that an almost wholly permissive immigration policy was a *part* of the Great American Idea. For practical purposes, however, the answer was given by the policy espoused.

Close as contemporaries were to the problem, it may well be that they sensed neither their evasions nor their decisions. It is more difficult to make similar assumptions about subsequent approaches. With deeper perspective, both the basic character of the early nationalism and the changes that were going on in this period should now be discernible more clearly than while they were occurring. But such recognition is reflected in few studies concerning themselves with the several aspects of the problem. Denigration of the view that commonly held ideas were essential to American unity, or presumably that unity itself was important, is the rule rather than the exception. In this sense nineteenth-century opponents of nativism understood the issues better than twentieth-century anti-Nativists. The former at least recognized that the basis of Americanism was essentially conceptual, and sought to turn the Nativist's own argument against him by insisting that for precisely this reason anyone could be an American. But to dismiss the Nativist as a dolt and a bigot for raising the question of whether the character of any immigration was consonant with the character of America came dangerously close to saying that this was a nonsense question because neither an immigrant group nor a national society can have a character—that nothing, whether ideas, birth, culture, or history, can create one. This is, indeed, the claim of some social scientists today. While awaiting proof of the thesis, the historian will have ample reason to concern himself with the actual situation in an age when *neither* the Nativist *nor* his opponents held to this view.

The period from 1865 to the 1890's is transitional and, like most such times, mixed in its commitments to the past and to the future. The Civil War had demonstrated that previous conceptions of the national ideology had been too ample. Until then United States political consensus had expressed itself in a willingness to place the power of the state into the hands of the majority, confident that it would respect the principles on which the unity of the state had originally been predicated. Probably only in this way could the principle of the consent of the governed be reconciled with majority rule. Formulas for state-making do not include instructions on what to do when the prescribed steps do not produce the anticipated results. But this was what happened to the United States when the original commitment to common values and purposes was gradually replaced by a whole series of deep-seated divisions. The failure was not, as has been said too often, one of compromise, but of a continuing national consensus. Questions about who had departed from original ideals first and more frequently do not call for discussion here. But the sequel merits some attention because of its bearing on American nationalism. The answer was bound to be a tragic one, because each side in the conflict had to violate one of the foundation principles, consent of the governed or majority rule, in the effort to support the other. In the process, the character of American national ideas was permanently changed. Brave reassertion of erstwhile assumptions about basic agreement on social-political ideology never was convincing after 1865, was tacitly abandoned from the last decade of the century until 1954, and has been embarrassingly troublesome since.

Although the change was fundamental enough, Americans were neither intellectually nor psychologically prepared to accept it. After Appomattox pre-Civil War theories of voluntary political association were pure myth. American nationalism had been transformed at its very base in the name of saving the nation. Perhaps this was unavoidable, and the irony therefore wholly unintentional. But the denial that it had happened was by intent, and could have been avoided. The majority of the people simply preferred to believe that they had preserved or re-established their former way of life. That this was not true constituted no obstacle to its being believed. Indeed, it was such a popular article of faith that at least a generation would have to pass on before the United States could accept what had been the case ever since the war. In this air of unreality, the vital relationship between the role of the new national state and the question of what made it national or whether it was, could not be frankly explored. False reverence could not restore what had been destroyed, but it could thwart any efforts to replace it with something honest and responsible. Consequently the metamorphosis was carried out behind a screen that hid it from the public view.

In the generation following the end of the conflict, leadership in intellectual and political life was passing into the hands of groups that repudiated the doctrines which had supported the nationalism of the republic's formative years. Permanence of values, the obligation of government to reflect those held by the people, sanctity of certain rights, and the very notion of democratic responsibility—all were under attack from one quarter or another. Relativist trends in philosophical thought, scientific theories and their social implications, industrial or governmental technicians with ideas about their mission to engage in human engineering, and simple exploiters of the power to be derived from the new position of the government in the national hierarchy of values contributed to the disintegration of the previous pattern of society, and the establishment of the new. Under this dispensation, the nation was neither something grandly to create, nor something patriotically to defend, but something to manipulate in order to produce the illusion that there was a meaningful relation between it and policies predetermined by a political elite.

In such an intellectual, political, and social context, the questions of relationship between nationalism and immigration did not disappear, but they became entirely different questions. Certainly the issues over which the pre-war generation had gotten most excited were becoming less and less relevant. Anyone who insisted on reviving the debates of an earlier day would have a hard time getting a comparable hearing. The revival of post-Civil War nativism would be relatively briefer and notably less successful. It was not that what the alien or the native thought or felt was unimportant. On the contrary. It was essential that he should have the right attitudes. But public opinion was a product, not a source, of decision. That was what the eager battlers about ideas had not understood in an earlier day.

Into this very different kind of America, Europe continued to send her surplus population at an unprecedented rate. But if the native-born did not realize most of the changes occurring, the immigrants could hardly be expected to detect them. They were not quite of the same character as before the war, but then neither was the United States. So far as the Germans were concerned, they came in force for fifteen years after 1865. But the changes that were afoot were less in evidence in the immediate post-war period than they were later. By then German immigration was declining and being superseded by others. Until about 1890, however, the Germans blended in well enough, and did not suspect that they were walking into a very different kind of country than their predecessors had entered twenty or twenty-five years before. After all, few of them read Henry Adams or Henry Cabot Lodge. Now, they had new partners, such as the heavy Scandinavian immigration of the period. If anything, this created less friction than being paired with the Irish.

So the German immigrants multiplied and prospered. But the former political verve was not in evidence by the turn of the century. Old firebrands would have been appalled at the comparative apathy of 1900. The late German immigration, in its turn, would not have understood the Forty-eighters and their affectionate wrangle with the earlier generation. They had known no other America, and were led to believe that there had been none. The illusion that they were living in a society where certainly opinion and normally action were free individual choices would continue until rudely shattered after 1914. It was possible to sit out the Mexican War, if one chose, but not World War I. Then they would learn that Americans did not really regard all immigrants as equally desirable and that the United States had something it would fight for, even if it was neither a "national character" that was derided, or national interests that were denied. They would also learn that on occasion attitudes and opinions were presumed to be as much "*zu Befehl*" in the new United States as in the "old country." But all that lay in the future.

Meanwhile, the vanguard of the new immigration was arriving. It overlapped the last great wave from northern Europe and then engulfed it. Here was the ideal matériel for the new-style nation-maker. For now the re-definition of American nationalism, so long overdue, could be undertaken in the name of humanitarianism. The timing was perfect. With the generation that had fought the Civil War no longer around to protest, with the German immigration beginning to taper off, and in any case not as obstreperous as the arrivals of an earlier day, and with no common denominator for the new immigration save its desperate needs, the opportunity had come to have done with the old thesis that wished to proceed from common values to a political society that should reflect them. Repudiation of the vaguely democratic and still venerated dogma simply as a matter of public correction or personal preference might have been difficult. The argument went much better when the claim could be made that the United States admitted the immigrant on humanitarian grounds. Thus anyone who questioned whether the policy was desirable from the viewpoint of American nationalism, or, for that matter, any other viewpoint, was by definition not humanitarian. Of course, the old nationalism had passed away years before. Restatement would have been necessary soon in any case; already it was a generation delayed. Few were changing their ideas out of compassion for the poor immigrant, least of all Judge Gary. But for years a majority could be fashioned for a broadly permissive policy. And everyone felt better for putting a good light upon it.

IMMIGRANTS, NEGROES, AND THE PUBLIC SCHOOLS

COLIN GREER

CURRENT concern over the failure of the American Negro to become a viable part of the post-industrial society has found vigorous expression within the framework of the traditional American faith in public education. Now that it is totally unprofitable for the nation to support a large reserve unskilled labor force, self-interest has reforged an old alliance with altruism in a concerted effort to claim the Negro as a technological independent.

Political and social energy has been spent in an increasingly more determined effort to effect change in precisely that area where the roots of future national and ethnic progress are believed to lie: namely, in the classroom, where reading achievement promises freedom from welfare dependency and racial isolation. Indeed integration has been the flagstaff of both Negro and white impatience. But while the civil rights movement is generally recognized as having been of signal import in finally making a citizen of the ex-slave— always with regret for the tardiness—the typology of "cultural deprivation" describes the deficits of that tardiness and finds alarmingly far-reaching debilitation stretching from plantation to city ghetto.

Of late, the perspective of a quasi-historical comparison spanning more than fifty years of industrial explosion has

REPRINTED by permission of the publisher from Colin Greer, *Cobweb Attitudes: Essays on American Education and Culture* (New York: Teachers College Press, copyright 1970 by Teachers College, Columbia University), pp. 1–8.

83

been employed to stress the similarity of condition between the newly urbanized immigrant to America at the turn of the century and his latter-day Negro counterpart. The myth has emerged that the miracle of the American melting pot, clearly to be seen in the ostensible accommodation of immigrant groups in the modern nation, has been accomplished with the school acting as prime agent in the process, because it was in the public school that a longstanding fear of the foreigner and the economic need of him combined to refurbish the traditional American faith in the social power of free public education. And if public education could do it for the immigrant, then why not for the Negro? For some this provides the basis for an invidious comparison; for others it offers reassurance in the power of the American city to assimilate widely diverse groups. As a result, it is wishfully expected that the Negro, despite totally different circumstances, should be able to respond to the readiness of white America to accept his change in status and welcome him into the economic mainstream.

The only period in which such historical comparisons can be meaningfully undertaken is at the turn of the century when both foreign-born immigrant and Negro migrant left the rural and tradition-bound structures during the same period of time and in unprecedented numbers. They came to the Yankee North to find economic and social breathing space amid its growing urban centers. Although the Negro's exodus from the southern states has customarily been regarded as a function of the greater and lesser migrations which followed World War I and the cessation of large-scale foreign immigration, it should not be forgotten that there were almost 100,000 Negroes in New York in 1910 (a 51 per cent increase since 1900, following a 79 per cent increase in the previous decade) and that they were largely a migrant population. Philadelphia and Chicago, too, contained increasingly Negro populations after 1800. After all, the nation was on the move cityward and the Negro was a part of it, although the numbers were relatively small seen against the flood-like proportions of foreign immigration. By 1910, only Washington, D.C., had a larger urban Negro population than New York, and the Negro's movement northward had already aroused the concern of a number of contemporary observers. Professor Kelly Miller of Howard University could speak of the "prevailing dread"[1] of this migration in the North. In 1909, William Bulkley maintained that "the majority of them [Negroes in northern cities] were more or less recent arrivals from the South";[2] and in 1911, Mary White Ovington found most Negro neighborhoods in New York City populated by southerners.[3]

A significant number of Negroes, then, were attempting to set a foot on the very occupational rungs of the ladder the immigrant was mounting, and amid the same deplorable conditions of urban poverty and tenement squalor. With varying degrees of speed, the diverse foreign ethnic groups successfully joined the ongoing society and proceeded to grow with it and adapt to its demands (though at very different rates for each group). In this period of early industrial investment, the Negro remained on the periphery; as a strike-breaker and menial service worker he became the "slave of industry," not a partner in it. Economic dependence and familial dislocation took on a new relevance and have continued to deny him the gradual preparation for the demands of the technological, highly literate society he is now being invited so anxiously to join.

In the momentous years at the turn of the century, the assumption of Anglo-Saxon superiority and a demanding machine economy led to a tremendous investment in the efficacy

[1] Kelly Miller, "The Industrial Condition of the Negro in North," *The Annals,* Vol. 27 (May, 1906).

[2] William L. Bulkley, "Race Prejudice as Viewed from an Economic Standpoint," *Proceedings of the National Negro Conference,* New York: 1909.

[3] Mary White Ovington, *Half a Man: The Status of the Negro in New York,* New York: 1911.

of an open door on immigration—contingent always on the ability of the melting pot to melt. The ethnocultural structure never really did melt; but as a general behavioral conformity became established, urbanization was easily mistaken for Americanization and the public school has consistently maintained a hallowed place in the process. The factory, the union, and the promise of material well-being (real or vicarious) laid important ground rules for this level of cultural unity, just as they played their part in expanding the urban condition itself.

The twin myths of melting pot magic and public school alchemy grew out of a constant need for manpower and a corollary faith that a culturally diverse population could be Americanized. Despite periodic lapses of faith in them, the myths have hardened into dogma. Before the fear for internal security that surrounded the World War I years, and the "Red Scare" phenomenon that followed close upon its heels, social critics and educational reformers made clear that they trusted the effectiveness of the school system in the nation's cities. As one immigrant herself put it, "the public school has done its best for us foreigners and for the country, when it has made us into good Americans." A federal commissioner of education expressed his wonder at the "marvelous" job done by the schools. To Jacob Riis, faith in the real and symbolic power of the "flag flying over the schoolhouse" seemed more than justified. Below the surface, however, and not too far below, the reality was very different.

New York's Superintendent Maxwell called in vain for public response to the problems of immigrants. Settlement house workers tried desperately to fill the gap while waging a campaign to broaden the commitment of public education. With the outbreak of war in Europe, the mystique of melting pot and public school began to lose power. Xenophobes lamented the schools' failure to assimilate immigrants and schoolmen reacted anxiously, and of course, defensively; some renewing their commitment and some trying to place blame for the schools' perceived breakdown on politics, finances, and the immigrants themselves. It was almost as if the fact of ethnic diversity itself demanded attention; indeed, the continuing diversity would later be used as evidence of an America made vital by the strains of "pluralism." Suddenly, in 1916, the U.S. Department of the Interior ran a series of conferences to discuss the role of education in the acculturation of foreigners. Programs were developed to bring schooling into factories to reach those who had no time at the end of the working day. By 1918 the president of New York's Board of Education agreed with the many who complained that the schools had failed miserably in dealing with the problems of heavy foreign immigration.

New York's Board of Estimate commissioned a comprehensive study of the city's public schools in 1911. Fifty thousand dollars was to be spent in response to Superintendent Maxwell's feverish attempts to persuade the Board of Estimate that the schools must take a fuller responsibility for the city's school-age children. Paul Hanus of Harvard University conducted the survey and found, as successive studies continued to find, that the schools with the largest number of immigrants were totally unprepared to deal with the rapidly multiplying needs that confronted them.

Contemporary public and private welfare records show that all the evils characteristic of an unemployed urban lower class today were disastrously well known to a high proportion of immigrant families caught in the disrupting pressures of poverty and squalor, and the flutterings of the business cycle. Of twelve and a half million families in the United States, eleven million had an annual income below $380 per annum. When jobs were not available to the men of a family for a long period of time, the woman and child might be deserted or forced to become breadwinners. It was these conditions which Lillian Brandt, like many of her settlement house colleagues, found when she reported the dire effects of urban poverty on the immigrant family. According to the Hanus survey and reports of school superintendents from 1904 to 1922, between 32 and 36 per cent of public school pupils were "over-age" and making "slow progress" in any given year. Schoolmen regularly pointed out that school failure was a district phenomenon; "excessive retardation," they claimed, was the perennial correlate of lower-class life. Statistical methods varied so that improvement was now affirmed and now denied, but on the whole, the rates of school failure were astronomical in a city whose educational standards were, in the opinion of the State Department of Education, considerably better than elsewhere in the nation.

While almost all school pupils, immigrant and native born, were drop-outs, school drop-outs were employable most of the time. (Fewer than ten per cent of the school population graduated from high school in 1915.) Indeed, it was for this very reason that the majority of new immigrants made their homes in urban centers. New York's Board of Health noted that the immigrant and his offspring sustained an astonishing degree of "mortality," and were encouraged to become truants, even during their elementary school years, by the ready employment to be found in expanding "manufacturing and mechanical pursuits." Compulsory education laws for those beyond 14 years of age referred only to those without "permanent employment." When higher education finally opened up it was a result of completion rates in elementary and high schools—the percentage of high school graduates who attain some college and college entrants who graduate has not increased greatly, even by 1960 figures. George Counts reported, in 1922, how few and how socially select were the children who continued their education to the high school level, making it clear that American education was still much more involved in the production of healthy, minimally literate labor. That same year, in his annual report, New York City's school superintendent, William Ettinger, set about "Facing the Facts," the same facts, in the system he supervised. This survey committee found progressive failure in the high school grades. A 1927 study of truancy in the city echoed the findings of a similar study carried out in 1915, in which Elizabeth Irwin described the high incidence of truancy (and truant employment) in a West Side section of Manhattan "noted for its large proportion of broken homes." Public education had broadened its efforts to care for the health needs of its charges, but few of them found the specifically educational effort relevant to their place in society. Typically, school success came after the establishment of an indigenous ethnic stability (e.g., ethnic business and political organizations grounded in the community) and the subsequent need of a high school diploma education to advance it.

Data compiled for the 1920 census, the last before the door on European immigration was slammed tightly shut, show clearly that the years of schooling attained by native whites of native parentage is separated from those of foreign parentage by a proportion similar to that which separates the adult employment rate of the former group from the latter. In fact, the level of employment is in proportion to the rate of school retention beyond compulsory attendance age and breaks down with a revealing differential even between native born of foreign parentage and the foreign born. For example, foreign-born groups as a whole showed a level of adult unemployment smaller only than that of the Negro, while bearing, at the same time, the greatest proportions of 15, 16 and 17 year olds out of school.

Most of the students who now drop out *would never have been* in high school fifty years ago. Students remained in grade school until acceptable standards or school leaving age were attained. Public education was the rubber stamp of economic improvement; rarely has it been the bootstrap. The economic value of an education has been at once a cause and a consequence of its scarcity.

During these years, manpower was the important factor; the factory and the union, rather than the school, were the assimilating agents. In 1909 a Greek language newspaper told its readers to "become citizens and join labor unions." In Manhattan, only 47 per cent of the school population was even registered at the high school level. The secretary of the City Census Board informed Hanus that the elementary school graduate and the elementary school drop-out were generally to be found in "blind alley" occupations in the factory and the shop.

Economic stability for the group preceded its entry onto the broader middle-class stage via education. The correlation between school achievement and economic status was so high that in school surveys carried out in the mid-West during the 1920's, it became necessary to separate Scandinavian-Americans from other "ethnic" Americans because the school performance of their children so outdistanced other foreign mid-West groups. Census figures reveal that the degree of economic security among farm-holding Scandinavians and storekeeping Jews (surprisingly high even in 1920) was much greater than among more characteristically wage-laboring groups. As Theodore Saloutos points out, the Greeks, too, were among the first to make this transition.[4] Similarly, in 1940 the relatively recently arrived San Francisco Japanese community —tightly organized around their own business enterprise— ranked high on school achievement measures. It was not until the 1950's that the Irish began to enter universities in large numbers. They remain predominantly "blue collar" in status and, like many high schoolers of Italian origin, sustain a high incidence of poor school performance. The erstwhile lower class who are now moving into the hundreds of non-elite colleges across the country are not being prepared for professional middle-class life, but for manning the newly industralized sector of lower management, pre-college teaching, and the I.B.M. machines. There is a hard core of reality behind the story which depicts the entry of the Eastern

[4] Theodore Saloutos, *The Greeks in the United States,* Cambridge, Mass.: Harvard University Press, 1964.

Immigrants, Negroes, and Public Schools

European Jewish immigrant into the small business enterprise and then of his son into the university and the professions. The "business" quality of the ethnic community has
not itself been the vital ingredient; the key factor is more
probably the indigenous grounding of the unit within the
ethnic boundary, that is, the establishment of an ethnic
middle-class before scaling the walls of the dominant society.
In this perspective, one is less ready to mythologize the role
of the public school.

While school drop-outs were generally employable, the
Negro for the most part worked sporadically and as a reserve
force. If the immigrant was vulnerable in his lower-class status, it was usually the individual, not the group, who was
throttled by swings of the economic pendulum. For the
Negro, caste, through color, added a much more pervasively
ethnic dimension to the rigors of lower-class life.

As one might expect, the marginal place of the Negro was
accurately reflected in the educational arena. With no evidence of any considerable economic progress, and with a history of circular justifications for Negro inferiority, the Negro
was eminently suited to being placed outside the general
faith in both the melting pot and the public school. The
Hanus survey and the conditions which made it necessary notwithstanding, complaints of school personnel led the school
system to have Frances Blascoer undertake a study of its
"Colored School Children" during the very time (1915) when
the Hanus findings were being reported. There were less than
8,000 Negro school children in a school population of more
than 700,000, yet a separate study seemed to be justified. Both
reports found the rates of truancy in the city (among the total
school population in the case of Professor Hanus, and among
Negroes only for Miss Blascoer) to be outrageously high.
Among the populations surveyed in the two reports, school
retardation was discovered to be progressive: the child was
performing less adequately at the end of his school career
than at the beginning. Hanus placed the blame on the combi-

nation of inappropriate family preparation among immigrants, the exploitation of children by parents, and the totally inadequate conditions with which the school was prepared to meet its new responsibilities. At least 33 new school buildings were needed, provisions were long overdue for about two per cent of the school population which could be classified as mentally defective, and ungraded classes were immediately required to accommodate 15,000 children. Having agreed with the Hanus observations and acknowledging the particular prejudice which made school that much more painful and ineffective for the Negro child, Frances Blascoer reported that the Negro's unique educational problems demanded a rather different educational treatment. The separate definition which followed meant that the society, which denied more than minimal education to most, denied the Negro even the pragmatic justification for this denial.

Miss Blascoer advised the Negro to give up hope of the factory floor and develop a small, separate, and self-employing ghetto economy. While one may be tempted to acknowledge Miss Blascoer's recommendations as pertinent to the Negro's need for independence and indigenous growth, she made it clear that despite her sincere concern for the urban poor, this was a "child race," as yet unready to compete in a highly "civilized" world. She castigated the Urban League for its efforts to train Negro social workers because it was clear to her that the Negro worker would do only serious harm; the white worker alone must provide regenerative help. The Negro was advised to move away from the areas of employment which left him standing as a blatant scar, the very areas where real industrial progress was being made. Blascoer's vision for the school went no further than the economy that excluded the Negro so extensively, instead of using the school as a way of leading to Negro mobility. The separate definition of Negro failure in school may be seen as a symbol of the failure and the animosity which underlined his life within the city and as an accurate measure of the school's extremely limited power to cope with broad social issues.

The Hanus and Blascoer surveys were carried out during a time when several of the nation's other cities were examining their school systems. The first decades of the century found schoolmen across the country searching for greater efficiency in dealing with greatly increased populations. Philadelphia, too, looked Janus-like, with one face toward the system as a whole and another toward the Negro. With a sophistication that must, at the very least, make for unease in the mind of the modern educator, Philadelphia's study of Negro school children showed sympathetic understanding of the problems that beset the ex-slave; perhaps the issue was really one of basically different cultures. Very possibly, the Negro performed laudably by measures other than those used to judge the "superior" [5] white race. Apparently, different measures were applicable and, in a sense, justified, because to whites, school failure had meaning in the economic marketplace; to blacks, it bore no relevance to the improvement of their place in society.

Comparisons such as those I criticized at the outset as quasi-historical tend to ignore the push and pull of events at any given time. Abstracted from time, sociological parallels may confuse rather than clarify. We should realize that urban Negroes at the turn of the twentieth century (and later) were confronted by very different conditions than were the foreign immigrants at the turn of the century. The gap between Negro and European immigrant, as groups, has steadily widened so that the difference in their respective rates of progress has been intensified by changing economic demands and by the appropriateness of the tools with which the lower classes, at any given time, have met those demands.

The school system which served the expanding industrial

---

[5] *My* quotes, *their* tone.

society has changed little in the interim, but success within it has become essential to security and status for those who had been able in the past to leave school success to their children. Big city public schools have never, in fact, done the job they are now expected to do. In the face of today's urban poor, nostalgia for 1910 is at best a tempting but suspiciously convenient method of presenting facts.

NEGROES AND JEWS: THE NEW CHALLENGE TO PLURALISM

NATHAN GLAZER

IF today one re-reads the article by Kenneth Clark on Negro-Jewish relations that was published in *Commentary* almost nineteen years ago,[1] one will discover that tension between Negroes and Jews is neither of recent origin nor a product of the civil rights revolution. In that article Dr. Clark described the bitter feelings of the masses of Northern Negroes toward Jews. Not that these feelings hampered cooperation between Negro and Jewish leaders—an effective cooperation which was to play an important role in the following years in bringing fair-employment, fair-housing, and fair-education legislation to many communities, and indeed to most of the large Northern and Western states. But whatever the relationships were at the top, the fact was that down below, the Negro's experience of the Jew was not as a co-worker or friend or ally, but, in a word, as an exploiter.

As Dr. Clark wrote: "Some Negro domestics assert that Jewish housewives who employ them are unreasonably and

FROM: Nathan Glazer, "Negroes and Jews: The New Challenge to Pluralism," *Commentary* (December 1964), pp. 29–34. Reprinted by permission of the author.

[1] "Candor on Negro-Jewish Relations," *Commentary*, February 1946.

brazenly exploitative. A Negro actor states in bitter terms that he is being flagrantly underpaid by a Jewish producer. A Negro entertainer is antagonistic to his Jewish agent, who, he is convinced, is exploiting him. . . . Antagonism to the 'Jewish landlord' is so common as to become almost an integral part of the folk culture of the Northern urban Negro." And, of course, one would have to add to this catalogue the Jewish merchants in the Negro business districts, believed by their customers to be selling them inferior goods at high prices and on poor credit terms (a charge the merchants might answer by explaining that they were simply covering the greater financial costs—through payment delinquency and robbery—of doing business in a Negro area, plus compensation for the physical danger involved).

In any case, long before many of those Negro youths were born who took part last summer in the destruction and looting of Jewish businesses in Harlem and Bedford-Stuyvesant and Philadelphia, Dr. Clark explained clearly enough the basis for the anti-Semitism prevalent in the Negro ghettos. It was, he said, a special variant of anti-white feeling, encouraged by the more direct and immediate contact that Negroes had with Jews than with other whites, and encouraged as well by the inferior position of Jews in American society, which permitted the Negro to find in the luxury of anti-Jewishness one of his few means of identifying with the American majority. Two years later, also in *Commentary,* the young James Baldwin told the same story in one of his first published articles,[2] underlining the point with his elegant acidity: "But just as a society must have a scapegoat, so hatred must have a symbol. Georgia has the Negro and Harlem has the Jew." One still feels the shock of that cold ending: is *that* what the Jew was to Harlem in 1948?

If, however, we knew decades ago that the ironic historic confrontation of Jew (as landlord, merchant, housewife, busi-

---

[2] "The Harlem Ghetto: Winter 1948," *Commentary,* February 1948.

nessman) with Negro (as tenant, customer, servant, and worker) in the North had produced hatred on the part of many poor and uneducated Negroes, we now have to record two new developments in this confrontation. First, the well of ill-feeling has moved upward to include a substantial part of the Negro leadership, mainly some of the newer leaders thrown up in the North by the civil rights revolution; and second, Jewish feeling toward the Negro has undergone changes of its own.

There is little question that this feeling has never been hatred. It has ranged from passionate advocacy of Negro rights by Jewish liberals (and Communists and Socialists too), through friendly cooperation on the part of Jewish leaders who saw Negroes as allies in the fight for common goals, to a less effective but fairly widespread good will on the part of ordinary Jews. The hatred of poor Negroes for Jews was not reciprocated by Jews; in the way that Harlem "needed" the Jew, the Lower East Side, Brownsville, and Flatbush perhaps needed the *goy*, but they never needed the Negro. If there was prejudice against Negroes (and, of course, there was), it was part of the standard Jewish ethnocentrism which excluded all outsiders. The businesslike adoption of the norms of behavior of the white world (in refusing to rent to Negroes in New York, or serve them in department stores in the South) was just that—businesslike rather than the reflection of a deeply held prejudice. The Irish had had experiences which had taught many of them to dislike or hate Negroes: their competition with Negroes for the worst jobs in the early days of immigration, their antagonism to a Civil War draft that forced them to fight—as they thought—for Negroes. But the Jews had never come into direct competition with Negroes, in North or South. The tenant or customer might hate the landlord or storekeeper—the feeling was not mutual.

In the North, then, in the late 40's and 50's, well-staffed and well-financed Jewish organizations usually had the support of much more poorly staffed and poorly financed Negro organizations in fighting for legislation that advanced the interests of both groups, even though they stood on very different steps in the economic and occupational ladder. For the same law permitted a Jew to challenge exclusion from a Fifth Avenue cooperative apartment and a Negro to challenge exclusion from a much more modest apartment building.

This situation is now changing. As the Negro masses have become more active and more militant in their own interests, their feelings have become more relevant, and have forced themselves to the surface; and Jewish leaders—of unions, of defense and civil rights organizations—as well as businessmen, housewives, and home-owners, have been confronted for the first time with demands from Negro organizations that, they find, cannot serve as the basis of a common effort. The new developments feed each other, and it would be impossible to say which came first. The resistance of Jewish organizations and individual Jews to such demands as preferential union membership and preferential hiring, and to the insistence on the primacy of integration over all other educational objectives, breeds antagonism among former Negro allies. The "white liberal," who is attacked as a false friend unwilling to support demands which affect him or his, and as probably prejudiced to boot, is generally (even if this is not spelled out) the white *Jewish* liberal—and it could hardly be otherwise, in view of the predominance of Jews among liberals, particularly in major cities like New York, Chicago, Philadelphia, and Los Angeles. This Jewish resistance, however, is often based not only on the demands themselves, but on a growing awareness of the depths of Negro antagonism to the world that Jewish liberalism considers desirable.

One important new element in the situation, then, is that the feelings of the Negro masses have become politically relevant and meaningful in a way that they were not in 1935 or 1943. In those years, too, the Negroes of Harlem rioted, and broke the show windows of the Jewish-owned stores, and looted their contents. But these earlier outbreaks—which in terms of the feelings involved were very similar to the outbreaks of last summer—were not tied up with a great civil rights movement. While the Negro leaders of today could deny all responsibility for such outbreaks, and could point out that this kind of hoodlumism had been endemic in the Negro ghettos since the Depression, the growing tendency toward militancy in the civil rights movement meant that the leadership would inevitably be charged with responsibility— as they were not in 1935 and 1943 (except for Communists and race radicals). Moreover, the feelings of the Negro masses were now in greater measure *shared* by middle-class and white-collar and leadership groups. And this is also strikingly new.

For the Negro no longer confronts the Jew only as tenant, servant, customer, worker. The rise of Negro teachers, social workers, and civil servants in considerable numbers means another kind of confrontation. Once again, the accidents of history have put the Jew just ahead of the Negro, and just above him. Now the Negro teacher works under a Jewish principal, the Negro social worker under a Jewish supervisor. When HARYOU issued its huge report, *Youth in the Ghetto,* last summer, only one of some 800 school principals in the New York system was a Negro, and only four of the 1,200 top-level administrative positions in the system were filled by Negroes! But as significant as these ridiculously tiny percentages is the fact that most of the *other* principalships and administrative positions are filled by Jews who poured into the educational system during the 30's and are now well advanced within it, while thousands of Negroes, comparative latecomers, have inferior jobs. And what makes the situation even worse is that part of the blame for the poor education of Negro children can be placed on this white (but concretely Jewish) dominance. As the HARYOU report states (though indicating that this is only one possible point of view):

Negroes and Jews

Public school teachers in New York City come largely from the city colleges, which have a dominant pupil population from a culture which prepares the child from birth for competition of a most strenuous type. These students are largely white, middle-class, growing up in segregated white communities where, by and large, their only contact with the Negro finds him in positions of servitude. . . . Responsible positions, even within the neighborhood schools, are in the main held by people who perceivably differ from [the Negro pupils]. The dearth of Negro principals, assistants and supervisors is a most glaring deficit and one which leaves a marked, unwholesome effect upon the child's self-image. . . . The competitive culture from which the bulk of the teachers come, with the attendant arrogance of intellectual superiority of its members, lends itself readily to the class system within the school . . . which in effect perpetuates the academic pre-eminence of the dominant group.

This new confrontation of middle-class Negroes, recently arrived at professional status, and middle-class Jews, who got there earlier and hold the superior positions, is most marked in New York, because of its huge Jewish population. It is there that the animus against the white liberal reaches its peak, and where the white liberal tends most often to be a Jew. But the confrontation is only somewhat less sharp in Philadelphia, Detroit, Chicago, Los Angeles, and other cities with substantial Jewish populations. Perhaps the only place where the term "white liberal" is not used to mean the "Jewish liberal" is in San Francisco. The reason is that radicalism in San Francisco has a peculiarly non-Jewish base in Harry Bridges's International Longshoreman's and Warehouseman's Union; moreover, the Jewish group there contains many early settlers who are closely identified with San Franciscans of the same class and origin. Indeed, in San Francisco, there was never even a Jewish ghetto available to become transformed into a Negro ghetto; yet the fragment of a Jewish ghetto that did exist is now part of a Negro ghetto.

And this brings us to yet another new twist in the historic confrontation of Jew and Negro. I do not know why in so many American cities Negro settlement has concentrated in the very areas that originally harbored Jewish immigrants. There are possibly three reasons. First, Jews have on the whole favored apartment-house living, and apartments provide cheap quarters for newcomers. Second, Jews have been economically and geographically more mobile than other immigrant groups who arrived around the same time (for example, Italians and Poles), and consequently their neighborhoods opened up to Negroes more rapidly. And finally, Jews have not resorted to violence in resisting the influx of new groups—in any case, most of them were already moving away.

But as Jews kept retreating to the edges of the city and beyond, the Negroes, their numbers and in some measure their income rising, followed—in recent years, as far as the suburbs. This is a problem, of course, for the same reasons that it is a problem for any white property-owner or home-owner: fear of the declining real-estate values that can be occasioned by a flight of panicky white residents; fear of changes in the neighborhood affecting the schools and the homogeneity of the environment. Obviously, Jews are not the only people caught up in such concerns; but since migrating urban groups generally follow radial paths outward (a pattern that is not so marked in New York, broken up as it is by rivers and bays, but that is very clear in inland cities like Detroit, Chicago, Cleveland, and Cincinnati), this new Negro middle class has moved into Jewish areas far more often than statistical probability alone would lead one to expect. Here again, therefore, a novel type of tension—specifically involving middle-class groups and home-owners—has been introduced.

In a number of suburbs Jewish home-owners of liberal outlook have banded together in an effort to slow down the outflow of whites and thus create an integrated community (which, of course, also helps to maintain the value of their homes). But to create an integrated community not only means slowing down the outflow of whites; it also means reducing the influx of Negroes. In some cases these good—

from the Jewish point of view—intentions (and they usually *are* good) have looked, from the Negro point of view, like just another means of keeping Negroes *out,* but this time using the language of liberalism instead of race prejudice. We are all acquainted with the paranoia of persecuted minorities, and many jokes that used to be told of Jews (for example, the one about the stutterer who could not get a job as a radio announcer because of "anti-Semitism") could now be told of Negroes—and would be just as true.

All this forms part of the background of Negro-Jewish relations today. But in the immediate foreground are the new demands that have come to be made in the North and West by the civil rights movement. Negroes are acutely aware of how few of their young people even now get into the good colleges, and they see as a critical cause of this the small proportion of Negroes in good public elementary and high schools; they are acutely aware that their large-scale entry into the ranks of the clerks and typists of our huge public bureaucracies has not been accompanied by any equivalent entry into the higher positions of the civil service; they know that their new junior executive trainees in the large corporations are matched by hardly any Negroes higher up in these great private bureaucracies. And since political pressure and organized group pressure have been effective in breaching segregation in the South, and in bringing about some of these entries in the North, they see no reason why similar pressures should not be equally effective in making good the deficiencies that continue to be apparent. If whites say, "But first you must earn your entry—through grades, or examinations," Negroes, with a good deal more knowledge of the realities of American society than foreign immigrants used to have, answer, "But we know how *you* got ahead—through political power, and connections, and the like; therefore, we won't accept your pious argument that merit is the only thing that counts."

There is some truth to this rejoinder; there is, I believe, much less truth when it is made to Jews. For the Jews have, indeed, put their faith in the abstract measures of individual merit—marks and examinations. Earlier, before school grades and civil-service test scores became so important, they depended on money: it, too, could be measured, and the man who had it could manage without any ties of blood or deep organic connection to the ruling elite of the land. In addition to this, the reason merit and money have been the major Jewish weapons in overcoming discrimination, rather than political power and pressure, is that only in exceptional cases (New York City is one of them) have they had the numbers to make these latter means of advancement effective. As a result, their political skills are poor (where are the master Jewish politicians in America?), but their ability to score the highest grades in examinations and to develop money-getting competence still shows no sign of declining.

The ideologies that have justified the principle of measurable individual merit and the logic of the market place, where one man's money is equal to any other man's, have always appeared to Jews, even more than to other Americans, almost self-evidently just and right. And the *New York Times,* which most of the newer Negro leaders dislike intensely, expresses this liberal ideology in its purest form. The *Times* has never been tolerant toward the accommodations that others have sometimes seen as necessary in our mixed and complex society—the balanced ticket, for example, which has nothing to do with the abstract principles of merit.

But the liberal principles—the earlier ones arguing the democracy of money, the newer ones arguing the democracy of merit—that have been so congenial to Jews and so much in their interest are being increasingly accepted by everyone else nowadays under the pressures of a technological world. We are moving into a diploma society, where individual merit rather than family and connections and group must be the basis for advancement, recognition, achievement. The rea-

sons have nothing directly to do with the Jews, but no matter
—the Jews certainly gain from such a grand historical shift.
Thus Jewish interests coincide with the new rational approaches to the distribution of rewards.

It is clear that one cannot say the same about Negro interests. And so the Negroes have come to be opposed to these
approaches. But when Negroes challenge—as they do in New
York—the systems of testing by which school principals and
higher officials in the educational bureaucracy are selected
and promoted, they are also challenging the very system
under which Jews have done so well. And when they challenge the use of grades as the sole criterion for entry into special high schools and free colleges, they challenge the system
which has enabled Jews to dominate these institutions for decades.

But there is another and more subtle side to the shift of
Negro demands from abstract equality to group consideration, from color-blind to color-conscious. The Negroes press
these new demands because they see that the abstract color-
blind policies do not lead rapidly enough to the entry of
large numbers of Negroes into good jobs, good neighborhoods, good schools. It is, in other words, a group interest
they wish to further. Paradoxically, however, the ultimate
basis of the resistance to their demands, I am convinced—
certainly among Jews, but not Jews alone—is that they pose
a serious threat to the ability of other groups to maintain
their communities.

In America we have lived under a peculiar social compact.
On the one hand, publicly and formally and legally, we recognize only individuals; we do not recognize groups—
whether ethnic, racial, or religious. On the other hand, these
groups exist in actual social fact. They strongly color the activities and lives of most of our citizens. They in large measure determine an individual's fate through their control of
social networks which tend to run along ethnic, racial, and

103

religious lines. Even more subtly, they determine a man's fate by the culture and values they transmit, which affect his chances in the general competition for the abstract signs of merit and money.

This is not an easy situation to grasp. On the one hand (except for the South) there is equality—political equality, equal justice before the law, equal opportunity to get grades, take examinations, qualify for professions, open businesses, make money. This equality penetrates deeper and deeper into the society. The great private colleges now attempt to have nationally representative student bodies, not only geographically, but socially and economically and racially. The great private corporations reluctantly begin to accept the principle that, like a government civil service, they should open their selection processes and their recruiting procedures so that all may be represented. On the other hand, these uniform processes of selection for advancement, and the pattern of freedom to start a business and make money, operate not on a homogeneous mass of individuals, but on individuals as molded by a range of communities of different degrees of organization and self-consciousness, with different histories and cultures, and with different capacities to take advantage of the opportunities that are truly in large measure open to all.

Here we come to the crux of the Negro anger and the Jewish discomfort. The Negro anger is based on the fact that the system of formal equality produces so little for them. The Jewish discomfort is based on the fact that Jews discover they can no longer support the newest Negro demands, which may be designed from the Negro point of view to produce equality for all, but which are also designed to break down this pattern of communities. We must emphasize again that Jewish money, organizational strength, and political energy have played a major role in most cities and states in getting effective law and effective administration covering the rights to equal opportunity in employment, housing, and education. But all this past cooperation loses its relevance as it dawns on Jews, and others as well, that many Negro leaders are now beginning to expect that the pattern of their advancement in American society will take quite a different form from that of the immigrant ethnic groups. This new form may well be justified by the greater sufferings that have been inflicted on the Negroes by slavery, by the loss of their traditional culture, by their deliberate exclusion from power and privilege for the past century, by the new circumstances in American society which make the old pattern of advance (through formal equality plus the support of the group) less effective today. But that it *is* a new form, a radically new one, for the integration of a group into American society, we must recognize.

In the past, the established groups in American society came to understand, eventually, that the newer groups would not push their claims for equality to the point where the special institutions of the older groups would no longer be able to maintain their identity. There were certainly delicate moments when it looked as if the strongly pressed and effectively supported Jewish demand for formal equality, combined with Jewish wealth and grades, would challenge the rights of vacation resorts, social clubs, and private schools of the old established white Protestant community to serve as exclusive institutions of that community. But after a time the established Protestant community realized there were limits to the demands of the Jews, as there were limits to the demands of the Catholics. They realized that Jews and Catholics could not demand the complete abolition of lines between the communities because they too wanted to maintain communities of their own. Most Jews wanted to remain members of a distinctive group, and regardless of how consistent they were in battering against the walls of privilege, they always implicitly accepted the argument that various forms of division between people, aside from those based on the abstract criteria of money and achievement, were legitimate in America. Thus, when John Slawson of the American Jewish

Committee argued against the discriminatory practices of various social clubs, he did not, I believe, attack the right of a group to maintain distinctive institutions. He argued rather that Jews in banking or high politics could not conduct their *business* if they were not accepted as members of these clubs. He did not attack social discrimination as such—he attacked it because of its political and economic consequences and suggested it was abetting economic and political discrimination. The grounds he chose for his attack are revealing, for they indicate what he felt were the legitimate claims that one group in American society could raise about the way the other groups conducted their social life.

Now it is my sense of the matter that with the Negro revolution there has been a radical challenge to this pattern of individual advancement within an accepted structure of group distinctiveness. The white community into which the Negro now demands full entrance is not actually a single community—it is a series of communities. And all of them feel threatened by the implications of the new Negro demand for full equality. They did not previously realize how much store they set by their power to control the character of the social setting in which they lived. They did not realize this because their own demands generally did not involve or imply the dissolution of the established groups; they never really wanted to mingle too closely with these established groups. They demanded political representation—which assumed that the group continued. They demanded the right to their own schools, or (like the Catholics today) support for their own schools—which again proceeded from the assumption of group maintenance. They demanded equal rights in employment, in education, in housing. But as a matter of fact many of their jobs were held in business enterprises or in trades controlled by members of their own group. Many of them set up their own educational institutions to create the kind of higher education they thought desirable for their young people. If freedom of housing became an issue on occasion, such freedom was nevertheless used as much to create voluntary new concentrations of the group as to disperse it among other people.

The new Negro demands challenge the right to maintain these sub-communities far more radically than the demands of any other group in American history. As Howard Brotz has pointed out, the exclusion of the Negro from his legitimate place in American society was so extreme, so thoroughgoing, so complete, that all the political energy of the Negro has been directed toward beating down the barriers. The corollary of this exclusive focus is that most Negroes see nothing of value in the Negro group whose preservation requires separate institutions, residential concentration, or a ban on intermarriage. Or rather, the only thing that might justify such group solidarity is the political struggle itself—the struggle against all barriers. What other groups see as a value, Negroes see as a strategy in the fight for equal rights.

We have become far more sophisticated in our understanding of the meaning of equality, far more stuble in our understanding of the causes of inequality. As a result, political equality alone—which the Negro now enjoys in most parts of the country—is considered of limited importance. The demand for economic equality is now not the demand for equal opportunities for the equally qualified: it is the demand for equality of economic *results*—and it therefore raises such questions as why some businesses succeed and others fail, and how people are selected for advancement in large organizations. When we move into areas like that, we are not asking for abstract tolerance, or a simple desisting from discrimination. We are involving ourselves in the complex relationships between people, and we are examining the kinds of ties and judgments that go to make up our American sub-communities. Or consider the demand for equality in education, which has also become a demand for equality of *results*, of *outcomes*. Suppose one's capacity to gain from education depends on going to school with less than a majority of one's own group? Or suppose it depends on one's home background? Then how do we achieve equality of results? The answers to this question and many similar ones suggest that the deprived group must be inserted into the community of the advantaged. For otherwise there is no equality of outcome.

The force of present-day Negro demands is that the subcommunity, because it either protects privileges or creates inequality, *has no right to exist.* That is why these demands pose a quite new challenge to the Jewish community, or to any sub-community. Using the work of Oscar Handlin and Will Herberg, the Jewish community has come up with a convenient defense of Jewish exclusiveness—namely, that everyone else is doing it, too. The thrust of present-day Negro demands is that everyone should *stop* doing it. I do not interpret Jewish discomfort over this idea as false liberalism—for Jewish liberalism, even if it has never confronted the question directly, has always assumed that the advancement of disadvantaged groups, both Jews and others, would proceed in such a way as to respect the group pattern of American life. But the new Negro leaders believe Negroes cannot advance without a modification of this pattern. The churches, one of the major means by which group identities maintain themselves, are challenged by the insistent Negro demand for entry into every church. And if the Jews, because their church is so special, are for the moment protected against this demand, they are not protected against demands for entry on equal footing into their institutions which are the true seats of Jewish exclusiveness—the Jewish business, for example, the Jewish union, or the Jewish (or largely Jewish) neighborhood and school. Thus Jews find their interests and those of formally less liberal neighbors becoming similar: they both have an interest in maintaining an area restricted to their own kind; an interest in managing the friendship and educational experiences of their children;

an interest in passing on advantages in money and skills to them.

The Negro now demands entry into a world, a society, that does not exist, except in ideology. In that world there is only one American community, and in that world, heritage, ethnicity, religion, race are only incidental and accidental personal characteristics. There may be many reasons for such a world to come into existence—among them the fact that it may be necessary in order to provide full equality for the Negroes. But if we do move in this direction, we will have to create communities very different from the kinds in which most of us who have already arrived—Protestants, Catholics, Jews—now live.

CHOOSING A DREAM
MARIO PUZO

AS a child and in my adolescence, living in the heart of New York's Neapolitan ghetto, I never heard an Italian singing. None of the grown-ups I knew were charming or loving or understanding. Rather they seemed coarse, vulgar, and insulting. And so later in my life when I was exposed to all the clichés of lovable Italians, singing Italians, happy-go-lucky Italians, I wondered where the hell the moviemakers and storywriters got all their ideas from.

At a very early age I decided to escape these uncongenial folk by becoming an artist, a writer. It seemed then an impossible dream. My father and mother were illiterate, as were their parents before them. But practising my art I tried to view the adults with a more charitable eye and so came to the conclusion that their only fault lay in their being foreigners; I was an American. This didn't really help because I was only half right. I was the foreigner. They were already more "American" than I could ever become.

But it did seem then that the Italian immigrants, all the fathers and mothers that I knew, were a grim lot; always shouting, always angry, quicker to quarrel than embrace. I did not understand that their lives were a long labor to earn their daily bread and that physical fatigue does not sweeten human natures.

And so even as a very small child I dreaded growing up to be like the adults around me. I heard them saying too many cruel things about their dearest friends, saw too many of their false embraces with those they had just maligned, observed with horror their paranoiac anger at some small slight or a fancied injury to their pride. They were, always, too unforgiving. In short, they did not have the careless magnanimity of children.

In my youth I was contemptuous of my elders, including a few under thirty. I thought my contempt special to their circumstances. Later when I wrote about these illiterate men and women, when I thought I understood them, I felt a condescending pity. After all, they had suffered, they had labored all the days of their lives. They had never tasted luxury, knew little more economic security than those ancient Roman slaves who might have been their ancestors. And alas, I thought, with new-found artistic insight, they were cut off from their children because of the strange American tongue, alien to them, native to their sons and daughters.

Already an artist but not yet a husband or father, I pondered omnisciently on their tragedy, again thinking it special circumstance rather than a constant in the human condition. I did not yet understand why these men and women were willing to settle for less than they deserved in life and think that "less" quite a bargain. I did not understand that they simply could not afford to dream, I myself had a hundred dreams from which to choose. For I was already sure I would make my escape, that I was one of the chosen. I would be rich, famous, happy. I would master my destiny.

And so it was perhaps natural that as a child, with my father gone, my mother the family chief, I, like all the children in all the ghettos of America, became locked in a bitter struggle with the adults responsible for me. It was inevitable that my mother and I became enemies.

As a child I had the usual dreams. I wanted to be handsome, specifically as cowboy stars in movies were handsome. I wanted to be a killer hero in a world-wide war. Or if no wars came along (our teachers told us another was impossible), I wanted at the very least to be a footloose adventurer. Then I branched out and thought of being a great artist, and then, getting ever more sophisticated, a great criminal.

My mother, however, wanted me to be a railroad clerk. And that was her *highest* ambition; she would have settled for less. At the age of sixteen when I let everybody know that I was going to be a great writer, my friends and family took the news quite calmly, my mother included. She did not become angry. She quite simply assumed that I had gone off my nut. She was illiterate and her peasant life in Italy made her believe that only a son of the nobility could possibly be a writer. Artistic beauty after all could spring only from the seedbed of fine clothes, fine food, luxurious living. So then how was it possible for a son of hers to be an artist? She was not too convinced she was wrong even after my first two books were published many years later. It was only after the commercial success of my third novel that she gave me the title of poet.

My family and I grew up together on Tenth Avenue, between Thirtieth and Thirty-first streets, part of the area called Hell's Kitchen. This particular neighborhood could have been a movie set for one of the Dead End Kid flicks or for the social drama of the East Side in which John Garfield played the hero. Our tenements were the western wall of the city. Beneath our windows were the vast black iron gardens of the New York Central Railroad, absolutely blooming with stinking boxcars freshly unloaded of cattle and pigs for the city slaughterhouse. Steers sometimes escaped and loped through the heart of the neighborhood followed by astonished young boys who had never seen a live cow.

The railroad yards stretched down to the Hudson River, beyond whose garbagey waters rose the rocky Palisades of New Jersey. There were railroad tracks running downtown on Tenth Avenue itself to another freight station called St. Johns Park. Because of this, because these trains cut off one side of the street from the other, there was a wooden bridge over Tenth Avenue, a romantic-looking bridge despite the fact that no sparkling water, no silver flying fish darted beneath it; only heavy dray carts drawn by tired horses, some flat-boarded trucks, tin lizzie automobiles and, of course, long strings of freight cars drawn by black, ugly engines.

What was really great, truly magical, was sitting on the bridge, feet dangling down, and letting the engine under you blow up clouds of steam that made you disappear, then reappear all damp and smelling of fresh ironing. When I was seven years old I fell in love for the first time with the tough little girl who held my hand and disappeared with me in that magical cloud of steam. This experience was probably more traumatic and damaging to my later relationships with women than one of those ugly childhood adventures Freudian novelists use to explain why their hero has gone bad.

My father supported his wife and seven children by working as a track man laborer for the New York Central Railroad. My oldest brother worked for the railroad as a brakeman, another brother was a railroad shipping clerk in the freight office. Eventually I spent some of the worst months of my life as the railroad's worst messenger boy.

Choosing a Dream

My oldest sister was just as unhappy as a dressmaker in the garment industry. She wanted to be a school teacher. At one time or another my other two brothers also worked for the railroad—it got all six males in the family. The two girls and my mother escaped, though my mother felt it her duty to send all our bosses a gallon of homemade wine on Christmas. But everybody hated their jobs except my oldest brother who had a night shift and spent most of his working hours sleeping in freight cars. My father finally got fired because the foreman told him to get a bucket of water for the crew and not to take all day. My father took the bucket and disappeared forever.

Nearly all the Italian men living on Tenth Avenue supported their large families by working on the railroad. Their children also earned pocket money by stealing ice from the refrigerator cars in summer and coal from the open stoking cars in the winter. Sometimes an older lad would break the seal of a freight car and take a look inside. But this usually brought down the "Bulls," the special railroad police. And usually the freight was "heavy" stuff, too much work to cart away and sell, something like fresh produce or boxes of cheap candy that nobody would buy.

The older boys, the ones just approaching voting age, made their easy money by hijacking silk trucks that loaded up at the garment factory on Thirty-first Street. They would then sell the expensive dresses door to door, at bargain prices no discount house could match. From this some graduated into organized crime, whose talent scouts alertly tapped young boys versed in strong-arm. Yet despite all this, most of the kids grew up honest, content with fifty bucks a week as truck drivers, deliverymen, and white-collar clerks in the civil service.

I had every desire to go wrong but I never had a chance. The Italian family structure was too formidable.

I never came home to an empty house; there was always the smell of supper cooking. My mother was always there to greet me, sometimes with a policeman's club in her hand (nobody ever knew how she acquired it). But she was always there, or her authorized deputy, my older sister, who preferred throwing empty milk bottles at the heads of her little brothers when they got bad marks on their report cards. During the great Depression of the 1930s, though we were the poorest of the poor, I never remember not dining well. Many years later as a guest of a millionaire's club, I realized that our poor family on home relief ate better than some of the richest people in America.

My mother would never dream of using anything but the finest imported olive oil, the best Italian cheeses. My father had access to the fruits coming off ships, the produce from railroad cars, all before it went through the stale process of middlemen; and my mother, like most Italian women, was a fine cook in the peasant style. . . .

I had to help support my family by working on the railroad. After school hours, of course. This was the same railroad that had supplied free coal and free ice to the whole Tenth Avenue when I was young enough to steal with impunity. After school finished at 3 p.m. I went to work in the freight office as a messenger. I also worked Saturdays and Sundays when there was work available.

I hated it. One of my first short stories was about how I hated that job. But of course what I really hated was entering the adult world. To me the adult world was a dark enchantment, unnatural. As unnatural to the human dream as death. And as inevitable.

The young are impatient about change because they cannot grasp the power of time itself; not only as the enemy of flesh, the very germ of death, but time as a benign cancer. As the young cannot grasp really that love must be a victim of time, so too they cannot grasp that injustices, the economic and family traps of living, can also fall victim to time.

And so I really thought that I would spend the rest of my life as a railroad clerk. That I would never be a writer. That

Choosing a Dream

I would be married and have children and go to christenings
and funerals and visit my mother on a Sunday afternoon.
That I would never own an automobile or a house. That I
would never see Europe, the Paris and Rome and Greece
I was reading about in books from the public library. That I
was hopelessly trapped by my family, by society, by my lack
of skills and education.

But I escaped again. At the age of eighteen I started
dreaming about the happiness of my childhood. As later at
the age of thirty I would dream about the joys of my lost adolescence, as at the age of thirty-five I was to dream about
the wonderful time I had in the army which I had hated
being in. As at the age of forty-five I dreamed about the
happy, struggling years of being a devoted husband and loving father. I had the most valuable of human gifts, that of retrospective falsification: remembering the good and not the
bad.

I still dreamed of future glory. I still wrote short stories,
one or two a year. I still *KNEW* I would be a great writer
but I was beginning to realize that accidents could happen
and my second choice, that of being a great criminal, was
coming up fast. But for the young everything goes so slowly, I
could wait it out. The world would wait for me. I could still
spin out my life with dreams.

In the summertime I was one of the great Tenth Avenue
athletes but in the wintertime I became a sissy. I read books.
At a very early age I discovered libraries, the one in the
Hudson Guild and the public ones. I loved reading in the
Hudson Guild where the librarian became a friend. I loved
Joseph Altsheler's (I don't even have to look up his name)
tales about the wars of the New York State Indian tribes, the
Senecas and the Iroquois. I discovered Doc Savage and the
Shadow and then the great Sabatini. Part of my character to
this day is Scaramouche, I like to think. And then maybe at
the age of fourteen or fifteen or sixteen I discovered Dostoev-
sky. I read the books, all of them I could get. I wept for

Prince Myshkin in *The Idiot,* I was as guilty as Raskolnikov. And when I finished *The Brothers Karamazov* I understood for the first time what was really happening to me and the people around me. I had always hated religion even as a child but now I became a true believer. I believed in art. A belief that has helped me as well as any other.

My mother looked on all this reading with a fishy Latin eye. She saw no profit in it but since all her children were great readers she was a good enough general to know she could not fight so pervasive an insubordination. And there may have been some envy. If she had been able to she would have been the greatest reader of us all.

My direct ancestors for a thousand years have most probably been illiterate. Italy, the golden land, so loving to vacationing Englishmen, so majestic in its language and cultural treasures (they call it, I think, the cradle of civilization), has never cared for its poor people. My father and mother were both illiterates. Both grew up on rocky, hilly farms in the countryside adjoining Naples. My mother remembers never being able to taste the ham from the pig they slaughtered every year. It brought too high a price in the marketplace and cash was needed. My mother was also told the family could not afford the traditional family gift of linens when she married and it was this that decided her to emigrate to America to marry her first husband, a man she barely knew. When he died in a tragic work accident on the docks, she married my father, who assumed responsibility for a widow and her four children perhaps out of ignorance, perhaps out of compassion, perhaps out of love. Nobody ever knew. He was a mystery, a Southern Italian with blue eyes who departed from the family scene three children later when I was twelve. But he cursed Italy even more than my mother did. Then again, he wasn't too pleased with America either. My mother never heard of Michelangelo; the great deeds of the Caesars had not yet reached her ears. She never heard the great music of her native land. She could not sign her name.

Choosing a Dream

And so it was hard for my mother to believe that her son could become an artist. After all, her one dream in coming to America had been to earn her daily bread, a wild dream in itself. And looking back she was dead right. Her son an artist? To this day she shakes her head. I shake mine with her.

America may be a fascistic, warmongering, racially prejudiced country today. It may deserve the hatred of its revolutionary young. But what a miracle it once was! What has happened here has never happened in any other country in any other time. The poor who had been poor for centuries— hell, since the beginning of Christ—whose children had inherited their poverty, their illiteracy, their hopelessness, achieved some economic dignity and freedom. You didn't get it for nothing, you had to pay a price in tears, in suffering, but why not? And some even became artists.

Not even my gift for retrospective falsification can make my eighteenth to twenty-first years seem like a happy time. I hated my life. I was being dragged into the trap I feared and had foreseen even as a child. It was all there, the steady job, the nice girl who would eventually get knocked up, and then the marriage and fighting over counting pennies to make ends meet. I noticed myself acting more unheroic all the time. I had to tell lies in pure self-defense, I did not forgive so easily.

But I was delivered. When World War II broke out I was delighted. There is no other word, terrible as it may sound. My country called. I was delivered from my mother, my family, the girl I was loving passionately but did not love. And delivered WITHOUT GUILT. Heroically. My country called, ordered me to defend it. I must have been one of millions, sons, husbands, fathers, lovers, making their innocent getaway from baffled loved ones. And what an escape it was. The war made all my dreams come true. I drove a jeep, toured Europe, had love affairs, found a wife, and lived the material for my first novel. But of course that was a just war as Vietnam is not, and so today it is perhaps for the best that the revolutionary young make their escape by attacking their own rulers.

Then why five years later did I walk back into the trap with a wife and child and a civil service job I was glad to get? After five years of the life I had dreamed about, plenty of women, plenty of booze, plenty of money, hardly any work, interesting companions, travel, etc., why did I walk back into that cage of family and duty and a steady job?

For the simple reason, of course, that I had never really escaped, not my mother, not my family, not the moral pressures of our society. Time again had done its work. I was back in my cage and I was, I think, happy. In the next twenty years I wrote three novels. Two of them were critical successes but I didn't make much money. The third novel, not as good as the others, made me rich. And free at last. Or so I thought.

Then why do I dream of those immigrant Italian peasants as having been happy? I remember how they spoke of their forebears, who spent all their lives farming the arid mountain slopes of Southern Italy. "He died in that house in which he was born," they say enviously. "He was never more than an hour from his village, not in all his life," they sigh. And what would they make of a phrase like "retrospective falsification"?

No, really, we are all happier now. It is a better life. And after all, as my mother always said, "Never mind about being happy. Be glad you're alive."

When I came to my "autobiographical novel," the one every writer does about himself, I planned to make myself the sensitive, misunderstood hero, much put upon by his mother and family. To my astonishment my mother took over the book and instead of my revenge I got another comeuppance. But it is, I think, my best book. And all those old-style grim conservative Italians whom I hated, then pitied so patronizingly, they also turned out to be heroes. Through no desire of mine. I was surprised. The thing that amazed me most was their courage. Where were their Congressional Medals of Honor? Their Distinguished Service Crosses? How did they ever have the balls to get married, have kids, go out to earn a living in a strange land, with no skills, not even knowing the language? They made it without tranquillizers, without sleeping pills, without psychiatrists, without even a dream. Heroes. Heroes all around me. I never saw them.

But how could I? They wore lumpy work clothes and handlebar moustaches, they blew their noses on their fingers and they were so short that their high-school children towered over them. They spoke a laughable broken English and the furthest limit of their horizon was their daily bread. Brave men, brave women, they fought to live their lives without dreams. Bent on survival they narrowed their minds to the thinnest line of existence.

It is no wonder that in my youth I found them contemptible. And yet they had left Italy and sailed the ocean to come to a new land and leave their sweated bones in America. Illiterate Colombos, they dared to seek the promised land. And so they, too, dreamed a dream.

Forty years ago, in 1930, when I was ten, I remember gas light, spooky, making the tenement halls and rooms alive with ghosts.

We had the best apartment on Tenth Avenue, a whole top floor of six rooms, with the hall as our storage cellar and the roof as our patio. Two views, one of the railroad yards backed by the Jersey shore, the other of a backyard teeming with tomcats everybody shot at with BB guns. In between these two rooms with a view were three bedrooms without windows—the classic railroad flat pattern. The kitchen had a fire escape that I used to sneak out [on] at night. I liked that apartment though it had no central heating, only a coal stove at one end and an oil stove at the other. I remember it as comfortable, slum or not.

My older brothers listened to a crystal radio on homemade headsets. I hitched a ride on the backs of horses and wagons, my elders daringly rode the trolley cars. Only forty years ago

119

in calendar time, it is really a thousand years in terms of change in our physical world. There are the jets, TV, penicillin for syphilis, cobalt for cancer, equal sex for single girls; yet still always the contempt of the young for their elders.

But maybe the young are on the right track this time. Maybe they know that the dreams of our fathers were malignant. Perhaps it is true that the only real escape is in the blood magic of drugs. All the Italians I knew and grew up with have escaped, have made their success. We are all Americans now, we are all successes now. And yet the most successful Italian man I know admits that though the one human act he never could understand was suicide, he understood it when he became a success. Not that he ever would do such a thing; no man with Italian blood ever commits suicide or becomes a homosexual in his belief. But suicide has crossed his mind. And so to what avail the finding of the dream? He went back to Italy and tried to live like a peasant again. But he can never again be unaware of more subtle traps than poverty and hunger.

There is a difference between having a good time in life and being happy. My mother's life was a terrible struggle and yet I think it was a happy life. One tentative proof is that at the age of eighty-two she is positively indignant at the thought that death dares approach her. But it's not for everybody that kind of life.

Thinking back I wonder why I became a writer. Was it the poverty or the books I read? Who traumatized me, my mother or the Brothers Karamazov? Being Italian? Or the girl sitting with me on the bridge as the engine steam deliciously made us vanish? Did it make any difference that I grew up Italian rather than Irish or black?

No matter. The good times are beginning, I am another Italian success story. Not as great as DiMaggio or Sinatra but quite enough. It will serve. Yet I can escape again. I have my retrospective falsifications (how I love that phrase). I can

Choosing a Dream

dream now about how happy I was in my childhood, in my tenement, playing in those dirty but magical streets—living in the poverty that made my mother weep. True, I was a deposed dictator at fifteen but they never hanged me. And now I remember all those impossible dreams strung out before me, waiting for me to choose, not knowing that the life I was living then, as a child, would become my final dream.

CHAPTER 2

Most (Un) Favored Peoples*

THE NORDIC JUNGLE: INFERIORITY IN AMERICA

MICHAEL NOVAK

I'VE noticed it in others—sometimes in Jews, just around the corner of attention. Everything is going well; they've forgotten the familiar feeling. Then something you say prompts uneasiness in their eyes, the eyes of one hunted, almost found, in danger. Swiftly it passes. Intelligence resumes its high performance.

You can generate that uneasiness in the eyes of almost any American, except a wealthy WASP: in Poles, Italians, Chicanos, Blacks, in Greeks, Armenians, the French. . . . Unworthiness was stamped upon their souls. Red-hot branding irons singe a calf's new skin. The trauma can be traced, reopened.

NOT A MELTING POT—A JUNGLE

Louis Adamic grew up in a small village in Carniola, Slovenia. All through his childhood—he was born in 1899—his imagination was fired by America. His parents did not want

REPRINTED with permission of Macmillan Publishing Co., Inc. and Curtis Brown, Ltd. from *The Rise of the Unmeltable Ethnics* by Michael Novak, pp. 72–115. Copyright © 1971, 1972 by Michael Novak.
  * See also Appendix III.

him to go. His father's farm was small but adequate; he looked forward to help from his children, of whom Louis was the oldest. (Over the years, the number of children reached nine.)

As Louis grew up, he saw many men come back broken from America. Some had diseases no one had ever heard of: rheumatism and asthma. Many others had gone to America and disappeared like stones in a deep, dark well. No one ever heard from them again. News of horrible accidents in which others were involved came back frequently: many died in mills or mines. His mother had a special dread concerning those who worked and died underground.

Louis was not a very religious boy. He was an observer rather than a participant in life—cool, detached, often moved with affection. He loved the almost pagan religion of his mother, her joy in life and fatalism in disaster. He did not see in Catholicism—although he did not like it—what its American critics saw. The feeling for religion among Slavic and Italian peoples is almost totally different from the feeling of WASPS or Irish Catholics: more pagan, more secular, closer to earth, aesthetic rather than moral, meditative rather than organizational. . . .

Laughing in the Jungle he called his autobiography. Not "melting pot." Jungle. From 1913 until 1931 he observed all across America the destruction of the spirit of the immigrants. He saw their broken bodies. He saw American soldiers firing upon American civilians. He saw Slavic pride in hard work frozen into steel and concrete buildings.

Even in his native village, when Louis was ten, a man of broken health had pointed to a picture of New York.

I—we helped to build these buildings—we Slovenians and Croatians and Slovaks and other people who went to America to work. We helped to build many other cities there, cities of which you have never heard, and railroads, and bridges, all made of steel which our people make in the mills. Our men from the Balkans are the best steelworkers in America. The framework of

123

America is made of steel. And this smoke that you see here—it comes from coal that we have dug up; we from the Balkans and from Galicia and Bohemia. . . .

Three times I was in accidents. Once, in Colorado, I was buried for four days three thousand feet underground. There were seven other men buried with me—three of them Slovenians like myself, two Poles, one Dalmatian, one American. When they dug us out, the Dalmatian and I were the only two still living. Once, in Pennsylvania, a rock fell on me in a mine and broke my right leg. The leg healed and I went back to work. I worked two months, and another rock fell on me. It almost broke my left leg.

Then his friend told him of walking the streets of New York just before sailing for home:

I looked up, and can hardly describe my feelings. I realized that there was much of our work and strength, my own work and strength, frozen in the greatness of New York and in the greatness of America. I felt that, although I was going home to Blato, I was actually leaving myself in America.

America is a jungle. That's how Adamic was warned to think of it. "American industry uses you, then casts you off."

Adamic records the histories of some who survived the jungle, and some who did not. In San Pedro, California, the Slovenian who was "the most American" among those Louis had met in America died by violence one night. He was running a rum-runner through the darkness and smashed directly into the looming side of an unseen freighter. In the gas explosion that followed, he was trapped in the wooden cabin for two minutes, was broiled, and died on his way to shore. His wife Josie, in her eighth month, had a miscarriage.

The crucial question is why it was so important to "old Americans" to put down the new Americans? Serious economic, social, and political dislocations were involved. But cultural differences were of highest interest. What was the American-Nordic norm, to whose dimensions the new immigrants were supposed to chop or stretch themselves? How did an "old American" think about himself, imagine his situation? What was his "feel" for life and destiny?

The subject, of course, is too vast. Crèvecoeur, de Tocqueville, D. W. Brogan, Commager, and others have tried to state it. But our interest is special. How did the "old American" appear *in the eyes of the new immigrant?* What new aspects of the American character were brought out by the immigrants from southern and eastern Europe? . . .

Closure, certainly. The restrictive immigration laws of 1917, 1921, 1924, and even 1952. The explicit boldness of Nordic racism: certain races are more "American" than others.

It is the springs of this racism that we must now explore. I am not eager to increase the quotient of Anglo-Saxon guilt. One of the most winning traits in the American character is its willingness to hear criticism of itself, to take that criticism to heart, to try more earnestly still to *become perfect*. Nothing is easier than to play upon the guilt feelings of Anglo-Saxon Americans. The ideals to which they are committed are so high.

Moreover, we must make certain distinctions. At best, we shall be able to describe the ideal-typical norm, the secret set of expectations implicit in American culture as the immigrants faced it. Only toward the end of the nineteenth century were the "old Americans" themselves beginning to become aware of their special identity. The very word "race" was just beginning to take on a modern meaning. Differences between English and American character were ever more strongly felt. The prospect of an America not dominated by "old American" consciousness was just being faced. The enormous revolution of bureaucratization was creating havoc in the self-identity and values of Americans, especially in the cities. Lacking the feudal traditions of Europe, Americans tended to believe, genuinely believe, in their own equality one with another. But the unchecked excesses of industry were generating a sharp conflict between management and labor, and the first profound stirrings of class consciousness were being felt. The aftermath of the Civil War occasioned deep guilts and repressions concerning the relations of blacks and whites. The economy oscillated wildly between panic and prosperity.

For our purposes, let us set to one side the intellectuals of the period 1880–1924. Their attitudes toward the immigrants were ambivalent—at times enormously sympathetic (Jane Addams at Hull House in Chicago), at other times distressed. In any case, the immigrants seldom met them.

Mostly, the immigrants encountered the factory owners and the workers, the farmers, and the people of the small towns in the northeast and the middle west. They met three levels of WASP culture: the established, educated, wealthy, and middle-class culture of the cities; the "older" American culture of the small towns; and the tough, direct culture of the farmhands and laborers. When, for example, they heard the word "Protestant," it meant all three. In the interstices, more often than not acting as political brokers, were the Irish. For most immigrants, the word "American" was first applied to an Irish neighbor. Ralph Perrotta, a young lawyer who served in the Civil Rights Division of the Justice Department, recalls a feeling still powerful in the 1930s: "You're brought up with a feeling that you're not quite American and develop feelings of self-hatred. One of my earliest recollections is my mother referring to the Irish families on the block as 'the Americans.'" It is a recollection almost every ethnic American shares.

Although Catholic, the Irish seemed to share a WASP disdain for swarthier peoples. Even today, an Irish bishop in Pennsylvania will not scruple to refer to part of his flock as "hunkies" and another part as "dagos." Not untypically, he will regard the Irish as deeper in the faith, more devout, richer in vocations. As the "others" are not quite fully American, so they are also not quite fully Catholic. How, statistically, the Irish rate southern and eastern Europeans I do not know. But to many of the latter the way it *feels* is not liberating or encouraging; the feeling tone generates the self-hatred Perrotta speaks of. The ethnic animosity within the Catholic church has scarcely been given tongue, let alone explored.

But the American Irish have also suffered from "Americanization." "No Irish Need Apply." They, too, have quite profound feelings of resentment towards native Americans, feelings that are extremely important in American politics. Kevin Phillips in *The Emerging Republican Majority* voices his resentment indictment by indictment.

What were the pressures that generated this resentment? The character of "the old American" was in certain respects very different from anything that the Catholic immigrant, even the one from Ireland, had ever known before. It would be easy enough to recount the familiar characteristics: the incredible mobility, the hucksterism, the fervid evangelism of the frontier, the pragmatism, the moneymaking schemes, the reduction of metaphysics to a single test: success, the confidence men, the greed, the righteousness, the free speech. The old Americans of English stock believed that the English, as the proudest flower of the Teutonic race, had been given certain skills in self-government and certain defenses of individual liberties unequalled by any other race. This the immigrants were usually delighted to discover, to revel in, and to be re-made by. Mary Antin wrote in *The Promised Land* (1912): "I have been made over. I am absolutely other than the person whose story I have to tell." Andrew Carnegie dedicated his *Triumphant Democracy* (1887) "to the country which has removed the stigma of inferiority which his native land saw proper to impress upon him at birth, and has made him in the estimation of its great laws as well as in his own estimation (much the more important consideration), the peer of any human being who draws the breath of life, be he pope, kaiser, priest, or king—henceforth the subject of no man, but a free man, a citizen."

America was an intoxicant. "*America! America!*" cries Elia Kazan in 1961. Yet the price was steep: the reconstruction of the self. More like a religion than like a nation, America required conversion of soul. . . .

First, the new immigrant had to learn loneliness. To be sure, men often came to America in advance of their families. Most came alone. But what was different about America was that loneliness was encouraged; it was a way of life. Industrialization even in Europe meant that the "network people" of the countryside were atomized. Men no longer worked with their sons. They came home exhausted to their wives. In America, however, men were not *supposed* to value family or ethnic or neighborhood community more than their own independence and advancement. It was assumed that older people and older ways were less "American," and that with every generation a new and better type of man was steadily emerging. . . .

Oscar Handlin stresses the feelings of loneliness induced by the symbolic ocean crossing, the landing on a strange land in strange cities, the novelties of moving farther and farther from roots and families and friends so that one could imagine oneself dropping from sight without a trace. The loneliness, I suspect, was such a violation of primordial biological needs for community that Americans also acquired a new and distinctive sort of guilt. They were "foreigners" on earth, a new type of human—and there was pride in that. But they were also trespassing ancient boundaries. There was an ominous sense of possible retribution. In any case, Americans have long had a novel and overwhelming need to be reassured that they are a moral and good people. American soldiers give chewing gum to little children. We *need* to think of ourselves as good, in a manner distinctively American. It is as though affection, once bonded to family and tribe but now cut loose, floats free: America needs to be reassured that fellow-feeling has not vanished. . . .

What first struck later immigrant consciousness, therefore, was the solitariness of Protestant consciousness. In order to become American, one had to learn to be alone. One had to learn to *value* being alone. Separate bedrooms, separate TV, separate auto—the contemporary centrifugal forces of American life were splitting apart the later immigrants' internal networks from the very first. . . .

What course lay open to the victims—Indians, Blacks, Orientals, Chicanos, Jews and, in our context, Poles, Italians, Greeks, Slavs? How desperately many tried to prove they were proper, reliable, chaste, self-disciplined, controlled. How earnestly they worked against their instincts, impulses, gestures, feelings, drives, and perceptions. How urgently they worked to find sex "dirty." The melting pot was a cauldron of lead for the purging and the encasement of passion. If one could not be a WASP, one could make oneself into a good metallic soldier.

MANY KINDS OF WASP

Growing up in America is a series of new social-cultural explorations. The undifferentiated "them" beyond one's own family; neighborhood; ethnic, religious, and economic group turns out to be exceedingly various. One evening in Boston I attended a party with black families in Roxbury; went for cocktails and dinner at the home of an assistant to the governor in a sheltered, quiet, sylvan hideaway in Cambridge; and finished up with dessert at the small suburban home of a genial Irish lawyer (a federal attorney) who had moved out from an Irish neighborhood to Wellesley. The manners, vocabulary, interests, courtesies, jokes, speech patterns, facial expressions varied from place to place.

When I first came to New York, general schemes like "Jews" shattered in my hands. I wasn't prepared for Jewish cab drivers or Jewish poverty; not for militantly conservative Jews in a teachers' union; not for countless factions, classes, political views, and neatly elaborate hierarchies of status. High in one status did not mean high in another; Jewish

disdain—escaping from compressed lips—is crisp. A relatively small number of Jews in New York and Los Angeles set
a style for Jewishness that may be foreign to Jews in Cleveland or Utica.

Just as clearly it has become plain to me that there are
many different kinds of WASP. In the West Virginia hills
there may be bitter hostility to Catholics or indeed to all outsiders, and four or five generations of residence are required
before one is accepted as other than an interloper. But West
Virginia WASPs would have an attitude toward Boston Brah-
mins or Wall Street bankers very much like that of Catholics
in Dorchester, or Okies in the Southwest. WASP history is
often internally tragic and bitter. Poor, forgotten, excluded
persons abound.

In a brilliant short study of a single Massachusetts town,
Stephen Thernstrom opened my eyes to the poverty and degradation exercised by upper-class WASPs for lower-class
WASPs. He helped me to see more vividly how threatening
to poor WASPs cheap immigrant labor must have been. One
can sympathize with their terror. Thernstrom also shows how
the image of a small-town community, where everyone knew
everyone, slipped from uneasy reality into sheer fantasy two
centuries ago. Far from being free and egalitarian, early
American culture was severely based on class power, authority from on high, and little or no participation by the poor:

In the 18th-century community the political structure encouraged
habits of obedience and deference, habits promising stability and
unity. Parties were abhorred, "fashions" despised. Repeated unani-
mous votes in their town meetings revealed the powerful centripetal influence of local political institutions.

At mid-century the town meeting disappeared, the size and
complexity which made Newburyport a city demanded a more rationalized, impersonal form of government. Voting became an
anonymous act, and social constraints supporting political deference were thereby weakened. Party competition was now fierce
and chaotic.

The competing political parties were not sharply polarized along class lines in 1850, and both were controlled by respectable middle-class citizens. . . . Not a single laborer was included on an 1852 list of the 72 members of the Democratic vigilance committees in the wards. The lower class was politically passive; laborers and operatives exercised their franchise less frequently than citizens of higher status.[1]

The extent to which upper-class WASP convictions rest upon high authority, distance, and direct application of force runs so contrary to the stated ideology of the Constitution, the Declaration of Independence, and the Gettysburg Address that the swift dependence of silver-haired establishmentarians on brute force always jangles one's mental images forcibly. Upper-class WASPs picture themselves as defending uniquely Anglo-Saxon liberties and a distinctive egalitarianism. Still, in the eyes of many of them, they are clearly defending order, *their* order, and they believe in beating down challenges swiftly and efficiently. The White House, GOP leaders assembled, and the Republican governors meeting in San Juan speedily came to Governor Rockefeller's defense after he had bloodily crushed the prisoners' rebellion at Attica. He did "what he had to do." They commended his "forcefulness."

The old WASP family, like other ethnic families, had a tradition of subjection. Thernstrom notes: "The seventeenth-century Puritan family had been not only 'a little church and a little commonwealth,' but also 'a school wherein the first principles and grounds of government and subjection are learned.' Every member of the community had to belong to some family, the agency through which social stability was maintained." This tradition of stability, subjection, the severe internalization of order, seems to lie behind a certain WASP suspicion of other looser ethnic groups, and gives historical depth to our perception of the symbolic meaning of "law and order." The point of force is "to teach a lesson" that was, un-

[1] Stephen Thernstrom, *Poverty and Progress* (Cambridge: Harvard University Press, 1964), pp. 52–3.

fortunately, not learned in the family. People of good families, meanwhile, seldom feel the weight of the law even when they err, for there are many testimonies to their "good character" and "upbringing." (The support of David Rockefeller for William Bundy as a suitable editor for *Foreign Affairs* is a classic of upper-class WASP solidarity. How could anyone impugn the character of "one of us"? Similarly, the Yankee grandmother of a young lawyer wanted for allegedly passing a gun to George Jackson at San Quentin tells a television audience that whatever the young man did, "he did from conscience.")

Upper-class WASP traditions of democratic liberty depended very highly on strict family discipline and internalized order. They flourished best in small towns and rural environments, where families could be in stricter control of their offspring. As *social* conceptions, these traditions have been under enormous strains, even among WASPs, for over a century. . . .

But there were other English conceptions, dear to a whole line of liberal thinkers, waiting to take up the slack:

The rise of the city and the spread of the factory across America was accompanied by a new social creed. According to this complex of ideas, American society was a collection of mobile, freely competing atoms; divisions between rich and poor could not produce destructive social conflict because the status rich or poor was not permanent. If society was in a state of constant circulation, if every man had an opportunity to rise to the top, all would be well.[2]

English conceptions of order, decorum, social planning, the free marketplace (of goods and of ideas), friction-free consensus, etc., dominate American life so thoroughly that most WASPSs seem unaware of them as ethnic preferences. For them, such matters are so much a part of their sense of reality, so integral to their own life story, so symbolically familiar, so inherently self-validating, that charges of partiality

[2] *Ibid.*, p. 56.

and bias must seem to them faintly insane. *Their* conception of sanity is, in fact, in question. They are being obliged to see themselves as ethnically one-sided for perhaps the first time. What used to be regarded as dignified reserve is now mocked as uptightness; what used to be regarded as good character is analyzed now for its "hangups"; the individualism of the Marlboro man, once a cherished aspiration, is regarded as alienation; the smooth-talking managerial style of liberal WASP authoritarianism is hissed as manipulative and venal; competitiveness is laughed at by those to whom it is closed. American cultural pluralism, fed by Jews, Blacks, Indians, and other ethnic groups, has thrown WASP ideals into a new and unflattering light. . . .

Still, one ought not to be too hard on others. All ethnic groups have their own confusions. All acceded for far too long to the pressures of Americanization—which was really WASPification. Many individuals eagerly accepted it. All have found some good and beautiful things in it.

Besides the many regional varieties of lower-class WASPs, moreover, we should also distinguish between two WASP elites who mutually, it appears, disdain each other: the WASPs of "the northeastern establishment" and the newly rich WASPs of what Kevin Phillips calls "the Sun Belt." The industrialists around Ronald Reagan, the oilmen and new technology of Texas, the booming real estate of Florida— over against the oak-panelled rooms, quiet voices, collections of art, and attachment to civil rights of the Rockefellers, Harrimans, Lodges, and others—may draw the contrasts in power and style clearly enough. And in between these two groups is a third: those small-town lawyers of little class, wealth, or power, whose armpits sweat and whose keys to Playboy clubs compensate for the strict morals of the midwestern Bible Belt, whose legwork is the backbone of Republican power across the land, and whose epigone is Richard Nixon—Nixon the outsider, the nonestablishmentarian, shifty, hardworking, fiercely controlled internally, making himself suffer to convince himself he's on a right path, tough, moralistic, "the last liberal," and president of the United States.

In the country clubs, as city executives, established families, industrialists, owners, lawyers, masters of etiquette, college presidents, dominators of the military, fundraisers, members of blue ribbon communities, realtors, brokers, deans, sheriffs—it is the cumulative power and distinctive styles of WASPs that the rest of us have had to learn in order to survive. WASPs have never had to celebrate Columbus Day or march down Fifth Avenue wearing green. Every day has been their day in America. No more.

EXODUS U.S.A.

THEODORE SALOUTOS

AMERICANS by reputation are a smug, self-satisfied people who find it difficult to believe that anyone, native or foreign-born, who has lived in their midst over a period of years would forsake their country for residence abroad. For years they gloried in their achievements as a nation, their spiritual and economic values, their bountiful resources, and their limitless opportunities. As proof they cited the millions of Europeans who settled in the United States during the nineteenth and twentieth centuries.

But in the process these same self-centered Americans overlooked the millions of aliens, and, to a much lesser extent, the naturalized citizens who left the United States to return to their native land. No one seemed to pay too much attention

FROM: O. F. Ander (ed.), *In the Trek of the Immigrant* (Rock Island, Ill.: Augustana College Library, 1964), Chap. 14. Reprinted by permission.

to them. "But these people," wrote one discerning observer, ". . . are going home. Disregarding all editorial assurance that America and Paradise are synonymous, they are going home. Unswayed by the spectacle of our superior civilization, they are going home. Unseduced by the siren song of our democracy, they are going home." [1]

The presumption has always been that the members of the older ethnic stocks were more inclined to remain than were the later arrivals from the countries of southern, central, and eastern Europe. Efforts to disprove this contention are made difficult by the absence of reliable statistical data on emigrant departures prior to 1908. Still it is reasonable to assume that the time required to cross the ocean and the difficulties of transatlantic travel during the nineteenth century discouraged departures that became commonplace during the twentieth.

Our lack of information about these emigrating aliens stems from the simple reason that they constituted an ignored and even a despised element in the United States and the countries to which they emigrated. The Americans viewed them as a negligible quantity in comparison with the incoming hordes who became the concern of the lawmakers, the welfare agencies, and the general public.

All indications are that aliens departed from the United States prior to 1908 for pretty much the same reasons they left in the later years. A clue as to the size of the emigrant traffic before 1908 is furnished by the statistics of the transatlantic passenger traffic. Third and steerage class passengers included many who went abroad temporarily or returned from short journeys, but as a rule they represented the bulk

---

[1] George Seibel, "Going Back—and Why," *Nation*, 109:493 (Oct. 11, 1919); 61st Congress, 3d Session, Sen. Doc. No. 748, *Reports of the Immigration Conditions in Europe* (Washington, 1911), p. 40; W. F. Willcox, "Restriction of Immigration—Discussion," *American Economic Review*, 2:68, Supplement (Mar., 1912).

of the immigrant and emigrant traffic; hence, they furnish a guide as to the outward movement, especially in periods of depression.[2]

In 1906 the Commissioner General of Immigration recognizing the importance of this emigrant traffic made an effort to obtain emigration data for the years 1890 to 1906. But in the absence of legislation requiring the shipmasters to provide lists of passengers, the Commissioner General realized that his efforts, at best, would be incomplete. Meanwhile, the value of this information had become so clear to the authorities that a provision finally was inserted into the immigration law of 1907 requiring the shipmasters of departing vessels to file accurate and detailed lists of their alien passengers. As a result, the Commissioner General of Immigration was able to issue the first official tabulation of aliens departing from this country for the fiscal year ending June 30th, 1908.[3]

A comparison of information released by immigration and steamship company authorities shows conclusively that emigration from the United States prior to 1908 was anything but new. This had been going on for years. Official statistics show that from 1887 to 1907, 2,231,961 Italians departed for the United States, while 972,695 returned to Italy. Immigration officials conjectured that the causes for the large movement out of the United States could not be attributed solely to the lack of employment opportunities, except in periods of depression. They assumed that dissatisfaction with life in the United States, poor health, the desire to be with relatives and friends, and the fulfillment of an ambition to make money and return home to lead a life of ease, influenced these departures.[4]

[2] Isaac A. Hourwich, *Immigration and Labor* (New York, 1912), p. 90.

[3] 61st Cong., 3d Session, Sen. Doc. No. 746, p. 43; *Annual Report of the Commissioner General of Immigration for the Fiscal Year Ended June 30, 1907* (Washington, 1907), p. 45.

[4] 61st Cong., 3d Session, *ibid.*, pp. 43–4; see also Matthew Simon, "The United States Balance of Payments, 1861–1900" in National Bureau of Economic Research, *Trends in the American Economy in the*

Exodus U.S.A.

During the twentieth century two periods stand out conspicuously in the emigration movement: the seven years prior to the outbreak of World War I, and the years immediately thereafter.

Those leaving prior to World War I were primarily of central, eastern, and southern European origins. The following table indicates that those departing in largest numbers from 1908 to 1914 were the Italians, Austrians, Hungarians, Russians, and Greeks:

TABLE 3
Emigrant Aliens Departing According to Country of Destination, 1908–1914 *

	AUSTRIA	HUNGARY	ITALY	RUSSIA	GREECE
1908	64,607	65,590	166,733	37,777	6,131
1909	27,782	21,631	83,300	19,707	5,606
1910	26,424	20,866	52,323	17,362	8,144
1911	45,160	41,182	72,640	27,053	9,376
1912	46,137	42,423	108,388	31,681	11,461
1913	28,760	29,904	88,024	26,923	30,603
1914	35,013	39,987	84,351	47,451	11,124

* United States Department of Labor, *Annual Report of the Commissioner General of Immigration, Fiscal Year Ended June 30, 1921* (Washington, 1921), pp. 110–11.

However, it remained for the panic years of 1907–1908 to focus the spotlight on these emigrating aliens. In November 1907 a total of 96,724 left; the homeward rush was so great that special trains had to be dispatched to carry the emigrants to New York where they often were compelled to wait until passage could be found. These mass departures continued through August 1908, except for the month of March. Then in September 1908 immigration once more exceeded emigration.[5]

Nineteenth Century (Princeton, 1960), pp. 685–9; U. S. Industrial Commission, *Reports of the Industrial Commission,* XV (Washington, 1901), pp. 161–4.

[5] *New International Year Book, 1907* (New York, 1908), pp. 246, 346; *Commercial and Financial Chronicles,* 86:444–5 (Feb. 22, 1908),

More important than these statistical revelations are the reasons behind these mass departures. Some left simply because they wanted to spend Christmas and the winter months at home; but the mass embarkations after the October panic were caused by unemployment and the possibility of living for less in the old country. The fear of being without jobs in a strange land had a chain reaction and prompted many of the insecure to follow in a sheep-like manner. These apprehensions were heightened in November 1907 when Pittsburgh manufacturers discharged about 15,000 Italians, Hungarians, and Slavs on the grounds that they were inefficient, and sent them home, expenses paid. The employers claimed that these employees were about half as efficient as their American, English, German, and Irish counterparts.[6]

But there were other compelling motives as well. Some had acquired a competence and were returning home to spend the remainder of their lives as they planned. Others expressed fear over the outcome of the presidential election of 1908 and the effects this would have on their future. Still others found living in the United States unsatisfying.[7]

Most Americans lamented these departures, not because these people were leaving but because they were taking so much money out of the country. This in turn brought about a loud clamor to bar the entry of such people into the United States. These foreigners were taking American-earned money out of the country instead of depositing it in American banks and American enterprises. Such persons, it was claimed, also made it difficult for American wage-earners to compete with them and contributed to bringing about industrial crises and depressed working conditions.[8]

690–91 (Mar. 21, 1908), 1006–7 (April 25, 1908), 1492–3 (June 20, 1908), 87:196–7 (July 25, 1908), 88:259–260 (Jan. 30, 1909), 89:319–20 (Aug. 7, 1909).

[6] *New York Tribune* (Nov. 21, 1907).

[7] C. S. Crowninshield to the Assistant Secretary of State, May 27, 1908.

[8] W. B. Bailey, "The Bird of Passage," *American Journal of Sociology*, 18:392–3 (Nov., 1912).

Exodus U.S.A.

Much of the resentment toward the departing immigrant stemmed from provincialism, bigotry, and misinformation; hindsight, if not common sense, bears out that the case against the emigrant alien was exaggerated if not misrepresented. Such short-sighted criticisms also obscured the commercial and cultural ties that he was helping forge between his country and the United States. He did not add to our burdens in times of trouble by swelling the army of the unemployed. One further doubts whether he had the adverse effect on wage-standards, especially on those of the organized skilled workers with whom he was in no position to compete.[9]

Even though the exodus of 1907–1908 was short-lived, its influence was felt in Europe. From Bremen and Hamburg came accounts of agitation and displeasure over the landing of thousands of homeless and penniless returning Poles, Russians, Lithuanians, and Hungarians. Caring for them had become a serious problem.[10]

Edward A. Steiner, a prolific student and writer on immigration topics, was among those rare individuals who concerned themselves with the influence that the much neglected returning immigrant was having on his native land. In his European travels he observed that almost every town or village of any size between Naples and Warsaw had a smaller or larger group of returned immigrants. He saw sharp differences between them and those who remained at home, especially in the countries in which the church had done very little for the masses. Residence and labor in an urban-industrial America had shaken the lethargy out of these repatriates. Manufacturers and landowners detected more efficiency in occupations which employed large numbers of returned immigrants.

[9] Allan McLaughlin, "Social and Political Effects of Immigration," *Popular Science Monthly*, 66:251 (Jan., 1905); Theodore Saloutos, *They Remember America* (Berkeley, 1956), pp. 117–31; Hourwich, *op. cit.*, pp. 284–310.
[10] *New International Year Book, 1907*, p. 246.

Steiner further noted that the repatriate purposely emphasized the differences between himself and those who never emigrated by wearing and doing everything which made him appear as if he were an American. His American clothes represented a new standard of living and a new standard of effort.

His influence was felt in still other ways. He bought land which the large landowners often were compelled to sell because they could not afford to hire labor. He lent money at a lower rate of interest. He sought the best goods that the market had to offer, often luxuries that were useless; he intro-

TABLE 4

Immigrant Arrivals and Departures, 1910–1914 [*]

	ARRIVALS	DEPARTURES
1910	1,041,570	202,436
1911	878,587	295,666
1912	838,172	333,262
1913	1,197,892	308,190
1914	1,218,480	303,338
	5,174,701	1,442,892

[*] *Commissioner General of Immigration, 1921,* pp. 110–11.

duced toothbrushes and dentifrices into some of the remotest areas. Gold in the teeth was a tell-tale sign of having been in the United States. So was sleeping with the windows open at night.[11]

A closer study of the five-year period prior to World War I shows that a total of 5,174,701 immigrants arrived as against 1,442,892 that departed. Roughly, this meant that one emi-

[11] Edward A. Steiner, "How Returning Emigrants Are Americanizing Europe," *American Review of Reviews,* 39:701–3 (June, 1909); "America Raising Europe's Standard of Living," *Charities,* 18:171–2 (Mary 4, 1902); see also 61st Congress, 3rd Session, Reports of the Immigration Commission. Sen. Doc. No. 748, *Emigration Conditions in Europe,* IV, pp. 228–35, 386–87.

grant alien left for every four immigrants that entered the country. The highest pre-war rate occurred during 1912 when one emigrant alien left for every two and two-thirds immigrants that came.

The reasons for these departures varied slightly from those of the panic years 1907–1908. Again it was a desire to see parents and the homeland after an absence of years, attend to property interests, acquire a wife, and settle down to the serious business of raising a family. Greeks, Serbians, Bulgarians, and Italians returned to fulfill their military obligations. Interspersed among these were those who were anxious to escape from the disappointments of America.[12]

As expected, the declaration of war in 1914 saw a drastic curtailment in emigration, except for the Italians and perhaps the Greeks. A total of 96,903 and 72,507 Italians left respectively during the fiscal years 1915 and 1916. Many of them were reservists responding to the call of duty.[13]

But few believed that this would be long-lived. As early as 1916 steamship companies were preparing for the great rush out of the country when peace was restored. They anticipated that about fifty per cent of the estimated 1,000,000 persons who left would remain abroad permanently and help rebuild their countries.

Thousands of Slavs, Hungarians, Poles, Austrians, and Germans throughout the United States placed small deposits on their passage, and held money in readiness so that they could sail at the first opportunity. When an account was published in the newspapers of the country that the *Deutschland* was returning to Germany, a mad rush took place to the steerage ticket offices in all principal cities by men and women anxious to book passage. They did not know what kind of a craft the *Deutschland* was, and did not inquire whether she trav-

[12] "War! Bulgar and Serb and Greek," *Survey*, 29:111–2 (Now. 2, 1912); see also the author's study, *The Greeks in the United States* (Cambridge, 1964), chap. 11, "The Military Obligations of the Immigrant"; Von Borsini, "Home-going Italians," *Survey*, 28:791–3 (Sept. 28, 1912).
[13] *Commissioner General of Immigration, 1921*, pp. 110–11.

elled above or below the surface, as long as she landed them in Europe.

Some predicted that there would be no comparable westward rush of aliens to the United States when peace was restored because the European governments would forbid the emigration of all able-bodied men, or were readying programs to encourage nationals living abroad to return home. Great Britain was preparing herself to give small plots of land and small sums of money to 2,000,000 demobilized soldiers in Australia, New Zealand, South Africa, and Canada as a means of discouraging emigration to the United States.[14]

Semi-official blessings were given these predictions of a mass exodus from the United States by New York Commissioner of Immigration, Frederick C. Howe, who estimated that at least 2,000,000 would return to Europe the first year after the war, if they could secure accommodations. Others privately expressed the opinion that as many as three, four, and five millions would leave. If true this would have been at a rate considerably in excess of the annual average emigrating before the war.[15]

Meanwhile, the war years witnessed something unusual in the departure of emigrant aliens who left to help in the liberation of their countries. This came in response to pleas of spokesmen for the emerging states of Yugoslavia, Poland, and Czechoslovakia. Comparable pleas from representatives of Greek liberals who wanted their compatriots to bolster the allied cause in the Balkans proved futile.[16]

British spokesmen inquired of the State Department late in the spring of 1917 about the prospects of raising a Polish army in the United States that could be shipped to Canada immediately for training. According to Polish sources, the

[14] *National Herald* (Dec. 14, 1915); *New York Times* (Aug. 14, 1916).
[15] *Ibid.*, Section 7:11–2 (Oct. 14, 1917).
[16] Newton D. Baker to Robert Lansing, Dec. 8, 1917.

Polish appeared very enthusiastic about the prospects of fighting with the United States Army.[17]

But Jean A. J. Jusserand, the French ambassador to the United States, countered with another proposal. He asked Secretary of State Robert Lansing if his government was prepared to permit Polish reservists who were not liable for conscription to leave for France where they could enlist in the autonomous Polish army organized by the French. These reservists were to wear a special uniform, be commanded by Poles, and fight under the Polish flag. Jusserand suspected that President Wilson's sympathy with the Polish cause would cause the President to look approvingly upon the existence of such an army. But Polish sources indicated that the Poles had too little confidence in the French to yield to such a proposal.[18]

Leaders of the Polish National Defense Committee in the United States, on the other hand, suggested the formation of "a Slav Army," consisting of Russians, Poles, Bohemians, and others, who could be transported into Siberia where they could help enforce order, establish local government, and recruit deserters from the Russian army.[19] This Slav contingent, it was felt, could be used to win the confidence of the Russians and perhaps persuade them to believe that the intentions of the Allies were altruistic.[20] At the same time, the Polish National Defense Committee opposed the formation of a Polish unit in the United States Army.[21]

Lansing responded that the formation of "a Slav Army" in the United States was impractical inasmuch as all efforts were being devoted to raising and equipping a strictly American Army. The only exception to this general policy was that

[17] Memorandum, Assistant Secretary of State, June 1, 1917.
[18] Jean A. J. Jusserand to Lansing, July 24, 1917; Memorandum, Assistant Secretary of State, June 1, 1917.
[19] G. J. Sosnowski to Woodrow Wilson, Mar. 28, 1918.
[20] William Wilder to Lansing, April 1, 1918.
[21] Wilder to Lansing, April 1, 1918.

the War Department, as a special concession, acquiesced to the Poles recruiting a force from nationals in this country who were not subject to the draft, and who could be used with certain forces that were fighting on the western front.[22]

Meanwhile, representatives of Serbia pursued a similar course. During the summer of 1917 they asked the United States government for permission to recruit, arm, train, and transport American Yugoslavs to the Salonika front and aid the Allies by defending Serbia. A similar plea came from the American legation in Corfu, Greece which called attention to Serbia's desperate need for recruits.[23] But again the War Department recommended that no assistance be given the project at this particular time owing to the large sums of money that had been allocated for military operations already decided upon.[24]

This refusal to sanction the recruiting of Yugoslavs did not deter those who wanted to volunteer from leaving the country. For late in August 1917 a contingent of 1,100 American volunteers reached Marseilles, France where they marched in review before military and civilian authorities.[25]

Lioubomir Mihailovitch, the Serbian minister to the United States, informed the State Department of the urgent need of gathering reserves in all allied or friendly countries in which Serbians lived. He said that several hundred thousand of these people were residents of the United States, but mostly citizens of enemy countries; and they were ready to liberate their country. Their appearance on the Balkan front would in no way interfere with the organization of the regular United States Army and would hearten the Serbian soldiers.[26]

The War Department, in response, advised the State De-

[22] Lansing to Wilder, April 15, 1918.

[23] Telegram, Henry P. Dodge to Secretary of State, Aug. 18, 1917; Dodge to Lansing, Aug. 23, 1917.

[24] Newton D. Baker to Lansing, Aug. 23, 1917.

[25] American Consulate General, Marseilles, France, to Lansing, Aug. 28, 1917.

[26] Lioubomir Mihailovitch to Lansing, Sept. 11, 1917.

Exodus U.S.A.

partment that since the United States was not at war with
Austria-Hungary, Bulgaria, and Turkey, against whose armies
the Serbian volunteers would have to fight, it was impractical
to approve the request of the Serbian minister.[27] No sooner
had this plea been rejected but that Mihailovitch submitted
another one in which he emphasized that the only sizable
number of reservists was found in the United States. "Co-na-
tionals" in England and France already had been sent to the
front, and an Austrian division that surrendered to the Russians could not be dispatched to Salonika.[28]

Late in 1917 Jusserand wrote Lansing pointing out that
since the United States actually was at war with Austria-
Hungary, the French government again was raising the question of bringing together and transporting American Yugoslavs to the Salonika front. He added that as a result of a
Franco-Anglo agreement in November 1916 the Yugoslav volunteers would go to Canada where they would sign contracts
of enlistment, and their transportation costs to France would
be assumed by England.

At the same time the French ambassador released some
statistical information on the Yugoslav volunteers arriving in
France. From January 1 to November 22, 1917, those arriving
from Canada (mostly from the United States) numbered 2,715
while those arriving from South America, Australia, and New
Zealand did not exceed 300. Yugoslav contingents that fought
with the Russian Army on the Rumanian front, and then were
transported to the Salonika front via France, numbered about
9,000.[29]

Then came the change. Late in January 1918, John Gabel-
ich, an American citizen of Croatian origin, was permitted to
gather a group of Serbians who were not citizens of the
United States and take them to the Salonika front. This was

[27] Newton D. Baker to Lansing, Oct. 11, 1917.
[28] Mihailovitch to William Phillips, Oct. 14, 1917; Phillips to Mihailovitch, Oct. 19, 1917.
[29] Jusserand to Lansing, Dec. 14, 1917.

being done in accordance with the provisions of the Act of May 7, 1917, that amended the neutrality laws of the United States.[30]

Meanwhile, charges of illegal recruiting activities were raised. One of the first complaints came from the American consul in Tunis concerning Yugoslav volunteers in training at Bizerte. According to the consul several men refused to take an oath of allegiance to Serbia because this meant they would forfeit their United States citizenship. And the consul, among other things, suggested that alien recruiting missions be placed under the supervision of federal officers who could advise American citizens of their rights, and compel volunteers to take their oath of allegiance to a foreign power and their physical examinations before they left American soil.[31]

George Horton, the American Consul General in Salonika, wrote in a similar vein. He said that after talking with many simple-hearted, honest Yugoslav volunteers, most of whom were naturalized citizens or had filed their declaration of intentions, he was convinced that the Serbian recruiting officers misrepresented matters to these men, either with respect to the kind of service they would render in the Serbian army or the provisions being made for their families in the United States. There were also charges of "bodily ill-treatment." Horton added that, "With all due respect to the Serbian nation and the fighting qualities of its armies, it must be stated that the majority of the officers, while often most charming to meet, practice the Prussian army rules of 'blow first and explanation (if any) afterwards' towards the soldiers." Men who came overseas of their own volition to fight for a principle were entitled to better treatment.[32]

Complaints of illegal recruiting activities within the United States were even more numerous. In Kansas City, Kansas, two

[30] War Department to Secretary of State, Jan. 28, 1918; Department of State to War Department, Feb. 4, 1918.

[31] Edwin D. Kemp to Lansing, Jan. 17, 1918.

[32] George Horton to Secretary of State, Aug. 10, 1918.

local Selective Service Board officials arbitrarily turned over the names and addresses of a number of men believed eligible to a Yugoslav recruiting officer. The Secretary of War, after being apprised of the actions of the overzealous clerks, recommended that the Serbian legation return all these men to Kansas City, where those eligible for enlistment in the Serbian army would be free to enlist.[33]

This chapter came to a close within two weeks after the Armistice when it was decided that all recruiting for foreign armies in the United States should cease.

This action alarmed certain influential elements of the Polish-American population. James C. White, the Director of the Associated Polish Press, assured the State Department that Poles from the United States were not being used for offensive military operations against the Bolsheviks or the armed forces of nations with whom the United States had declared an armistice. They were used as a stabilizing force within Polish territory and endangered Polish lives and property. ". . . we have from the first foreseen the development of a missionary spirit . . . these men although not American citizens are rapidly American in their beliefs [and] would dissipate the Eastside bolshevik villification of American ideals." [34]

The Yugoslav authorities, on the other hand, considered it proper that all foreign recruiting should cease in the United States. They even instructed members of their military mission to dismantle their activities and prepare to leave the country.[35]

The position of the Czechoslovaks was somewhat different. As a result of an agreement, about 2,000 Czechoslovaks who were not citizens were permitted to volunteer because of their age and to return to the United States after the war. The Czechoslovak authorities were of the opinion that it was

---

[33] War Department to State Department, July 10, 1918.
[34] James C. White to Phillips, Jan. 2, 1919.
[35] S. Y. Growitch to Frank L. Polk, Feb. 3, 1919.

possible for every soldier who was a resident of the United States before the war to return within one year after the ratification of the peace treaty. If he failed to take advantage of this opportunity, he would have to return as an ordinary immigrant. The United States was under no obligation to these men, but the Czechoslovaks were anxious to have them leave as soon as possible to spare them embarrassment.[36]

By comparison the publicity the Poles, Yugoslavs, and Czechoslovak volunteers received was trifling when compared with that given those preparing to emigrate from the United States. Journalists, labor leaders, employers, popular writers, and the man on the street were talking about it. One perceptive journalist observed that, "For centuries the flow of people has been westward . . . migration . . . has been toward the setting sun. Is the close of the war to mark the end of this era in history? Has man at last looked his fill on the lands of the West? And is migration now to take its flow, for the first time since the discovery of America, toward the rising sun? And if so, why?"

Some of the reasons given were old, some new; but they all displayed a certain restlessness, dissatisfaction, and a craving for something better. The return of peace brought with it a feeling of optimism and a determination to set things right.

First, this journalist detected the natural impulse to see friends and relatives with whom they had been out of communication during the war. If these channels had remained open they might have been content to remain in the United States, but they did not; and the imaginations of the immigrants were conjuring up the worst. Second, he saw the question of family property. Many immigrants had come to the United States because of dissatisfaction with the distribution of property in the old country, and now by returning they expected to obtain a more equitable division of it. Third, the

[36] Telegram from American Mission in Prague to Secretary of State, July 28, 1919; Zdenek Fierlinger to Richard Crane, Oct. 13, 1919.

drive to acquire cheap land at home was especially strong among the Russians, Poles, Hungarians, and other people from the Balkans who planned to benefit from the bankruptcy of the feudal proprietors and the other revolutionary changes. Fourth, many succumbed to the conviction that every European country from Ireland to the Black Sea was devising plans of encouraging those who lived abroad to return home. ". . . the days of absentee landlordism and of uncultivated estates, no matter who owns them, are probably over. Every European Government is awake to this condition." Fifth, many expected to leave because of unemployment and the feeling that they were unwelcome in the United States. "It has been said that the Texan hates the Slovak and the Northerner hates the 'greaser'; but, to both, it is America who has not welcomed them." [37]

Many agreed that these basically were the reasons the immigrants would depart, but they were not agreed on the dimensions that this exodus would take. They also suspected that conditions in Europe would not come up to their expectations, that they would have difficulty in adjusting themselves to living in their native country, and that exhausted and bankrupt countries would be unable to pay them high wages. After two years of peace, the outflow would return to normal pre-war levels.

For a time it appeared as though the predictions of Commissioner Howe would come true. Within two or three days after the Armistice, rumors spread that the United States government was preparing to lift restrictions on ocean travel. As a consequence, Russians, Italians, Hungarians, Austrians, Greeks, Syrians, and many others thronged the offices of the federal government and steamship companies asking for information and depositing money for accommodations on the very first vessel leaving port. But all were informed that the restrictions were still in effect. Agents of the Holland-Amer-

[37] *New York Times,* Section 7 (Oct. 14, 1917).

ica, the Norwegian-America, and the Scandinavian-American steamship companies announced that only the nationals of neutral countries would be permitted to travel on their ships, at least until a peace treaty was signed.

The exodus began slowly. Early in February 1919, steamships sailing for France and Italy carried away 4,460 passengers, most of them Italians, Greeks, and Spaniards. Anticipated departures were placed as high as 5,000,000, and shipping companies prepared for the greatest mass departures since 1907.[38]

During the spring and summer of 1919 aliens in large numbers preparing to emigrate poured into the old Chelsea district of New York City that centered on 23rd Street between 9th and 10th avenues. At all hours of the day one could see moustached Serbians, Croatians, and Slovenes wearing soft hats, soft shirts, and sometimes Victory loan buttons congregated on the steps and sidewalks of old homes that had been converted into boarding houses. The Yugoslav Consul General, whose office was in this district, claimed that a great percentage of the 1,000,000 he represented in the United States would leave. Letters from those who returned to Yugoslavia indicated that conditions there had improved, and this tended to stir those who remained behind. Men who arrived in 1910, 1911, and 1912—many of whom had worked in the mines of Montana and other western states—were departing at the rate of about 2,000 a month.[39]

News of these continued mass embarkations stirred up considerable resentment on the part of many Americans who were disturbed by reports that 1,500,000 foreign residents were preparing to take with them an estimated $5,000,000,000 they had earned in the United States. This prompted the Commissioner General of Immigration to speak out against the hysteria that was sweeping the country and to issue a statement showing that only 123,522 left the country during

[38] *Ibid.*, (Nov. 14, 1918); (Feb. 1, 1919).
[39] *Ibid.*, Section 7 (Aug. 24, 1919). 14.

the twelve months ending June 30, 1919. These departures, he pointed out, were perfectly normal, and the expectation was that many eventually would return to the United States.[40]

Employers voiced the fear that these departures would diminish the labor supply of the country. Some, as has already been implied, felt that this would adversely affect the merchant marine of the United States, the efforts of the government to redeem wastelands that were designed for occupancy by demobilized soldiers, and the reconversion of the economy to a normal peace-time basis. Officials of the Union Pacific Railroad Company, as a means of reversing this outward trend, arranged to help alien employees along its route buy farms on the installment plan. A couple of noted financiers even suggested the importing of 5,000,000 Chinamen.

Labor leaders and wage-earners naturally protested the idea of bringing 5,000,000 Chinamen into the country, and expressed the conviction that the return of these immigrants to their homeland was a good thing for the country. "In prosperous times . . . ," wrote one of their spokesmen, "two million workers are idle here; in hard times, six million. What harm, then, if two million quit us? . . ." Emigration instead of being a menace to the American laboring man would be a distinct advantage, for it would make more jobs available to those who needed them.

The super-patriots, however, predicted even greater benefits for these departures would result in "a better, because more American, America." Emigration promised "a weeding out of little Italys, little Hungarys, little Syrias, and foreign 'quarters' in general. The less Americanized will go. The more Americanized will stay." Those who left would be drawn from the bottom, not the top. As a consequence, those fittest for American citizenship would survive.[41]

[40] *New York Times* (Sept. 12, 1919).
[41] Rollin L. Hartt, "Emigration from America," *Outlook*, 121:186–7 (Jan. 29, 1919); Byron H. Uhl, "Emigration Scare Unfounded," *Forum*, 62:228 (Aug., 1919).

One of the immediate reactions was the formation of an Interracial Council with the view of checking the emigration movement, and, if practicable, reversing it. Comprised of business, labor, and "racial leaders," the council sought to aid "business America." However, its primary purpose was to bring "these foreign elements into harmony with American ideas," through the spread of "the native language" of the United States, an elementary knowledge of its history and government, and the "cooperation of the natives in bringing about a more complete coalescence." The Interracial Council in one of its prospectuses advocated the conversion of the United States into a "one language country," for suffering from a lack of political cohesion was far worse than suffering from a lack of labor.[42]

Poles, Hungarians, and Serbians who were anxious to quit the country as soon as they could became bitter toward the United States because of their inability to obtain passports. These men had accumulated savings which, at the prevailing rate of exchange, constituted fortunes. The reconstruction period provided them with opportunities of buying land in their native country at favorable prices or of establishing themselves in business under terms that would be unavailable to them in the future. Consequently their inability to leave when they wanted to embittered them.[43]

Another source of irritation was the income tax that had to be paid before they could leave the country. When news of this was broadcast many incensed Americans heaped additional denunciations on the emigrants; they viewed them as a new kind of profiteer who spent the war years in American munition plants, shipyards, and industries, and were trying to flee the country without paying their income taxes. "For the most part," observed one publication, "it has been necessary to stop these gentlemen on the piers at embarkation and col-

[42] *Literary Digest*, 63:96 (July 26, 1919); *World's Work*, 38:246 (July, 1919).
[43] *New York Times* (Sept. 15, 1919).

lect their income taxes, a ceremony which has disclosed that most are taking back at least $1,500 and some as much as $7,500, a neat profit for their few years sojourn in this country." [44]

Still another grievance was the exploitation to which they were subjected from the day they decided to emigrate. Agents reached into the smaller cities and mining towns promising them cheap travel and prompt departure from New York, if they left in groups of twelve. Upon reaching New York they usually were escorted to lodging houses operated by those who sought their patronage. When the prospective emigrant went out to book passage, the first question asked was whether they had passports. As a rule, the answer was "No," because this had not been called to their attention. However, the lodging house promoters assured them that in due time the passports would be obtained, which, of course, meant delays that were profitable to the proprietors of the rooming houses but costly to the emigrants. In some cases they waited two or three months before departing. [45]

Much to the surprise of many, those emigrating in the largest numbers were the nationals of Italy, Greece, and the people of the emerging states of Poland and Yugoslavia. The countries to which these people were heading had been allies of the United States or else had been aided by the allies in winning their freedom. The statistics in Table 5 bear this out.

These figures indicate that the Italians continued to depart after the war as they did before, but in steadily diminishing numbers, while the large number of Polish and Yugoslav departures may be attributed in part to the great promise of living in their liberated countries.

[44] Edward Hale Bierstadt, *Aspects of Americanization* (Cincinnati, 1922), pp. 42–6, 166–8, 188–90; U. S. Treasury Department, Bureau of Internal Revenue Digest A—Pt. IV, Income Tax Rulings Under the Revenue Act of 1921 and Prior Acts (Washington, 1932), pp. 1004–6.

[45] *World's Work*, 38:245 (July, 1919); reference here is to the Revenue Act of Feb. 24, 1919. Protests were filed by the British Embassy and the Dutch Legation. C. Barclay to William Phillips, April 17, 1919 and E. Brun to Secretary of State, April 18, 1919.

TABLE 5

*Emigrant Aliens Departing for Countries Identified
with the Allied Nations during World War I* [*]

	GREECE	IRELAND AND IRISH FREE STATE	ITALY	POLAND	YUGOSLAVIA
1919	15,482	988	38,245	—	—
1920	20,314	3,735	88,909	18,190	28,474
1921	13,423	1,905	48,909	45,572	13,034
1922	7,506	2,182	53,651	33,581	9,733
1923	2,988	1,368	23,329	5,439	2,064
1924	7,250	1,282	22,904	2,594	1,991
1925	6,574	1,133	27,151	3,721	2,464

[*] "Are Our Foreign-born Emigrating?" Survey, 43:539–40 (Feb. 7, 1920); see also S. Miles Bouton "What Is the Reason?" *Atlantic Monthly*, 127:40–3 (Jan. 1921).

The small number of departures among those considered enemy aliens during the war suggests that the indignities heaped upon them did not compel them to leave en masse as some predicted.

Many carried back a rather grim picture of life in the United States. Some left convinced that America no longer was "the home of liberty" that they once imagined it to be;

TABLE 6

*Emigrant Aliens Departing for Countries Identified
with Central Powers during World War I* [*]

	AUSTRIA	BULGARIA	GERMANY	HUNGARY	TURKEY IN EUROPE	TURKEY IN ASIA
1919	201	2,801	26	—	47	26
1920	2,272	3,587	3,069	—	1,812	1,731
1921	1,399	2,923	5,263	12,153	405	2,534
1922	576	660	4,362	4,307	201	1,731
1923	247	156	1,529	895	125	733
1924	217	233	1,178	522	128	211
1925	466	208	3,646	875	100	40

[*] United States Department of Labor, *Annual Report of the Commissioner General of Immigration, Fiscal Year Ended June 30, 1930*, pp. 224–5.

they resented having been subjected to years of "suspicion and espionage, coerced into buying Liberty Bonds, and forced to endure official and private surveillance of their churches, schools, and social organizations." They found it difficult to forget the race riots and how the victims went without redress; and they were positive that the naturalized citizen was adjudged inferior to the native-born, that most Americanization schemes simply were the devices of employers and politicians to assure themselves of a cheap labor supply and means of controlling the votes. Their inability to obtain beer or wine was viewed as an invasion of their personal liberty.[46]

Russians being transported back to the homeland at the expense of the Kerensky government pointed to a series of shortcomings with the American way of life. American methods of education, except those on the university and graduate school level, were found wanting. Too much money, they claimed, was spent on those who, in most cases, were able to pay for it themselves, and too little on those who could least afford it. The best buildings, the best teachers, and the best equipment went into those portions of the city in which the well-to-do lived, and the schools of the higher grades. The care of the aged was scandalous compared with the affectionate care they received in Russia and other European countries.

These same Russians were bewildered by the power conferred upon public service corporations. They found it difficult to understand why cities provided sewers, street work, fire protection, and free schools at the expense of the taxpayers, and then permitted income-bringing utilities such as water, gas, electricity, and street car systems to pass into the control of a few corporations. Why were these profit-making corporations not compelled to pay for the operations of

---

[46] *Ibid., Fiscal Year Ended June 30, 1921,* pp. 110–111; *ibid., Fiscal Year Ended June 30, 1930,* pp. 224–5.

the other non-profit-making agencies for which the people were taxed?

This was not all. They complained about the adulteration of food, the lax morals of the American people, the maltreatment of illegitimate children, the hard work, low wages, and unsanitary conditions under which Americans labored.

Many Americans viewed this as an unbalanced picture of life in the United States; but these Russians said a number of things that probably rankled the minds of the many inarticulate others who remained in the country.[47] These criticisms were voiced by others before and after. Still, the undeniable fact is that they fed the passions of those who had been highly critical of America.

Some actually left firm in the conviction that the United States was an undesirable country in which to rear a family. A couple that decided to return to Poland after spending ten years in America wanted to protect their children from the extravagance, restlessness, and ungratefulness of American youth. In their opinion, the American child had few virtues. The social costs of raising a family in the United States were too high for those who wanted their children to be obedient, contented, and hard working.[48]

The attitudes of some of the returning women varied. The older ones seemed indifferent to the subject of going back, while the younger ones opposed it. One young woman remarked that she liked America because of its facilities for housework, and also because here "A man can kick a woman once; the second time she calls the cop." [49]

Except for what is written about the Greeks who left the United States, very little is known about how the other nationalities fared in their native land. The problems they faced

[47] George Seibel, "Going Back—and Why," *Nation*, 109:492–3 (Oct. 11, 1919); "Emigrants and Immigrants," *ibid.*, 111:316 (Sept. 18, 1920).
[48] Ada French, "Alien Impressions of America," *Survey*, 43:540–1 (Feb. 7, 1920).
[49] Lily Winner, "American Emigrés," *Nation*, 112:714 (May 18, 1931).

in many instances were similar. One has reason to suspect that what befell the repatriated Greeks also befell the Italian-Americans, the Polish-Americans, the Yugoslav-Americans, and the rest. Encounters with the customs officials, the military authorities, and the sharpsters who waited for their American prey left them with an indelible impression of their first few months in the old country. If the Greek experience is any kind of an indicator, one has little reason to believe that their native land became a land of opportunity or the realization of an unfilled dream. They all felt the menacing hand of inflation, political instability, and the spread of totalitarianism. Most likely the differences in experiences were ones of degree, not kind, the particular time one repatriated himself, and not of nationality.[50]

As a rule, the returned immigrant was known as the American; and he was looked upon as a sort of curiosity, apart in a way from the rest. For a time he wore different clothes, walked differently, and did things in a manner that made him stand out conspicuously.[51]

The repatriate probably minimized or underestimated the problems he was likely to face in the old country. While in the United States he often dwelled on the scenic beauty of his native land, the hours of relaxation this would give him, the leisurely and festive features of his village, and the nearness of his family. He contrasted all this with the nerve-racking, money-mad pace the Americans set for themselves, their endless hours of toil, the absence of strong family ties, and other uncomplimentary aspects of American life. His almost childlike expectations of a happy and secure life on native soil, reinforced by American-earned dollars, blinded him to many of the difficulties of adjustment. He left the most advanced industrial nation in the world and in most cases returned to a

[50] "What Some Home-bound Immigrants Think of America," *Literary Digest*, 65:51 (June 19, 1920).
[51] *Ibid.*

retarded agrarian economy where the opportunities were fewer and the margin of permissible economic error negligible.

Hindsight probably convinced him that once he decided to return to his native country, he should have reconciled himself to a lower standard of living, political and economic instability, war, and even poverty. He should have abandoned the optimism acquired in an abundant economy such as the United States, and supplanted it with a realism often found among people living in a marginal or sub-marginal state. It was equally foolish for him to have expected to find the same personal freedom that he took for granted in the United States.

One can only speculate as to the economic fortunes of these repatriates. If they were small proprietors in the United States the chances are that they invested their money in homes, land, hotels, apartment houses, and a wide variety of mercantile establishments.[52] The presumption is that most of these repatriates settled in or near the larger cities, and did not return to their native villages.

Many displayed poor business judgment. Such persons disposed of their commercial and property interests in the United States, withdrew their savings from American banks and converted them into the currency of their native country. Or perhaps they invested in enterprises that could not be reconverted into American dollars very readily. The shrewder ones as a rule invested in real estate instead of commercial ventures they were ill-prepared to handle.

The misfortunes these earlier repatriates endured as an aftermath of inflation, confiscatory government decrees, bank failures, political instability, and eventually war served as a warning to those who repatriated themselves after World War II. Many of them were covered by social security pay-

[52] "Our Coney Island Ideals," *New York Times* (June 18, 1922).

ments they could collect abroad. Those having savings and investments in the United States as a rule took enough funds to maintain themselves in their native land, but they did not withdraw all of their personal savings. Sometimes they left their real estate and commercial interests in the United States intact, and had sums forwarded to them at regular intervals.

Apprising the influence of these people on their native land is difficult. They did pump new wealth into the economies of their respective countries; they introduced or popularized American business methods, foods, and became relentless propagandists for the American point of view. They organized American periodicals or had them sent by friends and relatives in the United States. For a time an American club in Athens had branches and chapters scattered throughout Greece. Similar groups were formed in other European countries as a means of keeping alive memories, contacts, and standards.

Repatriation never attained the proportions it assumed prior to and after World War I. Nothing comparable to a mass movement developed during "the great depression" of the 1930's, and for obvious reasons relatively few were tempted to repatriate themselves after the holocaust of World War II.[53]

Still the subject of repatriation is a fertile field that merits the attention of the historian. Much can be learned from the foreign-language press of the United States, the consular and diplomatic dispatches of the State Department, the immigration records of foreign countries, and the returned immigrants themselves. During and after World War II American G-Is in Europe, scholars interested in American influences abroad, policymakers seeking to promote better relations between the United States and other countries, and others found the repa-

[53] *Ibid.*

triates worthy objects of study. The historian who sets his
sights in this direction will also find his labors rewarded.[54]

[54] Harold Fields, "America's Emigrants," *Current History*, 45:62
(Oct. 1936); *New York Times* (April 17, May 1, June 20, Aug. 8, 1932;
Aug. 6, 1933); see also Fields in *South Atlantic Quarterly*, 32:227–36
(July, 1933).

BRITISH IMMIGRANTS
IN INDUSTRIAL AMERICA
ROWLAND BERTHOFF

"THE manufactures of America are yet in their infancy," an
English resident of that country in 1823 warned British
"weavers, cotton-spinners, and working manufacturers." Such
men, when they could get work, received good wages, but
many tramped up and down the country without finding any
call for their special skills.[1] Yet the time when they could be
sure of employment only during the harvest season was fast
ending. Factories were already springing up to rival Lancashire; within another decade the American industrial revolution would be turning under a full head of steam. Soon from
nearly all those trades which together had made Britain the
world's workshop a hundred kinds of skilled hands would
cross the ocean.

In Great Britain textile manufacturing—of cotton in
particular—had heralded the new factory age. As weaving,
spinning, and carding successively became mechanized and
powered by water or steam during the late eighteenth and

EXCERPTED by permission of the publishers from *British Immigrants in
Industrial America, 1790–1950* by Rowland T. Berthoff, (Cambridge,
Mass.: Harvard University Press), pp. 30–56, 110–133, Copyright 1953
by the President and Fellows of Harvard College.

[1] Isaac Holmes, *An Account of the United States of America* (London, 1823), p. 126.

early nineteenth centuries, workingmen and their wives and children left household wheels and looms and worked within factory walls. By 1850 cotton handloom weaving practically disappeared. The new industrial age concentrated most of the half million cotton operatives in the towns of Lancashire, Cheshire, and the valley of the Clyde.[2]

When New England merchants in the 1790's began to invest in cotton mills, Great Britain determined to maintain her lead by forbidding both the export of textile machinery and the emigration of skilled artisans. But British workingmen would not be held back when America offered fortune and fame. Samuel Slater, superintendent of an early Lancashire mill, memorized the plans of the new machinery, slipped out of England, and set up mills in Rhode Island and Massachusetts; ultimately he became one of America's leading manufacturers.[3] During the following decades Lancashire specialists likewise introduced calico printing and other processes new to the United States.[4] In 1825, when Parliament repealed the ban on the departure of artisans, a Lowell cotton-mill owner, by offering a salary nearly twice his own, secured a Manchester expert to supervise his new print works. Lancashire calico printers soon filled "English Row" in Lowell. Other new print works there and in Lawrence, Fall River, and New York State also relied on English or Scottish superintendents and craftsmen.[5] During the late 1820's and the

[2] Paul Mantoux, *The Industrial Revolution in the Eighteenth Century* (London, 1928), pp. 193–257; J. H. Clapham, *An Economic History of Modern Britain* (Cambridge, 1926–1930), I, 441–442, 551–553; II, 28–30; Laurance James Saunders, *Scottish Democracy 1815–1840* (Edinburgh, 1950), pp. 101–104, 125–126.

[3] *Dictionary of American Biography* (New York, 1928–1937), XVII, 205–206.

[4] Herbert Heaton, "The Industrial Immigrant in the United States," *Proceedings of the American Philosophical Society*, XCV (1951), 521–524.

[5] Charles Cowley, "The Foreign Colonies of Lowell," *Contributions of the Old Residents' Historical Association*, II (1883), 168–169; H. C. Meserve, *Lowell, an Industrial Dream Come True* (Boston, 1923), pp. 71–72; Henry Ashworth, *A Tour in the United States, Cuba, and Canada* (London, 1861), p. 149; *Cotton and Its Manufacture: The Industries*

1830's American employers paid many calico printers' passage from Liverpool and were said to be encouraging operatives to bring British machinery with them.[6]

British immigrants also appeared among the ranks of ordinary American mill hands during the 1820's. The original New England operatives were the sons, and more often the daughters, of Yankee farmers.[7] But as handloom weavers in England lost their livelihood to the new power looms, they hastened by the shipload to leave for America before being completely immobilized as their savings dwindled. In these years English and northern Irish handloom weavers, attracted by wages three or four times those at home, established the fine cotton-goods trade of Philadelphia.[8]

Although during the 1830's English, Scottish, and Irish operatives began to supplant the famous American mill girls of Lowell, not until the 1840's did immigrant labor dominate New England factories. Then it was Irish refugees from an overpopulated and famine-scourged island who, though they lacked industrial experience, tried their hands as mill laborers. English and Scottish hands also immigrated during the later 1840's and the 1850's; less numerous but more experienced than the Irish, they were welcome to take the better jobs.[9] When the Wamsutta Mill, New Bedford's first, opened

---

of Fall River (n.p., n.d.,), p. 123; Dictionary of American Biography, XII, 305.

[6] "Third Report from the Select Committee on Emigration from the United Kingdom," Parliamentary Papers, 1826–27, V (550), Q. 2174; Walter F. Willcox, ed., International Migrations (New York, 1931), II, 252.

[7] Melvin Thomas Copeland, The Cotton Manufacturing Industry of the United States (Cambridge, 1912), pp. 3–8, 12–13.

[8] Ibid., p. 31; Arthur Redford, Labour Migration in England 1800–1850 (Manchester, 1926), pp. 154–155; Massachusetts Bureau of Statistics of Labor, Third Annual Report (1872), pp. 395–397; "Third Report from the Select Committee on Emigration from the United Kingdom," pp. 301–302, Q, 2174, 2239; Textile Record of America, I (1880), 2.

[9] Copeland, pp. 13, 118; "Reports of the Immigration Commission," Senate Document, 61 Cong., 2 sess., no. 633 (June 15, 1910), X, 30, 225–226.

in 1846, many employees were English.[10] A few years later mills in Holyoke imported two or three hundred Scotswomen with training as weavers.[11]

During the Lancashire "cotton famine" brought on by the American Civil War blockade, unemployed English operatives clamored for assistance to emigrate, while the American labor shortage led Northern manufacturers to recruit hands in Scotland and England.[12] After the war American cotton workers returning from the army often found skilled foreigners in their old jobs. One Yankee mule spinner complained that, in consequence, many of his sort had become tramps: "They cannot get work: English help are preferred." [13]

With unemployment, wage cuts, and strikes throughout Lancashire in 1869, trade unions helped hundreds of their members to emigrate, and thousands more pressed to follow.[14] This slump was soon over, but New England's need for trained hands permitted no slackening of migration. Especially notable was the rush of mill building about Fall River in the 1860's and 1870's and in New Bedford in the 1880's; consequently southern Massachusetts drew the incoming Englishmen. While foreigners also manned the more slowly expanding cotton mills of Rhode Island, the Merrimack valley, and Maine, they were usually either Irishmen joining their countrymen already there or French Canadians from neighboring Quebec. Irish and French came also to Fall River and

[10] "Report of the Industrial Commission," *House Document*, 57 Cong., 1 sess., no. 183 (December 5, 1901), XIV, 544.

[11] Constance McLaughlin Green, *Holyoke, Massachusetts* (New Haven, 1939), pp. 48–49; *Scottish-American Journal*, February 4, 1875.

[12] Green, p. 76; Sylvia Chace Lintner, "A Social History of Fall River 1859–1879" (unpublished doctoral thesis, Radcliffe College, 1945), pp. 64–67; Daniel Creamer, "Recruiting Labor for the Amoskeag Mills," *Journal of Economic History*, I (1941), 42–46; W. O. Henderson, *The Lancashire Cotton Famine 1861–1865* (Manchester, 1934), pp. 115–118; Charlotte Erickson, "Encouragement of Emigration by British Trade Unions 1850–1900," *Population Studies*, III (1949), 255–256; *Fall River Weekly News*, March 18, 1875.

[13] Massachusetts Bureau of Statistics of Labor, *Tenth Annual Report* (1879), p. 135.

[14] Erickson, pp. 256–258, 262.

New Bedford, but the English influx made those cities a second Lancashire.[15]

The name of Fall River soon became synonymous with "America" among the spindles and shuttles of Preston and Oldham. Emigrant operatives encouraged friends at home to follow them. Ben Brierley, the Lancashire dialect writer, saw many of the latter on a voyage from Liverpool in 1885:

I looked down among the steerage passengers . . . an' seed three or four faces ut looked like gradely uns.

'Wheere dun yo' come fro'?' I axt 'em.

'Owdham an' Mossley,' they said.

'Wheere are yo' goin' to?'

'To Fall River.'

'Han yo' shops to go to?'

'Nawe, but we'n friends theere.' [16]

"When they reach Newfoundland or about there," an old hand observed in 1884, "the first question they ask is, 'Where is Fall River?'" The nightly boat from New York made Fall River the easiest cotton-mill town for most English newcomers to reach; "picked help" who landed at Boston also were soon there.[17] In Fall River Brierley saw so many Lancashire lads that he wrote, "I soon forgeet wheere I wur, an' fancied I're i' England, an' wur th' only Yankee i' th' company. I towd 'em I wouldno' forget 'em when I geet back to Ameriky." [18]

[15] Copeland, pp. 27–30; Lintner, pp. 1–53; "Reports of the Immigration Commission," X, 30, 38–47; "Study of a New England Factory Town," *Atlantic*, XLIII (1879), 690; Maine Bureau of Industrial Labor Statistics, *Second Annual Report* (1888), p. 121, and *Twenty-second Annual Report* (1908), p. 4; *Report of the Committee of the Senate upon the Relations between Labor and Capital* (Washington, 1885), III, 6, 28; Evelyn H. Knowlton, *Pepperell's Progress* (Cambridge, 1948), pp. 163–164; *Fall River Weekly News*, March 11, 1875; *New York Herald*, October 19, 1875.

[16] Benjamin Brierley, *Ab-o'th'-Yate in Yankeeland* (Manchester, 1885), p. 19.

[17] *Report of the Committee of the Senate upon the Relations between Labor and Capital*, I, 632; III, 496.

[18] Brierley, p. 135.

Some of these Lancashire people in Fall River were more Irish than English. Since the 1820's Irish laborers had been crossing over into the Lancashire mill towns. Though unskilled peasants when they arrived there, they or their children often had become mill operatives. While those who subsequently came to America generally remained Irish in religion and sentiment, at least their economic role in Fall River, derived from Lancashire rather than Mayo, rested on an English foundation.[19]

Good years and bad, the English kept coming during the 1880's and 1890's. Some old-country unions regularly helped unemployed members to emigrate, despite the protests of Fall River union officials.[20] The British Cotton Spinners' Society gave an emigration benefit to "members who have become marked men, or 'victims,' for taking an active part in the society's business, or who have been prominent in any trade dispute." [21] British machine manufacturers forwarded lists of prospective emigrants to American employers along with consignments of new looms or mules; they sometimes paid operatives' passage to America if they would install such equipment there.[22] In such ways, until federal law in 1885 forbade importation of alien workers under contract, American mill owners continued to secure British operatives. . . .[23]

When during the 1880's the trade was prosperous in America but depressed in Yorkshire, emigration was brisk. Operatives left Bradford at the rate of fifty a week, almost all for the States; one organized group of 750 sailed together.[24] Bradford emigrants, said the American consul there, were "almost wholly of the high artisan class . . . expert wool-sorters

---

[19] *New York Herald,* October 13, 1875.

[20] *John Swinton's Paper,* January 6, 1884. Cf. Erickson, pp. 265–267.

[21] "Report from the Select Committee on Colonisation," *Parliamentary Papers,* 1889, X (274), 92.

[22] "Diplomatic and Consular Reports on Emigration," *House Miscellaneous Document,* 50 Cong., 1 sess., no. 572, pt. 2 (1889), p. 15.

[23] New York Bureau of Statistics of Labor, *Third Annual Report* (1885).

[24] *American Manufacturer,* October 3, 1879, June 3, 1881.

. . . machinists, foremen, managers, and supervisors . . . whom the mills here are as loth to lose as we are pleased to gain." [25] From Huddersfield, Leeds, Morley, and other West Riding towns came men of the same caliber.[26]

As in cotton, however, American woolen manufacturers were anxious to dispense with skilled handworkers, especially the English hand-jack spinners. During the 1870's most mills introduced woolen mules, already in use in England, which allowed unskilled men or even boys to supplant the old spinners. Yet other techniques changed slowly; the Northrop loom was not adapted to wool until 1905, eleven years after its introduction in cotton weaving. Such delays probably account for the fact that in 1890 only one-fifth of the country's foreign-born cotton operatives but fully one-third of those in woolen were British. Although between 1890 and 1910 green European hands gradually took over all the simpler processes, experienced British newcomers, with some Germans and French, still found niches as expert operatives and as overseers.[27]

When the worsted section of the woolen trade suddenly began to expand in the 1860's, employers relied on standard British equipment operated by Yorkshire tykes.[28] Thus Lawrence, the rising worsted center, attracted many Englishmen and Scotsmen too.[29] A Yorkshireman visiting this "Bradford of America" in 1880 found the mills full of Bradford workmen, managers, and machinery; Bradford men even ran saloons and stores. Although travelers from the West Riding doubted whether American living costs left their countrymen of

[25] "Diplomatic and Consular Reports on Emigration," p. 33.

[26] Ibid., pp. 18–19; "Endorcement of Alien Contract Labor Laws," House Executive Document, 52 Cong., 1 sess., no. 235, pt. 2 (February 22, 1892), p. 88.

[27] Arthur Harrison Cole, The American Wool Manufacture (Cambridge, 1926), II, 88–91, 95–98, 112–113; Eleventh Census of the U.S. (1890), II, 486–488.

[28] Cole, I, 277–278; II, 81–83.

[29] "Reports of the Immigration Commission," X, 745–746.

166

Lawrence much better off than at home, the immigrants seemed content.[30] New worsted mills in Philadelphia likewise depended on newly arrived English overseers about 1880. . . .[31]

In carpet weaving, a still more intricate process, Kilmarnock in Ayrshire divided the nineteenth-century British trade with Kidderminster in Worcestershire. In the carpet works of New England and the Middle Atlantic states, therefore, Scots were as prominent as Englishmen. After the first American manufacturer of Brussels or Wilton carpets hired Kidderminster weavers for his Philadelphia mill about 1815, English, Scottish, and northern Irish artisans made the Kensington section the city's carpet center.[32] In Lowell weavers and overseers from Paisley established the ingrain carpet industry in 1829.[33] The Connecticut carpet village of Thompsonville, to which Kilmarnock operatives flocked in 1828, became virtually a Scottish town. . . .[34]

In 1903 an English visitor discovered a large Philadelphia carpet mill full of Kidderminster weavers and Lancashire machines.[35] As late as 1907 a New Jersey factory commenced with men hired in Kidderminster.[36] When Philadelphia added tapestry carpet weaving to its textile trades after 1900, most of the weavers were of English or Scottish origin.[37]

Another Philadelphia fine textile trade, upholstery and dra-

---

[30] James Burnley, *Two Sides of the Atlantic* (London, 1880), pp. 62–66; William Smith, *A Yorkshireman's Trip to the United States and Canada* (London, 1892), pp. 130–132.

[31] "Report of the Industrial Commission," XIV, 214–215.

[32] Pennsylvania Bureau of Industrial Statistics, *Seventeenth Annual Report* (1889), pp. D3–D4.

[33] Cowley, pp. 171–172.

[34] *Scottish-American Journal*, November 2, 1882; Arthur H. Cole and Harold F. Williamson, *The American Carpet Manufacture* (Cambridge, 1941), p. 38.

[35] *British Californian*, November 1903, p. 9.

[36] Cole and Williamson, p. 84.

[37] Gladys L. Palmer, *Union Tactics and Economic Change* (Philadelphia, 1932), p. 29.

pery fabrics, in the 1870's brought its first weavers, adept in a variety of cloths, from Yorkshire and Scotland. Later some skilled newcomers were Belgian, German, and French. In 1906 about a quarter of the industry's employees were English and Scottish; as late as the 1920's the trade relied on British weavers.[38]

Hosiery, despite the early start which the sixteenth-century stocking frame gave to machine knitting, became a factory industry decades after most other textiles. But by 1840 the heyday of framework knitting by Midland cottagers was long past; power-driven machinery gradually substituted factory operatives for the stockingers of old.[39] As English handframe knitting declined, emigrants took the old skill to America. In the 1830's Nottingham and Leicester knitters came to Philadelphia, where Germans had already introduced the trade. As in England, manufacturing in the workers' homes persisted to some extent throughout the century in Kensington and Germantown. Small mills gradually took over the bulk of the trade, but in 1880 they too depended on English, and some German and French, machines, workmen, and even mill proprietors. . . .[40]

Nearly the whole English silk industry migrated to America after the Civil War. Introduced into London by Huguenot refugees in the seventeenth century, silk was always a tariff-protected exotic in England, although the first textile trade to adopt power and factory organization. Lacking the natural economic advantages enjoyed by other British textile manufacturers, the industry, by then centered at Macclesfield, dwindled after the Cobden Treaty of 1860 opened the door to French silks. Some unemployed operatives shifted into other

[38] Gladys L. Palmer, *et al.*, *The Philadelphia Upholstery Industry* (Philadelphia, 1932), pp. 6, 15; Pennsylvania Bureau of Industrial Statistics, *Thirty-Fourth Annual Report* (1906), p. 256.

[39] F. A. Wells, *The British Hosiery Trade* (London, 1935), pp. 54–85, 128–159.

[40] *Textile Record*, I (1880), 2; III (1882), 195; "Report on the Foreign Commerce of the United States," pp. 294–296.

British textiles, but many emigrated to new mills in the United States.[41]

Although in 1860 a few factories constituted the entire American industry, they had already used immigrant skill— English, French, and German. A new company at Mansfield, Connecticut, in 1827 constructed its machinery from plans drawn by an English throwster. But ultimately the American trade clustered at Paterson, New Jersey, where a Macclesfield weaver in 1840 established the first successful mill. During the next twenty years several other Englishmen started factories at Paterson and elsewhere.[42]

. . . English and Scottish spinners and weavers climbed into managerial jobs and even to proprietorship. All together, as mill owners, superintendents, overseers, carders, spinners or throwsters, weavers or knitters, dyers or printers, British immigrants formed the strong warp threads of the rising American textile industry.

PICK AND POWDER CHARGE

Coal and ore miners were workingmen as skilled as any of the British immigrants who helped establish American industries. Labor underground and life in isolated mining villages set them apart from other men. Even if not born into the calling, one usually entered it as a boy and, having learned to work and survive in the depths, was unlikely to leave for the lower pay of some unskilled job. Only news of more promising mines abroad led a miner to emigrate. Since coal-hewers and ore-diggers had unlike skills, each group went to its own kind of pit in America. And, like the textile operatives, miners immigrated only when their own skills were in demand. . . .

[41] Mantoux, pp. 197–201; Ratan C. Rawlley, *Economics of the Silk Industry* (London, 1919), pp. 271–273.

[42] L. R. Trumbull, *A History of Industrial Paterson* (Paterson, 1882), pp. 164–191; Agnes Hannay, *A Chronicle of Industry on the Mill River* (Northampton, 1936), pp. 89, 93.

From its ever-growing labor force British collieries had miners to spare for the United States. . . . After Pennsylvania in 1885 required mine foremen to pass an examination for certificates of competency, the state's anthracite examiners and most of the successful candidates had Welsh, Irish, or English names, and some others, Scottish and German.[43] Scotsmen managed nine large bituminous mines in western Maryland.[44] The names of many Ohio superintendents and foremen were Welsh.[45] Welsh immigrants ran half the collieries of Washington State in 1894.[46] In several states the mine inspectors, appointed to enforce the new safety codes of the 1870's, were onetime immigrant British miners.[47] In 1903, in fact, the seven Illinois inspectorships were divided among five Englishmen, a Scot, and a Welshman, all with lifelong experience in the mines, while the head of the state mining board was an erstwhile Lancashire collier who had become the leading coal operator of the Peoria district.[48] Although it was difficult to become an owner and employer, at least one Welsh miner, James Jones, made a million shipping coal.[49]

But while the British and Irish and their sons bossed the mines, the proportion of their countrymen in the working force steadily declined. As elsewhere, American methods eventually rendered British training obsolete. It was cheaper to blast the coal "from the solid" than to undercut the vein

[43] Pennsylvania Inspectors of Mines of the Anthracite Coal Regions, *Reports*, 1887 *et seq*.

[44] *Scottish-American Journal*, October 9, 1884.

[45] Ohio State Mine Inspector, *Annual Reports*, 1876 *et seq*.

[46] W. P. Morgan, "The Welsh in the United States," *Wales*, III (1896), 22.

[47] *Ibid.*; Andrew Roy, *A History of the Coal Miners of the United States* (Columbus, 1907), p. 422; *Iron Molders' Journal*, August 10, 1878; *Druid*, December 26, 1912.

[48] Illinois Bureau of Labor Statistics; *Twenty-Second Annual Coal Report* (1903), pp. 134–140; *Thirty-Second Annual Coal Report* (1913), p. 73.

[49] *Druid*, December 17, 1908.

with the pick. For necessary undercutting the American industry also rapidly developed mining machinery. . . .[50]

These technological advances heralded the advent of Italian and Slavic laborers among the mineworkers, beginning in the mid-1870's. . . .[51] British miners, already disgruntled with American conditions, began to leave the industry. Down to the Scranton depot on their way back home tropped scores of Welshmen in 1890, their American citizenship forgotten.[52] And while most British-American colliers stayed in the United States, new arrivals no longer kept their ranks full.

TABLE 7

Reading Coal and Iron Company Employees, 1890–1896 °

NATIONALITY AND PARENTAGE	1890 NUMBER	1890 PER CENT	1895 NUMBER	1895 PER CENT	1896 NUMBER	1896 PER CENT
English	2,088	8.4	1,960	7.0	1,799	6.3
Welsh	1,282	5.2	1,112	4.0	1,037	3.7
Scots	210	0.9	223	0.8	168	0.6
Irish	6,887	27.8	6,450	23.0	6,025	21.3
German	3,709	15.0	3,471	12.4	3,207	11.3
"New immigrants"	5,819	23.6	9,000	32.2	10,286	36.2
Native American	4,719	19.1	5,765	20.6	5,838	20.6
Total	24,714	100.0	27,981	100.0	28,360	100.0

° G. O. Virtue, "The Anthracite Mine Laborer," *Bulletin of the Department of Labor*, no. 13 (November 1897), 751.

[50] Illinois Bureau of Labor Statistics, *Twenty-Fourth Annual Coal Report* (1905), pp. 138–151; Ohio Chief Inspector of Mines, *Eighteenth Annual Report* (1892), p. 48, and *Thirty-Second Annual Report* (1906), pp. 30–31.

[51] *American Manufacturer*, December 3, 1874, March 11, 1875, March 25, 1881, December 7, 1883, July 18, October 31, 1884; Virtue, pp. 750–753; "Reports of the Immigration Commission," VI, 254–255, 423–424, 534–535; XVI, 591–593, 659–661.

[52] "Report of the Select Committee on Immigration and Naturalization," *House Report*, 51 Cong., 2 sess., no. 3472 (January 15, 1891), II, 235. Cf. *Wilkes-Barre Record*, September 22, 1897; *Bulletin of the American Iron and Steel Association*, XXIV (1890), 92.

Many a skilled man landing in America after 1885 was suspected of having broken the law against prior contracts; deportation of a vociferous few further dissuaded others from coming.[53]

Exactly where in each state most of them settled is indeterminable. Unlike German or Scandinavian farmers in the Middle West, the English, Scots, or Canadians seldom huddled in communities of their own kind. Those who did band together are quickly listed. Most British-American rural colonies antedated the Civil War: Albion, Illinois, founded in 1817 by Morris Birkbeck;[54] Carlyle, Illinois;[55] Arena, Wisconsin, to which the British Temperance Emigration Society sent Liverpool mechanics in the 1840's;[56] and Welton, Iowa, similarly settled in 1850.[57] Scots came about 1820 to Caledonia, LeRoy, and Scottsville in western New York.[58] A group of Kintyre families thrived at Argyle, Illinois, from the late 1830's.[59] There were other prosperous colonies of Scottish farmers at Dundee and in Will, Boone, and LaSalle counties, Illinois,[60] near Janesville and Portage City, Wisconsin,[61] in northern Tama County in Iowa,[62] and even in Walton County, Florida.[63] Canadian

[53] C. P. Scott to Foreign Office, September 20, 1902, in F.O. 5/2506.

[54] George Flower, *History of the English Settlement in Edwards County, Illinois* (Chicago, 1882), *passim*.

[55] William Vipond Pooley, *The Settlement of Illinois from 1830 to 1850* (Madison, 1908), p. 503.

[56] Joseph Schafer, *The Wisconsin Lead Region* (Madison, 1932), p. 209.

[57] Grant Foreman, "English Emigrants in Iowa," *Iowa Journal of History and Politics*, XLIV (1946), 385–420.

[58] *Scottish-American*, December 27, 1916.

[59] Daniel G. Harvey, *The Argyle Settlement in History and Story* (Rockford, 1924), *passim*.

[60] Thomas C. MacMillan, "The Scots and Their Descendants in Illinois," *Transactions of the Illinois State Historical Society*, 1919, pp. 61–64; Pooley, p. 504.

[61] *Scottish-American Journal*, October 17, 1861, October 21, 1869.

[62] Janette Stevenson Murray, "Lairds of North Tama," *Iowa Journal of History and Politics*, XL (1942), 227–260.

[63] David Macrae, *America Revisited* (Glasgow, 1908), p. 94; *Scottish-American Journal*, April 10, 1884.

farmers moved into Polo and Farina, Illinois, in the 1830's and the 1850's.[64]

Like other foreign-language groups, the Welsh settled together to a much greater degree than the rest of the British. Their rural communities in Oneida County, New York—which made "Welsh butter" famous—and in Cambria County, Pennsylvania, took root in the 1790's. In Ohio within a few years Welsh families, some from Pennsylvania and others directly from Wales, farmed at Paddy's Run in Butler County, the "Welsh Hills" of Licking County, several spots in Gallia and Jackson counties, at Gomer in Allen County, and at Radnor in Delaware County.[65] During the 1830's Welsh Ohioans who revisited the homeland renewed the America fever there.[66] For another twenty years families from Wales and from the eastern Welsh settlements spread to new colonies in Waukesha, Columbia, LaCrosse, and Winnebago counties, Wisconsin, in Blue Earth and Fillmore counties, Minnesota, in Howard and Iowa counties, Iowa in northern Missouri, and even in Tennessee.[67] Besides the countrymen from North Wales, some South Wales miners and ironworkers turned to farming in the United States.[68]

[64] Paul Wallace Gates, *The Illinois Central Railroad and Its Colonization Work* (Cambridge, 1934), p. 234; John Poole *et al., Canada Settlement* (Polo, 1939).

[65] Pomroy Jones, *Annals and Recollections of Oneida County* (Rome, 1851), p. 307; William Harvey Jones, "Welsh Settlements in Ohio," *Ohio Archaeological and Historical Quarterly,* XVI (1907), 194–227; Paul DeMund Evans, "The Welsh in Oneida County" (unpublished master's thesis, Cornell University, 1914), pp. 10–16, 34–42.

[66] Benjamin W. Chidlaw, *Yr American* (Llanrwst, 1839); *Cambrian,* X (1890), 99.

[67] Daniel Jenkins Williams, *The Welsh Community of Waukesha County* (Columbus, 1926), *passim;* Howell D. Davies, *History of the Oshkosh Welsh Settlement* (Amarillo, 1947), *passim;* Thomas E. Hughes *et al., History of the Welsh in Minnesota* (Mankato, 1895), *passim;* David Williams, *A History of Modern Wales* (London, 1950), pp. 259–260; *Cambrian,* V (1885), 73–78, 109–112, 137–141, 260; *Druid,* May 19, 1910; February 29, 1912.

[68] William Harvey Jones, p. 217; *Drych,* May 3, 1877, June 27, 1878; *Cambrian,* V (1885), 74.

After the Civil War the railroads and other land speculators recruited—among other peoples—Englishmen, Scots,
and Canadians for all parts of the West.[69] The Pennsylvania
Railroad and several western lines in 1870 opened a London
agency to sell "cheap and comfortable" passage to the West
and to help immigrants to select farms.[70] The Santa Fe set up
the Anglo-American Agricultural Company to dispose of
some of its lands.[71] In 1883, at the height of the Northern
Pacific's colonization campaign, that railroad employed
throughout the United Kingdom more than eight hundred
agents to recruit emigrants at town markets and country
fairs.[72] The American Land Company of London advertised a
hundred thousand acres in southwest Minnesota in 1876, and
the Land Colonisation and Banking Company of London in
1879 offered twenty thousand acres complete with town sites
and grain elevators in Minnesota and Iowa.[73] Similar companies brought British farmers to Kansas, Dakota, and Ore-
gon.[74]

Once again only a few British herded together. During the
late 1860's and early 1870's English farmers settled whole villages in Kansas; state officials hired several men to go back
home as recruiting agents.[75] In 1870 a band of three hundred
Sussex emigrants came to Geary County.[76] The Burlington

[69] James B. Hedges, "The Colonization Work of the Northern Pacific
Railroad," *Mississippi Valley Historical Review*, XIII (1926), 311–342,
and "Promotion of Immigration to the Pacific Northwest by the Railroads," *ibid.*, XV (1928), 183–203.

[70] *Anglo-American Times*, February 26, 1870.

[71] *Ibid.*, March 25, 1881.

[72] Hedges, "Promotion of Immigration," p. 198.

[73] *Anglo-American Times*, January 14, 1876; "Report on the Foreign
Commerce of the United States of America," *Parliamentary Papers*,
1880, LXXII (C. 2570), 207.

[74] *Arweinydd i Diroedd yr Union Pacific Railway* (Carmarthen,
1872); *Anglo-American Times*, January 29, 1870; *Scottish-American
Journal*, March 11, 1875, August 31, 1882.

[75] *Anglo-American Times*, August 21, 1869, July 23, 1870, September
30, 1871.

[76] W. H. Carruth, "Foreign Settlements in Kansas," *Kansas University
Quarterly*, I (1892), 76.

and Missouri Railroad organized a colony of English farmers. Sailing in 1872, the majority as steerage passengers, the 145 settlers included blacksmiths, wheelwrights, and a clergyman and brought £10,000 capital.[77] Scots in 1871 established a western Minnesota colony for raising purebred cattle.[78] In 1873 several hundred Somerset, Devon, and Yorkshire farmers and artisans, shepherded by a Dorset Congregational minister, took up eight townships of Northern Pacific and homestead land in Clay County, Minnesota, and gave their colony the Somerset name Yeovil.[79] The "Furness colony" in Wadena County was planted on forty-two thousand railroad acres in 1873 and 1874 by a tightly knit group of several hundred prosperous North of England farmers and tradesmen.[80] New Welsh farming communities sprang up at New Cambria and Dawn in Missouri, Arvonia and Bala in Kansas, Prairie Union in Nebraska, and in Washington Territory.[81] Even northeastern Pennsylvania got a new colony of sixty Scots in 1882. . . .[82] The "immigrant problem" had nothing to do with prosaic English, Scots, and Canadians, or even the more clannish and foreign-speaking Welsh.[83]

Thus the British escaped the usual American ridicule of foreigners, and they themselves saw nothing ludicrous in their

---

[77] *Workingman's Advocate*, April 27, 1872.

[78] *Anglo-American Times*, December 9, 1871.

[79] *New York Daily Tribune*, April 10, 1873; Harold F. Peterson, "Some Colonization Projects of the Northern Pacific Railroad," *Minnesota History*, X (1929), 138–140.

[80] *Ibid.*, pp. 140–142.

[81] Robert D. Thomas, *Hanes Cymry America* (Utica, 1872), pt. II, pp. 87–94, 103–107, 123–124, 128–134; William D. Davies, *America a Gweledigaethau Bywyd* (Merthyr Tydfil, 1899), pp. 65–261; *Arvonia, sef Sefydliad Cymreig yn Sir Osage* (Arvonia, 1869); "Report on the Trade and Commerce of the Puget Sound District and Washington Territory," *Parliamentary Papers*, 1886, LXVI (C. 4761), 745; *Cambrian*, X (1890), 99–100; *Druid*, March 11–18, November 18, 1909.

[82] *Anglo-American Times*, January 26, 1883.

[83] David W. Mitchell, *Ten Years in the United States* (London, 1862), p. 59; Edward Young, *Special Report on Immigration* (Philadelphia, 1871), p. vi; Massachusetts Commission on Immigration, *The Problem of Immigration in Massachusetts* (Boston, 1914), *passim; Miners' Journal*, May 26, August 18, 1855.

place in American society. On the vaudeville stage the caricature of the Irishman, German, Jew, or Italian was an exag-
geration of an actual lower-class type which any immigrant
or city-bred American could recognize. The "stage Englishman," however, was a titled fop, "vulgarly overdressed, almost invariably wearing white spats over his boots, with a
single eye-glass, with a walking stick, and silk hat. Whatever
his class in life he uses no h's and repeatedly exclaims, 'Don't
you know,' 'deucedly clever,' and the word 'blooming' in
every other sentence." [84] This incongruous dandy hardly represented anyone's notion—except for the "h's"—of the miners
and mill hands who settled in America.[85]

Nor did Americans tag the British with opprobrious names
as they did "micks," "dagoes," "hunkies," and the rest. One
who argued loudly for England might be called "John Bull"
—hardly likely to offend him.[86] "Cousin Jack," the Cornish
miner's sobriquet on Lake Superior, he himself had imported
from Cornwall.[87] Although a Welshman might object that
such names as "Taffy" or "goat" were the subject of "jests by
cheap wits," these also had the respectability of long usage in
the old country.[88] A Scot would feel more surprise than hurt
if some American knew enough to call him "Jock" or "Sandy."
As for the English, the British naval and merchant marine ra-
tion of lime juice to prevent scurvy inspired "lime-juicer" or
"limey," but these were not widely used, except for sailors,
before the first World War.[89] In Fall River the name "jick,"
implying more contempt than any of the others, was coined

[84] Frank Dilnot, *The New America* (London, 1919), pp. 63–64.
[85] Harold E. Adams, "Minority Caricatures on the American Stage,"
in George Peter Murdock, ed., *Studies in the Science of Society Presented to Albert Galloway Keller* (New Haven, 1937), pp. 6, 20–21.
[86] Sir Frederick Smith, *My American Visit* (London, 1918), p. 64.
[87] T. A. Rickard, *The Copper Mines of Lake Superior* (New York,
1905), p. 18; Erick Partridge, *A Dictionary of Slang and Unconven-
tional English* (London, 1949), p. 184.
[89] *Druid*, March 30, September 21, 1911, March 28, 1912.
[89] *Partridge*, p. 484. Cf. *ante*, p. 83.

by Portuguese mill laborers who resented their Lancashire overlords.[90] But few Americans used any such terms; they seldom thought of their English, Welsh, or Scottish neighbors as foreigners.

. . . British-American editors . . . opposed the coming of "thousands of hungry starving Italians, Hungarians," and other "general pests" or justified Russian pogroms as no more than the Jews deserved.[91] George Gunton attacked the "[J]ew clothiers" of Fall River and dismissed Disraeli as "the Dizz Jew." [92] The bias of the English often thwarted trade-union leaders who tried to unite them with foreign-speaking workmen. At an operatives' meeting in Fall River in 1878 a French Canadian who briefly addressed his fellow countrymen in French "was repeatedly insulted by the English-speaking audience, being hissed and hooted and laughed at." [93]

Skilled British craft unionists particularly disliked the European laborers who, sometimes as strikebreakers, after 1880 gradually took their places in American industry.[94] John Golden, the Lancashire Irish leader of the United Textile Workers, in 1906 contrasted "the English-speaking people" with "the foreign elements" overrunning the mills.[95] Indeed, dislike for the "new immigrants" discouraged British colliers from entering American mining, which by 1910 seemed "a Hunkey's job." [96] The early-twentieth-century rule that every newcomer to the mines had to work two years as a laborer made things still worse. As a visitor to Scranton observed: "It

[90] H. L. Mencken, *The American Language* (New York, 1946), p. 216; private information.

[91] *Scottish-American Journal*, January 5, 1882, October 3, 1888; *British Californian*, June 1903; *Western British-American*, March 5, 1905.

[92] *Labor Standard*, August 9, 1879, May 1, 1880, September 24, 1881.

[93] *Fall River Weekly News*, October 24, 1878. Cf. *American Silk Journal*, II (1883), 141; VI (1887), 140.

[94] *Drych*, April 10, 1873.

[95] United Textile Workers of America, *Proceedings of the Sixth Annual Convention* (1906), p. 28. Cf. *ante*, p. 58.

[96] "Reports of the Immigration Commission," *Senate Document*, 61 Cong., 2 sess., no. 633 (June 15, 1910), VI, 426.

goes against the grain in an English-speaking man to fetch and
carry for a Slovak or a Pole." [97]

[97] Stephen Graham, *With Poor Immigrants to America* (New York,
1914), pp. 133–134.

THE IRISH:
AN AMBIVALENT VIEW
ANDREW GREELEY

BY way of illustration, I now offer an ambivalent view of the
American Irish, or at least an ambivalent view of aspects of
the contemporary life of the Irish ethnic group—their politics, their self-image, their church.

1. Irish politics: Edwin Levine, in his book *The Irish and
Irish Politicians,* points out that the Irish politician is a nonideological man, choosing to play the role of the pragmatic
broker of power and to accomplish his social change well
within the framework of consensus that such power brokerage
makes possible. The cement by which he binds together his
political organization is not common ideological commitment
but personal loyalty. He does not enjoy the trappings or pre-
rogatives of power but merely its exercise and is frequently
content to play a behind the scenes role in the game so long
as he can play in the game. Given his pragmatic orientation,
the Irish political leader is not terribly concerned about
moral purity—save in matters of sex. Government is seen as a
complex, delicate, balancing act in which one must be sensitive to the faults and frailties of men. As long as a politician

is loyal to his friends and does not desert his wife and family, other evils may be tolerated as being an elemental part of the human condition. Given the strong good-government orientation of Protestants and Jews, this tolerant element of the Irish style seems corrupt and immoral. But the Irish political leader shrugs his shoulders in response and says that at least he is able to get things done and the good-government people usually are not.

Another aspect of the Irish political style has been described by Professor James Q. Wilson in his study of the behavior of Irish police. He discovered that given a choice of a formal bureaucratic mode of communication and an informal, unofficial and indirect method of communication, Irish police sergeants almost invariably choose the latter, while sergeants of other ethnic groups tend to choose the former. The Irish sergeant—characteristic, I would say, of most Irish who engage in the political game—prefers the subtle hint, the wink of the eye, the ambiguous sentence, and the delicate innuendo, to the direct order. He prefers to work on the margins of the system rather than through its clearly established channels. He prefers the flexibility that comes with ambiguity rather than the rigidity which he feels comes with clarity.

Both Wilson and Levine see explanations for this behavior in the Irish past. During the penal, post-penal and prerevolutionary times in Ireland the political system was hostile to the Irish Catholic who had to live with it whether he liked it or not. Survival and success depended on skills that were necessary to get around the system without seeming to violate it. In the Ireland of the eighteenth and nineteenth century there was little or no room for ideology and the formal regulations of the system were hostile and punitive. The Irish therefore became masters at operating on the margins and in the interstices, saying one thing and doing something slightly different, agreeing with their lords and deceiving them behind their backs, apparently accepting the law but using the weaknesses and ambiguities of the law to triumph over those who had made and enforced the law.

Visitors to contemporary Ireland are astonished at the Irish characteristic of responding to one question with another. One friend of mine, for example, claims that he never heard a declarative sentence in his whole two weeks in the land of his ancestors. He cites as a classical example of this his experience in an attempt to ask where the post office was. "Is it a stamp you want to buy?" responded the native—even though in fact the two of them were standing in front of the post office.

Levine suggests that the Irish political style has also been profoundly affected by the governmental style of the Catholic church. There can be no doubt that the informal, indirect, nonideological approach of the Irish ward committeeman or precinct captain does bear a certain similarity to the operations of the Roman curia though my own particular biases would suggest that the precinct captain and the ward committeeman have proved far more nimble in keeping up with social change than have the curialists. However, the traditions have different origins; the Irish, despite their loyalties to the Pope, have always had a profound distrust of the curia. There is no reason to deny that Irish ecclesiastical politicians are rather like their civil counterparts, but my own inclination is to think that the two are influenced by a common cultural background and that, if anything, the churchmen learn from the civil leaders; by and large, the civil leadership is far more effective at the political style than the ecclesiastical leadership or at least quicker on its feet.

A further aspect of the Irish political style is its desire to win. Its pragmatic roots in the penal past seem to have left the Irish style not only without a taste for ideology, but also without the ability to enjoy illusions. The Irishman wants to win so badly that he can taste it, so badly, in some instances, that he will stop at almost nothing in order that he might win. He might justify himself by saying that his ancestors had few victories in the past (though a critic would respond by saying one of the reasons they had so few victories is that they were not able to stop fighting themselves for sufficiently long periods of time to fight their common enemies). For him, a politics not oriented toward victory is a vain and foolish politics. . . . That winning might be less important than assuming an ideologically pure or morally correct position was something that my young friends found completely inconceivable.

2. Self-esteem and the Irish: The mythology about the Celt is contradictory. He is thought of as the happy-go-lucky, playful comedian singing Clancy Brothers songs and "heisting" a few on St. Patrick's day. But he is also thought of as the moody, melancholy William Butler Yeats, seen in the mists arising from the peat bog. The statistical data are contradictory, too. On most measures of emotional well-being the Irish score higher than many other American ethnic groups. On the other hand, the fascinating research on hospital behavior suggests that the Irish repress even the acknowledgement of pain or symptoms while other groups, such as the Italians, if anything, exaggerate their reaction to suffering in hospital situations. . . .

Obviously, many Irishmen have no trace of the leprechaun in their personality and still others manifest no part of the banshee syndrome. Nevertheless, there is a strong impression that there is something rather unique in Irish family life which does produce a strain of self-hatred which, while it may be different from Jewish self-hatred (there are no Irish Portnoys, not yet, anyhow), nonetheless is fairly common in the American Irish experience. The alcoholism data offer overwhelming evidence that there is something peculiar going on in the Irish family and personality structure. The Irish are twenty-five times more likely than the typical American to suffer from alcoholism (though, for whatever consolation it may bring, they are apparently somewhat less likely to be alcoholics than are Mormons).

Having dealt with the Irish in one capacity or another for most of my life, I feel on sound ground when I say that they have a powerful self-esteem problem rooted in the coldness, not to say harshness, of Irish familial relationships. If the Jewish mother, at least in the stereotype, controls her children by smothering them with affection, the Irish mother tends to control them by withholding affection. The characteristic Irish alcoholic syndrome is of the compulsive perfectionist who feels that he has never been loved for who he is but only for what he can do (the syndrome is especially prevalent in the Irish clergy).

I am not asserting that no affection is felt between husband and wife, between parent and child—particularly between mother and son—in the Irish family, but I am saying that there is a strong tendency to conceal affection. The domineering Irish mother, surrounded by bachelors and old maids, is far too common a figure in reality as well as in fiction to be lightly dismissed. I suspect that the large number of "vocations" to the priestly and religious life found among the Irish can in part be attributed to the fact that the Irish mother does not lose her priest son or her nun daughter to anyone else. Again, the light-hearted Irish wake so well known in fiction and the stony-hearted Irish wake which abounds in fact if not in fiction are manifestations of a personality which has not learned how either to celebrate or to mourn.

This repression of affect—save for an occasional release under the influence of John Barleycorn—may be in part attributed to religious faith though surely other national manifestations of Roman Catholicism take very different emotional forms. Cultural, historical and child-rearing practices are, I suspect, far more important than religious faith, though the frequently Jansenistic style of Irish Catholicism unquestionably rationalizes, reinforces and justifies the suspicion of emotion and affect which seems to be part of, if not the Irish personality, at least the personalities of many Irishmen. . . .

Some observers see a relationship between this lack of

affect among the Irish and the Irish method of birth control; in the old country late marriage seems to have been until very recently the principal means of controlling population. However, such a form of population control is a relatively recent phenomena. In the years before the potato famine the Irish married very young and had large families, producing the highest birth rate in any of the European countries. I suspect that far more is involved in their low affect and relatively demonic view of sex than simply a means of population control. We are on very uncertain ground in these speculations. Impressions, little bits of data, folklore (like the old saying that the Irish are great at hating but not very good at loving) hardly are a basis for any convincing descriptions of the relationship between child-rearing and adult personality in a given ethnic group. . . .

3. The Irish and their church: David L. Edwards, in his *Religion and Change,* points out that while social forces can empty churches, they can also fill them; for weal or woe, the social forces have filled the churches of Irish Catholicism. In the old country the identification of Catholicism with Irish nationalism—courtesy of mother England—assured Catholicism a hold over the devotion of the people, which generations of ecclesiastical tyranny, obscurantism and ineptitude have not weakened in the slightest. In the United States the hostility of the WASP establishment to the Irish Catholic immigrant guaranteed the continuation of this identification of Irish and Catholic, an identification which has not been notably weakened either by the pilgrimage from the immigrant slum to the professional suburb nor by the transformation of a counter-Reformation church to an ecumenical church. There is absolutely no sign of schism or apostasy within the American Irish Catholic population and no reason even to think that such a sign will be apparent any time in the present century. . . .

Members of other ethnic groups, of course, bitterly resent the disproportionate power and influence the Irish have both within the American church and as Catholic representatives beyond the church. But they have not been able to do anything about it largely, I suspect, for the same reasons that it has taken a long, long time for any of the other Catholic ethnic groups to begin to replace the Irish as the dominant figures in urban political life.

Whether this Irish dominance has been functional or dysfunctional for Catholicism in the United States, it has certainly facilitated the acculturation of the Catholic church into American styles. But it has done so at the price of antagonizing and occasionally alienating members of other Catholic ethnic groups from the church and also of inhibiting the contributions of these ethnic groups to a more pluralistic Catholicism.

Paradoxically, the radical critics, the innovators and the reformers within American Catholicism are also mostly Irish (with an intermingling of some Middlewestern Germans influenced partly by the populist tradition of the plains and partly by the social and liturgical reforms from the German church communicated to America principally through the Benedictine monasteries, and especially St. John's monastery in Collegeville, Minnesota). A look at the roster of the various editors of *Commonweal, The National Catholic* and the *National Catholic Reporter* and at the names of those clergy and laity who are most critical of American Catholicism and most likely to be the leaders of reform organizations shows that it is the Irish who are the ones most likely to be critics of Irish Catholicism.

If there is no sign of an appreciable exodus of the Irish from the American church—even though now they are truly in the final stages of the acculturation process—there are still some fascinating signs of a modification in the relationship between well-to-do Irish and their church. First of all, there has been a precipitous decline in recruitment to the priesthood and the sisterhood in the American church. What is not so generally well known is that this decline is limited almost entirely to the Irish. Other ethnic groups, the Italians and the Poles, for example, are probably contributing larger numbers of religious "vocations" than they have ever done in the past. There are a number of possible explanations for the phenomenon. The Irish may have reached that location in the acculturation process where the priesthood is no longer perceived as a means of social mobility nor even as a thoroughly responsible and respectable profession. It may also be that the Irish clergy are most likely to be affected by the present identity crisis affecting the Catholic clergy in the United States and hence, they may be the ones most likely to refrain from recruiting other men to the priesthood. Also, the antagonism that many suburban Irish feel toward their clergy may have substantially modified the image of the priesthood in the Irish Catholic home. Finally, the indecisiveness which I observe among the younger generation of Irish Americans. . . . may also make it difficult for them to engage in the permanent commitment which the priesthood and the religious life still require.

There is some statistical evidence [1] that respect for the clergy is notably decreasing among American Catholics. In 1952 Catholics had more respect for their clergy than did Protestants and Jews, whereas in 1965 they had less. My hunch is that this phenomenon is especially prevalent among Irish Catholics. Until better data and better explanations are advanced, I would hypothesize that the antagonism of the suburban Irish towards their clergy results from the professionalization of the Irish population and the nonprofessionalism of their clergy. The most frequent charge heard against the priests in suburban Catholic communities is that they are inept, untrained and bungling. A new, well-educated and successful suburban professional class is apt to be particularly rigorous in demanding professional behavior from others. Clergy are viewed, perhaps correctly, as glorified ama-

[1] Greeley, Andrew M., Martz, Martin, and Rosenberg, Stuart, *What Do We Believe?* (New York: Meredith Press, 1967).

teurs who are not particularly good at any one thing and perform inadequately most of the things they attempt to do, from financial planning to Sunday preaching. In addition, many of the suburban professionals seem very unsympathetic and even hostile towards the younger clergy in their "identity crises." As one sophisticated and quite liberal suburban matron put it, "Our young priests don't give a damn about us. We're not black, we're not poor, we're not drug addicts, we're not teenagers, we're not hippies, so we're assumed not to have any religious need. The only kind of religious activity which they seem to enjoy is denouncing us as corrupt, immoral members of the middle class." This woman's reaction is by no means atypical. The Irish are no longer willing to excuse "poor father's" problems on the grounds that however inept —or however alcoholic—he may be, he is still a priest. If my impressions are accurate, the phenomenon is extremely interesting. The professionalization of Irish suburbanites and the lack of professional skills in their clergy may have accomplished what a thousand years of British rule was unable to accomplish—turning the Irish into anticlericals.

JEWS IN NEW YORK CITY: URBAN ECONOMIC FRONTIERS 1890–1920

MOSES RISCHIN

BUSINESS AND THE TRADES

THE peddler's pack still provided the most direct introduction to American ways, the most promising school for the study of the country's speech, tastes and economic needs, and

REPRINTED by permission of the publishers from *The Promised City: New York's Jews, 1870–1914* by Moses Rischin, Cambridge, Mass.: Harvard University Press, Copyright, 1962 by the President and Fellows of Harvard College.

the broadest field for the play of the aspiring tradesman's imagination. Potential peddlers were warned of the decrease in opportunities, but few failed to put this caution to the test of personal experience. The lure of commercial success, starting from the humble peddler's role, was magnetic. In the late 1880's, along the East Side from the Battery to Harlem, merchants in shoestrings, neckties, and sausages could be seen vending their wares. "Suspenders, collah buttons, 'lastic, matches, hankeches—please, lady, buy," went a familiar refrain. Compared with the alternative of seasonal sweatshop labor, peddling proved exhilarating. The rebuffs of housewives, the torments of young rowdies, and the harassment of the police intimidated the less venturesome and the more sensitive. But the number of peddlers at any one time barely suggested the multitudes who passed through this apprenticeship.[1]

As the immigrant Jewish population swelled, the Lower East Side became the center of the pushcart trade. "Whole blocks of the East Side Jewry [were turned] into a bazaar with high-piled carts lining the curb," as few commodities failed to find a seller or buyer. "Bandanas and tin cups at two cents, peaches at a cent a quart, damaged eggs for a song, hats for a quarter, and spectacles warranted to suit the eye . . . for thirty-five cents." On Thursday night Hester Street, the chief market center, resounded to the cries of bawling wives making their purchases for the Sabbath. "Big carp, little carp, middle-sized carp, but everywhere carp." Here only the limitations of space contained the crowds engaged in commerce, as the pinched economies of hundreds of transplanted *shtetls* competed amid plenty. "Every conceivable thing is for sale, chiefly candles, dried fruit, and oilcloth;

---

[1] *New Yorker Idishe Volks-Zeitung*, November 5, 1886; H. Idell Zeisloft, *The New Metropolis* (New York, 1899), p. 531; *Fourteenth Annual Report, Board of Relief of the United Hebrew Charities, City of New York, 1888*, p. 40.

and the yolk or the white of an egg, or a chicken leg or wing, or an ounce of tea, coffee or butter is not an uncommon purchase." Peddlers, able to sell in small quantities—from a penny's worth up—accommodated a bargain-eager clientele with limited storage space for perishable foods. Avid competition among sellers, crippling to the peddlers, reduced living costs for many an immigrant family from two to three dollars weekly.

The pushcart traffic, regularly increased by a host of seasonally unemployed garment workers, counted 25,000 peregrinating tradesmen in 1900. Predominantly Jews, augmented by Greeks and Italians who dominated the fruit and vegetable trade, they spilled over into Little Italy and on Saturdays intruded upon the Irish West Side to form the Paddy's Market. Many an energetic pushcart peddler earned 15 to 20 dollars weekly and was able to advance to more settled types of commerce, leaving the itinerant trade to newcomers and to the less successful.

The Lower East Side developed a fervent commercial life, infused with a vitality that made it something more than a mass of tenements. "Hurry and push, . . . the optimistic, whole-souled, almost religious passion for business," permeated the community. In 1899, within the Eighth Assembly District (coinciding essentially with the tenth ward) 2897 individuals were engaged in 182 different vocations and businesses. A total of 631 food mongers catered to the needs of the inhabitants of this area. Most numerous were the 140 groceries which often sold fruits, vegetables, bread, and rolls as well as the usual provisions. Second in number were the 131 butcher shops which proclaimed their wares in Hebrew characters. The other food vendors included: 36 bakeries, 9 bread stands, 14 butter and egg stores, 24 candy stands, 62 candy stores, 1 cheese store, 20 cigar stores, 3 cigarette shops, 7 combination two-cent coffee shops, 10 delicatessens, 9 fish stores, 7 fruit stores, 21 fruit stands, 3 grocery stands, 7 herring stands, 2 meat markets, 16 milk stores, 2 matzo (unleavened bread) stores, 10 sausage stores, 20 soda water stands, 5 tea shops, 14 tobacco shops, 11 vegetable stores, 13 wine shops, 15 grape wine shops, and 10 confectioners.[2]

Religious laws concerning the preparation and handling of foods had a decided effect on choice of occupation. Especially strict requirements for meats drew many immigrants into the meat and poultry business where earlier Jewish immigrants already were prominent. Markens estimated that in 1888 approximately half of the city's 4000 meat retailers and 300 wholesalers were Jews. From among them had emerged Schwartzchild and Sulzberger, subsequently the Wilson Company, and other leading meatpackers. By the turn of the century 80 per cent of the wholesale, and 50 per cent of the retail, meat trade was reputedly handled by Jewish dealers. In a period when other Eastern cities had come to depend upon Midwestern abattoirs, the mounting demand for kosher meat kept New York an important slaughtering center.[3]

Bakery products also required ritual supervision. The 70 Jewish bakeries catering to the Lower East Side at the turn of the century soon grew to nearly 500 in the city. Those on the Lower East Side were bunched on Hester and Rivington streets, where peddlers sold much of the product, calling: "Buy Jews, buy wives, buy girls and buy young gents, buy fresh cakes, buy little white loaves and eat them in good health." Family enterprises competed for the Sabbath trade,

[2] Jacob Riis, *How the Other Half Lives* (New York, 1890), p. 90; W. McAdoo, *Guarding A Great City* (New York, 1906), p. 143; *Eighteenth Annual Report, Bureau of Labor Statistics, State of New York, 1900*, pp. 292–293; Bertha H. Poole, "The Way of the Pushcart," *The Craftsman*, 9:218f (November 1905); *Report of the Mayor's Push-Cart Commission, The City of New York* (New York, 1906), pp. 37, 89, 199f; *Social Reform Club Circular* (1898); Hutchins Hapgood, "The Earnestness That Wins Wealth," *World's Work*, 6:3459 (May 1903); *Yearbook, University Settlement Society of New York, 1899–1900*, pp. 89–90.

[3] I. Markens, *Hebrews in America* (New York, 1888), pp. 156–157; R. A. Clemen, *The American Livestock Industry* (New York, 1923), pp. 156f, 169, 453, 460; I. Kopeloff, *Amol in amerika* (Warsaw, 1928), p. 402f; cf. Faith M. Williams, *The Food Manufacturing Industries in New York and Its Environs* (New York, 1924), p. 20.

employee and employer laboring underground side by side continuously from early Thursday morning until Friday at noon. Investigators of factory conditions reported:

The bakers worked in deep and dark subcellars, without ventilation or hygienic conditions. The walls and ceilings were moist and moldy. The shops were infested with rats and reeked with dirt. The air was pestilential. The bake ovens were primitive. No machinery was used. The work was all done by hand.

In 1910 Goodman and Son with 114 employees, Gottfried and Steckler with 102, and Nathan Messing with 60, were the leaders. Five factories employing 20 to 34 people, among them Horowitz & Margareten and Rauch and Strumpf, specialized in the preparation of matzos.[4]

The flourishing soda water business was directly attributable to the nonalcoholic drinking habits of Jewish immigrants. In immigrant Jewish neighborhoods where saloons languished, the imputed health-giving propensities of "the workers' champagne" proved irresistible. Two Jewish soda water firms in 1880 grew to well over one hundred by 1907, and comprised 90 per cent of such establishments in the city, almost all on the Lower East Side. With a rise in the price of sugar, seltzer came to replace soda as the staple beverage of Yiddish New York. If saloons ministered largely to a transient trade, coffee houses, cake parlors, lunchrooms, and restaurants thrived on Jewish custom.[5]

While bakers, meat merchants, and sellers of soda water were building characteristically Jewish industries, many im-

---

[4] *Yearbook, University Settlement Society,* (1900), p. 35f; *Forward,* September 28, 1909; *Fourth Annual Report, Bureau of Statistics of Labor, State of New York, 1886,* p. 485f; *State of New York, Preliminary Report of the Factory Investigation Commission,* 1912, I, 209, 217–218; Williams, *Food Manufacturing Industries,* p. 24; *Forward,* April 23, 1910; *Second Annual Industrial Directory, New York,* 1913, pp. 574–575.

[5] *Forward,* April 27, 1906, April 23, 1910; *Wilson's Business Directory 1880–1881,* pp. 705–706; *The Trow Business Directory of Greater New York,* 1907, pp. 1039–1040; M. E. Ravage, *An American in the Making* (New York, 1917), p. 124f.

migrants sought less perilous opportunities for independence than those afforded in commerce. Skilled craftsmen were singularly blessed: "An artisan will sooner or later obtain work and will not be forced to work for someone else," counseled a popular immigrant guide book. But before 1900 artisans made up only a small fraction of the immigrants. In 1892 newcomers of less than a year's residence, placed by the United Hebrew Charities in 132 different branches of industry, were largely unskilled. These placements, the UHC employment bureau reported, were made "in addition to the lines that custom has made more prevalent among our immigrants, of which unfortunately report seems to assign as their sole means of making livelihoods, cigar-makers, tailors, drummers, clerks and salesmen." Skilled workmen were directed to places where their specialties could be employed but many qualified artisans were squeezed out by the factory system. The mechanization of the shoe industry, for example, prevented cobblers and bootmakers from exercising their crafts. Others, such as blacksmiths, found it difficult to resume the village routine amid the roar of a strange city. Many immigrants, without industrial experience, were intimidated by machines. One of the rules governing labor-employer relations in the needle trades reflects the workmen's awe of the sewing machine: owners, rather than workmen, were to maintain, clean, and oil the machines. Numerous artisans abandoned their craft as soon as an opportunity showed itself. As little as one-third of 225 heads of families, according to one study, retained their original vocations. Most accommodated their skills to the labor market, turning to those industries where they might adhere to their religious habits and where the stranger could not mock.[6]

[6] G. M. Price, *Di yuden in amerika* (Odessa, 1891), p. 12; *Eighteenth Annual Report, United Hebrew Charities*, pp. 25–26; United States Industrial Commission, *Reports* (Washington, 1900–1902), XIV, 1200; M. D. C. Crawford, *Ways of Fashion* (New York, 1948), p. 148; C. S. Bernheimer, "The Jewish Immigrant as an Industrial Worker," *Annals of the American Academy of Political and Social Science*, 33:399f (March 1909);

The arrival, after the turn of the century, of many skilled and semiskilled Jewish workmen from a growingly industrialized homeland transformed the Jewish economic structure. An estimated 66 per cent of the gainfully employed Jewish immigrants between 1899 and 1914 possessed industrial skills —a far greater proportion than that of any other immigrant group. Jews ranked first in 26 out of 47 trades tabulated by the Immigration Commission, comprising an absolute majority in 8. They constituted 80 per cent of the hat and cap makers, 75 per cent of the furriers, 68 per cent of the tailors and bookbinders, 60 per cent of the watchmakers and milliners, and 55 per cent of the cigarmakers and tinsmiths. They totaled 30 to 50 per cent of the immigrants classified as tanners, turners, undergarment makers, jewelers, painters, glaziers, dressmakers, photographers, saddle-makers, locksmiths, butchers, and metal workers in other than iron and steel. They ranked first among immigrant printers, bakers, carpenters, cigar-packers, blacksmiths, and building trades workmen.[7]

In the late 1880's, Harry Fischel, a pioneer East European tenement builder, encouraged Jews to enter the building trades by keeping the Sabbath and affording his employees half-pay on that day. Otherwise, religious observances, language barriers, differences in work standards, and the paucity of Jewish contractors discouraged newcomers from entering this field. Yet, as early as 1885 a society of Russian house painters had formed, and by 1890 nearly 900 Jewish painters and carpenters lived on the Lower East Side.

Jews flocked to this industry when the building boom hit the late nineties and first decade of the twentieth century, when migration from the Lower East Side filled the newly

---

cf. Ann Reed, "The Jewish Immigrants of Two Pittsburgh Blocks," *Charities and Commons*, January 2, 1909, 609f; *Forward*, April 8, 1913.

[7] L. Hersch, "International Migrations of the Jews," *International Migrations*, ed. Imre Ferenczi and W. F. Willcox (New York, 1930), II, 497–498, 504–505.

built sections of Harlem, Washington Heights, Brownsville, Williamsburg, and the Bronx. As mortgage credit kept pace with the housing needs of a mounting populace, immigrants were able to enter the construction industry with but a small fraction of the price for lot and buildings. Barred by the unions from well-paid new construction, immigrant iron workers, housesmiths, masons, plumbers, plasterers, electricians, carpenters, and painters concentrated upon alterations and the remodeling of old tenements.[8]

Auxiliary to the building trades were the swiftly developing metal trades. Formerly, brass work had been limited to trained craftsmen, "workmen of artistic tact . . . as well as mechanical skill." But the rising demand for brass supplies and the available cheap labor encouraged mass production. In 1890 Jewish "locksmiths and jobbing tinkers and plumbers with their keys and their tools strung on a wire heap that rests on one shoulder" numbered over 400 on the Lower East Side. Frederick Haberman's Central Stamping Company, employing over 2000 men in the manufacture of tin house-furnishings, included many Jewish immigrants. Jewish tinsmiths and locksmiths crowded into metal shops producing wash boilers, barrels, pipes, and kitchenware. Ironwork shops where structural steel, doors, gates, steps, and fire escapes were turned out also offered jobs to the newer immigrants. Others found employment in installing ironwork and cornices, in roofing, and the laying-in of skylights in new and renovated buildings. Small shops founded by former workmen readily hired green *lansman* (fellow townsmen) at a five- or six-dollar weekly wage. At the turn of the century when a

[8] H. S. Goldstein, *Forty Years of Struggle for a Principle* (New York, 1928), pp. 32–33; *the Hebrew American Directory and Universal Guide* (New York, 1892), p. 137; *Arbeiter Zeitung,* June 6, 1890; *Sixteenth Annual Report, Bureau of Statistics of Labor, State of New York,* p. 1046; *Thirteenth Annual Report, Bureau of Statistics of Labor, State of New York,* II, 388–389; *Forward,* February 20, June 12, 1914; Sol Blum, "Trade Union Rules in the Building Trades," ed. J. H. Hollander and G. E. Barnett, *Studies in American Trade Unionism* (New York, 1912), p. 300.

vogue for Russian brassware created a demand for workmen in copper, 100 skilled coppersmiths in a dozen Allen Street basement shops modeled and forged candle sticks, ash trays, kettles, and samovars. Toiling for a ten-dollar weekly wage, the city's newest artisans slaked the thirst for "imported Russian" utensils.[9]

Workmen in fine metals, jewelry, and the printing trades were to find a ready market for their skills. In 1890 specialists in hand-made ornamental metalware numbered 287 on the East Side. Collectively described as "goldsmiths" in the Baron de Hirsch study, they probably included all those engaged in the jewelry trades. A decade later, 2000 Jews comprised 40 per cent of the industry's labor force. Printers encountered little difficulty in gaining employment once the immigrant community attained sufficient size. In 1890 over 145 Jewish printers lived on the Lower East Side, offering to many immigrants opportunities in the collateral bookbinder trade as well. The expanding field of Yiddish journalism and job printing soon became saturated, but openings in general printing mounted in one of the city's top industries.[10]

[9] *Fifth Annual Report, Bureau of Statistics of Labor, State of New York*, p. 220; *Sixth Annual Report, Bureau of Statistics of Labor, State of New York*, p. 829; E. S. Martin, "East Side Considerations," *Harper's Magazine*, 40:861 (May 1898); A. Cahan, *Bleter fun mayn lebn* (New York, 1926), II, 95; *Arbeiter Zeitung*, February 10, 1893; Markens, *Hebrews*, p. 162; *Forward*, July 20, August 24, 1906, June 21, 1907, April 4, 1910, October 16, 1911, February 8, 1914; *University Settlement Studies* (October 1906), pp. 24–25.

[10] G. Weinstein, *The Ardent Eighties* (New York, 1928), p. 11f; S. Sheinfeld, *Zikhroines fun a shriftzetzer* (New York, 1946), p. 61; S. Sheinfeld, *Fuftsig yor geshikhte* (New York, 1938), pp. 48–49; *Thirteenth Census, 1910: Manufactures Reports for Principal Industries* (Washington, 1913); pp. 910–912; cf. A. F. Hinrichs, *The Printing Industry in New York and Its Environs* (New York, 1924), p. 16; H. S. Linfield, "Jews in Trade Unions in the City of New York," *The Communal Organization of the Jews in the United States, 1927* (New York, 1930), p. 129; *Forward*, December 22, 1915.

THE GREAT JEWISH METIER

Most immigrants, unequipped to earn a livelihood in trade or skilled industry, arrived in a period when the manufacture of such consumer goods as clothing, cigars, and household wares was becoming less skilled. As mechanization routinized production, dexterity, speed, patience, and regular habits became the prime work requisites. So endowed, undersized and underfed immigrants could compete without handicap. And for the shrewd and aggressive the closeness of workshop to sales counter opened doors into the world of business.

Jewish immigrants, separated by religious prescriptions, customs, and language from the surrounding city, found a place in the clothing industry where the initial shock of contact with a bewildering world was tempered by a familiar milieu. Work, however arduous, did not forbid the performance of religious duties, the honoring of the Sabbath, and the celebration of religious festivals. Laboring in small units, immigrants could preserve the integrity of their families.

The homes of the Hebrew quarters are its workshop also . . . You are made fully aware of it before you have travelled the length of a single block in any of these East Side streets, by the whir of a thousand sewing-machines, worked at high pressure from earliest dawn till mind and muscle give out together. Every member of the family, from the youngest to the oldest, bears a hand, shut in the qualmy rooms, where meals are cooked and clothing washed and dried besides, the livelong day. It is not unusual to find a dozen persons—men, women, and children—at work in a single small room.

However wretched the externals, here a measure of self-respect was attainable, while hearts beat and minds stirred with hopes and thoughts of a brighter future.

Despite the roles that poverty and lack of skill forced them to assume, few Jews were to be found employed at day labor.

These jobs were filled by physically more powerful immigrants of peasant stock, who flowed into the city. Certainly many young men, upon first landing in New York, put in a few weeks or months in day labor upon the docks, in factories, and on the railroad; some even idealized heavy physical labor, but their ardor soon passed when faced with reality. Others were employed on major bridge and tunnel construction projects. But as soon as they were able to regain their equilibrium they turned to more promising fields. A study based upon the occupational table of the United States Census of 1900 concluded that only 2 per cent of the Russians in New York were employed at common labor, while 10 per cent of the foreign-born and their sons were so employed.[11]

---

[11] *Report, Select Committee, H. R., Importation of Contract Laborers, Paupers, Convicts, and Other Classes* (Washington, 1889), p. 507; B. Weinstein, *Di idishe unions in amerika* (New York, 1929), p. 44; Sheinfeld, *Fuftzig yor geshikhte,* pp. 83–84; *Forward,* December 10, 1904; Jacob Planken, "The Jew as Proletarian," *United Hebrew Trades Souvenir Journal* (New York, 1933), p. 28; S. Rubinow, "Economic Conditions of the Jews in Russia," *United States Department of Labor* (Washington, 1907), pp. 502, 532; Frank J. Sheridan, "Italian, Slavic and Hungarian Unskilled Immigrant Laborers in the United States," *United States Department of Labor* (Washington, 1907), pp. 403–404; Maurice Fishberg, *The Jews* (London, 1911), p. 398.

THE NEGRO AT WORK:
BLACKS IN HARLEM, 1865–1920

SETH M. SCHEINER

LACKING freedom of choice during their period of enslavement, New York's Negroes were severely limited in their selection of an occupation. A few Negroes had been trained

REPRINTED by permission of New York University Press from *Negro Mecca: A History of the Negro in New York City, 1865–1920* by Seth M. Scheiner, Chap. 2. Copyright © 1965 by New York University.

as artisans during their years of slavery. But given the nature of slavery, the average Negro was prepared for little more than domestic service outside of farming. Nor was there any appreciable improvement in the Negro's status once the shackles of slavery had been broken. Freedom of person did not mean freedom of choice. His former master once again determined the Negro's occupational status. The Negro was left those jobs that whites considered distasteful and menial.[1]

Most New York Negroes worked as domestics and common laborers in the pre-Civil War period. They could be found in the homes of affluent whites working as butlers and coachmen, cooks and waiters, gardeners and general domestics. In the public sphere, they were employed as bootblacks, porters, waiters, cooks, longshoremen, hod carriers, seamen, washerwomen, dressmakers, and seamstresses.[2] At first Negroes and whites worked side by side, but before long prejudice developed and whites refused to work with the man of the darker skin. Economic competition drove a wedge between the two groups. Fearing the occupational challenge of the Negro laborer, white workers pressured the state into refusing licenses to Negro carmen and porters. With the great migration of Irish immigrants to New York City in the 1840s and 1850s, prejudice between white and Negro workers increased. The German immigrant, on the other hand, who was not the Negro's economic competitor, never developed the antipathy for Negroes that the Irish newcomer manifested.[3]

[1] George E. Haynes, *Negro at Work in New York* (New York, 1912), p. 47; Edwin Olson, "Negro Slavery in New York" (Unpublished Ph.D. dissertation, New York University, 1938), pp. 57–58; *Weekly Anglo-African*, August 12, 1865.

[2] Sterling D. Spero and Abram I. Harris, *The Black Worker: the Negro and the Labor Movement* (New York, 1931), pp. 12–18; Haynes, *Negro at Work*, pp. 67–68.

[3] Robert Ernst, "The Economic Status of the New York City Negro, 1850–1863," *Negro History Bulletin*, 12 (March, 1949), pp. 131–32; Arnett G. Lindsay, "The Economic Condition of the Negroes of New York Prior to 1861," *Journal of Negro History*, VI (April, 1921), 193–94; Leon F. Litwack, *North of Slavery: The Negro in the Free States* (Chicago, 1961), pp. 159, 167.

Initially, white employers professed a preference for Negro to Irish workers. The Irish were considered too truculent and independent. No doubt Protestant employers looked contemptuously upon Irish-Catholic employees. Advertisements in the New York press reflected this sentiment: "A Cook, Washer, and Ironer; who perfectly understands her business; any color or country except Irish." [4] Thus, two of New York society's outcasts struggled for the more menial jobs reserved for them. They developed a mutual antipathy that manifested itself in a number of pitched battles. When the Irishman forced the Negro out of certain jobs, the darker race was impelled to resort to strikebreaking when Irish employees went on strike. This precipitated a number of riots that culminated in the great draft riots of 1863. [5]

Despite the early preference of white employers for Negro labor, the Negro was displaced gradually by the Irish newcomer. In addition, economic innovations created new jobs that were filled by the Irish rather than the Negro. By 1850 there were more Irish servants than the entire Negro population of the city, whereas twenty years earlier Negro labor constituted a majority of the servant class. Hence, the Negro's already precarious position was made even more insecure. Still, a few Negroes were able to enter the skilled trades. Of the 3,688 employed Negroes in 1855, some 200 were in the trades. Most of these trained workers engaged in occupations that catered to the Negro community. Ministers, teachers, druggists, doctors, and musicians comprised the bulk of the skilled Negro class. [6] Discussions of Negro workers, however, were limited to those who serviced the white community, for

[4] Ernst, "The Economic Status of the New York City Negro," p. 140.

[5] Litwack, *North of Slavery*, pp. 163–64; Albon P. Man, Jr., "Labor Competition and the New York Draft Riots," *Journal of Negro History*, XXXVI (October, 1951), 384–402.

[6] Ernst, "The Economic Status of the New York City Negro," p. 142; Litwack, *North of Slavery*, pp. 165–66; Samuel R. Scottron, "The Industrial and Professional Pursuits of the Colored People of Old New York," *Colored American Magazine*, XIII (October, 1907), 265–67.

the white commentator rarely entered the Negro's world. The Negro caterer was the man most whites turned to when they planned a banquet. On the streets of the city, the Negro coachman, in private employment, was a common sight. A white man wishing a haircut or shave would most likely have gone to a Negro barber. Serving the white man, according to the Negro barber, caterer, and coachman, was more respectable than catering to the Negro community. Believing themselves superior to other Negro workers, these men formed their own organizations. Negro caterers, for instance, established the United Waiters' Mutual Beneficial Association in 1869. Despite its title, waiters were not admitted until the 1880s. The organization had a threefold purpose: first, it was to provide sick and death benefits for its members; second, it sought to maintain a high degree of proficiency among Negro caterers; and third, it served as an outlet through which its members manifested their higher status.[7]

After the Civil War, catering, barbering, and coaching among Negroes declined. The majority of the city's Negro domestics worked as waiters and servants. In 1874, an Irish traveler, Fergus Ferguson, commented on the frequent employment of Negro waiters in New York City. This observation was confirmed four years later by another visitor to Gotham, Sir George Campbell. Other foreign visitors commented on the high quality of service given by Negro waiters. According to George Rose, visiting the city in 1868, the Negro was "far better mannered and attentive" than the white servant. In 1870 another traveler touring the United States was pleasantly surprised to find Negro waiters "more active and obliging" than Irish waiters.[8]

[7] *Weekly Anglo-African*, August 12, 1865; J. Gilmer Speed, "The Negro in New York," *Harper's Weekly*, 44 (December 22, 1900), p. 1249; *New York Times*, March 2, 1869; Haynes, *Negro at Work*, p. 68.

[8] *Weekly Anglo-African*, August 12, 1865; *National Anti-Slavery Standard*, January 15, 1870; Fergus Ferguson, *From Glasgow to Missouri and Back* (Glasgow, 1879), p. 24; George Campbell, *White and Black: the Outcome of a Visit to the United States* (London, 1879), p.

The minority of New York City Negroes who worked outside of the domestic field in the late 1860s were generally unskilled laborers. According to a report of the National Labor Convention of 1869, the few skilled Negro workers were employed in such occupations as tobacco twisting, carpentry, masonry, and printing. However, this was a small number when compared to the 500 Negro longshoremen working on New York City's waterfront in that year. Before the Civil War, Negroes had been used as strikebreakers on the city's piers and a few of these men were retained after a strike was settled. By 1865 Negroes had secured a small place on the docks of New York City.[9]

A change, though, occurred in the Negro's economic status in the post-Civil War period. In 1884 the Negro *Globe* reported that many hotels had replaced Negro workers with white help. French, German, and Irish immigrants had been substituted for many Negro coachmen, footmen, valets, chambermaids, and waiters. Edward Money, an Englishman visiting New York in 1885, noted that Negroes were employed in second-class hotels. Jacob Riis wrote in 1890 that the Negro barber was becoming a "thing of the past."[10]

Though foreign-born workers had replaced some Negro domestics in the 1880s, most Negroes continued to work in the domestic and personal service field. According to the Census of 1890—the first such report to list the occupations of New York City Negroes—about 70 per cent of the city's Negro men were in domestic and personal service. On the other hand, only 20 per cent of the city's male population and 25

206; George Rose, *The Great Country; or, Impressions of America* (London, 1868), p. 70; James Macauley, "First Impressions of America and Its People," *The Leisure Hour*, XX (1871), 206.

[9] *National Anti-Slavery Standard*, January 15, 1870; *New York Times*, March 2, 1869; Spero and Harris, *The Black Worker*, p. 197. Negroes usually were relegated to the least skilled jobs on the waterfront. Charles B. Barnes, *The Longshoremen* (New York, 1915), p. 3.

[10] *New York Globe*, March 8, 29, 1884; Edward Money, *The Truth About America* (London, 1886), p. 41; Jacob Riis, *How the Other Half Lives* (New York, 1890), p. 149.

per cent of the foreign-born males were so employed. Negro women also were employed as domestic servants to a greater degree than the other elements of Gotham's population.[11] In 1890 most Negro domestics were employed as servants, waiters, laundresses, and janitors. Negroes constituted 19.9 per cent of the city's male servants and 5.3 per cent of the female servants. Some 20.3 per cent of the laundresses in New York City were Negro as were 15.1 per cent of the janitors. Only 30 per cent of the city's Negro men, however, made their living outside of the domestic and personal service fields. This was far less than the 75 per cent for foreign-born males and the 80 per cent of the total male population. Most Negro men were unskilled workers. Some 68 per cent of those working in the trade and transportation field were draymen, hackmen, teamsters, hostlers, porters, packers, and messengers. As the Colored Mission had remarked in 1885, Negroes were "shut out from nearly all of the trades." [12]

The European immigrant was the main competitor of the Negro. In 1890 the foreign-born element of New York City accounted for at least 50 per cent of the persons employed in occupations that contained a high percentage of Negroes. Not only did Negroes still vie with the Irish and German immigrant for jobs, but they now had to compete, to a lesser degree, with the Italians. Between 1890 and 1900 Italians became New York's bootblacks and barbers, positions that had been the province of the Negro. In addition, French cooks and German waiters replaced Negro help in the better New York restaurants. But foreign displacement of the Negro occurred in only a few areas. Negro workers continued to enter most of the positions they had held in previous years, and in those did so at a faster rate than did the European immigrant.[13]

[11] *Eleventh Census, Population,* I, pp. 640, 704.

[12] *Eleventh Census, Population,* I, 640, 704; New York Colored Mission, *Annual Report for 1885* (New York, 1886), p. 10.

[13] *Eleventh Census, Population,* I, 640, 704; Speed, "The Negro in New York," pp. 1249–50; *New York Age,* May 16, 1891; *New York*

Between 1890 and 1900 male Negro domestics increased by 109 per cent as opposed to 45 per cent for the foreign-born male. In 1900 Negroes constituted a larger percentage of the city's draymen, hostlers, housekeepers, and servants than in 1890, while the foreign-born proportion of workers in these occupations declined. Only among the city's barbers and seamstresses was there a decrease in the Negro's share and an increase in the foreign-born portion. Thus, in the 1890s the migration of southern and eastern Europeans to New York City failed to result in any sizable displacement of Negroes from occupations that they had acquired in earlier years. When they were supplanted, it was by west European immigrants—the Irish, German, and French. As in the 1880s, they continued to replace Negro servants and cooks in the better hotels and restaurants of the city. It was only as barbers, bootblacks, and whitewashers that the Italian gave the Negro serious competition, for most Italians entered the unskilled occupations of trade and industry where only a few Negroes worked.[14]

Though few Negroes were employed outside of the domestic trades, the number of Negroes in the professions, trades, and industry increased between 1890 and 1900. Negro professionals expanded by over 500 per cent as opposed to about a 200 per cent rise for both the entire population of the city and the foreign-born element. In the trade, transportation, and manufacturing fields the Negro also increased at a more rapid rate than the other major elements of New York City's population. These percentages, nevertheless, can be misleading. For example, Negro professionals increased by 600 persons,

---

Times, November 17, 1901. H. D. Bloch, "The New York City Negro and Occupational Eviction, 1860–1910," International Review of Social History, V (Part 1, 1960), 28–32, has taken a position opposite the one presented here. Mr. Bloch has made the conclusion that because there was competition between Negroes and European immigrants for jobs the Negro was displaced. The mere existence of competition did not mean displacement.

[14] Eleventh Census, Population, I, 640, 704; Twelfth Census, Occupations, pp. 634–41.

whereas foreign-born professionals rose by 12,000. For Negroes this was a greater percentage growth; however, as indicated, they were proceeding from a smaller base. Of the 8,000
Negroes employed outside the domestic field in 1900, a majority worked as unskilled laborers. For example, draymen,
hucksters, teamsters, messengers, and porters accounted for
79 per cent of the Negroes in the trade and transportation
field as opposed to 68 per cent in 1890. Thus, while the number of Negroes in the skilled trades had increased in actual
numbers between 1890 and 1900, their share of the city's
Negro working force had either decreased, or, at best, remained stationary.[15]

Oscar Handlin has taken the position that Negroes "had
made considerable progress" between 1870 and 1900. He has
asserted that "they had earned a minor but secure economic
position in the service trades of the city. There were few unskilled workers among them to compete for factory jobs
against the hordes of poor immigrants." While the findings of
this study cast doubt concerning the "secure position" of the
Negro domestic and his "considerable progress" between 1870
and 1900, they do agree with Professor Handlin's argument
that the small number of unskilled Negro factory workers limited the effect of the foreign-born laborer's competition. H. D.
Bloch, on the other hand, has argued that there was wholesale displacement of the Negro worker between 1870 and
1900. He also has made no mention of any economic progress
on the part of the Negro. As will be seen, the author takes a
position between Handlin and Bloch.[16]

Between 1900 and 1910 there was a decline in domestic
employment throughout the United States.[17] By 1910 male
Negro domestics were reduced to 50.3 per cent of New York

---

[15] *Eleventh Census, Population,* I, p. 640.

[16] Oscar Handlin, *The Newcomers* (Cambridge, 1959), p. 46; Bloch, "The
New York City Negro and Occupational Eviction," pp. 30–33.

[17] Harold U. Faulkner, *The Decline of Laissez Faire, 1897–1917*
(New York, 1951), p. 241.

City's Negro work force.[18] While Negro men engaged in the trades or manufacturing had increased by almost 100 per cent, those in domestic service decreased by about 4 per cent. Although some 1,700 had become waiters or servants between 1890 and 1900, less than 250 entered those occupations between 1900 and 1910. This reflected the movement of Negro men from the home and restaurant to the factory and the store. The years spent by the Negro in domestic service, it appears, may have prepared him for industrial labor. As Harold U. Faulkner has written, "much personal service had become industrialized" between 1900 and 1910. It must be remembered, though, that the majority of Negro men continued to work as domestics. In fact, the city's domestic work force contained a higher percentage of Negro workers in 1910 than in 1900. The vast majority of Negro women, too, still were working in domestic service. Most New York City Negroes, therefore, were still domestic workers; however, by 1910 there was a distinct tendency on the part of Negro men to enter into the trades and industry. The number of male Negroes listed as engaged in manufacturing and mechanical pursuits increased from 1,774 in 1900 to 4,504 in 1910, and the percentage of Negroes so employed from about 7 per cent to 14 per cent of the total Negro working force.[19] Hence, to a greater degree than is often supposed, Negroes had begun to enter the industrial life of New York City during the early 1900s rather than the World War I years.[20]

[18] *Eleventh Census, Population*, I, pp. 640, 704; Bloch, "The New York City Negro and Occupational Eviction," p. 36, has concluded that 70.1 per cent of the city's Negro population were domestics. This is correct when the figures for men and women are combined; however, a clearer picture of the Negro worker is obtained when the sexes are studied separately.

[19] *Twelfth Census, Occupations*, pp. 634–41; *Thirteenth Census, Population*, IV, 571–74; Faulkner, *Decline of Laissez Faire*, p. 241.

[20] Faulkner, *Decline of Laissez Faire*, p. 100; John Hope Franklin, *From Slavery to Freedom: a History of American Negroes* (rev. ed.; New York, 1960), p. 464.

In the first decade of the twentieth century, more Negroes became skilled artisans than in any previous decade since the Civil War. This large increase in actual numbers, however, only resulted in a small growth in the percentage of Negroes engaged in skilled jobs. Negro entrance into the trades as well as industry was restricted to some degree by foreign competition. Between 1900 and 1910 Negroes had become far more conscious of their foreign competitors than in the last thirty-five years of the nineteenth century. European immigrants continued to be at least 50 per cent of those employed in occupations that contained a large portion of New York City's Negro population. Comparison with earlier census reports, however, is not possible. The 1910 Census gave a more detailed listing of occupations than any previous report, and because of this change comparison with earlier documents has been impossible. For example, longshoremen were listed in the 1910 Census; however, in the reports for 1890 and 1900 they were included in the broad category of common laborers. Consequently, one must turn to the opinions of Negroes and whites of the 1900s to determine the degree of competition between Negroes and European immigrants.[21]

In 1904 the *Tribune* commented on the "persistence" of European immigrants in "seeking and keeping employment." Hungarians, Bohemians, and Italians, according to the newspaper, were the main competitors of the Negro. In the same year, Samuel Scottron, a Negro businessman, noted that Italians and Greeks had replaced Negro waiters. D. Macon Webster, a Negro lawyer, told the National Negro Business League Convention of 1905 that the New York Negro experienced his severest economic rivalry from immigrants. One year later Mary Ovington reported that "no first class hotels" and few "good restaurants" employed Negro help. William Archer, traveling through the United States in the same year

[21] *Twelfth Census, Occupations,* pp. 636, 638; *Thirteenth Census, Population,* IV, 571–74.

in which Mary Ovington wrote her article, observed that Negroes were "no longer at the best hotels and clubs." [22] In the first decade of the twentieth century, therefore, southern and eastern Europeans had replaced the immigrant from western Europe as the chief economic rival of the Negro. In the 1900s the "new" immigrants gave the Negro more serious competition as waiters, servants, and stewards than the west Europeans, for, while the Negro portion in these trades was declining, the foreign-born share was increasing. In addition, it appears that they vied with the Negro for industrial occupations as well as domestic jobs.[23]

Following the outbreak of World War I, the massive flow of foreign immigrants to the United States came to a virtual halt. Negroes entered industry to fill both the gap left by the decrease in foreign immigration and the needs of the expanding American industrial machine. James Weldon Johnson, Negro author, poet, musical composer, social critic, and race leader, reported that the demand for Negro labor was so great that the members of his race found little trouble in obtaining employment.[24] Negro women for the first time entered industry in large numbers. Employers who had never before used Negro labor were compelled to employ the black worker. As a result, the number of New York Negroes in the manufacturing, mechanical, trade, and transportation fields more than doubled in the decade 1910–1920. The proportion of employed male Negroes in these fields rose from 43.9 per cent in 1910 to 56.4 per cent in 1920. At the same time, the proportion of Negro men employed as domestics fell from 50.3 in 1910 to 37.4 in 1920. The war years also had their effect on Negro women. There was a decided decline in the

[22] *New York Tribune,* August 14, 1904; *New York Age,* August 24, 1905; Mary White Ovington, "The Negro in the Trade Unions in New York." *Annals of the American Academy of Political and Social Science,* XXVII (June, 1906), 557; William Archer, *Through Afro-America: an English Reading of the Race Problem* (London, 1910), p. 7.
[23] *Thirteenth Census, Population,* IV, 571–74.
[24] *New York Age,* June 7, 1917.

proportion of New York's Negro women working in domestic service—from 86.9 per cent in 1910 to 74.2 per cent in 1920. Consequently, there was a rise in the number of women in industry. New York Negro women in manufacturing and mechanical pursuits increased almost fourfold in the decade. Nevertheless, the smaller proportion of the Negro population engaged in domestic service had increased in its share of the city's domestic work force. Where Negro men constituted 8 per cent of the city's domestics in 1890, in 1910 they accounted for 11 per cent, and 14 per cent in 1920. A similar trend was evidenced among Negro women. But it was not as waiters and servants that Negroes showed the greatest increase—in fact, in these occupations the Negro proportion declined—it was in the more menial fields such as janitoring and portering that they made their greatest gains.[25]

Although more Negroes than ever were entering skilled trades, a still larger number were finding positions that required less training. Skilled workers accounted for 53 per cent the Negroes in manufacturing and mechanical pursuits in 1910, but fell to 48 per cent in 1920. The difference was filled by the semi-skilled and unskilled.[26] Negroes had entered new fields, but, in general, they were restricted to the lower paying and least skilled positions. Even many of the new-won positions in the skilled trades were limited to servicing the Negro community. Economic progress for the Negro race in the fifty-five years since the Civil War came to only a few. Many of the positions that Negroes had held in previous years, especially in domestic service, became the province of other groups. New York Negroes still found themselves restricted to the more menial occupations.

[25] *New York Age*, January 4, 1912; *New York Herald*, December 10, 1911; Consumers' League of the City of New York, *Report for 1918* (New York, 1919), pp. 6–8. George E. Haynes, "The Negro at Work, a Development of the War and a Problem of Reconstruction," *Review of Reviews*, LIX (August, 1919), 390.
[26] *Thirteenth Census, Population*, IV, 571–74; *Fourteenth Census, Population*, IV, 1157–62.

Foreign competition not only displaced the Negro from certain jobs, but was one factor in limiting the Negro's entrance into the skilled trades. Discrimination, however, appears to have had a greater effect than competition on excluding Negroes from the skilled trades. Throughout the fifty-five year period between 1865 and 1920, attempts by Negroes to enter the skilled occupations were met with constant obstructions. In 1868 a Brooklynite, Frederick Belson, remarked that Negroes were excluded from the mechanical trades. According to the Colored Mission in 1879, Negroes were "entirely excluded from the more lucrative branches of employment" and were "debarred from the trades." One year later, the Mission reported that "many of the various industries open to the foreigner" were closed "to the native colored man." [27] Restrictions upon the Negro's entrance into the skilled trades continued during the 1880s. In 1885 the Colored Mission took this view of the Negro's economic predicament:

The condition of the colored people of New York City is one that should claim the serious consideration of our citizens . . . shut out from nearly all of the trades (on account of color) there seems to be no career open to them except that of a less lucrative character which affords them a bare subsistence.[28]

Though some Negroes in the 1880s were employed as carpenters and masons, Negro leaders considered the number too small and contended that further entrance was next to impossible. In 1890 Jacob Riis stated that the average Negro was forced to take the "lower level of menial service"; but he blamed the Negro's "past tradition and natural love of ease" for his condition.[29]

[27] Frederick Belson, *Considerations in the Interests of the Colored People* (Brooklyn, 1868), p. 4; New York Colored Mission, *Annual Report for 1879* (New York, 1880), p. 5, and *Annual Report for 1880* (New York, 1881), p. 5.

[28] New York Colored Mission, *Annual Report for 1885*, p. 10.

[29] *New York Age*, March 16, 1889; Riis, *How Other Half Lives*, p. 149.

During the 1890s some commentators reported Negro advancement in the trades and professions. In 1891 the *Age* noted that Negroes were entering the professions in greater numbers; however, it complained that there "was a scarcity of skilled laborers . . . in comparison to the vast number" of Negroes engaged in the professions. "Those who imagine that the Negro population of this city is composed of peddlers, whitewashers, and bootblacks," wrote the *Times* in 1895, "would be considerably enlightened if they could observe the real progress which the race has made." At about the same time, the Colored Mission observed that "prejudice against" the Negro was "steadily waning" into the past.[30] But not all comments indicated that the Negro had improved his position in the 1890s. The *Age* in 1891 still complained that the Negro was limited to "menial employment." According to the *New York Post* in 1900, Negroes were excluded from most employments. In the same year, J. Gilmer Speed contended that the prospects for the New York Negro were not "very encouraging"; in fact, they were "less" bright than they ever had been.[31]

In the first two decades of the twentieth century, observers continued to mention both the Negro's exclusion from and entrance into the skilled trades. W. E. B. Du Bois, writing for the *Times* in 1901, complained of the obstacles "placed in the way" of attempts by Negroes to improve their position. A Joshua Barton, in a letter published in the *Tribune* of March 25, 1901, asserted that Negro "opportunities for advancement" were practically at a standstill. Three years later, the *Tribune* agreed with Barton's comments, declaring that "better class" Negroes were limited to working as elevator operators or porters. Also in 1904, Charles Morris, minister of the Abyssinian Baptist Church, spoke of the "barred doors" that New York Negroes faced in labor and business. "Outside of domestic

[30] *New York Age*, February 28, 1891; *New York Times*, July 14, 1895; *Milestones* (April, 1896), unpaged.
[31] *New York Age*, September 5, 1891; *New York Post*, August 17, 1900; Speed, "The Negro in New York," p. 1249.

employment," declared another Negro clergyman in 1913, "there is very little opportunity . . . except within the limited circle of their own people." Negroes complained that they were excluded from public transportation employment above the rank of porter. "The Negro gets a chance to work only when there is no one else," wrote the *New Republic* in 1916 of the New York Negro's occupational plight. "He is the last served; his are the industrial leavings and scraps." [32]

Negro leaders such as the educator William L. Bulkley, writing in 1906, contended that employment restrictions had a deleterious effect on Negro youths. The Negro boy had run "up against a stone wall in his attempts to learn a trade," argued Bulkley. Negro women, too, found the factory door closed to them, declared Mary Ovington.[33] Even when Negro women entered industry, they were limited to the "most poorly paid and the least desirable kinds of work." Many employers admitted that they employed the Negro female only when they could find no one else.[34] Though the prejudice of employers and even unions may have restricted the employment of Negro women in skilled jobs, their lack of training for industry as well as the trades was a serious impediment to their economic progress. Limited in the past to domestic service and the most menial positions in other fields, they lacked the background that was needed in the trades. But again, it was prejudice rather than the female's own predilection that was responsible for her inadequate training. For where there was no employment opportunity, there was little motivation to seek training.[35]

[32] *New York Times*, November 17, 1901, and June 15, 1904; *New York Tribune*, August 14, 1904; *New York World*, August 17, 1918; "The Superfluous Negro," *New Republic*, VII (June 24, 1916), 187.

[33] William L. Bulkley, "The Industrial Condition of the Negro in New York City," *Annals of the American Academy of Political and Social Science*, XXVII (June, 1906), 592; Mary White Ovington, *Half a Man* (New York, 1911), pp. 43, 162.

[34] Louise P. Kennedy, *Negro Peasant Turns Cityward* (New York, 1930), pp. 90–91.

[35] Consumers' League, *Report of 1918*, pp. 6–8.

Those Negroes who had received training in the skilled trades fared little better than the untutored members of their race. Negro artisans who migrated to New York City in the 1900s experienced difficulty in obtaining jobs in their chosen occupations.[36] In 1907 the *Age* warned southern Negroes to "think carefully" before coming to New York. It asserted that native New York Negroes were severely limited in their choice of "responsible positions of any sort." The steady stream of newcomers only complicated a difficult situation, the paper concluded. This opinion was supported one year later by Samuel Scottron. The Negro businessman said that Negro newcomers were arriving in the city "faster than they can be assimilated and adjusted." These people have discovered that "expressions of sympathy" are more "plentiful than employment," Scottron declared. According to a report of the *Times* in 1917, only one of about 2,800 skilled Negroes obtained employment in his chosen occupation.[37]

Though most Negroes in the first twenty years of the twentieth century experienced difficulty in their search for better employment opportunities, a few were able to enter the skilled trades. In 1907 the *Colored American Magazine* asserted that "despite the general belief to the contrary, now and then" a Negro mechanic was employed in the construction industry. According to Mary Ovington, by 1909 some Negroes had obtained skilled jobs. In support of Mary Ovington's observation, the *Age* in 1910 reported that Negroes were "not only holding their own," but they were "making progress." George Haynes, who was making a study of Manhattan's Negroes at this time, concluded that the "slight" entrance of Negroes into the trades was "prophetic of a proba-

[36] Bulkley, "Industrial Conditions of the Negro in New York City," p. 591; Helen A. Tucker, "Negro Craftsmen in New York," *Southern Workman*, XXXVI (October, 1907), 545–51 and XXXVIII (March, 1908), 130–44.
[37] *New York Age*, February 14, April 4, 1907, and May 24, 1908; *New York Times*, October 7, 1917.

ble widening scope of the field of employment open to them." [38]

Because of the opportunities afforded by industry during World War I, Negroes entered skilled jobs in greater numbers than ever before. But these gains were few. When compared to the status of most Negroes, they were more illusory than real. By 1920 the vast majority of the city's Negro population remained outside or on the periphery of the skilled trades.[39] The few Negroes who entered the skilled occupations were a small portion of the expanding Negro population of Gotham. This fact was illustrated by the Negro artisans who migrated to New York City but were unable to find employment in the fields for which they had been trained. Thus, although the Negro skilled worker increased in actual numbers, the proportion of skilled workers in the city's work force had expanded only slightly.

Even those gains made in the unskilled and semiskilled industrial positions during World War I were not guaranteed. Negro leaders feared that a renewed wave of European migration to the United States would deprive their race of those jobs they had obtained during the war. For this reason some Negroes supported immigration restriction proposals.[40] Still another threat to the Negro's industrial position was the returning white soldier. The first to feel the effects of a change from a war to a peace economy were Negro women. Negro war veterans, too, discovered that jobs were hard to come by. In cooperation with the Urban League, governmental agencies established employment offices in Harlem to help returning soldiers as well as civilian Negroes in their postwar adjustment. Although some Negroes retained those industrial positions secured during the war, others found them-

[38] *Colored American Magazine,* XIII (August, 1907), 87; Ovington, *Half a Man,* pp. 107–108; *New York Age,* August 18, 1910; Haynes, *Negro at Work,* p. 57.
[39] *Fourteenth Census, Population,* IV, 1157–62.
[40] *New York Age,* November 23, 1918, and February 8, 1919.

selves the "first fired and the last hired" when the nation was struck by a recession.[41]

Unemployment was not a new phenomenon for the Negro worker; it was something that he had faced for years. In the nineteenth century the seasonal nature of his work made for unemployment. In 1869 the *Times* reported that job opportunities were better for Negro servants and waiters during the summer than the winter. This compelled Negroes to live for an entire year on one season's pay, the paper asserted. The Colored Mission in 1871 took a position directly opposite to that of the *Times*. It claimed that Negro unemployment was greatest in the summer when the well-to-do families who used Negro help left the city.[42] Hence, it may have been possible for a Negro to find a job in the city for the winter and at the resorts in the summer. But the concern of the *Times* and the Mission for the unemployed Negro indicated that not all Negroes found both summer and winter work; in fact, it appears that Negro unemployment was high throughout the year. When the economic situation of the city deteriorated, the Negro faced more difficult times. During the panic of 1893, according to the Colored Mission, the Negro was subjected to trying days—"some were found actually dying of want." Negroes were so hard hit by the recession of 1915 that the Mayor's Unemployment Committee worked with the Urban League to assist Negro workers. Relief was provided, work projects were established, and some training of the unemployed was conducted by the League. When the industrial

[41] *Ibid.*, January 24, 1917; December 21, 1918; January 1, 1921; *Survey*, XLII (September 27, 1919), 900; *Crisis*, XVII (May, 1919), 13–14; Haynes, "The Negro at Work: a Development of the War and a Problem of Reconstruction," p. 390; United States Department of Labor, Women's Bureau, *Negro Women in Industry* (Washington, D.C., 1920), p. 15; U.S. Department of Labor, Division of Negro Economics, *The Negro at Work During the World War and During Reconstruction* (Washington 1921), pp. 95–96; Kennedy, *Negro Peasant Turns City-ward*, pp. 130–31.

[42] *New York Times*, March 2, 1869; New York Colored Mission, *Annual Report for 1871*, p. 8.

slump of 1921 occurred, Howard D. Gregg, industrial secretary of the Urban League, reported that Negro workers were the first to feel its effects. Their late entrance into industrial occupations and the prevalence of unskilled workers among the race contributed to the high rate of Negro unemployment. . . .[43]

By 1920, therefore, more organizations than ever before were working in behalf of Negro laborers. Philanthropic agencies composed of whites as well as blacks showed a greater interest in the Negro. The Negro community, outside of some cooperation with whites, restricted its self-help activities to private schools, private employment agencies, and the church. Of the three, the church contributed the least.[44] Employment agencies became a thriving business for their owners and to a lesser degree helped the Negro worker.[45] A necessary service was performed by Negro trade schools. Mme Beck's School of Dressmaking held day and evening classes. Negroes interested in chauffeuring and repairing automobiles could attend such trade schools as the Harlem River Auto School and Repair Shop, the Broadway Auto School, and the Cosmopolitan Automobile School.[46] But these educational institutions, despite all their efforts, could not fill the needs of a population that was deprived of training and employment because of the color of its skin. Little could be done for the Negro's economic plight before the most influential elements of the American economic system and the American public changed their attitudes toward the Negro. It is doubtful whether these agencies would broaden their outlook by themselves. Negro organizations and governmental agencies would

[43] New York Colored Mission, *Annual Report for 1893* (New York, 1894), pp. 14, 17; *New York Age*, April 22, 1915, and October 25, 1917; National League on Urban Conditions, *Report for 1913–1914 and 1914–1915*, p. 14.

[44] *New York Age*, February 19, April 30, 1914; *Crisis*, IV (May, 1912), 24–25.

[45] *Colored American Review*, (October, 1, 1915), 8–9, 15.

[46] *Ibid.*, I (December, 1915), 13; *New York Age*, March 2, 1911, and February 13, 1913; *Crusades*, V (November, 1921), 3.

have to conduct a massive campaign in behalf of Negro equality before there would be any appreciable improvement in the Negro's occupational situation.

CONTADINI IN CHICAGO
RUDOLPH J. VECOLI

IN *The Uprooted* [1] Oscar Handlin attempted an overarching interpretation of European peasant society and of the adjustment of emigrants from that society to the American environment. This interpretation is open to criticism on the grounds that it fails to respect the unique cultural attributes of the many and varied ethnic groups which sent immigrants to the United States. Through an examination of the south Italians, both in their Old World setting and in Chicago, this article will indicate how Handlin's portrayal of the peasant as immigrant does violence to the character of the *contadini* (peasants) of the Mezzogiorno. [2]

The idealized peasant village which Handlin depicts in *The Uprooted* did not exist in the southern Italy of the late nineteenth century. Handlin's village was an harmonious social entity in which the individual derived his identity and being from the community as a whole; the ethos of his village was one of solidarity, communality, and neighborliness. [3] The typical south Italian peasant, however, did not live in a small village, but in a "rural city" with a population of thousands

FROM: Rudolph J. Vecoli. "Contadini in Chicago: A Critique of *The Uprooted*," *Journal of American History*, LI (December 1964), 404–417.

[1] Oscar Handlin, *The Uprooted* (Boston, 1951).

[2] The Mezzogiorno of Italy includes the southern part of continental Italy, i.e., the regions of Abruzzi e Molise, Campania, Puglia, Basilicata, Calabria, and the island of Sicily.

[3] *Uprooted*, 7–12.

or even tens of thousands.[4] Seeking refuge from brigands and malaria, the *contadini* huddled together in these hill towns, living in stone dwellings under the most primitive conditions and each day descending the slopes to work in the fields below.

Nor were these towns simple communities of agriculturists, for their social structure included the gentry and middle class as well as the peasants. Feudalism died slowly in southern Italy, and vestiges of this archaic social order were still visible in the attitudes and customs of the various classes. While the great landowners had taken up residence in the capital cities, the lesser gentry constituted the social elite of the towns. Beneath it in the social hierarchy were the professional men, officials, merchants, and artisans; at the base were the *contadini* who comprised almost a distinct caste. The upper classes lorded over and exploited the peasants whom they regarded as less than human. Toward the upper classes, the *contadini* nourished a hatred which was veiled by the traditional forms of deference.[5]

This is not to say that the south Italian peasants enjoyed a sense of solidarity either as a community or as a social class.

[4] On south Italian society see Edward C. Banfield, *The Moral Basis of a Backward Society* (Glencoe, Ill., 1958); Robert F. Foerster, *The Italian Emigration of Our Times* (Cambridge, 1919), 51–105; Leopoldo Franchetti and Sidney Sonnino, *La Sicilia nel 1876* (2 vols., Florence, 1925); Carlo Levi, *Christ Stopped at Eboli* (New York, 1947); Leonard W. Moss and Stephen C. Cappannari, "A Sociological and Anthropological Investigation of an Italian Rural Community" (mimeographed, Detroit, 1959); Luigi Villari, *Italian Life in Town and Country* (New York, 1902); Arrigo Serpieri, *La Guerra e le Classi Rurali Italiane* (Storia Economica e Sociale della Guerra Mondiale, Publicazioni della Fondazione Carnegie per la Pace Internazionale, Bari, 1930), 1–21; Friedrich Vöchting, *La Questione Meridionale* (Casa per il Mezzogiorno Studi e Testi 1, Naples, 1955); Phyllis H. Williams, *South Italian Folkways in Europe and America* (New Haven, 1938); Rocco Scotellaro, *Contadini del Sud* (Bari, 1955).

[5] The following thought, which Handlin attributes to the immigrant in America, would hardly have occurred to the oppressed *contadino:* "Could he here, as at home, expect the relationship of reciprocal goodness between master and men, between just employer and true employee?" *Uprooted,* 80.

Contadini in Chicago

Rather it was the family which provided the basis of peasant solidarity. Indeed, so exclusive was the demand of the family for the loyalty of its members that it precluded allegiance to other social institutions. This explains the paucity of voluntary associations among the peasantry. Each member of the family was expected to advance its welfare and to defend its honor, regardless of the consequences for outsiders. This singleminded attention to the interests of the family led one student of south Italian society to describe its ethos as one of "amoral familism." [6]

While the strongest ties were within the nuclear unit, there existed among the members of the extended family a degree of trust, intimacy, and interdependence denied to all others. Only through the ritual kinship of *comparaggio* (godparenthood) could non-relatives gain admittance to the family circle. The south Italian family was "father-dominated but mother-centered." The father as the head of the family enjoyed unquestioned authority over the household, but the mother provided the emotional focus for family life.

Among the various families of the *paese* (town), there were usually jealousies and feuds which frequently resulted in bloodshed. This atmosphere of hostility was revealed in the game of *passatella*, which Carlo Levi has described as "a peasant tournament of oratory, where interminable speeches reveal in veiled terms a vast amount of repressed rancor, hate, and rivalry." [7] The sexual code of the Mezzogiorno was also expressive of the family pride of the south Italians. When violations occurred, family honor required that the seducer

---

[6] Banfield, *Moral Basis of a Backward Society*, 10. In his study of a town in Basilicata, Banfield found that both gentry and peasants were unable to act "for any end transcending the immediate, material interest of the nuclear family." On the south Italian family see also Leonard W. Moss and Stephen C. Cappannari, "Patterns of Kinship, Comparaggio and Community in a South Italian Village," *Anthropological Quarterly,* XXXIII (Jan. 1960), 24–32; Leonard W. Moss and Walter H. Thomson, "The South Italian Family: Literature and Observations," *Human Organization,* XVIII (Spring 1959), 35–41.

[7] Levi, *Christ Stopped,* 179.

be punished. The south Italian was also bound by the tradition of personal vengeance, as in the Sicilian code of *omertà*. These cultural traits secured for southern Italy the distinction of having the highest rate of homicides in all of Europe at the turn of the century.[8] Such antisocial behavior, however, has no place in Handlin's scheme of the peasant community.

If the south Italian peasant regarded his fellow townsman with less than brotherly feeling, he viewed with even greater suspicion the stranger—which included anyone not native to the town. The peasants knew nothing of patriotism for the Kingdom of Italy, or of class solidarity with other tillers of the soil; their sense of affinity did not extend beyond town boundaries. This attachment to their native village was termed *campanilismo,* a figure of speech suggesting that the world of the *contadini* was confined within the shadow cast by his town campanile.[9] While this parochial attitude did not manifest itself in community spirit or activities, the sentiment of *campanilismo* did exert a powerful influence on the emigrants from southern Italy.

During the late nineteenth century, increasing population, agricultural depression, and oppressive taxes, combined with poor land to make life ever more difficult for the peasantry. Still, misery does not provide an adequate explanation of the great emigration which followed. For, while the peasants were equally impoverished, the rate of emigration varied widely from province to province. J. S. McDonald has suggested that the key to these differential rates lies in the differing systems of land tenure and in the contrasting sentiments of "individualism" and "solidarity" which they produced among the peasants.[10] From Apulia and the interior of Sicily

[8] Napoleone Colajanni, "Homicide and the Italians," *Forum,* XXXI (March 1901), 63–66.
[9] Richard Bagot, *The Italians of To-day* (Chicago, 1913), 87.
[10] J. S. McDonald, "Italy's Rural Social Structure and Emigration," *Occidente,* XII (Sept.–Oct. 1956), 437–55. McDonald concludes that where the peasantry's "aspirations for material betterment were ex-

where large-scale agriculture prevailed and cultivators' associations were formed, there was little emigration. Elsewhere in the South, where the peasants as small proprietors and tenants competed with one another, emigration soared. Rather than practicing communal agriculture as did Handlin's peasants, these *contadini*, both as cultivators and emigrants, acted on the principle of economic individualism, pursuing family and self-interest.

Handlin's peasants have other characteristics which do not hold true for those of southern Italy. In the Mezzogiorno, manual labor—and especially tilling the soil—was considered degrading. There the peasants did not share the reverence of Handlin's peasants for the land; rather they were "accustomed to look with distrust and hate at the soil." [11] No sentimental ties to the land deterred the south Italian peasants from becoming artisans, shopkeepers, or priests, if the opportunities presented themselves. Contrary to Handlin's peasants who meekly accepted their lowly status, the *contadini* were ambitious to advance the material and social position of their families. Emigration was one way of doing so. For the peasants in *The Uprooted* emigration was a desperate flight from disaster, but the south Italians viewed a sojourn in America as a means to acquire capital with which to purchase land, provide dowries for their daughters, and assist their sons to enter business or the professions.

If the design of peasant society described in *The Uprooted* is not adequate for southern Italy, neither is Handlin's description of the process of immigrant adjustment an accurate rendering of the experience of the *contadini*. For Handlin,

---

pressed in broad associative behavior, there was little emigration. Where economic aspirations were integrated only with the welfare of the individual's nuclear family, emigration rates were high." *Ibid.*, 454.

[11] Kate H. Claghorn, "The Agricultural Distribution of Immigrants," in U.S. Industrial Commission, *Reports* (19 vols., Washington, 1900–1902), XV, 496; Banfield, *Moral Basis of a Backward Society*, 37, 50, 69.

"the history of immigration is a history of alienation and its consequences." [12] In line with this theme, he emphasizes the isolation and loneliness of the immigrant, "the broken homes, interruptions of a familiar life, separation from known surroundings, the becoming a foreigner and ceasing to belong." While there is no desire here to belittle the hardships, fears, and anxieties to which the immigrant was subject, there are good reasons for contending that Handlin overstates the disorganizing effects of emigration and underestimates the tenacity with which the south Italian peasants at least clung to their traditional social forms and values.

Handlin, for example, dramatically pictures the immigrant ceasing to be a member of a solidary community and being cast upon his own resources as an individual.[13] But this description does not apply to the *contadini* who customarily emigrated as a group from a particular town, and, once in America, stuck together "like a swarm of bees from the same hive." [14] After working a while, and having decided to remain in America, they would send for their wives, children, and other relatives. In this fashion, chains of emigration were established between certain towns of southern Italy and Chicago.[15]

From 1880 on, the tide of emigration ran strongly from Italy to this midwestern metropolis where by 1920 the Italian population reached approximately 60,000.[16] Of these, the *con-*

[12] *Uprooted*, 4.
[13] *Ibid.*, 38.
[14] Pascal D'Angelo, *Son of Italy* (New York, 1924), 54.
[15] These chains of emigration are traced in Rudolph J. Vecoli, "Chicago's Italians Prior to World War I: A Study of Their Social and Economic Adjustments" (doctoral dissertation, University of Wisconsin, 1963), 71–234.
[16] On the Italians in Chicago see Vecoli, "Chicago's Italians"; U.S. Commissioner of Labor, *Ninth Special Report: The Italians in Chicago* (Washington, 1897); Frank O. Beck, "The Italian in Chicago," *Bulletin of the Chicago Department of Public Welfare*, II (Feb. 1919); Jane Addams, *Twenty Years at Hull-House* (New York, 1910); Giuseppe Giacosa, "Chicago e la sua colonia Italiana," *Nuova Antologia di Scienze, Lettere ed Arti*, Third Series, CXXVIII (March 1, 1893), 15–33; Giovanni E. Schiavo, *The Italians in Chicago* (Chicago, 1928); Alessandro

tadini of the Mezzogiorno formed the preponderant element. Because of the sentiment of *campanilismo*, there emerged not one "Little Italy" but some seventeen larger and smaller colonies scattered about the city. Each group of townsmen clustered by itself, seeking, as Jane Addams observed, to fill "an entire tenement house with the people from one village." [17] Within these settlements, the town groups maintained their distinct identities, practiced endogamy, and preserved their traditional folkways. Contrary to Handlin's dictum that the common experience of the immigrants was their inability to transplant the European village,[18] one is struck by the degree to which the *contadini* succeeded in reconstructing their native towns in the heart of industrial Chicago. As an Italian journalist commented:

Emigrating, the Italian working class brings away with it from the mother country all the little world in which they were accustomed to live; a world of traditions, of beliefs, of customs, of ideals of their own. There is no reason to marvel then that in this great center of manufacturing and commercial activity of North America our colonies, though acclimating themselves in certain ways, conserve the customs of their *paesi* of origin.[19]

If the south Italian immigrant retained a sense of belongingness with his fellow townsmen, the family continued to be the focus of his most intense loyalties. Among the male emigrants there were some who abandoned their families in Italy, but the many underwent harsh privations so that they might send money to their parents or wives. Reunited in Chicago the peasant family functioned much as it had at home;

Mastro-Valerio, "Remarks Upon the Italian Colony in Chicago," in *Hull-House Maps and Papers* (New York, 1895), 131–42; Harvey Warren Zorbaugh, *The Gold Coast and the Slum* (Chicago, 1929), 159–81; I. W. Howerth, "Are the Italians a Dangerous Class?" *Charities Review*, IV (Nov. 1894), 17–40.

[17] Jane Addams, *Newer Ideals of Peace* (New York, 1907), 67.

[18] *Uprooted*, 144.

[19] *L'Italia* (Chicago), Aug. 3, 1901. See also Anna Zaloha, "A Study of the Persistence of Italian Customs Among 143 Families of Italian Descent" (master's thesis, Northwestern University, 1937).

there appears to have been little of that confusion of roles depicted in *The Uprooted*. The husband's authority was not diminished, while the wife's subordinate position was not questioned. If dissension arose, it was when the children became
somewhat "Americanized"; yet there are good reasons for believing that Handlin exaggerates the estrangement of the second generation from its immigrant parentage. Nor did the extended family disintegrate upon emigration as is contended.
An observation made with respect to the Sicilians in Chicago
was generally true for the south Italians: "Intense family
pride . . . is the outstanding characteristic, and as the family
unit not only includes those related by blood, but those related by ritual bonds as well (the *commare* and *compare*),
and as intermarriage in the village groups is a common practice, this family pride becomes really a clan pride." [20] The alliance of families of the town through intermarriage and godparenthood perpetuated a social organization based upon
large kinship groups.

The south Italian peasants also brought with them to Chicago some of their less attractive customs. Many a new chapter of an ancient vendetta of Calabria or Sicily was written
on the streets of this American city. The zealous protection of
the family honor was often a cause of bloodshed. Emigration
had not abrogated the duty of the south Italian to guard the
chastity of his women. Without the mitigating quality of
these "crimes of passion" were the depredations of the "Black
Hand." After 1900 the practice of extorting money under
threat of death became so common as to constitute a reign of
terror in the Sicilian settlements. Both the Black Handers and
their victims were with few exceptions from the province of
Palermo where the criminal element known collectively as
the *mafia* had thrived for decades. The propensity for violence of the south Italians was not a symptom of social disor-

[20] Zorbaugh, *Gold Coast*, 166–67. *Commare* and *compare* are god-
mother and godfather. See also Zaloha, "Persistence of Italian Customs,"
103–05, 145–48.

ganization caused by emigration but a characteristic of their Old World culture.[21] Here too the generalizations that the immigrant feared to have recourse to the peasant crimes of revenge, and that the immigrant was rarely involved in crime for profit,[22] do not apply to the south Italians.

To speak of alienation as the essence of the immigrant experience is to ignore the persistence of traditional forms of group life. For the *contadino,* his family and his townsmen continued to provide a sense of belonging and to sanction his customary world-view and life-ways. Living "in," but not "of," the sprawling, dynamic city of Chicago, the south Italian was sheltered within his ethnic colony from the confusing complexity of American society.

While the acquisition of land was a significant motive for emigration, the south Italian peasants were not ones to dream, as did Handlin's, of possessing "endless acres" in America.[23] Their goal was a small plot of ground in their native towns. If they failed to reach the American soil, it was not because, as Handlin puts it, "the town had somehow trapped them," [24] but because they sought work which would pay ready wages. These peasants had no romantic illusions about farming; and despite urgings by railroad and land companies, reformers, and philanthropists to form agricultural colonies, the south Italians preferred to remain in the city.[25]

Although Chicago experienced an extraordinary growth of manufacturing during the period of their emigration, few south Italians found employment in the city's industries.

[21] *The Italian "White Hand" Society in Chicago, Illinois. Studies, Actions and Results* (Chicago, 1906); Illinois Association for Criminal Justice, *Illinois Crime Survey* (Chicago, 1929), 845–62, 935–54; Vecoli, "Chicago's Italians," 393–460.

[22] *Uprooted,* 163.

[23] *Ibid.,* 82.

[24] *Ibid.,* 64.

[25] Vecoli, "Chicago's Italians," 184–234; Luigi Villari, *Gli Stati Uniti d'America e l'Emigrazione Italiana* (Milan, 1912), 256. Villari observed that even Italian immigrants who worked as gardeners in the suburbs of Boston preferred to live with their countrymen in the center of the city, commuting to their work in the country. *Ibid.,* 224.

Great numbers of other recent immigrants worked in meat-packing and steelmaking, but it was uncommon to find an Italian name on the payroll of these enterprises.[26] The absence of the *contadini* from these basic industries was due both to their aversion to this type of factory work and to discrimination against them by employers. For the great majority of the south Italian peasants "the stifling, brazen factories and the dark, stony pits" did not supplant "the warm living earth as the source of their daily bread." [27] Diggers in the earth they had been and diggers in the earth they remained; only in America they dug with the pick and shovel rather than the mattock. In Chicago the Italian laborers quickly displaced the Irish in excavation and street work, as they did on railroad construction jobs throughout the West.[28]

The lot of the railroad workers was hard. Arriving at an unknown destination, they were sometimes attacked as "scabs," they found the wages and conditions of labor quite different from those promised, or it happened that they were put to work under armed guard and kept in a state of peonage. For twelve hours a day in all kinds of weather, the laborers dug and picked, lifted ties and rails, swung sledge hammers, under the constant goading of tyrannical foremen. Housed in filthy boxcars, eating wretched food, they endured this miserable existence for a wage which seldom exceeded $1.50 a day. Usually they suffered in silence, and by the most stern abstinence were able to save the greater part of their meager earnings. Yet it happened that conditions became in-

[26] In 1901, for example, of over 6,000 employees at the Illinois Steel works only two were Italian. John M. Gillette, "The Culture Agencies of a Typical Manufacturing Group: South Chicago," *American Journal of Sociology*, VII (July 1901), 93–112. In 1915 the Armour Packing Company reported that there was not one Italian among its 8,000 workers in Chicago. U.S. Commission on Industrial Relations, *Final Report and Testimony* (11 vols., Washington, 1916), IV, 3530.

[27] *Uprooted*, 73.

[28] Chicago *Tribune*, March 20, 1891; Frank J. Sheridan, "Italian, Slavic and Hungarian Unskilled Laborers in the United States," U.S. Bureau of Labor, *Bulletin* XV (Sept. 1907), 445–68; Vecoli, "Chicago's Italians," 279–337.

tolerable, and the *paesani* (gangs were commonly composed of men from the same town) would resist the exactions of the "boss." These uprisings were more in the nature of peasants' revolts than of industrial strikes, and they generally ended badly for the *contadini*.[29]

With the approach of winter the men returned to Chicago. While some continued on to Italy, the majority wintered in the city. Those with families in Chicago had households to return to; the others formed cooperative living groups. Thus they passed the winter months in idleness, much as they had in Italy. Railroad work was cyclical as well as seasonal. In times of depression emigration from Italy declined sharply; many of the Italian workers returned to their native towns to await the return of American prosperity. Those who remained were faced with long periods of unemployment; it was at these times, such as the decade of the 1890s, that the spectre of starvation stalked through the Italian quarters of Chicago.[30]

Because the *contadini* were engaged in gang labor of a seasonal nature there developed an institution which was thought most typical of the Italian immigration: the padrone system.[31] Bewildered by the tumult of the city, the newcom-

[29] D'Angelo, *Son of Italy*, 85–119; Dominic T. Ciolli, "The 'Wop' in the Track Gang," *Immigrants in America Review*, II (July 1916), 61–64; Gino C. Speranza, "Forced Labor in West Virginia," *Outlook*, LXXIV (June 13, 1903), 407–10.

[30] U.S. Commissioner of Labor, *Italians in Chicago*, 29, 44; Rosa Cassettari, "The Story of an Italian Neighbor (as told to Marie Hall Ets)," 342–50, ms. on loan to the author; Mayor's Commission on Unemployment (Chicago), *Report* (Chicago, 1914); Vecoli, "Chicago's Italians," 279–337.

[31] On the padrone system see Grace Abbott, "The Chicago Employment Agency and the Immigrant Worker," *American Journal of Sociology*, XIV (Nov. 1908), 289–305; John Koren, "The Padrone System and the Padrone Banks," U.S. Bureau of Labor, *Bulletin* II (March 1897), 113–29; S. Merlino, "Italian Immigrants and Their Enslavement," *Forum*, XV (April 1893), 183–90; Gino C. Speranza, "The Italian Foreman as a Social Agent," *Charities*, XI (July 4, 1903), 26–28; Vecoli, "Chicago's Italians," 235–278; Giovanni Ermenegildo Schiavo, *Italian-American History* (2 vols., New York, 1947–1949), I, 538–40.

ers sought out a townsman who could guide them in the ways of this strange land. Thus was created the padrone who made a business out of the ignorance and necessities of his countrymen. To the laborers, the padrone was banker, saloonkeeper, grocer, steamship agent, lodginghouse keeper, and politician. But his most important function was that of employment agent.

While there were honest padrones, most appeared unable to resist the opportunities for graft. Although Handlin states that "the padrone had the virtue of shielding the laborer against the excesses of employers,"[32] the Italian padrones usually operated in collusion with the contractors. Often the padrones were shrewd, enterprising men who had risen from the ranks of the unskilled; many of them, however, were members of the gentry who sought to make an easy living by exploiting their peasant compatriots in America as they had in Italy. The padrone system should not be interpreted as evidence "that a leader in America was not bound by patterns of obligation that were sacred in the Old World"; rather, it was a logical outcome of the economic individualism and "amoral familism" of south Italian society.

In their associational life the *contadini* also contradicted Handlin's assertion that the social patterns of the Old Country could not survive the ocean voyage.[33] The marked incapacity of the south Italians for organizational activity was itself a result of the divisive attitudes which they had brought with them to America. Almost the only form of association among these immigrants was the mutual aid society. Since such societies were common in Italy by the 1870s,[34] they can hardly be regarded as "spontaneously generated" by American conditions. Instead, the mutual aid society was a transplanted institution which was found to have especial utility for the immigrants. An Italian journalist observed: "If associa-

---

[32] *Uprooted*, 69–70.
[33] *Ibid.*, 170–71.
[34] Franchetti and Sonnino, *La Sicilia*, II, 335.

tions have been found useful in the *patria,* how much more they are in a strange land, where it is so much more necessary for the Italians to gather together, to fraternize, to help one another." [35] Nowhere, however, was the spirit of *campanilismo* more in evidence than in these societies. An exasperated Italian patriot wrote: "Here the majority of the Italian societies are formed of individuals from the same town and more often from the same parish, others are not admitted. But are you or are you not Italians? And if you are, why do you exclude your brother who is born a few miles from your town?" [36] As the number of these small societies multiplied (by 1912 there were some 400 of them in Chicago),[37] various attempts were made to form them into a federation. Only the Sicilians, however, were able to achieve a degree of unity through two federations which enrolled several thousand members.

The sentiment of regionalism was also a major obstacle to the organizational unity of the Italians in Chicago. Rather than being allayed by emigration, this regional pride and jealousy was accentuated by the proximity of Abruzzese, Calabrians, Genoese, Sicilians, and other groups in the city. Each regional group regarded those from other regions with their strange dialects and customs not as fellow Italians, but as distinct and inferior ethnic types. Any proposal for cooperation among the Italians was sure to arouse these regional antipathies and to end in bitter recriminations.[38] The experience of emigration did not create a sense of nationality among the Italians strong enough to submerge their parochialism. Unlike Handlin's immigrants who acquired "new modes of fellowship to replace the old ones destroyed by emigration," [39] the South

[35] *L'Unione Italiana* (Chicago), March 18, 1868.

[36] *L'Italia,* Oct. 23–24, 1897.

[37] Schiavo, *Italians in Chicago,* 57.

[38] Giacosa, "Chicago," 31–33; Comitato Locale di Chicago, *Primo Congresso degli Italiani all'estero sotto l'atto patronato di S. M. Vittorio Emanuele III* (Chicago, 1908).

[39] *Uprooted,* 189.

Italians confined themselves largely to the traditional ones of family and townsmen.

The quality of leadership of the mutual aid societies also prevented them from becoming agencies for the betterment of the *contadini*. These organizations, it was said, were often controlled by the "very worse [sic] element in the Italian colony," [40] arrogant, selfish men, who founded societies not out of a sense of fraternity but to satisfy their ambition and vanity. The scope of their leadership was restricted to presiding despotically over the meetings, marching in full regalia at the head of the society, and gaining economic and political advantage through their influence over the members. If such a one were frustrated in his attempt to control a society, he would secede with his followers and found a new one. Thus even the townsmen were divided into opposing factions.[41]

The function of the typical mutual aid society was as limited as was its sphere of membership. The member received relief in case of illness, an indemnity for his family in case of death, and a funeral celebrated with pomp and pageantry. The societies also sponsored an annual ball and picnic, and, most important of all, the feast of the local patron saint. This was the extent of society activities; any attempt to enlist support for philanthropic or civic projects was doomed to failure.[42]

Since there was a surplus of doctors, lawyers, teachers, musicians, and classical scholars in southern Italy, an "intellectual proletariat" accompanied the peasants to America in search of fortune.[43] Often, however, these educated im-

[40] Edmund M. Dunne, *Memoirs of "Zi Pre"* (St. Louis, 1914), 18. Father Dunne was the first pastor of the Italian Church of the Guardian Angel on Chicago's West Side.

[41] Comitato Locale di Chicago, *Primo Congresso; L'Italia*, Feb. 18, 1888, Oct. 21, 1899.

[42] Beck, "The Italian in Chicago," 23; Comitato Locale di Chicago, *Primo Congresso; L'Italia*, Aug. 24, 1889, April 28, 1906.

[43] Amy A. Bernardy, *Italia randagia attraverso gli Stati Uniti* (Turin, 1913), 293; Giacosa, "Chicago," 31; *L'Italia*, Jan. 19, 1889.

migrants found that America had no use for their talents, and to their chagrin they were reduced to performing manual labor. Their only hope of success was to gain the patronage of their lowly countrymen, but the sphere of colonial enterprise was very restricted. The sharp competition among the Italian bankers, doctors, journalists, and others engendered jealousies and rivalries. Thus this intelligentsia which might have been expected to provide tutelage and leadership to the humbler elements was itself rent by internecine conflict and expended its energies in polemics.

For the most part the upper-class immigrants generally regarded the peasants here as in Italy as boors and either exploited them or remained indifferent to their plight. These "respectable" Italians, however, were concerned with the growing prejudice against their nationality and wished to elevate its prestige among the Americans and other ethnic groups. As one means of doing this, they formed an association to suppress scavenging, organ-grinding, and begging as disgraceful to the Italian reputation. They simultaneously urged the workers to adopt American ways and to become patriotic Italians; but to these exhortations, the *contadino* replied: "It does not give me any bread whether the Italians have a good name in America or not. I am going back soon." [44]

Well-to-do Italians were more liberal with advice than with good works. Compared with other nationalities in Chicago, the Italians were distinguished by their lack of philanthropic institutions. There was a substantial number of men of wealth among them, but as an Italian reformer commented: "It is strange that when a work depends exclusively on the wealthy of the colony, one can not hope for success. Evidently philanthropy is not the favored attribute of our

[44] Robert E. Park and Herbert A. Miller, *Old World Traits Transplanted* (New York, 1921), 104; Mastro-Valerio, "Remarks Upon the Italian Colony," 131–32; *L'Italia*, Aug. 6, 1887, April 5, 1890.

rich." [45] Indeed, there was no tradition of philanthropy among the gentry of southern Italy, and the "self-made" men did not recognize any responsibility outside the family. Projects were launched for an Italian hospital, an Italian school, an Italian charity society, an Italian institute to curb the padrone evil, and a White Hand Society to combat the Black Hand, but they all floundered in this morass of discord and disinterest. Clearly Handlin does not have the Italians in mind when he describes a growing spirit of benevolence as a product of immigrant life.[46]

If there is one particular in which the *contadini* most strikingly refute Handlin's conception of the peasant it is in the place of religion in their lives. Handlin emphasizes the influence of Christian doctrine on the psychology of the peasantry,[47] but throughout the Mezzogiorno, Christianity was only a thin veneer.[48] Magic, not religion, pervaded their everyday existence; through the use of rituals, symbols, and charms, they sought to ward off evil spirits and to gain the favor of powerful deities. To the peasants, God was a distant, unapproachable being, like the King, but the local saints and Madonnas were real personages whose power had been attested to by innumerable miracles. But in the devotions to their patron saints, the attitude of the peasants was less one of piety than of bargaining, making vows if certain requests were granted. For the Church, which they had known as an oppressive landlord, they had little reverence; and for the clergy, whom they knew to be immoral and greedy, they had little respect. They knew little of and cared less for the doctrines of the Church.

---

[45] *L'Italia*, Aug. 24–25, 1895; Luigi Carnovale, *Il Giornalismo degli Emigrati Italiani nel Nord America* (Chicago, 1909), 67; Comitato Locale di Chicago, *Primo Congresso.*

[46] *Uprooted*, 175–76.

[47] *Ibid.*, 102–03.

[48] Levi, *Christ Stopped*, 116–18; Leonard W. Moss and Stephen C. Cappannari, "Folklore and Medicine in an Italian Village," *Journal of American Folklore*, LXXIII (April 1960), 85–102; Banfield, *Moral Basis of a Backward Society*, 17–18, 129–32.

Contadini in Chicago

Nor was the influence of established religion on the south Italian peasants strengthened by emigration as Handlin asserts.[49] American priests were scandalized by the indifference of the Italians to the Church.[50] Even when Italian churches were provided by the Catholic hierarchy, the *contadini* seldom displayed any religious enthusiasm. As one missionary was told upon his arrival in an Italian colony: "We have no need of priests here, it would be better if you returned from whence you came."[51] As in their native towns, the south Italian peasants for the most part went to church "to be christened, married or buried and that is about all."[52]

Because they were said to be drifting into infidelity, the south Italians were also the object of much of the home mission work of the Protestant churches of Chicago. Drawing their ministry from Italian converts and Waldensians, these missions carried the Gospel to the *contadini*, who, however, revealed little inclination to become "true Christians." After several decades of missionary effort, the half dozen Italian Protestant churches counted their membership in the few hundreds.[53] The suggestion that Italians were especially vulnerable to Protestant proselyting was not borne out in Chicago. For the *contadini*, neither Catholicism nor Protestantism became "paramount as a way of life."[54]

According to Handlin, the immigrants found it "hard to believe that the whole world of spirits and demons had aban-

[49] *Uprooted*, 117.

[50] On the religious condition of the Italian immigrants, see the discussion in *America*, XII (Oct. 17, 31, Nov. 7, 14, 21, 28, Dec. 5, 12, 19, 1914), 6–7, 66, 93, 121, 144–45, 168–69, 193–96, 221, 243–46.

[51] G. Sofia, ed., *Missioni Scalabriniane in America, estratto da "Le Missioni Scalabriniane tra gli Italiani"* (Rome, 1939), 122.

[52] Church Census of the 17th Ward, 1909," Chicago Commons, 1904–1910, Graham Taylor Papers (Newberry Library).

[53] Palmerio Chessa, "A Survey Study of the Evangelical Work among Italians in Chicago" (bachelor of divinity thesis, Presbyterian Theological Seminary, Chicago, 1934); Jane K. Hackett, "A Survey of Presbyterian Work with Italians in the Presbytery of Chicago" (master's thesis, Presbyterian College of Christian Education, Chicago, 1943).

[54] *Uprooted*, 117, 136.

doned their familiar homes and come also across the Atlantic," [55] but the *contadino* in America who carried a *corno* (a goat's horn of coral) to protect him from the evil eye harbored no such doubts. The grip of the supernatural on the minds of the peasants was not diminished by their ocean crossing. In the Italian settlements, sorcerers plied their magical trades on behalf of the ill, the lovelorn, the bewitched. As Alice Hamilton noted: "Without the help of these mysterious and powerful magicians they [the *contadini*] believe that they would be defenseless before terrors that the police and the doctor and even the priest cannot cope with." [56] For this peasant folk, in Chicago as in Campania, the logic of medicine, law, or theology had no meaning; only magic provided an explanation of, and power over, the vagaries of life.

The persistence of Old World customs among the south Italians was perhaps best exemplified by the *feste* which were held in great number in Chicago. The cults of the saints and Madonnas had also survived the crossing, and the fellow townsmen had no doubt that their local divinities could perform miracles in Chicago as well as in the Old Country. Feast day celebrations were inspired not only by devotion to the saints and Madonnas; they were also an expression of nostalgia for the life left behind. The procession, the street fair, the crowds of townsmen, created the illusion of being once more back home; as one writer commented of a *festa*: "There in the midst of these Italians, with almost no Americans, it seemed to be truly a village of southern Italy." [57] Despite efforts by "respectable" Italians and the Catholic clergy to discourage these colorful but unruly celebrations, the *contadini* would have their *feste*. After the prohibition of a *festa*

[55] *Ibid.*, 110.

[56] Alice Hamilton, "Witchcraft in West Polk Street," *American Mercury*, X (Jan. 1927), 71; Chicago *Tribune*, Jan. 19, 1900; *L'Italia*, Oct. 3, 1903. See also Zaloha, "Persistence of Italian Customs," 158–63.

[57] *L'Italia*, July 28–29, 1894; Cassettari, "Story of an Italian Neighbor," 419. See also Zaloha, "Persistence of Italian Customs," 90–100.

by the Church was defied, a priest explained: "The feast is a custom of Sicily and survives despite denunciations from the altar. Wherever there is a colony of these people they have the festival, remaining deaf to the requests of the clergy." [58] The south Italian peasants remained deaf to the entreaties of reformers and radicals as well as priests, for above all they wished to continue in the ways of their *paesi*.

The *contadini* of the Mezzogiorno thus came to terms with life in Chicago within the framework of their traditional pattern of thought and behavior. The social character of the south Italian peasant did not undergo a sea change, and the very nature of their adjustments to American society was dictated by their "Old World traits," which were not so much ballast to be jettisoned once they set foot on American soil. These traits and customs were the very bone and sinew of the south Italian character which proved very resistant to change even under the stress of emigration. Because it over-emphasizes the power of environment and underestimates the toughness of cultural heritage, Handlin's thesis does not comprehend the experience of the immigrants from southern Italy. The basic error of this thesis is that it subordinates historical complexity to the symmetrical pattern of a sociological theory. Rather than constructing ideal types of "the peasant" or "the immigrant," the historian of immigration must study the distinctive cultural character of each ethnic group and the manner in which this influenced its adjustments in the New World.

[58] Chicago *Tribune*, Aug. 14, 1903.

ROTATING CREDIT ASSOCIATIONS

IVAN H. LIGHT

THE single most prominent argument advanced to explain the black American's underrepresentation in small business has fastened on his special difficulty in securing business loans from institutional lenders, especially from banks. This explanation is 200 years old.[1] It asserts that, because of poverty, lack of capital, and inability to borrow, blacks have been unable to finance business ventures. In its most straightforward form, this argument holds that black business failed to develop because prejudiced white bankers were unwilling to make business loans to black applicants at all or were willing to make loans but only on terms very much less favorable than those extended to white borrowers with equivalent business credentials. In a more sophisticated version, the argument maintains that black borrowers were relatively disadvantaged in the capital market simply by virtue of their impoverishment and the marginal status of their businesses. Impecunious blacks opening solo proprietorships were objectively higher risks than were the typically wealthier whites operating larger businesses. Hence, quite apart from discriminatory treatment at the hands of white bankers, blacks did not receive loans at all or received them only at a higher price than did whites. The humble stature of black business

FROM: Ivan H. Light, *Ethnic Enterprise in America* (Berkeley: University of California Press, 1973), pp. 19–36. Originally published by the University of California Press; reprinted by permission of The Regents of the University of California.

[1] Abram L. Harris, *The Negro as Capitalist*, p. 22; John Hope Franklin, *From Slavery to Freedom*, 2d ed. (New York: Alfred Knopf, 1963), p. 309.

implicated borrowers in a vicious cycle of smallness, credit difficulties, smallness.

However, the discrimination-in-lending theory has lately lost the preeminent place it formerly occupied among explanations of Negro business retardation. In the first place, studies of small businessmen have shown that, contrary to expectation, loans from institutions have been relatively insignificant among the financial resources actually employed by proprietors in the capitalization of small firms. Only a small percentage of proprietors have reported seeking or obtaining bank loans in order to open a small business; by far the greater percentage rely entirely on their personal resources, especially their own savings, and loans from kin and friends· "Small new enterprises are financed primarily by owners, their relatives and friends, and by suppliers of materials and equipment. Banking institutions extend only slight accommodation to small new businesses."[2] These findings do not support the familiar argument that institutional discrimination in lending produced black difficulties in small business. On the contrary, these findings suggest that even had racial discrimination been exceptionally severe in commercial lending, it could have had only a minor impact. Since bank credit has been so insignificant a resource for new proprietors in general, even complete denial of bank credit could hardly account for the Negro's singular difficulties in small business.[3]

Reviewing the relevant arguments, Gunnar Myrdal observed that "the credit situation has certainly been one of the major obstacles barring the way for the Negro businessman." Yet Myrdal also complained that the credit theory appeared

[2] Alfred R. Oxenfeldt, *New Firms and Free Enterprise* (Washington, D.C.: American Council on Public Affairs, 1943), pp. 146, 160. Also see Kurt B. Mayer and Sidney Goldstein, *The First Two Years* (Washington, D.C.: U.S. Small Business Administration, 1961), p. 53; Joseph A. Pierce, *Negro Business and Business Education* (New York: Harper, 1947), pp. 187–88.
[3] Eugene P. Foley, *The Achieving Ghetto* (Washington, D.C.: National Press, 1968), pp. 136–40.

highly inadequate when the Negro's actual involvement in small business was contrasted with that of foreign-born whites, and especially with that of Americans of Japanese or Chinese descent.[4] If discrimination in lending accounted for black underrepresentation in business, then the Orientals ought also to have been underrepresented relative to more advantaged foreign-born whites. In turn, one would expect the foreign-born whites to have been underrepresented relative to native-born whites. If smallness or poverty accounted for the Negro's difficulties in securing commercial loans, then smallness ought to have interfered with foreign-born whites and Orientals as well. But, in fact, both foreign-born whites and Orientals were overrepresented in business relative to native whites, who presumably suffered no discrimination in lending. If Orientals and foreign-born whites were able to overcome these handicaps, then why were black Americans not also able to surmount them?

Accounting for these anomalies has necessitated a reconsideration of black business history in which the emphasis has shifted from financial to social causes. E. Franklin Frazier's "tradition-of-enterprise" hypothesis stands out as the general paradigm for research in this area: "Although no systematic study has been undertaken of the social causes of the failure of the Negro to achieve success as a businessman, it appears from what we know of the social and cultural history of the Negro that it is the result largely of the lack of traditions in the field of business enterprise."[5] "Experience in buying and selling" was apparently the tradition Frazier thought relevant, for he explicitly deemphasized the role played by "such economic factors as . . . availability of capital," evidently because of Myrdal's earlier discussion.

In his discussion of Negro business, Eugene Foley has fol-

[4] Gunnar Myrdal, *An American Dilemma* (New York: Harper, 1944), Vol. 1, pp. 308, 314.
[5] E. Franklin Frazier, *The Negro in the United States* (New York: Macmillan, 1957), pp. 410–11.

lowed Frazier's lead in interpreting Negro business from the perspective of traditions; however, Foley singled out a different tradition: "In the final analysis, the fundamental reason that Negroes have not advanced in business is the lack of business success symbols available to them." [6] Foley's theory has an advantage of concreteness relative to Frazier. However, Foley's view of the relevant traditions is flimsy and probably incorrect, for there is a very old tradition of successful Negro businessmen in the United States. This tradition is, to be sure, one of successful individuals, rather than one based on collective experience. But it is withal a tradition that offers "business success symbols" to Negroes. Around the turn of the century Booker T. Washington undertook an energetic campaign to bring these black entrepreneurs to popular attention. But the subsequent decline of Negro business despite the vigorous turn-of-the-century popularization of business success symbols suggests that the problems of Negro business were independent of popularized success symbols.

ROTATING CREDIT ASSOCIATIONS

Regarding questions of finance as purely economic and, therefore, beyond the pale of sociological analysis, Frazier failed to follow up lines of inquiry suggested by his own conclusion. That is, Frazier did not inquire into cultural traditions relevant to the capitalization of small business even though he had himself singled out "tradition" as of overriding importance in accounting for Negro underrepresentation in business. Recent anthropological studies of economic development have generated renewed scholarly interest in traditions of informal financial cooperation in many areas of the non-Western world. Although these are practical economic

[6] Eugene P. Foley, "The Negro Businessman: In Search of a Tradition," *Daedalus* 95 (Winter 1966), p. 124. Cf. Booker T. Washington, *The Negro in Business* (Boston: Hertel, Jenkins, 1907), *passim.*

traditions, they are a part of functioning cultures. Hence they are of sociological as well as of economic interest. These informal methods of financial cooperation are of considerable importance in fulfilling Frazier's program of research, because they constitute concrete traditions relevant to the financing of small business enterprises.

Although the details of such financial cooperation differ by region, Clifford Geertz has shown that a basic model can be extracted from the manifest diversity of ethnic customs. This basic model he has appropriately labeled the "rotating credit association." [7] In a comprehensive review of rotating credit associations throughout the world, Shirley Ardener has agreed with Geertz that basic principles of rotating credit can be extracted from the diversity of customs, but she has slightly restated the formula for expressing the essential rotating credit idea. She defines it as "an association formed upon a core of participants who agree to make regular contributions to a fund which is given, in whole or in part, to each contributor in rotation." [8] Within the limits of the rotating credit association as defined, Ardener was also able to specify the axes of variation which distinguish local customs from one another. That is, local rotating credit associations frequently differ with regard to membership size and criteria of membership, organization of the association, types of funds, transferability of funds, deductions from the fund, and sanctions imposed on members. But despite variations in these important respects, the rotating credit association may be taken as a generic type of cooperative financial institution. In many parts of the non-Western world, this type of association serves or has served many of the functions of Western banks. Such associations are, above all, credit institutions which

[7] Clifford Geertz, "The Rotating Credit Association: A 'Middle Rung' in Development," *Economic Development and Cultural Change* 10 (April 1962), p. 213.

[8] Shirley Ardener, "The Comparative Study of Rotating Credit Associations," *Journal of the Royal Anthropological Institute* 94 (1964), p. 201. Italicized in original.

lend lump sums of money to members. In this activity, rotating credit associations are found frequently to "assist in small scale capital formation." [9]

Of especial importance to this discussion are the rotating credit associations of southern China, Japan, and West Africa. Immigrants to the United States from southern China and Japan employed traditional rotating credit associations as their principal device for capitalizing small business. West Indian blacks brought the West African rotating credit association to the United States; they too used this traditional practice to finance small businesses. American-born Negroes apparently did not employ a similar institution. Hence, the rotating credit association suggests itself as a specific tradition in the field of business which accounts, in some measure, for the differential business success of American-born Negroes, West Indian Negroes, and Orientals.

HUI IN CHINA AND IN THE UNITED STATES

The generic term for the Cantonese rotating credit association is *hui*, which means simply "association" or "club." Several variants of hui existed in China, but the rotating credit principle was everywhere strongly pronounced. Such associations are thought to be about 800 years old in China.

D. H. Kulp described a simple form of hui used in southern China.[10] Greatly more complex variants of hui also existed; but the simple lottery scheme described by Kulp illustrates the basic principle of the Cantonese hui. A person in need of a lump sum of money would take the initiative in organizing a hui by securing from friends or relatives an agreement to

[9] *Ibid.*, p. 217.
[10] Daniel H. Kulp, *Country Life in South China* (New York: Columbia University Press, 1925), 190 ff.; also see Kenneth Scott Latourette, *The Chinese: Their History and Culture*, 3rd ed. (New York: Macmillan, 1946), p. 593; Max Weber, *The Religion of China* (Glencoe, Ill.: Free Press, 1951), p. 99; Gideon Sjoberg, *The Preindustrial City* (Glencoe, Ill.: Free Press, 1960), p. 215.

pay a stipulated sum of money—say, $5—every month into a common pool. In a hui of ten members, the organizer himself received the first lump sum created, or $50, which he employed as he pleased. A month later the organizer held a feast in his home for the ten contributors. At the feast the ten members again contributed $5 each to create a fund of $50. A lottery determined which member (excluding the organizer) would receive the lump sum. Since a member could receive the lump sum only once, at each subsequent feast the pool of members still in the lottery narrowed until, finally, at the tenth feast the outstanding member automatically received the lump sum of $50. The organizer never contributed to the money pool; his repayment was exclusively in the form of the ten feasts, each of which was supposed to have cost him $5. At the conclusion of the ten feasts, each member would have dribbled away $55 in cash and would have received one lump sum of $50 and ten 50-cent feasts. Also, the organizer of the hui had received the interest-free use of $50 when he needed it, eight of the ten members had received an advance on their contribution (credit), and all of the participants had enjoyed ten sumptuous feasts in convivial company.

If the membership chose, a hui could be organized on less benevolent lines. Instead of a lottery to determine which member of the club would take the pot, each eligible member might submit a sealed bid indicating how much interest he was prepared to pay to have the use of the money.[11] The high bidder received the pot. This system of hui operation placed a clear premium on not needing the money. Those who wanted the money in the early rounds of the hui would have to compete and pay a high interest. On the other hand, wealthier members who were not in need of money could collect the high interest paid by members who needed the use of their surplus. This form of hui created an investment opportu-

[11] Hsiao-tung Fei, *Peasant Life in China* (London: Routledge & Kegan Paul, 1939), pp. 273 ff.

nity for the wealthy and tended to enlist the profit motive in the extension of credit. Of course, even in this more capitalistic form of mutual aid, the interest actually paid by members in need of money tended to be less than what they would have paid for equivalent funds obtained from the town moneylender.

Cantonese in the United States employed the hui as a means of acquiring capital for business purposes.[12] The extent of the practice is impossible to ascertain with precision, but the evidence suggests that the traditional hui was widely used and of first importance in the funding of small business enterprises. An early reference to what was probably a hui is found in Helen Clark's discussion of Chinese in New York City; [13] however, the earliest discovered reference to what was certainly a Cantonese hui appears in Helen Cather's history of the Chinese in San Francisco:

The Chinese have a peculiar method of obtaining funds without going to commercial banks. If a responsible Chinaman needs an amount of money, he will organize an association, each member of which will promise to pay a certain amount on a specified day of each month for a given length of time. For instance, if the organizer wants $1,300 he may ask 12 others to join with him and each will promise to pay $100 each month for 13 months. The organizer has the use of the $1,300 the first month. When the date of the meeting comes around again, the members assemble and each pays his $100, including the organizer. All but the organizer, who has had the use of the money, bid for the pool. The man paying the highest bid pays the amount of the bid to each of the others and has the money. This continues for 13 months. Each man makes his payment each month but those who have already used the money cannot bid for it again. By the end of the 13-month period, each

---

[12] Chinese immigrants in Britain have also employed the device for this purpose. See Maurice Broady, "The Chinese in Great Britain," in *Colloquium on Overseas Chinese*, ed. Morton H. Fried (New York: Institute of Pacific Relations, 1958), p. 32.

[13] Helen F. Clark, "The Chinese of New York Contrasted with Their Foreign Neighbors," *Century* 53 (November 1896): 110.

will have paid in $1,300 and have had the use of the whole amount.[14]

Cather did not name the institution she described, but it was clearly a Cantonese hui of the bidding type. In regard to the origins of the practice, she learned from informants that "This is a very old Chinese custom and is still [1932] practiced by the Chinese in San Francisco. Since a man may belong to several of these associations at one time, it is not hard for a Chinaman to secure funds on short notice, for he can estimate from past bids about how much he must bid to secure the money." [15]

In his history of San Francisco's Chinatown, Richard Dare mentions the *yueh-woey* custom which was frequently used to secure business capital.[16] Like the institution described by Cather, Dare's yueh-woey was of the bidding and interest-paying type. In New York City's Chinatown, Virginia Heyer also found a bidding type of hui in operation. Memberships were usually limited to persons from the same village in China:

Sometimes members of small associations form loan societies to provide capital for fellow members who hope to start businesses. Each member contributes a fixed amount of money to a common fund. The one who offers the highest rate of interest in secret bid gets to borrow the whole fund, though first he must repay the full interest. . . . This method of financing business ventures was frequent in the past, but in recent years [1953] it is said to have been less common.[17]

Betty Lee Sung has recently described a hui of the bidding type which was popular among the Chinese in New York be-

[14] Helen Virginia Cather, "The History of San Francisco's Chinatown" (Master's thesis, University of California, Berkeley, 1932), pp. 60–61.

[15] *Ibid.*, p. 61.

[16] Richard Kock Dare, "The Economic and Social Adjustment of the San Francisco Chinese for the Past Fifty Years" (M.A. thesis, University of California, Berkeley, 1959), pp. 12–13.

[17] Virginia Heyer, "Patterns of Social Organization in New York City's Chinatown" (Ph.D. thesis, Columbia University, 1953), pp. 60–61.

fore 1950. One hundred members of the hui (all of the same clan) paid $10 a week for 100 weeks. Each week members bid for the $1,000 pot. If there were no bidders, a lottery among the outstanding members determined which one would receive the total fund subscribed at a stipulated low rate of interest. The hui described by Sung did not include conviviality, and the number of members greatly exceeded that characteristic of the hui in South China. In American Chinatowns, the hui had evidently become more commercial and less fraternal: "The *hui* in effect served as a systematic savings method for the thrifty and as a source of credit for those who needed a lump sum in cash for business or other reasons. Few Chinese utilized American banks." [18] The economic importance of the hui in the Chinese-American small business economy was emphasized by Gor Yun Leong, who observed that, "without such societies, very few businesses could be started." [19]

KO IN JAPAN AND IN THE UNITED STATES

Variously called *ko, tanomoshi,* or *mujin,* the Japanese form of the rotating credit association was probably adapted in the thirteenth century from the Chinese institution.[20] In Japan, ko clubs among rural villagers included from twenty to fifty persons, whereas, according to Hsiao-tung Fei, the Chinese hui

[18] Betty Lee Sung, *Mountain of Gold* (New York: Macmillan, 1967), pp. 141–42.

[19] Gor Yun Leong, *Chinatown Inside Out* (New York: Barrows Mussey, 1936), pp. 177–78; also see Paul C. P. Siu, "The Chinese Laundryman: A Study of Social Isolation" (Ph.D. diss., University of Chicago, 1953), pp. 112, 116–17. For a novelist's treatment of *hui* among immigrant Chinese in New York City, see Lin Yutang, *Chinatown Family* (New York: John Day, 1948), pp. 249–50.

[20] John F. Embree, *Suye Mura* (Chicago: University of Chicago Press, 1939), pp. 138 ff.; Koichi Hosono, "Outline of Small Business Financing in Japan," in *Small Business in Japan,* ed. Tokutaro Yamanaka (Tokyo: Japan Times, 1960), pp. 339–40. Also see Hugh T. Patrick, "Japan, 1868–1914," in *Banking in the Early Stages of Industrialization,* ed. Rondo Cameron et al. (New York: Oxford University Press, 1967), p. 245.

243

normally included only eight to fourteen persons. Unlike the hui, the Japanese institution sometimes included unrelated persons. Ko clubs met twice yearly, but the hui met monthly. Since the ko typically included more members than the hui, the Japanese clubs sometimes carried on as long as twenty years before each of the participants had received his portion. Ko was an extremely popular financial institution in rural Japan as late as the 1930s. According to John Embree, richer villagers and those in special need of funds belonged to several clubs. More of the villagers' money was tied up in ko than in commercial banks, credit unions, or postal savings.

Both a bidding system and a lottery system of ko were practiced.[21] Only the bidding system provided for the payment of interest by early drawers to late drawers. Under the rules of the bidding system, an organizer would receive the first portion. Meetings were held at the organizer's residence where refreshments were served and business was combined with sociability. At the second meeting, bidders for the combined fund indicated the amount of payment they were willing to receive from the other participants. The lowest bidder received the fund thus created. Having once received the fund, persons were obligated to pay back at the regular meetings the full stipulated contribution. Thus, as the ko wore on, fewer and fewer persons were bidding for the fund and fewer and fewer could be released by a low bid from the necessity of paying back the stipulated rate.

In the United States the memberships of ko associations were usually composed of immigrants from the same prefecture or village in Japan. Religious organizations, Buddhist and Christian alike, also organized clubs for the benefit of their congregants. But congruent with the Japanese traditions of neighborliness, neighborhood and friendship groups also

[21] Sometimes the bidding and lottery forms were combined so that half of the pots were allocated on the basis of bidding and half on a lottery basis. See Guenther Stein, "Made in Japan—I," *Forum* 94 (November 1935): 290–94.

started clubs. Although the larger ko clubs required each member to furnish guarantors, the meetings of the clubs were social as well as financial occasions. Sake was served before dinner and members entertained one another with friendly conversation. Interest payments were tendered as gifts rather than as payments for the use of money.[22]

In Hawaii, northern California, and the Pacific Northwest, Japanese settlers referred to the rotating credit associations as *tanomoshi*. In southern California the term *mujin* prevailed. Exactly how extensively these clubs were used is difficult to ascertain, but Fumiko Fukuoka referred to the mujin as "a common and popular form of mutual financial aid association among the Japanese in Southern California." She observes that this "ancient form of mutual aid association" had been "brought to America by the Japanese immigrants." [23] Of foreign-born Japanese sampled in California in the course of a 1965–66 survey, almost one-half reported having participated in some form of economic combination involving the pooling of money. Of the participating half, 90 percent had taken part in a tanomoshi.[24] According to Embree, Hawaiian Japanese organized tanomoshi which met monthly rather than biannually as in Japan and in which larger sums were invested.[25]

In 1922 Schichiro Matsui charged that white-owned banks in California discriminated against Japanese businessmen and farmers. Nonetheless, the tanomoshi permitted Japanese to capitalize business enterprises on their own. "Very popular

[22] Bradford Smith, *Americans from Japan* (Philadelphia: J. B. Lippincott, 1948), p. 58; Shotaro Frank Miyamoto, *Social Solidarity Among the Japanese in Seattle* (Seattle: University of Washington Press, 1939), pp. 75–76.
[23] Fumiko Fukuoka, "Mutual Life and Aid Among the Japanese of Southern California" (Master's thesis, University of Southern California, 1937), p. 33.
[24] John Modell, "The Japanese of Los Angeles" (Ph.D. thesis, Columbia University, 1969), p. 95.
[25] John F. Embree, "Acculturation Among the Japanese of Kona, Hawaii," *Memoirs of the American Anthropological Association* 59 (1941): 91.

among the Japanese in every line of trade," the tanomoshi was helpful because " a merchant without security may thus obtain credit."[26] Two decades later S. F. Miyamoto also stressed the economic importance of tanomoshi among Japanese in Seattle:

Few [Japanese] . . . were able to expand their business individually to any great extent. Possibly without a system of cooperative financing the Japanese would not have developed the economic structure that they did. Fortunately, they met their needs through adaptions of Japanese customs, such as the money-pool known as the *tanomoshi*. . . . It is difficult to ascertain the extent to which such pools were used by the Japanese immigrants . . . but from the wide-spread recognition of its use, it was probably no inconsequential part of their financing practices. The largest hotel ever attempted by the Japanese, a transaction involving some $90,000, . . . was financed on the basis of a *tanomoshi*.[27]

Commentators agreed that the rotating credit associations were more popular with Japanese of the immigrant generation than with their American-born offspring, the nisei, especially those with college degrees. For purposes of financing business operations, the nisei preferred the impersonal credit union or savings and loan association.[28] According to a nisei informant, Japanese in the San Francisco Bay region no longer employ the tanomoshi for purposes of business capitalization. However, the custom survives. Its purposes are now social, and only small sums are invested. This information agrees with the findings of Minako Kurokawa's recent study of Japanese small businessmen in San Francisco. She noted that, as a source of business capitalization, "the traditional institution of mutual aid [tanomoshi] . . . was not mentioned by

[26] Schichiro Matsui, "Economic Aspects of the Japanese Situation in California" (Master's thesis, University of California, Berkeley, 1922), pp. 86–87.

[27] Miyamoto, *Social Solidarity*, p. 75; also see Harry H. L. Kitano, *Japanese Americans*, pp. 19–20.

[28] Ruth Masuda, "The Japanese Tanomoshi," *Social Process in Hawaii* 3 (May 1937): 19; Smith, *Americans*, p. 58; Modell, "The Japanese," p. 96.

respondents." [29] On the other hand, a nisei informant in Los Angeles claims to be personally involved in an on-going tanomoshi, the members of which are still principally interested in securing capital for business purposes. According to this informant, the custom remains very widespread among Japanese in Los Angeles and retains its business significance.

ESUSU IN AFRICA, BRITAIN, AND THE AMERICAS

Anthropological research has documented the existence of rotating credit associations in many parts of Africa, including West Africa from which the progenitors of American Negroes were abducted as slaves. Although the details of administration and organization differ substantially among African regions and peoples, the essential rotating credit principle is virtually ubiquitous. However, one such rotating credit institution, the Nigerian *esusu,* is of especial importance here because of its historical influence on Negro business in the Americas. The esusu developed in southeastern Nigeria among the Yoruba people. Among the Yoruba's northern neighbors, the Nupe, the rotating credit institution is known as *dashi,* but the Nupe's custom differs little from the Yoruba's.[30] The antiquity of the esusu has not yet been finally established, but researchers are of the opinion that the custom was indigenously African. Certainly the Yoruba esusu existed as early as 1843, for it is mentioned in a Yoruba vocabulary of that date. In Sierra Leone, thrift clubs of some sort existed

[29] Minako Kurokawa, "Occupational Mobility Among Japanese Businessmen in San Francisco" (M.A. thesis, University of California, Berkeley, 1962), p. 70.

[30] S. F. Nadel, *A Black Byzantium* (New York: Oxford University Press, 1942), pp. 371–73; also see P. C. Lloyd, "The Yoruba of Nigeria," in *Peoples of Agrica,* ed. James L. Gibbs (New York: Holt, Rinehart, and Winston, 1965), p. 559; Kenneth Little, *West African Urbanization* (New York: Columbia University Press, 1965), p. 51; Michael Banton, *West African City* (London: Oxford University Press, 1957), pp. 187–88.

as early as 1794, but they cannot be positively identified as organized on the rotating credit principle.[31]

In his discussion of Yoruba associations, A. K. Ajisafe provides a statement of the esusu institution which summarizes its formal operation:

There is a certain society called Esusu. This society deals with monetary matters only, and it helps its members to save and raise money thus: Every member shall pay a certain fixed sum of money regularly at a fixed time (say every fifth or ninth day). And one of the subscribing members shall take the total amount thus subscribed for his or her own personal use. The next subscription shall be taken by another member; this shall so continue rotationally until every member has taken.[32]

In the principle of pooling funds and rotating the pot among the membership, the Yoruba esusu does not differ from either of its Oriental counterparts; however, in common practice, it exhibits some idiosyncracies. As W. R. Bascom observed, "anyone who wishes to do so may found an *esusu* group, provided that others are willing to entrust their money to him." [33] But the organizer or president of the esusu needed only to be known; he did not need to know all of the members personally. Once an organizer had announced his intention to sponsor an esusu, persons willing to entrust their money to him indicated a willingness to join. Such personal acquaintances of the organizer, if accepted, became in turn heads of "roads." There were as many separate roads as there were persons who had directly contacted the organizer and had been scrutinized and accepted by him. As heads of roads, these personal acquaintances of the organizer were entitled to contact their own friends and kin concerning membership in the esusu. Heads of the roads normally were responsible for "collecting the contributions and making the disbursements

[31] Ardener, "Comparative Study," p. 209.
[32] A. K. Ajisafe, *Laws and Customs of the Yoruba People* (London: George Routledge, 1924), pp. 48–49.
[33] William R. Bascom, "The *Esusu;* A Credit Institution of the Yoruba," *Journal of the Royal Anthropological Institute* 82 (1952), p. 64.

within their subgroups which consist of members who have applied to them rather than to the founder for admission." In this manner the Yoruba esusu delegated responsibility for the integrity of all members from the original organizer to managers known and appointed by and accountable to him.

The Yoruba esusu was apparently carried to the Americas by African slaves. Indeed Bascom bases his argument for the indigenous African origins of the esusu on the persistence in the West Indies of the same custom among the descendants of slaves. An early reference mentions the practice of *asu* in the British Bahamas in 1910:

Another method of promoting thrift is apparently of Yoruban origin. Little associations called "Asu" are formed of one or two dozen people who agree to contribute weekly a small sum toward a common fund. Every month . . . the amount thus pooled is handed to a member, in order of seniority of admission, and makes a little nest-egg for investment or relief. These "Asu" have no written statutes or regulations, no regular officers, but carry on their affairs without fraud or miscalculation.[34]

In the Trinidad village studied by M. J. Herskovits, residents referred to their rotating credit association as *susu*. As Herskovits observed, the term is clearly a corruption of the Yoruba word esusu. Trinidadians originally from Barbados and Guiana told Herskovits of the form of the susu in their birthplaces. In Barbados the rotating credit association was commonly known as "the meeting" and in Guiana as "boxi money." [35] According to Herskovits, the Trinidadian susu "takes the form of a cooperative pooling of earnings by those in the group, so that each member may benefit by obtaining in turn, and at one time, all the money paid in by the entire group on a given date. Members may contribute the same

[34] Harry H. Johnston, *The Negro in the New World* (New York: Macmillan, 1910), p. 303.
[35] Melville J. Herskovits, *Trinidad Village* (New York: Knopf, 1947), p. 292.

amount. The total of the weekly contribution . . . is called 'a hand.' " [36]

Jamaicans refer to their rotating credit association as "partners." The partners in Jamaica is headed by a "banker" and the membership is composed of "throwers." In operation the club is apparently identical to the susu of Trinidad. In the Jamaican setting, however, members apparently used their partnership portions for business capitalization, whereas rural Trinidadians appear to have made use of the fund only for consumption purposes. Many Jamaican petty traders used their partnership "draw" to restock their stalls with imported goods for which they were required to pay cash. The partnership constituted the "most important source of capital for petty traders." [37]

West Indian migration to the United States commenced around 1900 and continued until 1924. In 1920, at the peak of the immigration, foreign-born Negroes, almost exclusively West Indians, numbered 73,803, of whom 36,613 resided in New York City. Most of these migrants came from the British West Indies. West Indians in Harlem distinguished themselves from native-born Negroes by their remarkable propensity to operate small business enterprises.[38] The West Indians, W. A. Domingo observed, "are forever launching out in business, and such retail businesses as are in the hands of Negroes in Harlem are largely in the control of the foreign-

[36] *Ibid.*, p. 76.

[37] Margaret Katzin, " 'Partners': An Informal Savings Institution in Jamaica," *Social and Economic Studies* 8 (December 1959), pp. 436–40.

[38] This difference was persistently noted so long as West Indians remained a distinctive part of the Harlem population. See George Edmund Haynes, *The Negro at Work in New York City* (New York: Columbia University Press, 1912), p. 101; Gary Ward Moore, "A Study of a Group of West Indian Negroes in New York City" (M.A. thesis, Columbia University, 1923), p. 26; Ira De A. Reid, *The Negro Immigrant* (New York: Columbia University Press, 1959), pp. 120–21; Claude McKay, *Harlem: Negro Metropolis* (New York: Dutton, 1940), pp. 92–93; Roi Ottley, *New World A-Coming* (New York: World, 1943), p. 46; Gilbert Osofsky, *Harlem: The Making of a Ghetto* (New York: Harper and Row, 1963), p. 133.

born." [39] Moreover, the West Indians were more aggressive than the native-born Negroes in their choice of self-employment enterprises. Whereas native-born Negroes tended only to open noncompetitive service enterprises, the West Indians operated grocery stores, tailor shops, jewelry stores, and fruit vending and real estate operations in which they undertook direct competition with whites doing business in the ghetto. Only the Bajan, it was said, could withstand the competition of the Jew.

The thriftiness of the West Indians provoked resentment on the part of American-born Negroes who regarded the West Indians as stingy and grasping. Some of the West Indians' thrift expressed itself in patronage of orthodox savings institutions, especially the postal savings. However, the West Indians in Harlem also employed the traditional susu credit institution as a savings device. According to Amy Jacques Garvey, higher status West Indian migrants of urban origin "acquired the habit of accumulating capital" through the partners system from enforced contact with lower status West Indians of rural origins. Mrs. Garvey adds that in Harlem, "Women were mostly active in running the [partners] system —being bankers and collectors. Some 'threw a regular hand' for their husbands or brothers to enable them to operate small businesses. Later, the West Indian shopkeepers, barbers, etc. operated bigger 'pools' for setting up or capitalizing existing small business, or buying homes." [40] The partners draw also permitted a West Indian to purchase passage for relatives to the United States and to finance the secondary education of their children in the islands. As to the extensiveness of the practice of partners in Harlem, Mrs. Garvey observes that "the 'partners' system was fairly widespread in the 1920's and 1930's, but the Depression lessened its usage."

[39] W. A. Domingo, "The Tropics in New York," *Survey* 53 (March 1, 1925): 648–50.
[40] Personal communication of February 12, 1968. For a novelist's treatment of West Indian life in Harlem, see Paule Marshall, *Brown Girl, Brownstones,* (New York: Random House, 1959).

The significance of the partners as a factor in West Indian saving is further illustrated by postwar British West Indian migration to Britain. As in Harlem during the first several decades of the century, West Indians in Britain attracted attention because of their extraordinary frugality. Observers noted that West Indian migrants tended to "economize to a much greater extent than comparable English income groups." Investigating the savings habits of London's Jamaicans, Hyndman reported that the traditional partners played the leading role:

Methods of saving vary, but the most prevalent is the friendly cooperative effort normally referred to by Jamaicans as "partner." Other names for similar systems in the Eastern group of islands are "Sousou," "chitty," "syndicate." This is a simple method based on mutual trust between friends and relations, and complete confidence in the man or woman who is organizer—fifteen or twenty people pay a weekly sum of between one pound and five pounds to the organizers. Either by drawing lots or by prior arrangement, the total amount at the end of each week goes to one of the twenty. . . . In some instances the weekly payments necessitate a strenuous savings effort, but in most cases the "partners" is carried on time and again with satisfaction on all sides.[41]

R. B. Davidson's sample of Jamaican migrants in Britain also disclosed the persistence of the partners custom. At the end of the first year after arrival, 25 percent of Jamaicans sampled reported that they were presently involved in a partners or had recently been so involved. Other Jamaicans reported that they would participate in partners if only they could find an on-going group with a reliable membership and banker. One Jamaican claimed to be still participating by mail in a partners in Jamaica. "The urge to engage in some form of cooperative savings," observed Davison, "is strong among at least a substantial minority of the Jamaican community." [42]

[41] Albert Hyndman, "The West Indian in London," in *The West Indian Comes to England*, ed. by S. K. Rock (London: Routledge & Kegan Paul, 1960), p. 74.
[42] R. B. Davison, *West Indian Migrants* (London: Oxford University Press, 1962), pp. 95–96, 102–03.

Rotating Credit Associations

As in the United States, West Indians in Britain evinced a strong interest in real estate investment. In providing financial resources for such investment, the partners played a major role. Hyndman found that, by means of continuous participation in the partners, Jamaicans became able to "command a large sum of ready cash," which often provided "the initial payment on a house" or the passage to Britain of a family member. Racial discrimination in housing rentals apparently influenced the Jamaicans' schedule of priorities. West Indians scrimped in order "to achieve property ownership because of the difficulties experienced in providing adequate accommodation" for themselves and their families. Jamaicans came to own a substantial amount of real property in a relatively short time, especially in view of their impoverished origins. Of Davison's sample of Jamaicans, 75 percent were residing in houses "as tenants of Jamaican landlords." [43] Jamaican-owned housing thus clearly encompassed almost enough units to house the entire Jamaican population. Virtually all of this real estate had, of course, been purchased since 1945.

ROTATING CREDIT AS A TRADITION OF ENTERPRISE

The employment of the esusu by West Indian migrants in Harlem and again in Britain illustrates the manner in which a traditional economic custom encouraged the business activities of immigrants. The process was much the same among Chinese, Japanese, and West Indians. But unlike any of these immigrant groups, American-born Negroes in the United States did not employ any rotating credit institution, appar-

[43] The extent of business self-employment among West Indians in Britain is, however, less clear. Hyndman reported a few "one man or family businesses" ("West Indian," pp. 71–72). But Davison's sample turned up only one "successful, self-employed immigrant" (*West Indian,* p. 110).

ently because this African economic custom had vanished from their cultural repertoire. Since ethnographic accounts of black life in the United States did not consciously investigate the persistence of the Yoruba esusu or its variants, only negative evidence for this proposition exists. That is, lack of reference to rotating credit associations among Negroes in the United States may be taken as prima facie evidence that such practices were not, in fact, employed.[44] Students of this question have thus far been unable to locate any instance of rotating credit practices among American-born Negroes. Even Herskovits made no mention of rotating credit associations in the United States, although his own research in Trinidad had awakened him to the persistence of this Africanism.[45]

The persistence of the rotating credit associations among Chinese, Japanese, and West Indians provides tangible support for E. F. Frazier's contention that tradition played a critical role in the business success of "other alien groups" and that a lack of traditions inhibited Negro-owned business in the United States. Moreover, it makes possible an understanding of why racial discrimination in lending affected American-born Negroes more deleteriously than it did Orientals and foreign-born Negroes. Unlike the Chinese, Japanese, and West Indians, American-born Negroes did not have the rotating credit tradition to fall back on as a source of capital for small business enterprises. Hence, they were especially dependent on banks and lending companies for credit; and when such credit was for one reason or another denied, they possessed no traditional resources for making do on their own.

[44] Shirley Ardener, "The Comparative Study of Rotating Credit Associations," *Journal of the Royal Anthropological Institute* 94 (1964), 208.
[45] Melville J. Herskovits, *The Myth of the Negro Past*, p. 165.

CHAPTER 3

*Ethnicity and Class**

SLAVERY, RACE, AND THE POOR

J. H. PLUMB

RACISM does not create slavery. It is an excuse for it. Racism was a rampant feature of the centuries when slavery was being established in America and it was, therefore, easy to make it one of the justifications for the institution. But racism could be intense and not lead to slavery—and racism does not explain why the European nations found so little difficulty in adopting slavery in their colonies long after the institution had become insignificant in Europe's economic structure.

Although the institution had no economic relevance in contemporary Europe, the idea of slavery was both potent and entirely acceptable on stronger grounds than those of race. The English House of Commons did not even turn a hair at the suggestion that persistent English vagabonds should be enslaved by their fellow countrymen and they passed an Act in 1547 for this purpose: along, of course, with branding the victims with a large S. It failed and was repealed, but not on humanitarian grounds. No one wanted

FROM: J. H. Plumb, *In the Light of History* (Boston: Houghton Mifflin, 1972), pp. 108–113. Copyright © 1972 by J. H. Plumb. Reprinted by permission of Houghton Mifflin Company and Penguin Books Ltd.
° See also Appendix IV and Appendix V.

slaves—there was enough cheap labour without them, requiring no more food and less supervision. But the idea of white slavery was in no way repellent to the Tudors, or limited by them to savages and heathens. Indeed the condition of slavery had been accepted by the Church and by society from time out of mind; a part of that great law of subordination without which the whole edifice of society might crash to the ground. Without slave status, what would happen to bonded servants, to children sold as apprentices, to the indignant poor who had no rights in society except to labour? Slavery was only the most extreme of all servile conditions. Servant and slave were more than semantically linked.

The type of abuse that was hurled at the slave was hurled at the poor, particularly in English society, from which many Southern slave masters were drawn. Take these remarks of William Perkins, the popular puritan preacher of the early seventeenth century:

Rogues, beggars, vagabonds . . . commonly are of no civil society or corporation nor of any particular Church; and are as rotten legs and arms that drop from the body. . . . To wander up and down from year to year to this end, to seek and procure bodily maintenance is no calling, but the life of a beast.

or this from his colleague Sibbes: "They are the refuse of mankind: as they are in condition so they are in disposition."

These puritan divines were more charitable than many. The rogues and vagabonds were, of course, the wandering poor desperate for food. Their lot was bloody whippings, frequent branding and enforced labour. The early slave codes were very similar to the legislation designed to control the Elizabethan unemployed poor. Again, the poor, like slaves, were, it is now thought, neither expected to go to Church or be welcomed there. And as for cruelty, treatment of apprentices could be vicious, the floggings and brandings meted out to the "dregs of society" of Elizabethan and Stuart England almost as savage as anything the Negro knew; perhaps at times more so, for the poor were no man's property, and hence valueless if sick, weak or contumacious.

Again, miscegenation: the taboos against marrying the poor were formidable—for a woman it usually meant total ostracism—yet, of course, the young servant women, like slave Negresses, could be and were fair game for their masters. And even the Sambo mentality can be found in the deliberately stupid country yokel or the Cockney clown of later centuries. And so, too, the belief, as with Negroes, that they were abandoned sexually, given both to promiscuity and over-indulgence. Slave, servant, worker were the objects of exploitation, the sources of labour, therefore wealth; hence we should not be surprised to find similar attitudes, similar social oppressions operating against the poor as against the slave. Slavery and poverty in these centuries are not different in kind but different in degree, and the disadvantage was not always the slave's for, as property, he might be treated with greater consideration in sickness or in old age than the wage-slave. Because America did not know poverty, rural or urban, as Europe did in those early formative years, historians tend to attribute to slavery conditions which spring from the intensive exploitation of labour, whether "free" or servile. I do not doubt that racism gave an added intensity, a further degree of hopelessness and degradation to slavery and the slave's lot, but it is important to see the similarities in the treatment of slaves and the poor: otherwise one cannot realize how natural slavery was to the majority of men who practised it or accepted it.

To underline this, if underlining be needed, slavery was often—not always but often—at its cruellest where intensive economic exploitation was at its highest, namely on the great plantations. The comparatively mild slavery of Cuba turned into a far more vicious and disciplined form with the rise of the large sugar plantations, as Michael Banton points out in his admirable *Race Relations* [New York: Basic Books, 1968], a book which really deserves a far more extensive treatment than can be given it here. Just as a discussion of slavery without a consideration of the exploitation of other labourers tends to obscure fundamental issues, so too can racism and questions of civil rights obscure the deeper issues. No amount of civil rights can alleviate the Negro's lot, for much of the hatred of the black springs from the rich's fear of the poor and dispossessed. The basis of the problem is exploitation: the gross injustice which acquisitive society always inflicts on those who have nothing to offer but their body's labour. Hence the absence of an extended consideration of other labouring poor weakens to some extent the force of Jordan's book [Winthrop D. Jordon, *White over Black* (Chapel Hill: University of North Carolina Press, 1968)].

Once Jordan moves into the eighteenth century there is a greater sense of mastery, and he is particularly skillful in tracing the evasions of the Founding Fathers and the reasons why they could not face the question of abolition. Jordan analyses very subtly the conflict between the insistence on natural rights and the Lockeian concept of the holiness of property. The easiest escape was to defend natural rights negatively, and after the first flush of idealism, revolutionary America had little difficulty in pushing the question of slavery on to the sidelines. But this was as far as it could be pushed: for by 1800 white America's dilemma became both clearer and more devastating to its conscience. How could they keep the purity of white America free from Negro contamination? How could they preserve all that they thought was best in American society, even the inviolability of family life, if they allowed Negroes to be emancipated? And yet their revolutionary cultural heritage, their growing sense that Destiny had placed the moral future of the world in their hands "prohibited extreme, overt manifestations of aggression against them." Here were the roots both of a crisis of conscience and of its solution. Slavery was destroyed, yet racism preserved. And how this was achieved has been little understood.

The story of abolition, the reasons why the whole of Europe in the last third of the eighteenth century began to acquire a strong distaste firstly for the slave trade and even for slavery itself, is a vast question which none of the great historians of slavery—Davis, Jordan, Stampp, Genovese, Elkins— have yet attempted. It is a highly complex issue. The important factor is not the conversion of Quakers to anti-slavery attitudes, nor the convictions of a few intellectuals; voices, some weak, some powerful, had always been raised against slavery. The real question is why did abolition acquire a strong social basis, why did it become a passionate political issue? Again, I believe that this cannot be understood in isolation from the working class and the different attitude which was developing towards it. The most fertile ground for conversion to anti-slavery agitation, besides the Quakers, was in England amongst the entrepreneurs of the industrial revolution: the manufacturing districts (as against the commercial) were inclined to produce the subscribers, the speakers and the supporters of the anti-slavery movement; not all, of course, but it was an area of marked sympathy.

From the middle of the eighteenth century, and indeed far earlier amongst the Quaker industrialists, one can find a changing attitude to the poor labouring man, the attitude that he turned into a better, more profitable tool if he were given incentives, that is if he were encouraged to feel that his work possessed opportunities for self-advancement and better conditions, no matter how rudimentary. Furthermore, the new industrial methods required more self-disciplined skillful, better educated, literate labourers. The more imaginative, speculative manufacturers, such as Josiah Wedgwood, Jedediah Strutt and Robert Owen, experimented with higher wages, bonus schemes, better housing, works canteens, children's schools and the like. Instead of labouring men, exploiters now wanted tools, and far more tools than the old craftsman methods of industrial organization permitted: also their new tools needed to be more specialized and more limited. Master craftsmen were not wanted. Tools or "hands" were wanted, and they could be created from the labouring mass. Also a pool of labouring men, skilled, semi-skilled and un-skilled, selling their labour on a free market, was invaluable for keeping down wages. In a world of violent business cycles, "free" labour obviously had great advantages over unfree. Manufacturers' attitudes were rarely as crudely materialistic as this, any more than those of the slave owners. Many were devoted to their workers, helped them in harsh times and developed a patriarchal attitude, but this does not disguise the basic situation.

And so the whole attitude to exploitation began to change, very slowly but with gathering momentum, and the poor began to turn into the working class: but this working class, of course, was sharply differentiated within itself and, in a society that needed a mass basis of free wage-slaves, was treated often with a callousness which was no less evil than slavery and often justified by the same bogus quasi-scientific arguments that were used to justify racism: that the poor were biologically inferior. And, of course, racism did not die, indeed, given the right conditions, as with the influx of East European Jews into London's East End in the late nineteenth century, it intensified. And the same is true with Negroes in America.

The flourishing state of racism throughout the world, *post abolition*, should make us chary of explaining slavery in its terms. Yet slavery was abolished, the most powerful world leaders, for the first time in recorded history, deliberately set out to get both the slave trade and slavery suppressed. It became politically and socially viable for them to pursue such a policy. Slavery began to appear as archaic and its personal brutalities and restrictions were anathematized. Slavery became the antithesis of modernity. It cannot be an accident that the leadership of the anti-slavery agitation on a world-wide scale was conducted by the most industrialized nation in the world, namely Great Britain. However, that is another and a longer story. The point that I wish to emphasize is that a study of slavery, disengaged from the general history of the exploitation of labour, has inherent dangers, leading to a false emphasis and to a too simplified causation. It is even more confusing to see slavery entirely in terms of racism.

THE HIDDEN INJURIES OF CLASS
RICHARD SENNETT
AND JONATHAN COBB

IN the manufacturing cities of Western Europe during the nineteenth century, children of the countryside became the proletariat. The worker who was bred in city ways and comfortable in its crowds could indeed be found in the factories, but he did not dominate them. Even in England, where urban centers had been home to the new industrial order for generations, the working classes of Manchester or Birmingham were swelled each decade principally by people who could remember another way of life. Though Saint-Simon or Marx could speak of the "industrial era" as a fact taken for granted, less than a hundred years ago most people still had experience of rhythms of labor tied to the change of seasons, with diversity in human affairs measured by the boundaries of a village.

The rural influx to cities was not, four or five generations ago, a simple affair. People moved in complicated ways, often migrating in a chain from small farm to small town, then from town to cities of increasingly larger size. In Europe, a rural crisis forced vast population movements during the last decades of the nineteenth century. Large landholders no

FROM: *The Hidden Injuries of Class*, by Richard Sennett and Jonathan Cobb pp. 10–26. Copyright © 1972 by Richard Sennett and Jonathan Cobb. Reprinted by permission of Alfred A. Knopf, Inc.

261

longer found it profitable to keep peasants on their land; small farmers could no longer survive in an agricultural market swayed by international trade; local craftsmen could not compete with the cheaper commodities of factory production. The rhythms of rural life were disrupted by the magnet of the city, whose rulers capitalized on the disaffection of the rural young to draw in a supply of labor. More overt upheavals occurred through the persecution of minorities in villages, such as the Jews in Lithuania.

The American workers in cities of the Midwest and East Coast are predominantly men with this past. The majority of the 35 million white manual laborers in these cities have come from Ireland and Southern and Eastern Europe during the last four generations, and the chaos of the old country has cast a shadow across generations of these Americans still called "ethnics." It has commonly been thought that the settlement of Italians, Poles, or Greeks in little enclaves in American cities, in neighborhoods where the old language was spoken and the old customs kept, embodied a preservation of what the immigrant had known in his native land. But it is perhaps more accurate to say that these veterans of European turmoil found in the strange and alien cities of America a way to re-ignite some feeling of common custom and culture that had been disintegrating at home. "In the desert of America," a Russian Jew remarked in the 1920's, "it is easier to remain Russian in the old ways than among the iron mills in the Urals."

Yet this national crisis in the old country is not a sufficient explanation for the historic isolation of such ethnic groups. For this isolation also resulted from the impact these immigrants had on the economic life of the growing American cities.

Before the arrival of large numbers of immigrants, labor for industrial production was scarce, and machines were used in a special way to counteract the lack of sufficient urban workmen; machines were constructed to replace, wherever possible, *unskilled* labor, thus freeing scarce manpower for the jobs involving more skill, judgment, and complexity. When human labor was replaced by machines, as happened to the Lowell or Waltham mill girls, it occurred where workers performed unskilled tasks. The cost of unskilled human toil was greater than the cost of running machines.[1]

The influx of large numbers of destitute Europeans at the century's end changed this economic relationship. For example, Polish immigrants, looking desperately for work—any kind of work at any wage—arriving in the steel towns of western Pennsylvania, presented the region's industrialists with a substantial pool of cheap labor that would cost less to employ than the then-existing machines. Industrialists thereupon began to use machines to replace *skilled* labor in a situation where unskilled, unorganized labor was abundant.[2] In other words, this immigrant influx came to pose a serious, though indirect, threat to the jobs of established skilled workers—not only in steel, but in carriage-making, in printing, in textiles. And, not surprisingly, a deep hostility arose among the old Americans toward the newcomers.

The "social consciousness" of the new migrant was fixed on the problems he had left behind at home. In entering on the new experience of working for wages, he was concerned, beyond his own survival, with sending money back to relatives in the old country so that they could join him in the New World or survive the rural economic disaster in Europe.[3] The idea of formal labor organization was unknown to most of the immigrants. The ever-growing supply of unskilled labor made it almost impossible to organize stable industrial unions even when the idea was advanced—the skilled-crafts

[1] H. J. Habakkuk, *American & British Technology in the 19th Century* (Cambridge U. Press; n.d.) is an interesting discussion.
[2] David Brody, *Steelworkers in America: The Nonunion Era* (Russell; 1969).
[3] Oscar Handlin, *The Uprooted* (Grosset & Dunlap; 1957); *The Americans: A New History of the People of the United States* (Atlantic Monthly Press; 1963).

workers were, of course, uninterested in uniting with un-skilled foreigners. Indeed, employers used the threat of being reduced to the level of the immigrants to tame skilled-labor agitation. If the skilled worker was obedient and did not or-ganize, employers offered him the hope of at least semiskilled work, as machines took away his old job.

Although in the twentieth century skilled labor has re-asserted itself, this traumatic shift to a higher technology at the end of the last century established a native source of isolation for the urban immigrant of four generations ago: he came to the American factory at a moment when his presence allowed the growth of a new technology destructive to already-estab-lished workers. The hostilities sparked under these conditions left him only his countrymen for support.

It was perhaps no accident that a second force isolating the immigrant came into play at the same time. By the turn of the century, attitudes had crystallized toward foreigners whose closest equivalent is what we call today racism. These attitudes produced a kind of moral hierarchy of national and cultural differences in which the Western Europeans—with the exception of the Irish—stood at the top, diligent, hard-working, and for the most part, skilled laborers, and in which Slavs, Bohemians, Jews, and Southern Europeans stood lower, accused of dirtiness, secretiveness, or laziness. It is at this time that the image of the non-Teutonic or non-British immigrant as a potential criminal, at worst inclined to bomb-throwing and anarchism, but in any case brutish, surfaces in American folk mythology. Together with the schisms the immigrant brought from his own past, and the economic hostility he en-countered at the factory from established labor, national ster-eotypes forced the ethnic worker to turn to people like him-self for comfort and warmth, in little Italys and little Polands hostile to outsiders, "urban villages" stretching over time from the end of the nineteenth century to the middle of our own.[4]

[4] For a discussion of ethnic neighborhoods as "urban villages," see Herbert Gans, *The Urban Villagers* (Free Press; 1962).

The Hidden Injuries of Class

It was into this inward-turning urban world that most of the people we interviewed in Boston were born. Within its boundaries, people preserved a sociability little known on the outside. Its focus was the street. Almost all of the middle-aged adults with whom we spoke remembered their child-hood scenes as street scenes—family scenes, too, for their parents were there, shopping, talking to neighbors, sitting on stoops after the evening meal. Boston children growing up in the 1930's and 40's were planted in the midst of an especially vivid ethnic life, strong traces of which have survived. On Friday and Saturday, an open-air market still envelops the Italian section, where old men bargain hard and seldom in English; in South Boston, people still celebrate the Irish national holidays with fervor, and old men there who have never been to Ireland talk with Irish brogues.

Historians and sociologists have asked themselves repeatedly why the urban villages have lasted so long. A number of years ago, Nathan Glazer and Daniel P. Moynihan argued [5] that there is group will and choice embodied in this ethnic isolation, apart from economic tensions and turmoil in the mother countries. Ethnicity, they said, is a way of preserving some special identity in the midst of an American mass, a way of maintaining distinctive traditions and rituals even after a person has the practical opportunity to "melt" into "average" Americanness. Many observers have since taken issue with this thesis, arguing that isolation was in fact beyond the control of immigrant groups. Why do you talk about choice, they have said to Glazer and Moynihan, when the whole history of urban ethnic groups in American society shows an isolation bred of economic rejection in the old country and in the new? Father Andrew Greeley remarks, for instance, that although many people from ethnic backgrounds have made dramatic economic changes in their lives, the ethnic heritage that stays with them most powerfully is the memory of group

[5] In *Beyond the Melting Pot* (MIT Press; 1958).

traditions practiced in poverty in the teeth of a hostile native American culture.

This debate has given way to another. The urban villages which withstood native prejudice, the hostility of skilled native workers, and the economic shocks of the Great Depression have in recent years been subjected to a new set of forces, thrusting people into problems beyond the power of the old historic institutions to meet.

The urban "renewal" of central cities has been the most striking intrusion on the isolation of urban Americans of recent ethnic origins. The urban villages are often situated in areas where the housing is old, worn, and close to the central business district, and they have become prime targets for planners who dream of rivers of concrete connecting the office with the suburban bedroom, or of towers of glass as symbols of rebirth for the metropolitan economic order.

These communities have also been forcefully integrated into the larger society by national problems that are too powerful to be excluded. "Yes, you might call me an 'Italian-American,'" one woman remarked to us, "but it doesn't do me much good when I have to face my kids taking drugs." Inflation in rents and prices often forces people to move away from their old neighborhoods, as does the fear of crime.

Displacements caused by urban renewal often leave the uprooted with a sense of "grieving" akin to what they have felt when a member of the family has died, a grieving accentuated by the fact that they personally or their political representatives have been largely defeated in fights to stop "progress." [6] The fears of drugs and crime are similarly joined to a feeling that neither the individual nor the traditional institutions of the ethnic culture—the family, the Church, the local politicians—have much power to resist these threats.

One way to interpret this forced integration is that it is

[6] Marc Fried, "Grieving for a Lost Home," in Leonard J. Duhl, ed., *The Urban Condition* (Basic Books; 1963); Gordon Fellman, manuscript on highway protest, in preparation.

266

leading the mass of America's white laborers to become "workers" in the classic sense of the term. With the cultural shelter of the ethnic community crumbling—so this view runs —ethnic workers are now coming to grips with their true position in American capitalism: they are powerless in the hands of the economic and political forces controlling the cities. The wave of working-class protest in recent years would then appear as a groping to find a political voice as workers, rather than as Irishmen or Poles, a search that at first errs in choosing the wrong targets, like Blacks or radical students, for its anger.

This interpretation of the historical shifts in the experience of urban ethnic workers falls back on a calculus of material well-being; it prophesies a new, rebellious class consciousness arising from the shock American white workers are undergoing, as they are forced beyond the ethnic village into deprivations caused by living just as workers.

Critics following the logic of Arnold or Pfaff, on the other hand, can see in the breakup of the ethnic village support for their own pessimism. Herbert Gans argues, for example, that the ethnic enclaves have fragments at least in part by the voluntary desire of their inhabitants: as families make economic and occupational gains, they move out to the suburbs to join the ranks of the middle class. Much of the discontent voiced in the last few years by white workers, this view holds, is precisely against those who challenge the system. The historic changes in the lives of American blue-collar ethnics, on this account too, rest on a calculus of material self-interest.

In our own work, we began to see from the first interview on that urban laborers themselves, no less than their critics, are aware of the momentous change in their lives the decline of the old neighborhoods has caused; these working-people of Boston are trying to find out what position they occupy in America as a whole. To create images of their place, however, they use a language more complicated, more puzzling, than the computations of material well-being their interpreters use. For the people we interviewed, integration into American life meant integration into a world with different symbols of human respect and courtesy, a world in which human capabilities are measured in terms profoundly alien to those that prevailed in the ethnic enclaves of their childhood. The changes in their lives mean more to them than a chance, or a failure, to acquire middle-class *things*. For them, history is challenging them and their children to become "cultured," in the intellectual's sense of that word, if they want to achieve respect in the new American terms; and toward that challenge they feel deeply ambivalent. Perhaps the best way to illustrate this ambivalence is to describe what occurred in our first interview.

Frank Rissarro,[7] a third-generation Italian-American, forty-four years old when we talked with him, had worked his way up from being a shoeshine boy at the age of nine to classifying loan applications in a bank. He makes $10,000 a year, owns a suburban home, and every August rents a small cottage in the country. He is a man who at first glance appears satisfied—"I know I did a good job in my life"—and yet is also a man who feels defensive about his honor, fearing that people secretly do not respect him; he feels threatened by his children, who are "turning out just the way I want them to be," and he runs his home in a dictatorial manner.

Rissarro was born in 1925, the second-eldest child and only son of parents who lived in a predominantly Italian section of Boston. His father, an uneducated day laborer, worked hard, drank hard, and beat his wife and children often. As a young boy, Rissarro was not interested in school—his life was passed in constant fear of his father's violence. He was regarded by his family as a spoiled brat, with no brains and no common sense. His sisters and cousins did better than he

[7] This is not his real name, nor are the details that follow about his job, age, and income precisely accurate.

scholastically, all finishing high school. Yet even as a child, Rissarro worked nights and weekends helping to support his family. At sixteen he quit school, feeling incapable of doing the work and out of place. After two years in the military, he worked as a meat-cutter for nearly twenty years.

Rissarro was and is a man of ambition. The affluence spreading across America in the decades following the Second World War made him restless—he wanted to either get a butcher shop of his own or get out. The capital for a small business being beyond his reach, he had a friend introduce him to the branch manager of a bank setting up a new office in his neighborhood. He won a job processing loans for people who come in off the street; he helps them fill out the forms, though he is still too low-level to have the power to approve or disapprove the loans themselves.

A success story: from chaos in the Depression, from twenty years of hacking away at sides of beef, Rissarro now wears a suit to work and has a stable home in respectable surroundings. Yes, it is a success story—except that *he* does not read it that way.

As we explored with Rissarro the reasons why these good things have come to him, we found the declarations of self-satisfaction almost instantly giving way to a view of himself as a passive agent in his own life, a man who has been on the receiving end of events rather than their cause: "I was just at the right place at the right time," he says again and again. "I was lucky," he claims, in describing how he emotionally withstood the terrors of his father's home.

Is this modesty? Not for him. He feels passive in the midst of his success because he feels illegitimate, a pushy intruder, in his entrance to the middle-class world of neat suburban lawns, peaceable families, happy friendships. Despite the fact that he has gained entrée, he doesn't believe he deserves to be respected. In discussing, for instance, his marriage—to a woman somewhat more educated than he, from an Italian background equivalent to "lace-curtain Irish"—Rissarro told us something impossible to believe, considering his ungrammatical speech, his obsession with his childhood, his mannerisms and gestures: "My wife didn't know that I had no background to speak of, or else she would never have married me." The possibility that she accepted him for himself, and never made an issue of where he came from, he simply cannot accept.

Sociologists have a neat formula to explain the discontent caused by upward mobility; they call Frank's malaise a product of "status incongruity": Because Frank does not yet know the rules of his new position, because he is caught between two worlds, he feels something is wrong with him. This formula falls back on an image of the antithesis between working-class struggle and educated, "higher" culture.

The trouble here, however, is that Frank *doesn't* feel caught between two worlds. He knows what the rules of middle-class life are, he has played at them now for some years; furthermore, he is not in any way ashamed of his working-class past. Indeed, he is proud of it, he thinks it makes him a more honest person at work:

"I'm working, like I said, with fellows that are educated, college boys, in that office. I'm about the only one in there in any straits to say I'm educated. I'm enjoying this job, I'm going in with the big shots. I go in at nine, I come out at five. *The other fellows, because they got an education, sneaks out early and comes in late.* The boss knows I'm there, a reliable worker. 'Cause I've had the factory life, I know what it is. I mean, a man deserves—the least you can do is put your hours in and do your job. I'm a good employee. I know I am because I see others who are educated."

In fact, toward educated white-collar work itself, beyond all its symbolic connotations of success, Frank Rissarro harbors an innate disrespect: "These jobs aren't real work where you make something—it's just pushing papers."

Then why has he striven so hard to be upwardly mobile? One ready answer is that he wanted the house, the suit, the cottage in the country. And Rissarro himself gives that answer at first. After a few hours of talk, however, he conveys a more complicated and difficult set of feelings.

The poverty of his childhood he speaks about as something shameful, not because there was a lack of things, but rather because the people who had nothing acted like animals. He remembers this particularly in terms of his father—his father's poverty and his drunken brutality toward Frank and Frank's mother are interwoven in Frank's memory. Other images in his conversation concerning the poor, both white and black, similarly fuse material deprivation with chaotic, arbitrary, and unpredictable behavior; he sees poverty, in other words, as depriving men of the capacity to act rationally, to exercise self-control. A poor man, therefore, *has* to want upward mobility in order to establish dignity in his own life, and dignity means, specifically, moving toward a position in which he deals with the world in some controlled, emotionally restrained way. People who have been educated, on the other hand, are supposed to already possess this capacity. They are supposed to have developed skills for taming the world without force or passion.

Frank feels that it is such people on whom he ought to model the changes he wants in his own life. And yet, paradoxically, he doesn't respect the content of their powers: just as intellect gives a man respect in the world, the educated do nothing worth respecting; their status means they can cheat. In a further twist, Rissarro then proceeds to turn the paradox into a terrible accusation against himself: "As far as I'm concerned, I got through life by always trying to depend on the other guy to do my work. But when it came to my hands, I could do all the work myself."

Capturing respect in the larger America, then, means to Frank getting into an educated position; but capturing that respect means that he no longer respects himself. This contradiction ran through every discussion we held, as an image either of what people felt compelled to do with their own lives or of what they sought for their sons. If the boys could get educated, anybody in America would respect them; and yet, the fathers felt education would lead the young into work not as "real" as their own.

A workingman looks at the privileges high culture bestows in much the same light as does Ortega y Gasset or William Pfaff—that high culture permits a life in which material need can be transcended by a higher form of self-control; he looks at the claims of intellectual privilege, however, with the same jaundiced eyes as does Sartre. On this ground, the working-man's feelings about his leaving the isolated, poor ethnic community have the same ambivalence that the radical intel-lectual experiences when he seeks to define his place in rela-tion to the workingman.

Yet, why should Frank Rissarro be worrying about his le-gitimacy? And why has he chosen as a "prestige model" a kind of work activity he despises?

This paradox might, of course, be read simply as a conflict in the individual personalities of men like Frank Rissarro. It is more accurate, however, to see it as an issue introduced into their lives by the America outside the urban village. The story these workingmen have to tell is not just who they are but what are the contradictory codes of respect in the Amer-ica of their generation.

How Frank Rissarro talked to his interviewer provides some beginning clues in this regard.

Frank Rissarro did not so much grant an interview as give a confession. The interviewer began by asking a neutral ques-tion, something about what Rissarro remembered of Boston while he was growing up. He replied by talking with little in-terruption for more than three hours about intimate feelings and experiences to this stranger whom he had never met be-fore. Rissarro talked to the interviewer in a peculiar way: he treated him as an emissary from a different way of life, as a representative of a higher, more educated class, before whom he spread a justification of his entire life. At various points where he spoke of situations where he felt powerless and the interviewer sympathized, Rissarro would suddenly respond to him as simply a human being, not as an emissary sent in judgment; but then, as he returned to the story of his life, which he seemed to live through again as he described it, the interviewer once again became a representative of a class of people who could do what they wanted and who made him feel inadequate. It was Rissarro's chief concern throughout to show why circumstances had not permitted him to take charge of his life in the same way.

Yet this man is someone who feels he has done a good job in establishing a stable family and margin of security in contrast to the life of poverty and turmoil he knew as a child during the Depression. Why then is he so defensive?

The word "educated" as used by Rissarro, and by other men and women we talked to, is what psychologists call a "cover term"; that is, it stands for a whole range of experiences and feelings that may in fact have little to do with formal schooling. Education covers, at the most abstract level, the development of capacities within a human being. At the most concrete level, education meant to the people we interviewed getting certificates for social mobility and job choice, and they felt that American society parcels out the certificates very unequally and unfairly, so that middle-class people have more of a chance to become educated than themselves. But if the abstract is connected to the concrete, this means middle-class people have more of a chance than workers to escape from becoming creatures of circumstance, more chance to develop the defenses, the tools of personal, rational control that "education" gives. Why should one class of human beings get a chance to develop the weapons of self more than another? And yet, if that class difference is a *fait accompli*, what has a man without education got inside himself to defend against this superior power?

Rissarro believes people of a higher class have a power to

judge him because they seem internally more developed human beings; and he is afraid, because they are better armed, that they will not respect him. He feels compelled to justify his own position, and in his life he has felt compelled to put himself up on their level in order to earn respect. All of this, in turn—when he thinks just of himself and *is not comparing himself* to his image of people in a higher class— all of this is set against a revulsion against the work of educated people in the bank, and a feeling that manual labor has more dignity.

What does he make of his contradiction in his life? That he is an imposter—but more, that the sheer fact that he is troubled must prove he really is inadequate. After all, he has played by the rules, he has gained the outward signs of material respectability; if, then, he still feels defenseless, something must be wrong with *him:* his unhappiness seems to him a sign that he simply cannot become the kind of person other people can respect.

This tangle of feelings appeared again and again as we talked to people who started life as poor, ethnically isolated laboring families, and have been successful in making the sort of material gains that are supposed to "melt" people into the American middle class.

BOSTON'S WEST END: AN URBAN VILLAGE

HERBERT J. GANS

AN HISTORICAL AND ECOLOGICAL OVERVIEW

TO the average Bostonian, the West End was one of the three slum areas that surrounded the city's central business district, little different in appearance and name from the North or the South End. He rarely entered the West End and usually glimpsed it only from the highways or elevated train lines that enveloped it. From there he saw a series of narrow winding streets flanked on both sides by columns of three- and five-story apartment buildings, constructed in an era when such buildings were still called tenements. Furthermore, he saw many poorly maintained structures, some of them unoccupied or partially vacant, some facing on alleys covered with more than an average amount of garbage; many vacant stores; and enough of the kinds of people who are thought to inhabit a slum area. If he ventured inside the area, he saw some old people who looked like European immigrants, some very poor people, some who were probably suffering from mental illness, a few sullen looking adolescents and young adults who congregated on street corners, and many middle-aged people who were probably mainly Italian, Russian Jewish, Polish, and Irish in parentage.

To the superficial observer, armed with conventional images and a little imagination about the mysteries thought to lie behind the tenement entrances, the West End certainly had all the earmarks of a slum. Whether or not it actually was a slum is a question that involves a number of technical housing and planning considerations and some value judgments. . . . For the moment, the West End can be described simply as an old, somewhat deteriorated, low-rent neighborhood that housed a variety of people, most of them poor.

In most American cities there are two major types of low-rent neighborhoods: the areas of first or second settlement for urban migrants; and the areas that attract the criminal, the mentally ill, the socially rejected, and those who for one reason or another have given up the attempt to cope with life.

The former kind of area, typically, is one in which European immigrants—and more recently Negro and Puerto Rican ones—try to adapt their nonurban institutions and cultures to the urban milieu. Thus it may be called an *urban village*. Often it is described in ethnic terms: Little Italy, The Ghetto, or Black Belt. The second kind of area is populated largely by single men, pathological families, people in hiding from themselves or society, and individuals who provide the more disreputable of illegal-but-demanded services to the rest of the community. In such an area, life is comparatively more transient, depressed if not brutal, and it might be called an *urban jungle*.[1] It is usually described as Skid Row, Tenderloin, the red-light district, or even the Jungle.

In sociological terminology, these are ideal types, and no existing neighborhood is a pure example of either. Moreover, since the people who occupy both types are poor and at the mercy of the housing market, they often may live in the same neighborhood, erecting physical or symbolic boundary lines to separate themselves. In some areas, especially those occu-

---

[1] These are purely descriptive terms, and should not be taken too literally. They are not ecological concepts, for neither in economic, demographic, or physical terms do such areas resemble villages or jungles. They are terms that describe the quality of social life, but do not definitively identify social structure or culture.

pied by the most deprived people, the village and the jungle are intertwined.

The West End was an urban village, located next to Boston's original and once largest skid row area, Scollay Square. During the early nineteenth century, the West End had been an isolated farm area, almost inaccessible from the North End and the central business district area that then constituted Boston. Later, some streets were cut through and developed with three-story single family homes of various price levels. Following the arrival of Nova Scotian and Irish immigrants, other streets were built up with three- and five-story tenements, until, by the turn of the century, the five-story tenement became the main building type. The structures built in the latter half of the nineteenth century were intended, like those in the North End, for the poorest tenants. Apartments were small and several units had to share bathroom and toilet facilities. The buildings constructed around the turn of the century, however, were intended for a somewhat higher income group. Instead of three- and four-room apartments, there were five- and six-room ones, each with private bath and toilet, and kitchens equipped with a large combination heating and cooking stove. The new and the old apartments were built at high densities—more than 150 dwelling units per net residential acre—as compared today with the 5 to 8 units in the average middle-income suburb. Land coverage was high, 72 per cent of the land being covered with buildings, and, in a quarter of the blocks, buildings comprised over 90 per cent of the land.[2] Some of the streets were shopping blocks with small stores on the ground floor of the tenements. A few industrial lofts that attracted small manufacturing and wholesale establishments were scattered through the shopping streets.

Physically, as well as socially, the development of the West End followed a typical ecological process. The West End is

[2] Boston Housing Authority, "West End Project Report," Boston: The Authority, 1953, p. 5.

located at the bottom of one slope of Beacon Hill. At the top of this hill are the apartments and townhouses inhabited by upper- and upper-middle-class people. As one descends the slope, the status of buildings and people decreases. The "Back of the Hill" area, once occupied by servants to the Hill aristocracy, now is inhabited by families who moved up from the bottom of the slope, and, increasingly, by young middle-class couples in modernized tenements or converted townhouses who are gradually erasing the social differences between the Back of the Hill, and the Hill itself.[3]

The West End is at the bottom of the slope. At one time, when the Back of the Hill was a low-income settlement, both it and the area below were called the West End. Then, with the widening of Cambridge Street in the 1920's, a physical boundary was created between the two areas that eventually led to the symbolic separation as well. Within the West End, the area nearest to Cambridge Street and the Back of Beacon Hill contained the better apartment buildings and the two major institutions in the area—Massachusetts General Hospital and St. Joseph's Roman Catholic Church. The hospital, traditionally an extremely high status institution, is one of the teaching hospitals for the Harvard Medical School. The church, originally Congregationalist, later became one of the higher status Irish churches, which served Beacon Hill as well. The area closest to Cambridge Street and that fronting on the Charles River was known as the "upper end." Then, as one descended to what was called the "lower end," dwelling units became older and the people, poorer. At one corner of the lower end, the West End fronted on the Scollay Square skid row, and provided rooming houses for the people who frequented its bars and eating places. At another corner, there were small commercial buildings which were part of

[3] For descriptions of this area, see Walter Firey, *Land Use in Central Boston*, Cambridge: Harvard University Press, 1947; and H. Laurence Ross, "The Local Community and the Metropolis," Unpublished Ph.D. Dissertation, Harvard University, 1959.

the industrial and wholesaling area that separated the residential portions of the West End from the North End.

Several times during its existence, the population of the West End has changed in a pattern typical of other urban villages. The North and the South End were the primary areas of first settlement for Irish, Jewish, and Italian peoples, in that order. The South End also served the other ethnic groups that settled in Boston, especially Chinese, Greek, and Syrian. The West End had somewhat more distinctive functions. First, it was an overspill area for those who could not find room in the North End; later, it became an area of second settlement for some of the groups who began their American life in the North End. Thus, the West End underwent approximately the same ethnic succession pattern as the North End. In the late nineteenth century, it was primarily an Irish area, with Yankees scattered through the upper end.[4] Then, around the turn of the century, the Irish were replaced by the Jews, who dominated the West End until about 1930. During this era, the West End sometimes was called the Lower East Side of Boston. In the late twenties, Italians and Poles began to arrive, the former from the North End, and they joined a small Italian settlement that had existed in the lower end of the area since the beginning of the century. Throughout the 1930's and early 1940's, the Italian influx continued until eventually they became the largest ethnic group in both the upper and lower portions of the West End. The changes in population are reflected in data taken from library registration cards.[5] In 1926, the area was estimated to be 75 per cent Jewish. In 1936, however, the library users were 35 per cent Italian, 25 per cent Polish, 20 per cent Jewish, and

[4] For a detailed description of the West End around the turn of the century as it appeared to Yankee settlement house workers, see Robert A. Woods, ed., *Americans in Process,* Boston: Houghton Mifflin, 1902. For a fictional description of Jewish life in the area in the second decade of the twentieth century, see Charles Angoff, *In the Morning Light,* New York: Beechhurst Press, 1952.

[5] From unpublished reports in the files of the West End Library.

20 per cent "miscellaneous." [6] By 1942, the Italians were in the majority. . . .

The Italians who came to America were not farmers or peasants, but town-dwelling farm laborers who worked for absentee owners and managers. Although there was some evidence of the existence of a clanlike extended family, the occupational role of the farm laborer made it impossible for the extended family to function as a unit. The farm laborer, who was paid in wages that barely supported even his wife and children, could exist only in a nuclear family household.

Since people lived under conditions of extreme poverty, and in a static social system from which escape—other than by emigration—was impossible, the overriding goal was the survival of the nuclear family. Moreover, as marriages were contracted to advance—or at least not to retrogress—the economic and social position of the families involved, they had to be arranged. Consequently, husband and wife were usually not as close as in partnerships based on love. Since children had to go to work at the earliest opportunity, they were raised to adult status as quickly as possible, which was accomplished by treating them as small adults from an early age.

The nuclear family is neither entirely self-sufficient nor independent; nor can it satisfy all the needs of daily life. It is particularly handicapped in dealing with emergencies. Consequently, other institutions must be available. But when every family was involved in a struggle to survive—as was the case with the Southern Italian farm laborer—few people could be called on for aid, or trusted to give it when their own families were equally in need. Nor could they be treated as friends and companions, for they might take advantage of this relationship to help themselves in the fight for survival.

[6] *Ibid.* Registration figures do not reflect the population distribution with complete accuracy. In all likelihood, Jews are overrepresented among library users; and all other ethnic groups, underrepresented.

Moreover, in order to attract friends, one had to be able to make a good impression. This required a dwelling unit to which people could be invited without shame, money to pay the cost of entertaining, and a considerable amount of trust over a long period of time. As one of Covello's respondents put it: "Friends are a luxury we cannot afford." Community agencies, were they churches, schools, or welfare agencies, could not be trusted because they were controlled by the employer. It made no difference when they had been founded for beneficial purposes; they were rejected by their intended clients as a matter of pride.

Under such conditions, relatives were the only source of group life and mutual aid. Being tied to each other by what were felt to be irrevocable ties of blood, they could face each other without putting on appearances, without feelings of shame, and without suspicion that the relationship would be exploited. In a society where no one could afford to trust anyone else, relatives had to trust each other. Moreover, when survival depended on the ability to work strenuously for long hours, older people were at a disadvantage. Possessing no special skills or traditional knowledge not also available to younger people, they had little influence in the group once they had become too old to support themselves. In addition, since relatives had to double as friends, people naturally gravitated to family members with whom they had the most in common. Consequently, they were drawn to peers.

The Southern Italian farm laborers lived not simply in poverty, but in poverty in the midst of a visibly higher standard of living enjoyed by the artisans, the middle class, and the gentry. In some areas they resorted to strikes and to class conflict; in others, to emigration.[7] But until these solutions were possible, most farm laborers lived in a state of extreme relative deprivation, a state made even more painful because

[7] John S. MacDonald and Lea D. MacDonald, "Migration Versus Non-Migration: A Typology of Responses to Poverty," paper read at the 1961 meetings of the American Sociological Society.

of the close proximity of more fortunate people. In such circumstances, the restriction of aspirations was emotionally a most functional solution—at least in the short range—since it prevented the development of frustrations, which were frequently harder to endure than physical deprivation. Parental lack of interest in education, detachment from the larger community, and unwillingness to fight the exploiting powers —all were practical solutions in a society in which mobility was so restricted that there was no reason to expect benefits from schooling, and where the oversupply of labor made it possible to starve out rebellious individuals. While these solutions were harsh and denying, they also reduced stress, and made life as bearable as possible. Since the achievement of object-goals was certain to be frustrated, children were reared to reject them. The development of empathy was also discouraged; too great a sensitivity to the problems of other people would have been hard to endure.

Many of the conditions that gave rise to this way of life accompanied the Southern Italians in their move to America. In Italy, they had labored from sunrise to sunset on the farms of landowners; in America, they worked long hours as laborers for factory owners or contractors. Moreover, since they did not gravitate to the highly mechanized and rationalized assembly line jobs, the nature of their work did not change radically either. Many worked with the earth—pick and shovel in hand—in both countries, although in America, they brought forth construction projects rather than farm products. In Italy, they had lived in densely built-up and overcrowded small towns, barren of vegetation; in America, they moved into equally overcrowded and barren tenement neighborhoods. Indeed, their trip across the ocean took them only from rural towns to urban villages.

Most of these parallels continued into the adulthood of the second generation. Not until World War II, in fact, and the subsequent prosperity of the postwar era, did their economic position differ radically from that of their forebears. Even then, many West Enders have been dogged by unemployment, layoffs, and other forms of economic insecurity. Since they—as well as their parents—have often been employed in marginal industries, they also have felt themselves to be exploited occupationally. Moreover, like their ancestors, they have been beset by serious illness, premature death, infant mortality, and by other of the sudden and unpredictable tragedies that so frequently hit low-income people.

Many other parallels exist between Southern Italy and Boston. The immigrants who settled in Boston found a society stratified not only by class but also by ethnic background and religion. In fact, in Boston—more so perhaps than in other cities—they encountered a hereditary aristocracy that at the time of the Italian influx still held considerable social, economic, and political power. Since then, its place has been taken by the Irish and by other groups, all of them culturally different from the Southern Italians. In short, the world outside the home was and still is dominated by people different in class and culture, by outsiders to be suspected and rejected.

Thus, the environment that the immigrants and the West Enders have encountered in America has differed in degree rather than in kind; it is less hostile and depriving, of course, but it is otherwise still the same. There have been no radical changes in the position of the working class vis-à-vis other classes, or in the position of minority ethnic groups vis-à-vis the majority. As a result, there have been as yet no strong pressures or incentives among the West Enders for any radical change in the basic social structure with which they respond to the environment.

A number of findings on group life and personality have suggested that many of the elements I have summarized . . . are found among working-class people generally, and one survey of American studies describes them as person-centered.[8] This article also notes the practice of personalizing bureaucracy and other outside world situations, as does an account of English working-class life. A study of American working-class women describes their problems in regard to self-control, and shows how lack of self-control encourages their children in turn to express anger through violence.[9] It also suggests that working-class adolescents express themselves motorically, or physically, while middle-class adolescents use conceptual and symbolic modes.[10] Another study of American working-class women stresses the importance of group life, the fear of loneliness, and their concern with what others think of them.[11] An analysis of lower-class interview respondents has described in considerable detail their tendency to be concrete and particularistic, to think anecdotally, to personalize events, and to see phenomena only from their own perspective: [12] they do not "assume the role of another toward still others." [13] The limited repertoire of roles also has been described in a study of an English group,[14] and the inability or unwillingness of people to adopt other roles has

[8] S. M. Miller and Frank Riessman, "The Working Class Subculture: A New View," *Social Problems*, vol. 9 (1961), pp. 93–94.

[9] Daniel R. Miller, Guy E. Swanson *et al.*, *Inner Conflict and Defense*, New York: Holt, Rinehart, and Winston, 1960, Chap. 14.

[10] *Op. cit.*, Chap. 15. A national survey reports that "respondents with less education tend to be less introspective about themselves, whether about strong points or shortcomings." G. Gurin, J. Veroff, and S. Feld, *Americans View Their Mental Health*, New York: Basic Books, 1960, p. 69.

[11] Lee Rainwater, R. Coleman, and G. Handel, *Workingman's Wife* (New York: Oceana Publications, 1959), pp. 64–66. See also Hoggart, *op. cit.*, p. 72.

[12] Leonard Schatzman and Anselm Strauss, "Social Class and Modes of Communication," *American Journal of Sociology*, vol. 60 (1955), pp. 329–338; and Anselm Strauss and Leonard Schatzman, "Cross Class Interviewing: An Analysis of Interaction and Communicative Styles," in Richard N. Adams and Jack J. Preiss, ed., *Human Organization Research*, Homewood, Ill.: Dorsey Press, 1960, pp. 205–213.

[13] Schatzman and Strauss, *op. cit.*, p. 331.

[14] Madeleine Kerr, *The People of Ship Street* (London: Routledge & Kegan Paul, 1958), Chap. 17.

been reported as lack of empathy in a . . . study of Middle Eastern peasants.[15]

A number of American studies have shown the scarcity of working-class participation in what I have described as community life.[16] For example, the West Enders' pattern of being religious but not being identified with the church has been found among other American groups, both Protestant and Catholic,[17] and in England as well.[18]

Both American and English studies have reported the working-class' detachment from work,[19] the concern with job security,[20] and the negative evaluation of white-collar workers and bosses.[21] The West Enders' ambivalence about education is also widely shared. The conception that school should teach children to keep out of trouble has been described by an English study; [22] that education must contribute to the occupational success of the individual, by many studies, includ-

[15] Daniel Lerner, *The Passing of Traditional Society*, New York: The Free Press of Glencoe, 1958.

[16] Floyd Dotson, "Patterns of Voluntary Association Among Urban Working Class Families," *American Sociological Review*, vol. 16 (1951), p. 688; Bennett Berger, *Working-Class Suburb* (Berkeley: University of California Press, 1960), p. 59; Rainwater, Coleman, and Handel, *op. cit.*, pp. 114 ff. See also Morris Axelrod, "Urban Structure and Social Participation," *American Sociological Review*, vol. 21 (1956), pp. 13–18.

[17] Berger, *op. cit.*, pp. 45 ff.; Rainwater, Coleman, and Handel, *op. cit.*, p. 123.

[18] Richard Hoggart, *The Uses of Literacy* (London: Chatto and Windus, 1957), pp. 94–97; Kerr, *op. cit.*, pp. 135–136.

[19] A concise review of studies of work patterns and attitudes of working-class and lower-class people is found in Joseph A. Kahl, *The American Class Structure*, New York: Holt, Rinehart and Winston, 1957, pp. 205–215.

[20] Ephraim H. Mizruchi, "Social Structure Success Values and Structured Strain in a Small City," paper read at the 1961 meetings of the American Sociological Association, mimeographed; Social Research, Inc., "Status of the Working Class in Changing American Society," Chicago: Social Research, Inc., February 1961, mimeographed, pp. 57–58.

[21] Katherine Archibald, "Status Orientations among Shipyard Workers," in Reinhard Bendix and Seymour M. Lipset, eds., *Class, Status and Power*, New York: The Free Press of Glencoe, 1953, pp. 395–403; Michael Young and Peter Willmott, *Family and Kinship in East London* (London: Routledge & Kegan Paul, 1957), p. 14.

[22] Hoggart, *op. cit.*, p. 98.

ing an American [23] and a Puerto Rican one.[24] Two studies have indicated that working-class mothers want more education for their children than do the fathers.[25]

[There exists also the] prevalence of the general conception that the outside world is not to be trusted. This extends also to a skepticism about caretakers,[26] a reluctance to visit settlement houses,[27] and a fear of doctors and hospitals that seems to be found in all countries.[28] Similarly, working-class people everywhere believe—or know—the police to be crooked, and politicians, corrupt. In America,[29] England,[30] and Mexico,[31] researchers have described the working- and lower-class antagonism toward law, government, and politics.

Conversely, the mass media are accepted, often more enthusiastically than by other classes. A recently published study of American television viewers has made this finding, and noted the working-class audience's interest in and identification with performers.[32] Several studies have also suggested the preference for action dramas over other forms of media content, not only in America, [33] but all over the world.[34] In

[23] Social Research, Inc., pp. 51–53; see also Archibald, *op. cit.*, p. 399; and Mizruchi, *op. cit.*

[24] Elena Padilla, *Up from Puerto Rico* (New York: Columbia University Press, 1958), p. 198.

[25] Herbert H. Hyman, "The Value System of Different Classes," in Bendix and Lipset, *op. cit.*, pp. 426–442, Tables III, IV; and Helen Icken, "From Slum to Housing Project," Commonwealth of Puerto Rico, Urban Renewal and Housing Administration, 1960, p. 34.

[26] Padilla, *op. cit.*, p. 264.

[27] Albert Cohen, *Delinquent Boys: The Culture of the Gang*, New York: The Free Press of Glencoe, 1955, pp. 116–117.

[28] Hoggart, *op. cit.*, p. 42; Kerr, *op. cit.*, p. 39; Oscar Lewis, *The Children of Sanchez* (New York: Free Press, 1958), p. xxviii.

[29] Miller and Riessman, *op. cit.*, p. 91.

[30] Hoggart, *op. cit.*, p. 87.

[31] Lewis, *op. cit.*, pp. xxvii, 351, 389. On the personalization of government, see Miller and Riessman, *op. cit.*, p. 93; Padilla, *op. cit.*, p. 256; and Lewis, *op. cit.*, p. 332.

[32] Ira O. Glick and Sidney J. Levy, *Living with Television*, Chicago: Aldine Publishing Company, 1962, Chap. III, VII.

[33] See, for example, Berger, *op. cit.*, pp. 74–75.

[34] Herbert J. Gans, "American Films and Television Programs on British Screens: A Study of the Functions of American Popular Culture

Green's study of a Polish group, the rejection of romantic films by young working-class adults was described as follows: "At the local movie house, when the hero pauses in pursuit of the villain to proffer the heroine a tender sentiment, whistling and footstamping greet his fall from grace." [35]

As I have not attempted to make a complete survey of the literature, I have mentioned here only some of the many similarities between the West Enders and other groups. Even so, it should be evident that, by and large, the peer group society is associated with working- and lower-class life. Moreover, the data show that many of its features are found among other ethnic groups who have come to America from Europe—notably the Irish and Polish—as well as among racially differentiated groups, such as the Negroes and the Puerto Ricans. Incidentally, the peer group society also cuts across religious lines, for many of its characteristics appear not only among Protestants in England and America, but among European and Latin Catholics as well.

Some differences—including a few ethnic ones—do exist between the West Enders and other working-class people. Yet many of these differences can be traced to class factors operating in past and present generations. Italian-Americans, for example, differ from the Irish-Americans in a number of ways. The Irish are more respectful of paternal authority, of the older generation, of the church, and of authority in general. Irish men are also much closer to their mothers than are Italian men, a fact that has a number of implications for family structure, family dynamics, and even for the ways in which mental illness is expressed.[36]

Abroad," Philadelphia: Institute for Urban Studies, 1959, mimeographed, Chap. 4.

[35] Arnold W. Green, "The 'Cult of Personality' and Sexual Relations," in Norman Bell and Ezra F. Vogel, eds., *A Modern Introduction to the Family* (New York: Free Press, 1960), p. 613.

[36] These differences between the Irish are reported in Ezra F. Vogel, "The Marital Relationships of Emotionally Disturbed Children" (Ph.D. thesis, Harvard University, 1958), and M. K. Opler and J. L. Singer,

Many of these differences can be related to the fact that the Irish immigrants came from landowning, peasant families. In Ireland, the father was the sole owner of the family farm, and thus was free to choose as to which of his sons would inherit it. As a result, sons were in a subordinate position.[37] One study of the Irish peasantry notes, in fact, that sons were called boys until the day the father surrendered the farm to one of them, even if they themselves were middle-aged adults.[38] The conditions which the Irish immigrants found in America evidently did not encourage any major change in family structure. Certainly, one could argue that those Irish-Americans who turned to politics and the priesthood found that the relationship between the political boss and his underlings and between the Bishop and his priests was much the same as that between the farm owner and his sons. Needless to say, not all Irish-Italian differences can be explained purely by class factors, or by cultural differences which developed from economic conditions in Europe. They do seem, however, to be of primary importance.

West Enders also differ from other working-class, and especially lower-class, groups in the role that the mother plays in family life. Studies of the English working class, for example, have stressed the importance of the "Mum" and the dominance of the mother-daughter relationship over all others, even when the daughter is married and has children of her own.[39] Similarly, studies of the Negro, Puerto Rican, and Ca-

---

"Ethnic Differences in Behavior and Psychopathogy," *International Journal of Social Psychiatry*, vol. 2 (1956), pp. 11–22. See also Mark Zborowski, "Cultural Components in Responses to Pain," *Journal of Social Issues*, vol. 8 (1952), pp. 16–30; and Paul Barrabee and Otto van Mering, "Ethnic Variations in Mental Stress in Families with Psychotic Children," *Social Problems*, vol. 1 (1953), pp. 48–53.

[37] Conrad M. Arensberg and Solon T. Kimball, *Family and Community in Ireland*, Cambridge: Harvard University Press, 1940, pp. 47 ff.

[38] *Ibid.*, pp. 51, 56.

[39] The previously cited studies by Young and Willmott, and by Kerr describe this relationship in great detail.

ribbean lower classes have shown the family to be what anthropologists call matrifocal.[40] The mother is the head of the household, and the basic family unit includes her, her children, and one or more of her female relatives, such as her mother or aunt. Often the man is a marginal and only intermittent participant in this female-based household.[41] American studies of the lower class have reported what Walter Miller calls "serial monogamy"—a pattern in which a woman lives and has children with a series of men who desert her or whom she asks to leave.[42]

The reason for this pattern among Negroes can be found in the fact that in past and present, they have lived under conditions in which the male's position in the society has been marginal and insecure. Under slavery, for example, the formation of a normal family was discouraged, although the female slave was allowed to raise her own children. Since the days of slavery, the Negro's economic position has been such as to maintain much of this pattern. The man who has difficulty in finding a steady job and is laid off frequently finds it difficult to perform the functions of a male breadwinner and household head. Moreover, when the woman is able to find steady employment or can subsist on welfare payments, she tends to treat the man with disdain and often with open hostility, especially if he complicates her life by making her pregnant. Under these conditions, there is no incentive for the man to remain in the family, and in times of stress he deserts. Moreover, when the male children grow up in a predominantly female household—in which the man is a powerless and

[40] See, for example, Raymond T. Smith, *The Negro Family in British Guiana*, London: Routledge and Kegan Paul, 1956; and for America, E. Franklin Frazier, *The Negro Family in the United States*, Chicago: University of Chicago Press, 1939.

[41] Walter B. Miller, "Lower Class Culture as a Generating Milieu of Gang Delinquency," *Journal of Social Issues*, vol. 14 (1958), p. 14.

[42] Walter B. Miller, "Implications of Urban Lower-Class Culture for Social Work," *Social Service Review*, vol. 33 (1959), p. 225.

scorned figure—their upbringing encourages ambivalence as to male functions and masculinity. Thus, the pattern is perpetuated into the next generation.[43]

The hypothesis that the female-based family can be traced to class and, more specifically, to occupational factors is supported by studies describing this family type among peoples who have not been slaves.[44] It has been found, for example, among Puerto Ricans, both on the island and in New York. It seems, however, to be more prevalent among Puerto Ricans from sugar cane areas, which have a plantation economy much like that under which the Negro endured slavery.[45] The hypothesis is supported in another way by the fact that a somewhat similar family constellation prevails when the man's occupation separates him from his family for long periods. Thus, a study of sailors' families in Norway indicates that the woman takes over the dominant role in the family, and overprotects her children.[46] Although the girls show no negative consequences, the boys seem to develop what Tiller calls a defensive feminine identification, and compensatory masculine traits. When such boys become adults, they thus favor occupations that stress masculinity and minimize female contact and the family role.

The female-based family, however, is not found among West Enders, and the reasons perhaps can also be traced to occupational factors. Although the West Ender's ancestors suffered from unemployment, the totally agrarian economy of Southern Italian society and the extremely strenuous character of farm labor created no employment opportunities for

[43] Walter B. Miller, "Lower Class Culture as a Generating Milieu of Gang Delinquency," *op. cit.*, p. 9.

[44] I have not been able to find any explanation of the dominant role of the "Mum" in the English working-class family. It should be noted, however, that this family is not female-based.

[45] I owe this suggestion to Howard Stanton. In the sugar cane economy, there is work for only three to four months a year.

[46] Per Olav Tiller, "Father Absence and Personality Development of Children in Sailor Families," Oslo: Institute for Social Research, 1957, mimeographed.

women. Indeed, the family could best survive if the woman
stayed home and bore a large number of children who could
eventually add to the family's income. As a result, the woman
did not take on an economic function, and the man maintained his position in the family even though he could not always support it adequately. This family constellation seems
to have been strong enough to endure in America during
those periods when the man was unemployed and the woman
could find a job. Needless to say, some family instability and
male marginality or desertion has occurred among the immigrants and the second generation, but such cases have been
considerably fewer than among newcomers with female-based
families.

Finally, the West Enders may be contrasted to the Jews, an
ethnic group which came to America at about the same time
as the Italians, but with a different occupational history.[47]
The Jews who emigrated from Poland and Russia around the
turn of the century were neither farm laborers nor peasants,
but peddlers, shopkeepers, and artisans with a more middle-
class occupational tradition. They also differed from their fellow immigrants in their belief in education, partly for reasons
related to this tradition. Although they worked initially as
unskilled and semiskilled laborers in America, they reacted
differently to their environment than did the ethnic groups
from peasant and farm labor origins. Superficially, the Jewish
family structure resembled the Italian one, with a nuclear
household surrounded by a large family circle. Because of the
high value placed on education, however, the immigrants did
not restrain their children from contact with the outside
world. They encouraged the children to use the schools and
settlement houses to prepare themselves for white-collar and
professional occupations. Thus, the Jewish young people
pursued careers that drew them apart from the parental

[47] This account draws on Marshall Sklare, *Conservative Judaism*,
New York: The Free Press of Glencoe, 1955; and Nathan Glazer, *American Judaism*, Chicago: University of Chicago Press, 1957.

generation at the same time that their Italian neighbors rejected such careers as "lonely ventures" that could only break up the cohesion of the family circle. Although the Jewish immigrants did bemoan the children's acculturation into styles of life congruent with their higher occupational level, they also took pride in the successful mobility of their offspring.[48]

I would not want to claim that the West Enders are like all other working-class and peasant ethnic groups, or that all differences between them and other populations can be explained by class factors. Indeed, many differences between the ethnic groups must be attributed to other factors in their cultural traditions and in their American experience.[49] Until comparative studies of these groups are made that hold class constant, however, we will not know exactly where these differences are located, nor how they can be explained.

[48] For a detailed study of differences between American-born Italians and Jews, see Fred L. Strodtbeck, "Family Interaction, Values and Achievement," in D. C. McClelland, A. Baldwin, U. Bronfenbrenner, and F. Strodtbeck, *Talent and Society*, Princeton: D. Van Nostrand, 1958, pp. 135–194. He compares Jewish values, such as the belief in education, the desirability of individual achievement, and the striving for mobility and for rational mastery of the world to the Italians' familism and fatalism. Even so, he suggests that "differences between Italians and Jews are greatly attenuated when class level is held constant." *Op. cit.*, p. 154, based on an unpublished study by B. Tregoe.

[49] See here especially Zborowski, *op. cit.*, and Opler and Singer, *op. cit.* Since the West End was a multi-ethnic neighborhood with relatively little variation in class, the studies now being conducted by the Center for Community Studies among the various ethnic groups may shed further light on these differences.

THE SOURCES OF STABILITY: THE IMMIGRANTS IN STEEL

DAVID BRODY

BEFORE 1880, "English-speaking" workmen had manned America's iron and steel plants. Then immigrants from South and East Europe began to arrive in increasing numbers. More than 30,000 were steelworkers by 1900. The newcomers soon filled the unskilled jobs in the Northern mills, forcing the natives and earlier immigrants upward or out of the industry. In the Carnegie plants of Allegheny County in March 1907, 11,694 of the 14,359 common laborers were Eastern Europeans.[1] The recent arrivals dominated the bottom ranks of the steel industry.

The Slavic influx shaped the labor stability at the unskilled level. A lowly job in the mills, however ill-paid and unpleasant, was endurable if it enabled the immigrant to leave in a few years with funds enough to resume his accustomed place in his native village. That was his original purpose. The majority, who in time decided to stay in America, usually had by then risen into higher paid jobs. In either event, the acceptance of the hard terms of common labor was the necessary prelude to a better life. Immigrant mobility was at the center of the peaceable adjustment of the unskilled steelworkers.

Fixed for centuries, by 1900 the peasant society of Eastern

REPRINTED by permission of the publishers from *Steelworkers in America: The Nonunion Era* by David Brody, Cambridge, Mass.: Harvard University Press, pp. 96–111. Copyright, 1960 by the President and Fellows of Harvard College.

[1] U.S. House Committee on the Investigation of the U.S. Steel Corporation, *Hearings*, 62 Cong., 2nd Sess. (1911–1912), IV, 2889–2893 (cited hereafter as Stanley Hearings). For the general movement of Eastern Europeans into the industry, see second chapters in all the sections of *Report on Immigration*, VIII, XI.

Europe had begun to disintegrate. The abolition of serfdom gave the peasant the right to mortgage and sell his land, and, later, to subdivide it. The falling death rate upset the ancient balance between population and acreage, leaving sons unprovided for or with insufficient land. Manufactured goods destroyed the peasant's self-sufficiency, raised his living standards and costs, and emphasized the inefficiency of his farming methods. When misfortune struck—a destructive storm, a drought, an outbreak of phylloxyra in the vineyards or disease in the livestock—he fell into debt, or, already mortgaged, lost his farm.

The peasant was linked to a chain of family inheritance and tradition. He had a name, a reputation, and a posterity. His self-esteem went with property, independence, and an assured social position. All this rested on his land, located in a certain village and held by his family from the immemorial past. The peasant with mortgage payments he could not meet faced an intolerable decline into the dependent, propertyless servant class. Rooted to the land, he saw his salvation only in emigration to a country from which men returned with money.

Inhabitants of the Western provinces of Austria-Hungary had long been accustomed to migrate seasonally to Germany for the harvests. To supplement meager farm incomes, Slovaks had peddled goods or followed wandering trades as wiremakers, potmenders, and glaziers. From the peasant viewpoint the longer move to America differed from seasonal migration only in degree. Men went to Germany to add to a slender livelihood. In America they would save enough to pay off the mortgage or to buy the land that would restore their social position. A Polish immigrant expected to "remain for some years and return with something to our country, so that later we might not be obliged to earn [as hired laborers]." [2] The Atlantic crossing meant a heavy investment,

[2] Raczkowski Series, April 8, 1907, W. I. Thomas and F. Znaniecki, *The Polish Peasants in Europe and America* (2 vols., New York, 1927),

a long absence, unaccustomed work in mill or mine; but the essential purpose did not differ from seasonal migration. The immigrant hoped to earn a stake and return to his village. With this end Slovaks, Poles, Croats, Serbs, Magyars, and Italians made the passage to America, and many found their way into the steel mills.

They entered the mills under the lure of wages. Earnings of $1.50 or $2.00 a day, it was true, would not support a wife and children. In the Pittsburgh district, where a family required $15 a week, two-thirds of the recent immigrants in the steel plants made less than $12.50, and one-third less than $10. The Pittsburgh Associated Charities in 1910 found that, if a steel laborer worked twelve hours every day in the year, he could not provide a family of five with the barest necessities. Every steel center had large numbers who earned much below the minimum for family existence.

But the immigrant steelworkers had not expected to support families in America. The vast majority came alone. One-third of those surveyed by the Immigration Commission were single, and rougly three-quarters of the married men who had been in the country under five years reported their wives abroad.[3] The minority with families supplemented its income by lodging the others.

A "boarding-boss system" developed, benefiting all except perhaps the overburdened women. The workmen paid the "boss" $2.50 or $3.00 a month for lodging, including cooking and washing. The wife, or occasionally a hired housekeeper,

---

I, 771, as well as similar statements in other series, I, 454, 1023, 1041, and letters to the Emigrants Protective Society in Warsaw, II, 1504–1509. The immigrants quotations in this chapter come from the collections of letters in these volumes, unless otherwise stated in the footnotes, and will not be individually cited.

[3] U.S. Immigration Commission, *Report on Immigration* (Washington, D.C., 1911), VIII, 139–151, also III, 47, for numbers of males and females coming to the United States, 1899–1910. The bulk of the statistical data in this chapter comes from vols. VIII and IX of the invaluable *Reports* of the Immigration Commission, covering the iron and steel industry, and will hereafter not be specifically cited in the footnotes.

bought the food for the household, and at the end of each month the total bill was divided among the adult males. There were variations. The boss might charge a flat monthly rate, or provide only a specified amount of food. In Granite City, Illinois, the Bulgarians economized by doing their own housework. But the system was essentially the same. A boarder could live for about $15 a month, and even after spending another $10 on clothing and trifles, could put aside $15. The boarding boss increased his income usually by more than half his mill earnings, and, in addition, was likely to be made a foreman.

The immigrants, moreover, counted the value of their hoards in terms of the increased buying power in their native villages. Mentally converting dollars into roubles, they estimated carefully that a few years of steady work would bring enough to buy a piece of land. "If I don't earn $1.50 a day," figured a prospective immigrant, "it would not be worth thinking about America." He could surely get that much in a steel mill. The large sums deposited in banks or sent home during prosperous years like 1907 verified the calculations. America, a Polish workman wrote home, "is a golden land as long as there is work." The wages in steel mills appeared to enable the peasant to achieve his purpose.[4]

The newcomers harbored no illusions about America. "There in Pittsburgh, people say, the dear sun never shines brightly, the air is saturated with stench and gas," parents in Galicia wrote their children. A workman in the South Works warned a prospective immigrant: "if he wants to come, he is not to complain about [reproach] me for in America there are neither Sundays nor holidays; he must go and work." Letters emphasized that "here in America one must work for three

[4] In 1907 immigrants in Johnstown and Steelton sent abroad $1,-400,000. In September 1907 one bank on the South Side of Pittsburgh had on deposit $609,000 in immigrant accounts. See Emil Lengyel, *Americans from Hungary* (Philadelphia, 1948), pp. 182–185, for functioning of Transatlantic Trust Company set up by the Hungarian Postal Savings Bank.

horses." "There are different kinds of work, heavy and light," explained another, "but a man from our country cannot get the light." An Hungarian churchman inspecting Pittsburgh steel mills exclaimed bitterly: "Wherever the heat is most insupportable, the flames most scorching, the smoke and soot most choking, there we are certain to find compatriots bent and wasted with toil." [5] Returned men, it was said, were worn out by their years in America.

Knowing about the taxing labor awaiting them, only the hardier men immigrated. Letters cautioned, "let him not risk coming, for he is still too young," or "too weak for America." The need to borrow for the trip tended to limit the opportunity to those who expected to make "big money." [6] This selectivity gave the steel mills the best of Europe's peasant population.

Accustomed to village life, the adjustment to the new world of the steel mills was often painful. An Austrian Jew recalled his first day in a plant.

The man put me in a section where there was [sic] terrible noises, shooting, thundering and lightning. I wanted to run away but there was a big train in front of me. I looked up and a big train carrying a big vessel with fire was making towards me. I stood numb, afraid to move, until a man came to me and led me out of the mill. [7]

Most weathered the first terror, the bewildering surroundings, the shouts in an unknown tongue. Appearing passive and unflinching they grew used to the tumult and became skillful in their simple tasks.

A fat pay envelope overshadowed heavy labor and long hours; a few years' hardship was a cheap enough price for the precious savings. "I should like to have piecework, for work is

[5] Peter Vay de Vaya und zu Luskod, *Inner Life in North America,* reprinted in Oscar Handlin, *This Was America* (Cambridge, Mass., 1949), p. 410.

[6] Emily G. Balch, *Our Slavic Fellow Citizens* (New York, 1910), p. 186.

[7] David J. Saposs, Personal Interviews with Steelworkers, 1920.

297

never too hard," wrote a Polish peasant. "The work is very heavy, but I don't mind it," a brick factory worker informed his wife, "let it be heavy, but may it last without interruption." Russian steel laborers in Pittsburgh told an investigator they were glad to work extra days. A majority voluntarily reported on Sundays in 1907 to clear the yards and repair equipment.[8] An immigrant characterized his twelve-hour position: "A good job, save money, work all time, go home, sleep, no spend." [9] Thus did the immigrant's purpose match the policies of the employers.

The hazards of the mill alone troubled the workmen. Dangerous to experienced men, steelmaking was doubly so to untutored peasants. The accident rate for non-English-speaking employees at the South Works from 1906 to 1910 was twice the average of the rest of the labor force. Almost one-quarter of the recent immigrants in the works each year—3,273 in the five years—were injured or killed. In one year 127 Eastern Europeans died in the steel mills of Allegheny County.[10] Letters told, sometimes in gory detail, the sudden end of friend or relative. The debilitating effects of industrial life took their quieter toll on the health of the immigrants.

In misfortune, the peasant had depended on his kin and parish, whose obligations to assist were defined and certain. He left this secure web of mutual help when he came to America. A Pole explained to his wife the hard lot of an immigrant.

As long as he is well then he always works like a mule, and therefore he has something, but if he becomes sick then it is a trouble, because everybody is looking only for money in order to get some of it, and during the sickness the most will be spent.

[8] *Pittsburgh Survey*, ed. P. U. Kellog (New York, 1909–1914), VI, 39–44.
[9] Charles R. Walker, *Steel: Diary of a Furnace Worker* (Boston, 1922), p. 28.
[10] Crystal Eastman, *Work-Accidents and the Law*, Vol. II of *Pittsburgh Survey*, p. 14.

Illness meant expenditure without income; a lengthy conva-
lescence drained his savings and completely frustrated his
ends.

Accidents were equally catastrophic. Illiterate, ignorant of
the law, unable to speak the language, the immigrant had
small likelihood of successfully presenting his compensation
claim. If he was killed, the chances of his dependents were
even more dubious. The Pennsylvania courts had ruled that
the liability statute did not extend to nonresident aliens.
Whatever the company's negligence, the victim's family in
Europe was helpless. More than one-fourth of the men killed
in Allegheny County in the year ending July 1907 had left
their dependents in Europe, and the families of a score more
departed soon after the funeral. Destitution awaited them.
Friends learned from letters that "the widow begs, and the
children are in rags," that the woman "works in the fields" or
has "gone out to service," or that the family returned to the
grandparents "who are old and have nothing." [11]

Very early, the immigrants sought to ease the heavy individual risks. As soon as a number gathered in a mill town,
they set up an informal mutual help society obligating each
member to assist at sickness or death. These became local in-
surance associations, in time affiliating with national benefit
societies which were able to provide better and cheaper coverage. For example, the National Slovanic Society for
monthly dues of 60 cents paid a death benefit of $1,000 and a
sick benefit of $5.00 for the first thirteen weeks and $2.50 for
another thirteen weeks. Immigrant steelworkers joined in
large numbers. The Polish National Alliance had thirty locals
in Pittsburgh in 1908. In Homestead 421 men belonged to the
Greek Catholic Union, 363 to the National Slovanic Society,
460 to the First Catholic Slovak Union, 130 to the National
Croatian Society.[12] In much the same way as the native steel-

[11] Eastman, pp. 132, 185; *Pittsburgh Survey*, VI, 44.
[12] Margaret F. Byington, *Homestead: A Complete History of the Struggle
of July 1892*, Vol. IV of *Pittsburgh Survey*, p. 162; Thomas and Znaniecki,

workers, the immigrants partially coped with the hazards of the new world.

Bleak prospects faced the newcomers outside the mill. They settled on the low ground never far from the smoke and clamor of the plant, but also within easy walking distance to work. At Lackawanna they occupied the marshy land surrounding the works, living in houses on "made ground" surrounded by stagnant, filthy pools. In the older mill towns they pushed the inhabitants of the dreariest streets into better neighborhoods. They huddled apart in enclaves often called Hunkeyvilles—in Gary, the Patch; in Granite City, Hungary Hollow; in Vandergrift, Rising Sun.[13]

Flimsy, dilapidated structures lacking the most elementary sanitary facilities sheltered the immigrants. The Pittsburgh Bureau of Health reported after its 1907 inspection of tenement houses:

The privy vaults were often found to be foul and full to the surface, sinks without trap or vent, the rain conductor serving to carry off waste water; damp, dark, and ill-smelling cellars used for sleeping purposes; cellers filthy; leaky roofs causing the walls and ceilings to become watersoaked, rendering the rooms damp and unhealthy; broken and worn floors; broken stair railings . . . plaster broken and paper torn and dirty.[14]

Conditions were little better outside urban centers. Croatian workmen in Johnstown occupied frame houses edging a courtyard. A low four-room closet serving over fifty groups stood in the center directly over an exposed cesspool. The

---

II, 1517–1521, 1570, 1577 ff. See also "The Slovaks in America," *Charities and the Commons*, Dec. 3, 1904, p. 242, on the history and functioning of the National Slovanic Society. Also, A. A. Marchbin, "Hungarian Activities in Western Pennsylvania," *Western Pennsylvania Historical Magazine*, XXIII (Sept. 1940), 163–174.

[13] Map of Johnstown showing immigrant settlements in *Report on Immigration*, VIII, 329; map of Steelton in *ibid.*, p. 659, and description of settlement process, *ibid.*, pp. 659–660; *ibid.*, p. 767, on Lackawanna; *ibid.*, IX, 44–45, on Granite City.

[14] *Pittsburgh Survey*, V, 90 ff.

houses were dark, poorly ventilated, and in bad repair. Similarly, families depended on outside hydrants in the dismal immigrant courts of Homestead's Second Ward.

The inadequate dwellings were greatly overcrowded. The boarding boss and his family slept in one downstairs room in the standard four-room frame house. The kitchen was set aside for eating and living purposes, although it, too, often served as a bedroom. Upstairs the boss crammed double beds which were in use night and day when the mill was running full. Investigators came upon many cases of extreme crowding. Thirty-three Serbians and their boarding boss lived in a five-room house in Steelton. In Sharpsburg, Pennsylvania, an Italian family and nine boarders existed without running water or toilet in four rooms on the third floor of a ramshackle tenement. According to the Immigration Commission report, the number per sleeping room in immigrant households averaged around three; a sizable portion had four; and a small number six or more.

Ignorance compounded the living problems. Country people, the immigrants could not fathom the ways of urban life. Before the Pittsburgh filtration plant went into operation in 1908, many contracted typhoid fever. Doctors complained of the refusal to boil water. Despite warnings, men persisted in going to the river to quench their thirst as they had at home. Nor did they easily adjust to crowded, indoor life. Investigators found their rooms filthy, windows shut tight, sanitary facilities neglected and clogged. The occasional indoor bathrooms were left unused or served as storerooms.

The landlords, for their part, considered the immigrants fair game. When the newcomers invaded neighborhoods, property depreciated and frequently passed into new hands. The speculators ignored housing regulations, made no repairs or improvements, and in the continuing housing shortage and animus against immigrants, charged exorbitant rents. In some instances they received an extra dollar a month for each boarder. For much inferior accommodations, immigrant steel-workers paid an average 20 per cent more per room than did English-speaking tenants.

The local courts also fleeced the immigrants. The "squires" of the aldermanic courts in Pennsylvania received no salary, but were entitled to the fees incident to minor criminal and civil cases. Untutored in the law, they were usually brokers or real estate agents who regarded their office as a source of easy profit. And their prey were the foreigners, ignorant, inarticulate, and frightened. On pay nights the aldermen reaped handsomely from the workmen corralled into their dingy "shops" on dubious charges. An investigation of two aldermen revealed that only a small part of their criminal cases justified indictment. A Ruthenian boarding boss who had been fined $50 for disorderly conduct commented scornfully:

Huh! The police are busy enough all right stopping disorder when the men have got money. But when there's hard times, like there is now, a man can make all the noise he pleases. . . . It ain't law they think about. It's money.

Indiana, Ohio, and Illinois justice was equally corrupt.[15]

Harsh as life in the mill towns was, room still remained for a happier side. The newcomers went usually to friends and relatives, and worked with men from their own villages. The benefit societies were convivial, and from them sprang other social organizations. Priests arrived as soon as there were people enough to support a church. The parish emerged to unite the activities of the ethnic, religious group into a coherent community. The later arrival in steel towns found his social needs relatively well satisfied.

There were other means of consolation. Intemperance, particularly during pay nights and marriage and birth celebrations, dismayed social workers. The immigrants had ready money, beer and whiskey cost little, and saloons served

---

[15] *Pittsburgh Survey*, V, 139–152, VI, 72, 378–379; E. A. Steiner, *The Immigrant Tide* (New York, 1909), pp. 250–251.

as social centers. Investigators counted 30 saloons in Duquesne, 65 in Braddock, 69 in McKeesport. Gary had one saloon for less than every hundred inhabitants; barrooms lined solidly the immigrant end of the main thoroughfare, known locally as Whiskey Row.

But the main consolation was the knowledge that the hard life was temporary, a few years' sacrifice in exchange for a competence at home.

The one essential was not wages, working conditions, or living standards, but employment itself. "When there is none," wrote one Polish laborer, America "is worth nothing." Prospective immigrants wanted to know only "whether work is good and whether it is worth while to go to America." Favorable reports emptied the villages. "An awful multitude of people are going from here to America," a Polish peasant informed his brother during the high prosperity of early 1907. The peak years of American industry—1892, 1903, 1907, 1910—matched the heights of immigration.

The newcomer's stay depended directly on his employment. "I have had no work for four months now," a workman wrote his brother in February 1904. "If conditions don't improve by Easter, we will go back to our country, and if they improve and I get work, I will immediately send a ship ticket and you will come." In depressed years immigration dropped sharply; one Polish woman reported in 1908 "whole throngs of people coming back from America." More Austro-Hungarians and Italians departed than arrived that year.

The effects of trade fluctuations were, if anything, exaggerated in the unstable steel industry. And the immigrants were the first to be let go. Non-English-speaking men constituted 48 per cent of the South Works labor force in 1907, 37 per cent in 1908.[16] Thirty per cent of the immigrant steelworkers surveyed by the Immigration Commission in 1908 worked less than six months, almost two-thirds under nine months. Ap-

[16] U.S. Bureau of Labor, *Report on Conditions of Employment in the Iron and Steel Industry*, IV (Washington, 1911–1913), 108, 166.

proximately 2,425 recent immigrants left Steelton, where only half the normal work force had employment. By the end of the depression, nine-tenths of the Bulgarians, the chief unskilled labor of Granite City, had departed.

Unemployment frustrated the immigrant's aims in much the same way as illness or injury. If the depression was prolonged, he might be reduced to real want. Granite City's Hungary Hollow came with reason to be called Hungry Hollow during 1908. But the boarding boss system mitigated the worst of extreme hardship; the fortunate boarders shared with the others, and the boss rarely forced a penniless workman to leave. In every case, nevertheless, the lost job meant the collapse of the immigrant's plan. Not only did his savings stop, but his accumulation quickly drained out. Unemployment, impossible to accommodate within the immigrant's purpose, alone disturbed the unskilled labor pattern. Otherwise, the Slavic steelworker found entirely acceptable the terms of work imposed by the system of economy.

The immigrants intended to return to their villages, and many did. From 1908 to 1910 (including a bad, middling, and prosperous year) forty-four South and East Europeans departed for every hundred that arrived; altogether, 590,000 left in the three years. But more remained.

Many forces turned the immigrant away from his homeland. He saw little enough of the new country, but he was nevertheless influenced by it. He at once discarded his peasant garb, and he sensed, despite the hard life and the hostility of Americans, the disappearance of clear lines of class and status. Nothing revealed more of the American influence than the complaints of the gentry that immigrants, when they returned, were disrespectful.

Migration weakened the familial solidarity of peasant society, clouded the purposes and inherited values of the immigrant, and, particularly after the wife arrived, dimmed the

304

image of the home village. Moreover, the presence of friends and relatives and the developing social institutions began to meet the needs of the immigrants. They in time regarded their jobs, not as temporary chances, but as their careers, and their goal became promotion rather than property at home.

The crucial fact was that in the steel mills immigrants did rise. Thomas Huras, for example, came to America in October 1910 and the following February found a job in the open-hearth department of the Gary Works. He transferred to the merchant mill, where there was more opportunity, gradually rose, and in 1918 was a catcher in the ten-inch mill. Walter Stalmaszck, at fifteen going to work on a blast furnace in the South Works, eventually became a straightener on No. 1 rail mill. When in 1914 the Joliet Works picked out men to serve as safety supervisors for their sections, many immigrant workmen received their first chance to advance.[17]

Statistics showed the process. At one large Pittsburgh mill in 1910 none of the recent immigrants with under two years' service had skilled jobs, 56 were semiskilled, 314 unskilled; between two and five years, 17 were skilled, 243 semiskilled, 544 unskilled; between five and ten years, 79 were skilled, 441 semiskilled, 475 unskilled; and over ten years, 184 were skilled, 398 semiskilled, 439 unskilled.[18] The income of immigrant steelworkers increased steadily. Less than one-tenth of any ethnic group resident less than five years earned over fifteen dollars a week; between 13 and 25 per cent resident from five to ten years; and 20 to 33 per cent resident over ten years. Altogether, 13 per cent of the recent immigrants

[17] *Gary Works Circle*, October 1918; *South Works Review*, June 1918, also, February 1918; *Joliet Works Mixer*, July 15, 1914. For example, Samuel Starkovitch, employed for five years in the yard now was promoted to safety man in the yard department. Many other issues give squibs on such safety workers, almost invariably immigrants.

[18] *Labor Conditions*, III, appendix C, 480 ff.; *Stanley Hearings*, IV, 2889–2893. See also *Report on Immigration*, VIII, 395–399, for figures on Cambria Works.

in the industry held skilled jobs, another 42 per cent semi-skilled.[19]

The pattern of life changed with lengthening residence and rising earnings. The immigrant steelworker sent for his family; two-thirds in America under five years reported wives abroad, one-third from five to nine years, and one-seventh after nine years. His living standards rose; more money went for food, clothing, and luxuries. He was willing to pay higher rent for better lodging, frequently moved his family out of the densest immigrant sections, and abandoned the boarding boss system. Habitually saving, he often bought his house. One-sixth of 1,674 immigrant steelworkers in the Immigration Commission survey owned their homes. In time he learned to speak English with fair fluency. Steve Augustinovitch, a Croat who immigrated at the age of eighteen, was typical. Foreman of a repair crew at the Gary Works at twenty-eight, he owned his house, had savings, a large family, and his first citizenship papers.[20]

In short, he merged with other skilled steelworkers. Distinguishable ethnically and perhaps socially, within the plant he moved in the same orbit of dependence and repression. If anything, the immigrants were more susceptible to the employers' strategy, for the peasant mentality sharply distinguished between independent farming and hired labor. The immigrant felt less secure in his job than the native steelworkers, whose experience encompassed only hired employment, and he therefore became a more docile, loyal employee.[21]

The stability in the unskilled ranks thus rested on mobility. The newcomers either moved up into the skilled force; or

[19] *Report on Immigration,* VIII, 54–55. Lowering the figure to $12.50 a week added 25 per cent to each group.

[20] *Gary Works Circle,* February 1918.

[21] See, for example, Saposs Interviews, Mike Stephan in McKeesport, July 29, 1920; Julius Danko, McKeesport; and blast furnace labor foreman in McKeesport, August 2, 1920.

they moved out at the first depression or with a satisfactory accumulation. Despite the harsh terms of work, therefore, steel companies enjoyed peaceful relations with their common laborers.

The employer's part in maintaining the pattern was essentially passive. He was generally ignorant of the reasons why the immigrants came to America. But he recognized them as a "floating supply of labor." [22] That simple, crucial fact governed his decisions.

Hiring and firing policies assumed the mobility of common labor. Employment officials did not investigate the immigrants, kept no detailed records, and observed individual capacity only for physical strength. When labor was plentiful, foremen usually picked likely men out of the jobless crowds that gathered before the mill gates at the changing of the shift.

To insure a steady supply, companies reached understandings with immigrant leaders. The employment manager, said the labor supervisor of the South Works,

. . . must not only be aware of the location of all the groups of foreign settlement in the community, but he must become personally acquainted with the individual boarding bosses, steamship agents, clergymen, and other influential agents. . . . These are his supply depots, and only by perpetual, personal reconnoitering can he remain familiar with the quality and quantity of available applicants.[23]

The steel plants in Granite City, for instance, had an agreement to employ all the applicants of a Bulgarian leader. Boarding bosses, when they were gang foremen, could hire as well as lodge workmen. Before the immigrant channels to mill towns developed, steel companies had sent agents to New York City docks or employed labor agencies. That was

[22] *Iron Age*, October 30, 1913, p. 987.
[23] A. H. Young, "Employing Men for a Steel Mill," *Iron Age*, November 16, 1916, p. 1108.

rarely necessary in later years except during serious short-ages.

Welfare efforts, designed to attach workmen to the company, did not extend to common labor. "The problem of maintaining a force of skilled workmen is realized by every employer" and "much attention has been given to" their welfare, observed the *Iron Age*, "but the unskilled employee of shop or foundry gets little attention." [24] The difference could be seen most clearly in housing programs. One company in the Eastern district provided excellent facilities at low cost for its higher paid men. For unskilled labor, the firm offered "shanties," an appropriate designation. Ten by fourteen feet, these were constructed of ordinary rough pine boards weatherstripped on the outside. Four men ate, washed, and slept in each shanty. Four "barracks," built like the shanties, housed twenty men each. All the structures were primitively furnished, and damp and cold in winter. According to the federal Bureau of Labor estimate, the rent amounted each year to more than 200 per cent of the company's original investment.[25] In less isolated areas employers generally ignored the housing problems of the immigrants.

The few efforts at improvement proved dismal failures. Lackawanna erected a village of monotonous but substantial houses around its new plant for low paid employees. And the Steel Corporation put up fifty dwellings—"double dry goods boxes"—for its laborers at Gary. But the men did not understand the need for sanitation and objected to the lack of amusements in the vicinity. The Gary houses were filthy, used as boarding houses, and greatly overcrowded. Within a few years the Corporation evicted the inhabitants of the notorious Hunkeyville and razed the houses.[26] The experiment was admittedly unsuccessful.

[24] *Iron Age*, February 19, 1914, p. 504.

[25] *Labor Conditions*, III, 420–426.

[26] G. R. Taylor, "Creating the Newest Steel City," *Survey*, April 3, 1909, pp. 20–36; J. A. Fitch, "Lackawanna," *Survey*, October 7, 1911, pp. 929–945; Gary *Post-Tribune*, May 23, 1923.

The Immigrants in Steel

The housing provided by the Corporation is perhaps better suited to the needs of the skilled workmen than to the wages of the unskilled laborers [who are] largely foreigners without families. These men earn low wages, out of which they seek to save the utmost amount possible.[27]

The Steel Corporation thereupon left the immigrant steelworkers to their own devices, erecting housing designed only for the higher ranks. Other measures to reduce labor turnover—pensions, profit sharing, stock purchase—likewise bypassed the unskilled.

The steel manufacturers had ready answers for the criticisms of reformers. The immigrants, they said, were eager to work the long hours for the greater earnings. They received wages higher than for similar work in Europe. Their living conditions were worse than the skilled workers' not because of smaller income, but because their wages were dissipated in "debauch." However bad their life appeared, said a Pittsburgh employer, it "is probably somewhat better than that to which such foreign workmen were accustomed in their own countries." [28]

It was not that steel manufacturers undervalued the immigrants. Although claiming natives to be superior workmen, employers understood very well their good fortune. They dealt with the immigrant steelworkers as they did because nothing else was necessary. Developing without any effort on their part, the unskilled labor pattern of mobility fitted perfectly into the scheme of economical steel manufacture. The steelmakers were content.

[27] U.S. Steel Corporation, Bureau of Safety, Sanitation, and Welfare, *Bulletin*, No. 5 (1927), p. 56.
[28] *Iron Age*, March 24, 1910, pp. 670–671 (a series of short statements by Pittsburgh employers in reply to charges by the Federal Council of Churches).

THE WORKING CLASS:
A BREAK WITH THE PAST

STANLEY ARONOWITZ

I

THERE are new currents in the working class, not the least of which is the rise of a generation of workers whose life experience has been radically different from all previous generations. Nor are the potentially revolutionary sectors of the working class sufficiently defined by Marx's famous concept of productive labor—that is, all those who own nothing but their labor power, but are engaged in the production of material commodities. The rise of corporate capitalism and its integration with the state, together with the rise of central bureaucracies as a critical locus of economic and social power, have broadened the working class, both in size and composition.

The traditional industrial working class remains a necessary condition for expanded capitalist production, and its centrality in the production of capital in most industries has been essentially unaltered despite its numerical stagnation. But the rise of the mass of workers employed in the public bureaucracies, in the distributive trades and in the services is a striking feature of late capitalism, illustrating its parasitic character. Moreover, the relationship between mental and physical labor has altered dramatically since World War II within the production sector itself, so that in several key industries knowledge has become the critical productive force. This development has not been even in all mass production industries, however. The assembly line of the auto industry is

FROM: Stanley Aronowitz, "The Working Class: A Break with the Past," *Liberation*, Vol. 17, Nos. 3–5 (August 1972), pp. 20–31.

still highly labor-intensive, and productivity is still measured in terms of the speedup of human labor. Despite recent technological advances in some giant corporations, the textile industry has barely scratched the surface of possible cybernetic technologies. But the oil and chemical industries, the electronics industry, and important branches of the paper industry are examples of dramatic shifts in the composition of the labor force. Here the absolute number of technically trained wage and salary workers has begun to approach the size of the unskilled and semi-skilled work force. In the oil industry, no newly hired production worker has lacked a high school diploma for the past 20 years, and most of them aspire to college or technical school degrees so that they can work in the laboratories and as supervisors. Chemicals, oil, electronic equipment, synthetic fibers and some kinds of paper and food products are no longer produced by human physical labor, except for the maintenance workers who perform repair work. The production worker is a watcher of heat and volume gauges and his major task is to know the respective tolerances well enough to stop the flow of work when necessary. In the older plants, the production worker still adjusts some continuous flow operations by hand, but the recent expansion of the chemical and paper industries have made self-adjusting mechanisms more common. In plants where continuous-flow operations predominate, the key production workers are the chemist, the engineer, and the quality-control technician, not the machine watcher. It is not only the importance of the so-called research and development activities which define the growing importance of knowledge, but the production process itself.

Modern capitalism requires ever more investment outlets to absorb the tremendous output made possible by this rising productivity. These opportunities for investment are not only provided by foreign markets, but by the systematic exploitation of the home market. In the 1950s and 1960s, this plunder was accomplished by the well known device of making the government a consumer of capital through military expenditures paid for by taxes, by expanding the sales effort, shortening the amortization of durables by lowering quality, and enlarging public employment as a partial disguise for the disutility of vast quantities of human labor and capital within the productive sphere.

The distinction between the classical concept of productive and unproductive labor is still important for certain types of analyses. But it does not make sense in an era where the concentration of capital and its international integration has become the significant feature of the world capitalist system. The divisions within the capitalist class have not been healed, but they are far less important than the unity of the collective capitalist against the collective laborer.

On the other hand, differences within the working class on the basis of race, nationality, sex, skill and industry are not obliterated by late capitalism. On the contrary, they constitute antagonisms which still act as a brake on the development of revolutionary consciousness within the working class. But the collective worker is emerging as the direct antagonist of the collective capitalist. What I shall describe in this article should be understood as tendencies in this direction, not accomplished historical changes. In my opinion, the direction is clear: the objective possibility for the emergence of a new revolutionary subject is in the process of formation. Not the old working class, which, as has been pointed out by Marcuse and others, was not a class in "radical chains" in America because it actually did become *of* society as well as in it. Nor is the new revolutionary subject only the controversial new technical and scientific worker. Knowledge has indeed become a productive force in our society, but it is widely disseminated among the whole new generation of workers, which is better educated than any in history. The new revolutionary subject is simply this generation of collective labor. It was created by the conjuncture of capital's own development and the struggles of previous generations of workers to limit

312

the arbitrariness of capital. Its needs and aspirations are radically different from its ancestors. Its demands, not yet articulated, may be too far-reaching for capitalism to satisfy.

II

The most important change from all previous generations is the emergence of a homogeneous working class in America, a country which, as Daniel Bell has noted, corresponds more exactly to Marx's classic model than any other capitalist nation except Britain. This homogeneity is a result of 1) the decline of ethnicity as a critical factor of American political and social life; 2) the common experience of the generation of workers of being separated from the gnawing poverty or the constant threat of it that suffused the consciousness of its elders; 3) the decline of commodity culture as a determining ideology among workers; 4) and the weakness of the fundamental institutions of authority, such as the family, schools, religion, and labor unions.

Among the most persistent demographic influences stultifying working-class consciousness has been the fact that a huge sector of the basic industrial working class in America was formed out of the waves of immigration between the end of the Civil War and the end of World War I. In the early days of trade union organizing, a frequent complaint of militants was that the task of bringing "unskilled" and semi-skilled workers into labor unions was made extremely difficult by ethnic splits within the working class. These splits were nearly all encompassing. Different nationalities were recruited into different industries: Italians and Jews into the garment industry; Italians and Portuguese into the New England textile industries, with a minority of Irish; Irish into the transport industry; Eastern Europeans into the steel industry. Within the same industrial plant, the technical division of labor was also organized along ethnic lines. Germans became foremen and skilled workers, closely followed by the Irish. Eastern and southern Europeans of all nationalities were relegated to the hottest, hardest and lowest-paid jobs, until the blacks occupied these positions after the First World War.

The tremendous growth of American capitalism between 1865 and 1920 was made possible by the agricultural crisis in Europe (and later within the U.S.) which forced millions of rural laborers to pour into European and American cities. The hierarchical organization of immigrant labor within our country, corresponding to the stratification of labor within the workplace, reinforced cultural and ethnic divisions.

The southern and eastern European migration to the United States did not begin in earnest until the 1880s. It is important to realize, however, that southern and eastern Europeans were brought to this country to occupy job categories in precisely the same industries that had prompted the migration of the earlier groups of immigrants from northern and western Europe. As mass production of iron, textiles, and mining replaced artisan methods, the demand increased for unskilled workers in these industries. In Pennsylvania's Schuykill Field, an important mining area where foreign-born workers constituted the great majority of laborers, only 4 percent of the immigrants were from eastern and southern Europe in 1880. By 1890 their ratio had increased to 25 percent, and, by 1900, they constituted more than half the foreign-born workers in the field—their increase corresponding to the mechanization of mining.

Similarly, in textiles, as the old crafts of the mule spinner and weaver were replaced by power-driven looms, the proportion of workers from England, Scotland, and Wales decreased as these workers were replaced in the production process by Italians, Irish, and later by Portuguese. In the iron industry, the ratio of northern Europeans to the total number of foreign-born decreased in direct proportion to the modernization of this industry, that is the relative decline in the numerical and technical significance of skilled labor. In 1870 the northern European immigrants constituted 75 percent of the foreign-born; among these the Irish constituted almost one-half the total number, a reflection of the growing significance of unskilled labor. A decade later, the proportions of all these groups dropped as the Slavs and Hungarians rose among the ranks of the unskilled, and by 1890, the significant change in the ethnic composition of the labor force in this industry was the decline of the proportion of unskilled Irish workers.

Within the next two decades the eastern Europeans were well on the way to occupying the preponderance of unskilled categories. As a result of the introduction of the open hearth process, the need for unskilled labor expanded dramatically and employers chose to recruit from among the Slavs and Central Europeans rather than the Irish. The Italian immigration in the early years of the twentieth century was a product of the full flowering of the steel industry, the further expansion of unskilled rail construction labor, the rise of the clothing industry in the same period, and the growing importance of building construction concomitant with the growth of the cities.

The replacement of skilled by unskilled and semi-skilled labor in the industries that constituted the economic matrix of the country transformed the social position of skilled workers made up, to a very great extent, of earlier immigrants. They were no longer the core of productive labor. Indeed, in the wake of mechanization, they were increasingly threatened. The union scale among the highly organized skilled steel workers, for example, once respected by employers eager to use their invaluable skills, now became an anachronism. Steel barons like Andrew Carnegie and Charles M. Schwab resolved to break the economic power of the artisans in proportion to the already evident decline of their technical power. Skilled workers were replaced, on the one hand, by semi-skilled, "new" immigrant workers and unskilled laborers.

The 1892 Homestead Strike became a symbol of the economic and social changes experienced by American industry.

315

Although supported by many of the eastern European immigrants occupying the least skilled jobs, the strike was essentially a protest by the skilled workers against the employers' assault upon their privileged position in the mills. Carnegie and his cohorts demanded nothing less than the proletarianization of the crafts. But, despite his victory, neither industry nor the skilled workers were prepared to surrender the hierarchical division of labor within the factory.

Skilled workers still occupied those niches within the remaining sectors of American industry which were less susceptible to mechanization. German craftsmen dominated the printing industry and the still-undeveloped machine tool industry where machines were as yet unable to displace the requirement for hand precision. The English and the Welsh became weighers, foremen, and technicians in the mining industry, gang bosses on the railroads (together with the Irish who moved up as the Slavs, Italians, and blacks replaced them in common labor), and loom fixers in textiles. In the iron industry, Germans were heavily represented among the machinists; the Scotch Irish and the English remained skilled workers in the steel fabricating section of the industry that manufactured by-products of basic steel and were employed as maintenance mechanics in the basic steel industry. Typically, the Irish and English were the foremen of labor gangs in this industry. According to David Brody, by 1910 13 percent of the recent immigrants had achieved skilled jobs and another 42 percent of these workers were holding semi-skilled jobs. Although he represents this development as evidence that the southern and eastern immigrants actually had attained social mobility, and thereby accounted for their lack of class consciousness and presumed docility, the fact remains that in 1910 75 percent of the unskilled labor force in the steel industry consisted of southern and eastern European immigrants.

In 1910, even though the northern European immigration (exclusive of Scandinavia) accounted for about 40 percent of the total male, white immigrants in the labor force, they comprised more than 62 percent of the skilled immigrant workers. Workers from Great Britain and Germany were to be found in greater proportion than all foreign-born in the crucial occupational categories of the skilled, the professionals, and small proprietors. The Irish rose rapidly within the hierarchy of occupations, except among proprietors. As for the eastern and southern Europeans, they occupied significant proportions of the unskilled and semi-skilled ranks well into the twentieth century. Brinley Thomas has commented:

Evidence has been presented . . . to show that by the end of the century, the sons of immigrants who had come from Britain and northwestern Europe were consolidating their hold on the better class jobs in a society that was gradually becoming more stratified.

In contrast, among the Slav, Italian, and Hungarian immigrants, more than 70 percent were unskilled. In 1907, in the Homestead Mill, Slavs earned $12 a week, English-speaking immigrants were in occupations earning $16, native-born whites were making $22.

These differential wage rates corresponded to the stratification of labor based, in part, on the ethnic distribution within the hierarchies of occupations. Nearly the entire middle and upper management stratum within the steel industry, mining, textiles, and railroads were native-born or descended from earlier northern European migrants, particularly from England, Scotland, and, to a much lesser extent, Germany. ("Native-born" referred to two distinct groups: those whose parents had been born in the United States and those whose parents arrived in the United States prior to 1850. Managers in basic industries were clearly members of the first group.)

The consolidation of labor stratification meant that most southern and eastern European immigrants remained at the unskilled and semi-skilled levels. In most cases (notwithstanding the economic heterogeneity in the working class made

317

possible by the mobility of a successful but relatively small minority within each group) their "native-born" children did not become skilled workers, professionals, or proprietors. Instead, first generation workers from these nationality groups re-entered the mills as unskilled or semi-skilled labor or became workers in service industries and in the public sector; entrance into skilled occupations was restricted as trade unions established mechanisms such as separate seniority lists that distinguished between crafts and the rest of the labor force—a separation which was reinforced in the early part of the twentieth century by employers, too.

But the waves of immigration made possible some mobility within the working class itself. As long as the system kept expanding, the frontier myth could be sustained on the basis of the chance for upgrading as well as real and imagined opportunities for small-business ownership. Even if only a few workers ever left the shop or reached the exalted status of foreman, it was difficult to persuade workers that their own class solidarity was the best guarantee for change. The efforts of radicals to educate workers to the principle that they should rise *with* their class, rather than above it, were always counteracted by the differential access of different ethnic groups to opportunities within the system.

Trade union hierarchies remain an important indication of the relative status of respective immigrant groups. Nearly all major trade unions established after the Civil War have been dominated by skilled workers of northern European origins. The leadership of the Mine Workers Union has followed a typical pattern. Here, despite the decline in the numerical importance of Irish, English and Welsh miners after 1890 and the simultaneous rise of the Slavs and Italians, no significant national leaders of the union or challengers to leadership were of eastern or southern European origin up to and including the 1960s.

The leaders of the rail unions, even of those unions such as

318

the American Railway Union that attempted to organize workers on the basis of industry rather than craft were recruited from among the most skilled categories of workers—again, usually of northern European extraction. Eugene Debs, the founder of the A.R.U., was a skilled worker, having been a member of the Firemen's Union before attempting the amalgamation of all groups.

Textile unionism, in its early years had been characterized by leadership drawn from among loomfixers, weavers, and other skilled workers. Despite the recent recruitment of Italians and some Jews to top positions, native born and northern European workers have been dominant in union leadership for the past half century. Emil Rieve, a skilled hosiery worker and leader of the Textile Union during the rise of the C.I.O., was succeeded by William Pollock, a Philadelphia weaver of Scottish parentage.[1]

The C.I.O. was organized principally by leaders of the mining and clothing workers unions that had successfully established themselves as industrial organizations in the first decades of the century, although it relied heavily on the support of the unskilled workers in the key mass production industries. Indeed, a close examination of the ethnic, racial, and skill composition of its principal leadership on the national level as well as in the shops reveals an enormous disparity between its democratic ideology and its practice, as borne out by the following table of the principal leaders of important C.I.O. unions in 1950:

---

[1] One notable exception to this pattern was in the needle trades unions, but here Jewish hegemony was possible only after the Irish-led United Garment Workers, an A.F.L. affiliate composed largely of cutters, was successfully ousted. Even after overthrowing the old regime, both the International Ladies Garment Workers and the Amalgamated Clothing Workers remained in the hands of the skilled workers: cutters and highly paid sewing machine operators. Both David Dubinsky and Sidney Hillman, as well as those who have succeeded them as union leaders, were from the "craft" categories in an industry where the overwhelming majority of operatives are employed as section workers.

Steelworkers: Phillip Murray, Irish miner
United Auto Workers: Walter Reuther, first generation German toolmaker
United Auto Workers: Homer Martin, minister, first U.A.W. President of English origin
Rubber: L. S. Buckmaster, English skilled worker
Rubber: S. Dalrymple, skilled tire worker, Scotch-English descent
Oil: O. A. Knight, Scotch-Irish skilled worker
Miners: John L. Lewis, Welsh skilled worker
Amalgamated: Jacob Potopsky, Jewish cutter
Maritime: Joseph Curran, Irish seaman
Longshoremen: Harry Bridges, Australian
Electrical: James Carey, Irish, worked briefly in industry
Transport: Michael Quill, Irish

It is much the same tale told by the ethnic identification of leadership of the A.F.L. unions that organized large numbers of industrial workers in the 1940s and 1950s:

Meatcutters: Pat Gorman, Irish, skilled
Machinists: Al Hayes, Scotch-Irish, skilled
Garment workers: David Dubinsky, Jewish cutter
Teamsters: Dan Tobin, Irish

Currently, the ethnic and skill composition of the leadership of these unions has not changed radically in the wake of the large influx of black workers, the relative stability in number and proportion of skilled workers in each industry, and the decline in the proportion of workers of northern European origins. The machinists, teamsters, autoworkers, steelworkers, oilworkers, electrical workers, and miners are still led by men of northern European origins although the nationality of the top officers has changed in some cases.

Where mass unionism was successful among immigrants, such as in the steel industry after World War I, organization could only proceed by taking ethnic differences into account, that is, by organizing separately by nationality as well as together by class. William Z. Foster, the chief organizer of the great steel strike of 1919, described the immense obstacles

The Working Class: A Break with the Past

presented by ethnic divisions. Characteristically, after having achieved a degree of unity among the diverse groups comprising the basic steel labor force, employers resorted to herding black scabs, an explicit admission of the significance of race and nationality as an employer tool for dividing the working class.

But the fact of cultural diversity was not sufficient to explain the low level of class consciousness among immigrant groups (except for skilled workers, many of whom shared socialist and anarchist leanings or activities in the old country). Equally important was the exquisite sense of the promise of American life deeply embedded among the foreign born. To the extent that historians have dealt with the impact of immigration on the development of social and political life, emphasis has been placed on the importance of the frontier or Horatio Alger myths as determining the conservatism of the immigrants. But the ideology of social mobility was more than a myth. It corresponded to the real opportunities for advancement within and from the ranks of the unskilled made possible by the rapid expansion of American capitalism at home and abroad.

My grandfather fled the Czarist military draft for the war with Japan to come to America. His family were Jewish peasants in Lithuania who were able to make a living on the land, but never had the security of daily life in the literal sense of the phrase. Most immigrants were victims of famines or other forms of agricultural crises, or were similarly victimized by repressive regimes. Many European peasants filled the cities of their native lands. For others, like my grandparents, there was no room in Amsterdam or London. The United States may not have been the promised land, but there was a chance to live.

Some immigrants had been imbued with the revolutionary traditions of the old country. When they came to America they sought out the labor and socialist movements. Others were attracted, after some years of life and labor in the

321

United States, to the militant and idealist movements of immigrants and native born. Having fled from oppression, they were determined not to endure it all over again. But the majority saw a chance in America, if not for themselves, at least for their children. And this country did provide an opportunity for some of their children. Of course, the route of higher education was not available to most first- and second-generation children of the immigrants. But many of them found their way into the skilled trades or out of the lower-paid industrial jobs. America was not exactly the land of milk and honey, but it was certainly better than Sicily or County Cork.

The irony of the immigration was that its conservative influence was entirely misperceived by both radicals and the government. The rise of nativistic movements seeking to exclude immigrants from this country on the basis of their alleged radicalism and/or laziness was belied by the fact that American capitalism was built on the backs of black and white imported labor. Government suppression of immigration was prompted more by the slowing growth rate of the economy and the appearance of frequent economic crises after the turn of the century than by the clear and present danger of revolution. But it is important not to underestimate the significance of the anti-radical impulse behind nativist ideology. As with the emergence of the permanent war economy in the 1940s and 1950s, the "red menace" provided the rationale for government suppression of not only radicals but the entire working class as well. The most militant of the industrial workers movements, the IWW, organized among immigrant groups as well as the native born. Although it never achieved a solid base of support among either group, its successful strikes were conducted as much among foreign-born workers in Lawrence, Massachusetts, as native Americans working in the lumber camps of the Northwest. The IWW did not disappear under the weight of its internal conflicts or the failure of its ideology or organizing tactics. It was defeated by a determined repressive state apparatus during the First

The Working Class: A Break with the Past

World War when patriotism was rampant within liberal and socialist ranks, paralleling the jingoism rampant among large segments of the general population.

The last great waves of immigration came to our shores during the three years following World War I. In the wake of the Palmer raids against radicals, the government clamped down on immigrants and only permitted a trickle after 1921. Exceptions were to be made for the victims of the fascist terror in the late 1930s, the refugees of the Hungarian uprising in the late 1950s, and the Cubans after the rise of the socialist regime. Still, first-generation workers are often influenced by the attitudes of their parents, even though the mass culture of 20th-century America, together with the expansion of compulsory schooling, has created important differences between the generations. The rapid acculturation of new Americans was a key objective of the corporate-minded liberals at the turn of the century. Settlement houses, adult evening classes in English, the emphasis on public education, and the patriotic orientation of the ethnic social and fraternal clubs which sprang up to help immigrants make a successful adjustment to their new environment, were all assisted by large corporations and the government in the quest for a docile labor force.

Even though socialist-minded nationality groups were a powerful influence among some new arrivals and formed a significant part of the socialist and communist movements well into the 20th century, most foreign-born workers belonged to such organizations as the Polish Falcons or the Sons of Italy, which were strongly conservative, if not downright reactionary. These ethnic organizations preserved the contradictory goals of the American ruling class: on the one hand, homogenization seemed to be a strong preference of corporate and government planners; on the other, within industrial towns and plants, ethnicity was an important industrial-relations tool for the employers.

The Democratic party in the later 19th century developed into another powerful representative of ethnic interests. Apart from its role in national politics, the party built its popular support on the basis of its links with the everyday needs of immigrants thrust into a hostile urban environment with few resources to deal with the bewildering welter of problems facing them. Because it often competed with socialist groups for the loyalty of the immigrant populations, it became a further factor in reducing the strength of radical movements among foreign-born workers.

It was not until the second and third generations of native-born workers that the process of homogenization was complete. Although many workers born in the 1920s were already well on their way to breaking from the hyphenated-American syndrome, a second important event in American life prevented the emergence of mass working-class consciousness.

III

Among the most commonly held shibboleths of radical thought is the notion that misery brings revolutionary awakening. Unfortunately, this has long been proven false. There is convincing evidence that the leading forces in the rise of industrial unionism in this country were the native-born younger workers—who actually did not suffer as greatly from the Depression as their elders, but rather occupied the better semi-skilled jobs—the skilled trades workers within industrial plants, and the most stable of the older semi-skilled workers in the mines and the largest mass production shops. The skilled workers had suffered deterioration in their living conditions during the early years of the Depression, as did the basic work force in the mines. But none of the crucial elements in the general strikes in Minneapolis and San Francisco or in the Flint sit-down strike were the down-and-outers. The persons who were crushed by the Depression—older people thrown off the lines and out of their jobs—were part of the solid support for the New Deal, which offered them a life-raft. The impulse behind industrial unionism was somewhat different. It was born of the resentment of workers who had suffered setbacks during the Depression, particularly as a result of the boldness of employers in cutting wages and speeding up the work. The workers who conducted the mass textile, mining and transportation strikes during the early years of the New Deal did not perceive the government as a friend, much less a savior. These mass strikes were genuine expressions of self-activity and remarkable class solidarity. It was the trade unions which tried to channel the explosive protest against blatant employer attempts to use New Deal institutions to make surplus profits into bureaucratic molds.

For the mass of Americans, the Depression was a deeply traumatic experience which resonated long after the economy resumed its upward movement. The fear of unemployment and outright starvation haunted the working class for at least another generation. My father reached his industrial coming-of-age in the late 1920s, on the eve of the Depression. He spent a year in college, but quit to work on a newspaper as a cub reporter. Since he was the son of immigrant parents, he always had one foot in the ghetto and the other in the American mainstream. The contradictory part of his Lower East Side childhood was his inheritance of a passion for social justice alongside a gnawing yearning for economic security. The gnarled, decrepit tenements of his childhood stamped themselves indelibly on his social consciousness. In his boyhood, he helped his father deliver cases of seltzer to customers living in fifth-floor walkup apartments.

Although my father resolved to escape the ghetto, first through sports and then through journalism, these avenues proved too risky in economic terms. After the newspaper he worked for folded in 1931, he worked briefly for the Associated Press, but he finally left the low-paid and extremely shaky newspaper business. After some time in a textile factory and in the WPA, he finally landed a clerical job with the city.

Most of the rest of his life was spent in the choking confines of the civil service and, at the end, back in the factory. He died having worked and worried himself to death, but with some savings.

My father loved Walt Whitman's America, but lacked his recklessness. He respected the muckrakers and the radicals, but could not summon either the energy or courage to join their ranks. The spectre of the 1930s was never far from his nightmares and so he died an angry and frustrated man, unable and unwilling to take chances to realize his aspirations.

Even the members of my own generation were too close to the scarcity mentality of the Depression to transcend it. I rebelled against my family's neurotic lust for upward mobility, so I remained a worker. My mother had been a member of the CIO retail union, having participated in the sit-down strikes in the 1930s. She was always more "class" conscious than my father. Her family was intimately tied to the labor and socialist wings of Jewish immigrants. Her father was a cutter in a men's clothing factory for much of his working life. He was an extremely unstable man, capable of blowing his whole pay on a pinochle game or his savings on an ill-fated venture into the candy-store business. Grandpa was a lousy businessman. He *gave* candy to the kids, and they robbed him blind besides. But momma always worked and fought for her union. She feared the bosses, but hated them more. I guess my propensity to take chances was learned from my mother and her family. My father's sisters married businessmen and that fact put a hell of a lot of pressure on him to match their achievement in some way. On the other hand, my mother was crazy enough, according to my father, to quit her department store job in the middle of the second depression in 1938, after the defeat of the strike. I was five years old then. And I didn't understand all this until recently. But looking at my childhood friends in the East Bronx and the second-generation workers I encountered in my years as a shop-worker and union organizer, it seemed that few of them went much beyond the aspirations of their parents.

But most white kids born after 1940 never experienced real hunger. For them, the struggles for union security, health benefits and pensions were taken for granted. They could not get hot for welfare capitalism or the guarantee of a job, because they really had no sense of what it is like not to find a job for a good part of their lives. Instead, they were reared on the doctrines of infinite opportunity within an expanding economic system and the expectation that they would not starve, no matter what. Just as the workers of the 1930s often took factory or clerical jobs as a temporary cushion to ride out the storm of the Depression, so many high school and college graduates took these jobs in the 1960s as an aid to finishing college, technical or professional school. The relative freedom of this generation from the expectation that hard times are a permanent condition, interspersed with the opportunities provided by war, made the need for decent, satisfying jobs more important than the goals of decent income and job property rights guaranteed by a union contract.

The older generation was often grateful for the chance to work, even though it became necessary to rebel against the excesses of the companies, which took advantage of the plentiful labor supply to wring the last drop of profit out of the workers. But behind the gratitude was the eternal hope of escape into the middle class. The wartime and postwar expansion of U.S. capitalism, bringing steady work and rising wage levels, revived the expectation that some workers could escape the shop into their own tavern or small construction contracting business. Most of the postwar working class became quickly smitten (but also burdened) by huge mortgages, time payments for mechanical gadgets, and finally, college tuition for their children. Thus, steady work bringing regular paychecks helped to repress the realization that the distance between their rising educational levels or vocational aspirations and the routine character of their work was widening.

APPENDIXES

APPENDIX I

KAREN LARSEN'S review of *The Uprooted* is an important contemporary critique of the book whose significance has been seriously reflected on in most ethnic and immigrant studies of the last two decades.

REVIEW OF OSCAR HANDLIN'S *THE UPROOTED: THE EPIC STORY OF THE GREAT MIGRATIONS THAT MADE THE AMERICAN PEOPLE*

KAREN LARSEN

A story of vast proportions is unfolded before us in this book. Professor Handlin sketches the disintegration of the time-honored Old World village society which drove thousands upon thousands to take refuge in emigration. He describes the miseries of the crossing, the cold welcome and disillusionment that were in store for the immigrants as most of them were "trapped," so to speak, in the city slums, never reaching the farm land of which they had dreamed. The reaction of the immigrants to each new experience is pictured with the emo-

FROM: *The American Historical Review,* Vol. 57 (April 1952), pp. 703–704.

tional warmth and psychological insight of one who has been close to the newcomers. In the midst of innumerable individual tragedies, the movement as a whole was saved from becoming tragic by the tenacity and, at the same time, flexibility with which the immigrant groups were able to attain a certain harmony, unconscious perhaps, between the efforts to maintain their cultural identity and the struggle to find their place in the land of their adoption. Emphasis is placed upon their exploitation, the ideal of the "melting pot," Know-Nothingism, the smug hundred-percentism which reached a climax in World War I, and the policy of exclusion that followed it.

It is hardly correct to call this "the first study to examine the meaning of immigration . . . from the point of view of the people who were involved in it," but, as far as I know, there is no similar study of such wide scope. Nevertheless, Professor Handlin has not fulfilled his promise. Instead of showing the effects of immigration on the 35,000,000 people who came to our shores in the nineteenth century, his book is actually a study of those immigrants only who came from the village background of central and southern Europe and were stranded in our eastern cities, notably New York. It is questionable how far the sweeping generalities of the book have a universal application, even to this group. There are, for example, authentic accounts showing that the crossing was not always an unmitigated horror and that the milk of human kindness was not entirely lacking in the reception accorded the new arrivals.

The serious weakness of the book, however, lies in the feeble attempts to include other immigrant groups which, though numerically smaller, are important and have a history all their own. To illustrate: in discussing the European background, the author uses misleading examples (pp. 21 and 36) from Norway, a country which did not conform to the pattern of his description; and in the chapter entitled "The Ghettos," only a hasty detour is made from the slums of New York to the sod huts of the prairie. There is very little to indicate the diversity in the life of the immigrants: to show, for instance, that the farmers of the Midwest, who brought with them political training and took an interest in national affairs from the first, did not share the experience of slum population enmeshed in ward politics. The author apparently knows only those immigrants who never got far from the Battery. It is to be doubted whether all of these lived frustrated lives.

APPENDIX II

OSCAR HANDLIN'S contribution to the special issue of *Daedalus* on the Negro American characterizes what one reviewer noted then as Handlin's immediate, "practical usefulness" in recognizing the true nature of black organization and its parallel with other ethnic-group political forces; but it also represents what I consider to be a diversionary and unwarranted persuasion of an historic and manifest expansion of economic opportunity and political democracy for all—regardless of class, creed, or color.

THE GOALS OF INTEGRATION
OSCAR HANDLIN

THE view of integration as racial balance rests on two fallacious assumptions—that the position of the Negro is absolutely unique in the American experience and that racist prejudice is so thoroughly ingrained in the people of the United States that only positive exertions by the government will assure the colored man his rights. Neither proposition conforms to the evidence.

The Negro is unique, it is argued, because his color sets him off from the majority more decisively than the traits of

FROM: Oscar Handlin, "The Goals of Integration." Reprinted by permission of *Daedalus,* Journal of the American Academy of Arts and Sciences, Boston, Mass. Winter 1966, *The Negro American—2.*

other ethnic groups did and because slavery crippled him so seriously that he cannot compete on equal terms and needs a crutch to help him along.

Certainly slavery was a more traumatic experience than the centuries of persecution, the hardships of migration, and the generations of depressed proletarian existence from which the Irish peasants suffered. But the argument slights the Negro's powers of recuperation and exaggerates the extent to which the damage caused more than a century ago remains a permanent part of his character. There has been a tendency to underestimate the extent of his achievements even in the fifty years immediately after emancipation, under conditions immensely more difficult than those of the present. When one considers the backwardness of the Southern economy after 1865, the exclusion from political power, the racist prejudices, and the bitterness left by a great war, it was a respectable accomplishment to have formed stable family units, to have developed productive skills, and to have created an array of churches, lodges, and media for cultural expression, with the limited resources the group possessed. Few people released from bondage in any society have performed as creditably.[1]

The disadvantages from which the Negro suffers in 1965 are less the products of the plantation than of the great migration to the city in the past fifty years; and that experience he shares with the other ethnic groups who have participated in American urbanization. Of course the Negroes are different from the Poles or Italians or Jews, just as those peoples differ among, and from, each other. The differences, however, are not of kind but of degree, and they are largely explained by the recency of arrival of the colored men, by their greater numbers, and by their dense concentration in a few cities. The problems of prejudice and acculturation from which the

[1] Reconstruction literature generally focuses on the failures and the missed opportunities rather than on the achievements. See E. Franklin Frazier, *The Negro in the United States* (New York, 1957), pp. 135, 142; W. E. B. Du Bois, *Black Reconstruction in America* (New York, 1935).

most recent newcomers suffer had their counterparts among the earlier arrivals.[2]

Nor is color the sole and unique sign of ethnic visibility. It is no doubt the most prominent mode of social recognition; but much depends upon the social assessment of this as of other physical traits. The Japanese-Americans are far less visible in 1965 than they were in 1940 although their color has not changed. And the Kennedys are still identified as Irish after five generations in the New World, and despite their wealth, prominence, and whiteness.

The assumption that color has a unique differentiating quality rests upon the argument that American society is inherently racist, its promise of equality reserved only for the white man. It has become fashionable in the past few years to sneer at Myrdal's statement of the American creed of equality and to urge that only forceful measures will restrain the propensity to prejudice.

There was a racist period in American history in the sixty years after the end of the Civil War; but the hatreds of that period were peculiar to the time and place. Much more significant is the deeper tradition of equality before and since that interlude. The agony with which slaveholders like Thomas Jefferson and George Mason considered their own situation, the tortured efforts of early scientists to understand color differences, and the torment the abolitionists caused in the North and the South were the results of the inability to square the existing labor system with the belief in the brotherhood of man and the commitment to equality. And the changes since 1945 have been the result not of fear either of the Negroes or of Africans but of the awareness that equality is a necessary ideal of the Republic.

Furthermore, the Negro, while the most prominent, was not the sole target even in the racist period. Prejudice was not limited by race, creed, national origin, or previous condition

[2] Oscar Handlin, *The Newcomers: Negroes and Puerto Ricans in a Changing Metropolis* (New York, 1959).

of servitude. The majority of the victims of lynchings in those years were Negroes; but there were 1,293 white victims of the rope and faggot as against 3,436 black. Italians in New Orleans, a Jew in Georgia, and Greeks in Omaha also met the fury of mob violence. The Ku Klux Klan of 1924 was more concerned with Catholics and Jews than with colored men.[3]

Above all, the response of Americans to the crisis of the past decade reveals the effectiveness of the appeal to the creed of equality. Even Bogalusa is not South Africa; and the inability of the open advocates of racism to attract support is the best evidence of the extent of commitment to that creed.

In estimating the meanings of integration, therefore, it is entirely appropriate to examine the analogous if not identical experience of other ethnic groups. Their process of acculturation will throw light on the need for defining the goals and the strategy of the civil rights movement.

Barring a major overturn of the American social system, which at the moment appears neither probable nor desirable, change will come within definable limits and will involve choices among alternatives. And decisions on this matter will be more effective if they come within an informed context that makes it possible to envision their results.

The inequities which survive from the past cannot be understood or remedied without a comprehension of the social order that produced them. They are the pathological manifestations of a mechanism of adjustment which permitted that order to function. Their successful removal requires a consideration of the function they serve; otherwise, the alternatives are grim. Either the order will collapse to the injury of everyone, white as well as black, or else uncontrolled alternative modes of adjustment will recreate and perpetuate the diseased condition.

[3] Walter White, *Rope & Faggot* (New York, 1929), pp. 20, 227, 230 *ff.*; James E. Cutler, *Lynch-Law* (New York, 1905), pp. 170 *ff.*; J. E. Coxe, "New Orleans Mafia Incident," *Louisiana Historical Quarterly*, Vol. 20, No. 4 (October 1937), pp. 1067 *ff.*; Theodore Saloutos, *Greeks in the United States* (Cambridge, Mass., 1964), pp. 62–69.

This was the error of most of the abolitionists, who thought they could extirpate slavery without considering the effects upon Southern society. The result by 1900 was the restoration of the Negro's subordination in other forms than slavery.[4]

Hence, the importance, in any effort to foresee future developments, of an understanding of segregation, of its relationship to equality, and of the probable effects of integration.

Popularly speaking, segregation was a response to the dissolution of earlier forms of stratification. In a slave regime, the physical separation of the dominant and subordinate populations was superfluous and inconvenient. In other relatively static societies, where places were rigidly defined and the symbols of status clearly fixed by law or custom, groups could mingle with considerable promiscuity because there were no problems of recognition and no dangers to the established hierarchy of persons and groups.[5]

In the South, segregation was a response to the abolition of slavery and to the threat to white superiority posed by Reconstruction. The pattern that emerged in the last quarter of the nineteenth century used the law to fix the identity of the Negroes and to confine them to inferior social places. To those ends it established a rigid etiquette of behavior and separate institutions that restricted the opportunities of the former slaves for education and employment. Within the limits thus established, residential separateness was unnecessary. The measures that implemented segregation were deliberate on the part of the whites; the purposes were clearly understood at the time. As for the Negroes, their wishes were of no consequence; once they were excluded from political power,

---

[4] See Dwight L. Dumond, *Anti-Slavery* (Ann Arbor, Mich., 1961); Martin Duberman, *The Antislavery Vanguard* (Princeton, N.J., 1965), pp. 137 *ff.*; James M. McPherson, *The Struggle for Equality* (Princeton, N.J., 1964); Willie Lee Rose, *Rehearsal for Reconstruction* (Indianapolis, Ind., 1964).

[5] See Frank Tannenbaum, *Slave and Citizen* (New York, 1946); Stanley M. Elkins, *Slavery* (Chicago, 1959).

violence induced their acquiescence. The result was a kind of order, the price of which was inequality of rights.[6]

In the freer, more fluid, and more mobile sections of the country, segregation was achieved by withdrawal rather than by restraint and was voluntary rather than compulsory. As the Northern cities expanded with the influx of waves of heterogeneous newcomers, the old residents moved away, and the new arrivals sorted themselves out in neighborhoods that reflected their own sense of community. Education, employment, religious affiliation, and associational life fell within lines that were not imposed by law or by violence but were shaped by informal and largely spontaneous connections of kinship or community.

Although the Northern Negro suffered from prejudice as did the Southern, society was not polarized but fragmented; and he found himself but one of many groups comparably situated, some of which suffered from disabilities similar to his own. Negroes did not confront a homogeneous white community with a single chain of command leading up to a unified leadership. They found a place among numerous communities, each with its own power structure and its own leaders.[7]

The function of separateness in this context was not to establish or to perpetuate the inferiority of one group, but rather to accommodate diverse patterns of life that were the products of differences in ethnic and sectional heritage, or in economic and social background. By reducing contacts at the points of potential tension, this adjustment permitted each group to organize its own institutions without the oversight or interference of others, and yet was flexible enough to pre-

[6] C. Vann Woodward, *The Strange Career of Jim Crow* (New York, 1957) describes the process.

[7] See T. J. Woofter, *Negro Problem in Cities* (New York, 1928), pp. 177 *ff.*; Howard Brotz, *The Black Jews of Harlem* (New York, 1964); John Daniels, *In Freedom's Birthplace* (Boston, 1914), pp. 133 *ff.*; W. E. B. Du Bois, *The Philadelphia Negro* (Philadelphia, 1899), pp. 197 *ff.*, 389 *ff.*; St. Clair Drake, *Churches and Voluntary Associations in the Chicago Negro Community* (Chicago, 1940); St. Clair Drake and Horace R. Cayton, *Black Metropolis* (New York, 1962), Vol. I, pp. 174 *ff.*

serve some degree of order in a highly complex society. Furthermore, the expanding cities possessed enough free space and their organization was so loosely articulated that individuals who preferred not to affiliate could refrain from doing so and could get along in whatever degree of detachment they wished. The ghetto arrangement was therefore totally different in intention as well as in form from the segregation of the South.

Indeed the fact that the pluralistic order took account of actual differences within the population made it possible to preserve the *concept* of equality. Not every man was equally qualified in terms of inherited capital, cultural traits, personality, and intelligence to pursue equally the goals of success in American life. But the pursuit of happiness was not a single, unified scramble in which every individual sought the same prizes and in which only a few could be winners while the rest were doomed to frustration. In the stated beliefs of the society, every boy could grow up to be President—of the United States or at least a railroad. Americans could cling to faith in that useful proposition because they never subjected it to the test of practice. In reality the disparity of aspirations and career lines drew only a few persons into the competition for those lofty places while relatively independent subsystems, with their own values and rewards, provided satisfying alternatives to many more. The children of Irish or Italian parents did not count themselves failures if their lives did not follow a course identical with that of the children of the Yankees. They had their own criteria of achievement and their own sources of gratification.

The result was to take the edge off the harshly competitive psychological and social conditions of an open society. Pluralism permitted the deployment of the population in an intricate network of relationships and associations that facilitated cooperation at some points, but that left large areas free for the withdrawal of individuals and groups and that therefore minimized conflict-provoking contacts. There were manifestations of prejudice, discrimination, and occasional violence among many of the ethnic and occupational groups. Measured against the potential explosiveness of the situation, however, those were relatively minor. Until the migrations of the past half-century, Negro life in Northern cities was not essentially different from that of other ethnic groups. It had some distinctive problems as every other group did; but relatively small numbers and generally favorable conditions permitted an accommodation on essentially the same terms.

Neither in the North nor in the South is integration in the sense of racial balance a meaningful guide to proximate future action. Desegregation is likely soon to eliminate the vestiges of discrimination inherited from the Jim Crow era; and it may open the way to full participation by Negroes in the political and economic life of the nation, but it will do so within the terms of some approximation of the group life already developed. Integration, defined as the elimination of differences, on the other hand, demands of both Negroes and whites an impossible surrender of identity. The deletion of all memory of antecedents, the severance of all ties to the past, and the liquidation of all particularistic associations is not only unfeasible but undesirable. It would curtail the capacity of this society to deal with its problems under the conditions of freedom; and significantly some of its advocates are either altogether nihilistic or else do not flinch from the totalitarian methods and consequences that would be involved in achieving this version of integration.[8]

Only a small minority of Negroes, however, think in these terms. The vast majority understand that they are a group and will remain so; they seek an expansion of their rights and opportunities, but show neither a desire to merge with the whites nor any expectation that that will soon happen. Desegregation is a genuine issue; racial balance is a vague and

[8] See, for example, Howard Zinn, *SNCC, The New Abolitionist* (Boston, 1964), pp. 216–241.

confusing abstraction that turns their attention away from the genuine political, economic, and social problems they and other Americans confront.

The issue is perhaps clearest in the field of political action. No right is more basic than that to full and equal participation in the governmental process; and Negroes were quick to exercise the privileges of citizenship once they secured access to the ballot either through migration to the North or through the leveling of barriers in the South. Apathy was no more widespread among them than among other voters new to the suffrage. The colored people promptly assimilated the techniques of machine organization, and their power has increased steadily as their numbers have. With the appearance of a second generation, native to the city, they have begun to move into elective office at about the same pace as their predecessors did.

Three related factors continue to limit the effectiveness of their use of political power. The lack of competent leadership has enabled self-serving hacks and demagogues to push to the fore and has wasted on the quest for petty privilege the effort and energy that might have gone into improving the status of the whole group. The modes of collaboration with other blocs of voters have been slow to develop; and since the Negroes remain a minority, the ability to use their strength depends on alliances with others. Finally, Negroes have had difficulty in perceiving where their true interests lay when it came to such complex questions as education, urban renewal, and economic policy. In all three respects, they are repeating the experiences of earlier groups drawn into the processes of American democracy.

Nor is it to be expected that these people will be more enlightened in the use of power than their predecessors. Politics is not the cure-all that some naive observers consider it to be.[9] Post-Civil War Negroes in the South did not use their

[9] For example, Charles E. Silberman, *Crisis in Black and White* (New York, 1964).

strength any more effectively than did the Irish of Boston in the first quarter of the twentieth century. The same sentimental temptation to idealize the underdog that once built up exaggerated expectations of the proletariat now sometimes leads to hopes for a panacea in the activities of the Negro citizen. There is no more reason to expect political wisdom from the black than from the white resident of a slum or from either than from the suburban commuter. The vote is not an abstract exercise in either intelligence or benevolence but a means of exercising influence on the processes that shape governmental decisions. For some time yet, Negroes will use it to serve narrowly defined group interests.

The removal of surviving restraints on the right to vote is obviously important; but integration is an irrelevant distraction which disperses energy and inhibits the development of responsible leadership which can take a full and active role in politics at every level. Political effectiveness will grow not through the weakening of the sense of identity but through the development of institutions that can clarify the group's interests, provide organized means of ascent to leadership, and retain the loyalties of the growing middle-class and professional elements in the colored population.

Integration in the sense of the elimination of distinctiveness is no more relevant to the economic plight than to the political plight of the mass of Negroes. The demands for preferential hiring, for assigned quotas of desirable jobs, and for a Black Man's Marshall Plan are sometimes presented as if they were the means of attaining racial balance and therefore of furthering integration. Actually, they are calls for the recognition of the special character of the group; and to the extent that they are heeded, they strengthen identification with it.

Measurement of the rate of Negro progress is difficult because of the recency of this migration to the cities and because gross comparisons of whites and nonwhites distort the actual situation. A large proportion of urban Negroes have

343

been where they are less than twenty years, almost all of them, less than fifty years. The analogous migration from Eastern and Southern Europe began in the 1890's and reached its peak between 1900 and 1910. The mass of Poles, Italians, and Russian Jews even in the prosperous 1920's, much less in the depression 1930's, had not made more rapid progress. Furthermore, the limitations of the census categories which recognize only whites and nonwhites obscure the genuine differences in occupation and income among the former and make comparisons invidious. Unfortunately, more refined data are difficult to come by.

It is undeniable, however, that a large percentage of American Negroes are confined to unskilled and poorly paid occupations at a time when technological changes reduce the demand for their labor. They therefore suffer more than do other sectors of the population from unemployment, low incomes, and the consequent social deprivations. Furthermore, the same economic forces that contract the demand for their services and their position as late arrivals prevent them from developing the protected trades through which other groups maintained quasi-monopolistic control of some employment opportunities.

The difficulty is that no occupation in the United States—hod-carrier, teamster, machinist, shopkeeper, physician, or banker—ever represented a cross-section of the whole population. The social and cultural conditions that influenced recruitment to these callings did not prevail identically in all ethnic and sectional groups. Entirely apart from prejudice or discrimination, therefore, the chances that a given individual would follow one career line rather than another were likely to depend on an environment and on connections shaped by family influences.

Conceivably this pattern of recruitment could change. Since Jefferson's day, various utopians have dreamed of a mandarin system within which all infants start on equal terms and are directed by successive competitive tests of ability to their appropriate niches in life. This is the ultimate model of integration; and it would certainly put Negroes on terms of parity with all others. But, desirable or not, this solution is visionary. It is hardly necessary to attempt to estimate the social and psychological costs of such a system or even to speculate about the difficulty of defining ability (intelligence?) in that context. The dominant tendencies in American life have consistently broken down any effort to create the rigid controls upon which development in that direction depends. The likelihood is slim that those tendencies will change enough in the near future to offer any promise of relief to the Negroes' problems.

A general assault on the problems of poverty may, in time, mitigate the difficulties from which Negroes suffer along with the other unskilled and therefore superfluous elements in American society. But some Negroes at least are not content to wait for that happy outcome and are struggling now for better chances as a group. Pressure on employers to assign a quota of desirable places to colored people may result in a kind of tokenism, advantageous to a few without easing the hardships of the many. But such adjustments do help the few; and both the tactic and its outcome sustain and strengthen the sense of group solidarity. There are already contexts—in some levels of government employment, for instance—in which there is an advantage to being black, a condition which puts a premium on affiliation with the group.

In the last analysis, the welfare of the Negroes depends upon the health of the whole economy and its capacity to produce and distribute goods according to an acceptable pattern. But the last analysis is remote indeed. In the interim, the Negroes will use what power they can muster as a group for their own advantage. Preferential treatment in some high-prestige forms of employment will be justified not because it will improve the lot of the great mass of the unskilled, but because it is a means of opening some avenues of escape for the most qualified. At relatively little cost in efficiency, this device can create a pool of potential leaders with a stake in social order and at the same time break the identification of the race with poverty.

Hence the importance of education upon which, increasingly, access to the more desirable places depends. The Negroes started with the initial disadvantage of dependence on the weakest schools in the country—those of the South. Migration compounded their difficulties, and the environment of poverty adds to their handicaps. The need for improvement is unarguable.

The methods of effecting that improvement are by no means clear, however. The pressure for integration has called attention to the problem; but it has also confused the solution. For some elements in the civil rights movement, integration in the form of racial balance has become an end in itself more important than the quality of the schools. Martin Luther King's hit-and-run involvement in this issue in Boston, Chicago, and Cleveland shows the danger of the thoughtless transference of the tactics of one kind of struggle to another.

Partly this outcome is the result of the historic development of the school issue in the South, where segregation was a means of perpetuating educational inequality and Negro inferiority. There desegregation was an essential step toward equality. However, the slogans of that effort were uncritically applied to the separateness of the Northern schools which had an altogether different function. The imbalance of the Northern schools was not designed to create or maintain Negro inferiority; and its result was not always to lower the quality of the education available to colored people.[10] Yet

[10] A misleading impression is often the result of gross comparisons of selected Negro schools or school districts with a general white average. It is necessary to take account also of variables other than race that affect performance. An analysis of achievement in Boston district high schools, for instance, shows that schools in certain white neighborhoods are as deficient as those in Negro neighborhoods (reported in *Boston Globe*, December 14, 1964, pp. 1, 13).

there was no forethought about the consequences of the attempt to end what came to be termed *de facto* segregation.

Furthermore, in this matter, there is a striking division of opinion among Negroes, covered up by the appearance of unity on such occasions as the school strikes. The most vocal persons in the civil rights movement are the most mobile, those whose aspirations reach furthest, those most irked by the identification of their color. Integration expresses their not fully understood desire to sever their ties with the past; and racial balance is a means toward that end.

This desire does not reach very far among the mass of Negroes. In such cities as New York and Boston, where open-enrollment plans offered parents an opportunity to send their children outside the districts of their residence, only a very small minority chose to do so. However the lack of response may be explained away, it reveals the limited scope of the appeal of racial balance.

Yet this issue in many places has overshadowed the far more important factors that enter into the Negroes' educational deprivation. And it is likely that time and energy will continue to be dissipated on the question of racial balance that might more usefully be expended on the quality of the schools and on the orientation of the educational process to the needs of the colored students.

The demand for racial balance has sometimes had a blackmail effect; it has forced concessions on municipal authorities willing to spend more heavily on slum schools than they might otherwise have in order to stave off the drive for bussing. But this tactic has also had the adverse effect of exaggerating the deficiencies of schools in Negro neighborhoods and thus of frightening away experienced teachers, of hastening the flight to the suburbs and increasing the rate of withdrawal to private and parochial schools. The insistence upon integration is thus self-frustrating, as the experience of Washington, D.C., shows. Further pressure toward racial balance will certainly weaken the public schools and leave the Negroes the greatest sufferers.

The dilemma is unnecessary. There is no evidence that racial balance itself improves the capacity of the underprivileged to learn; nor that the *enforced* contact of dissimilar children has significant educational advantages. There is abundant evidence that deprived children have distinctive needs that require the special attention of the school. Yet the drive for integration has obscured, and sometimes actually impeded, the task of providing for those needs. Indeed the argument is now often being made that racial balance is desirable to meet the needs of white children.

Here, too, an awareness of the group's identity and a determination to deal with its problems is the most promising path to equality. The Negro deserves preferential treatment in education because his needs are great. But to receive it calls for the recognition of the special character of his situation, not for costly efforts artificially to commingle his children with others in the interest of the ideal of balance.[11]

Since the desegregated, but unintegrated, school is a neighborhood school, there is a relationship between the range of residential choices and the conditions of education. The Negroes suffer from poverty, from their recency of arrival, and —in housing, more than in any other sphere—from prejudice. It remains unfortunately true that some whites willing to work side by side with the Negro or even to vote for him

---

[11] There is abundant evidence that significant improvement can come in the performance of Negroes in desegregated but racially unbalanced schools. The Banneker experiment in St. Louis, the experience of Washington, D.C., and the results in Louisville, Kentucky, point to the same conclusion. Of course, improvement can also come in balanced schools. However, the essential element is not balance, but the allocation of adequate educational resources to compensate for the disadvantaged situation of the Negro. See also Frank G. Dickey, "A Frontal Attack on Cultural Deprivation," *Phi Delta Kappan*, Vol. 45, No. 8 (May 1964), p. 398; *New York Times*, May 17, 1965. A good deal of the literature is summarized in T. F. Pettigrew, *A Profile of the Negro American* (Princeton, N.J., 1964), although the conclusions drawn are different.

in an election will boggle at accepting him as a neighbor. That hesitation is connected with the fact that the residential district, especially in the middle-class areas of the city, is also the setting of a distinctive communal life, with group-derived values and activities of its own. The presence of any outsider is a potential threat, exaggerated in the case of the Negro by fears of a mass inundation.

Something has been done—by law and persuasion—to quiet these fears; a good deal more can be done by these methods. But it would help if the fearful were aware that there is no widespread desire among Negroes for residential intermixture as such. Colored people are primarily concerned with the quality of housing; they do not value highly propinquity to whites. Talk about racial balance not only distorts the actuality of Negro intentions, but it heightens the very fears that may limit the freedom of the occasional black family that wishes to move to a mixed neighborhood. A recent study of middle-income Negro families, for instance, expressed surprise at the preference for ghetto residence and suggested that whites be moved in to encourage integration, as if that were a necessary and desirable end in itself. A state legislative committee on low-income housing uncritically adopted the same goal. These proposals repeat the errors of New York City's experiment with benign quotas which deprived Negroes of the quarters they needed in order to save room for whites, all out of the concern with balance.[12]

Integration is a false issue. The problem is housing—how can adequate space up to present-day standards of decency be made available to the poor? How can all other colored families get fair value up to the level of their incomes, without being penalized for their race? For most Negroes these are the primary issues. They are difficult enough without

[12] Lewis G. Watts, *et al*, *The Middle-Income Negro Family Faces Urban Renewal* (Boston, 1964); Massachusetts Special Commission on Low-Income Housing, *Summary Report* (Boston, 1965), and *Final Report* (Boston, 1965).

the complications of racial balance. The control of the urban renewal process, the role of government as entrepreneur, and problems of design and form will set the framework within which the character of the Negroes' future housing will be determined. And group cohesiveness will be of great importance in influencing decisions in these matters.

The development and strengthening of Negro communal institutions may also help normalize the situation of the colored family. The disorderly features of that position are well known—the absence of a male head, frequent illegitimacy and dependence—as well as their relationship to juvenile delinquency, crime, and narcotic addiction. But these characteristics have been too readily associated with the effects of the slave heritage. The servitude of the plantation may have left elements of weakness in the families of the freedmen; but the extent to which sound family life developed among the Negroes between 1865 and 1915 is impressive, as is the extent to which it still prevails in the rural South closest to the slave setting.

A more plausible source of disorder is the effect of rural-urban migration with low income and slum housing at its destination. That correlation conforms to what is known about the changes in family life in other societies in which slavery has not been a factor.[13] It conforms also to the experience of earlier groups of migrants to American cities. Less than a half-century ago, the foreign-born residents of Irish, Jewish, or Polish slums faced comparable problems of matriarchal households and delinquency.

It was not alone the tradition of solidarity and discipline that contained the damage among these peoples, but also the fact that their families were encased in social and cultural in-

[13] See, for example, B. A. Pauw, *The Second Generation: A Study of the Family among the Urbanized Bantu in East London* (Cape Town, Union of South Africa, 1963); Raymond T. Smith, *The Negro Family in British Guiana* (London, 1956).

stitutions which imposed restraints upon recalcitrant individuals, established norms of behavior, and disposed of weighty sanctions for conformity. Negroes have been slower to develop similar institutions, partly because this migration came at a moment when government absorbed some of these functions, but also because in their experience separation meant segregation and bore the imputation of inferiority. Yet those men who, in the name of integration, deny that there is a significant role for the Negro press, or for Negro churches, or for Negro associations are also denying the group of its media for understanding, for expression, and for action. They would thereby weaken the capacity of the people who need those media to act on their own behalf.[14]

It is the ultimate illogic of integration to deny the separateness of the Negro and therefore to inhibit him from creating the communal institutions which can help cope with his problems. Delinquency, poverty, slums, and inadequate housing of course concern all Americans; and the attempt to eradicate them calls for common efforts from every part of the nation. But history has given the Negroes a special involvement in these matters; and to deny the actualities of the group's existence is to diminish its ability to deal with them. To confuse segregation, the function of which is to establish Negro inferiority, with the awareness of separate identity, the function of which is to generate the power for voluntary action, hopelessly confuses the struggle for equality.

Clarification of the goals of the civil rights movement has immediate tactical implications. Desegregation is not the same as integration; Selma is not Harlem, Bogalusa, not Chicago.

Where violence, exclusion from the ballot, or state power has deprived the Negro of his equal rights as a man and a citizen, it is his obligation and that of all other Americans to de-

[14] See, for example, Louis E. Lomax, *The Negro Revolt* (New York, 1962), pp. 204, 205.

mand an immediate end to the discriminatory measures that aim at his subordination.

Desegregation will not solve any of the other important economic, social, and political problems of American life; it will only offer a starting point from which to confront them. The inadequacies of the political system, unemployment, inferior education, poor housing, and delinquency will still call for attention. In some of these matters the peculiarities of the Negroes' situation call for special treatment. But with reference to none of them is integration a meaningful mode of action; and the call for it which echoes from a different struggle on a different battleground only produces confusion.

Whatever may happen in the more distant future, Negroes will not merge into the rest of the population in the next few decades. Those who desire to eliminate every difference so that all Americans will more nearly resemble each other, those who imagine that there is a main stream into which every element in the society will be swept, are deceived about the character of the country in which they live. As long as common memories, experience, and interests make the Negroes a group, they will find it advantageous to organize and act as such. And the society will better be able to accommodate them as equals on those terms than it could under the pretense that integration could wipe out the past.

APPENDIX III

THESE short items are newspaper accounts on the current experience of not-yet-making-it among those white-ethnic segments of the population on whom the immigrant success story is largely built.

ETHNIC POWER: HOPE FOR THE MIDDLE AMERICAN

RECENTLY in Washington, D.C., at a gathering of a group called the Task Force on Urban Problems, which has become a clearing house for "White Ethnic Communities in Pluralistic Urban America," a white community action organizer from Baltimore, Md., summed up the frustrations of ethnics: "he is sick of being stereotyped as a racist and dullard by phony white liberals, pseudo black militants and patronizing bureaucrats."

This rejection of a widespread accusation that ethnic Americans are the primary exponents of racism in our society was expressed in the 1970 Labor Day statement of the U. S. Catholic Bishops. "It is obvious," the statement said, "that if there is to be a resolution of the racial crisis which currently grips our society, a critical role will be played by white ethnic working class communities." The Bishops' statement also ad-

FROM: *Steel Labor* (September 1970), pp. 8–9. *Steel Labor* is published by the United Steelworkers of America.

dressed itself to a central issue which has almost universal endorsement within the white urban communities of America: "We believe that white society at large should spend less time looking for a scapegoat for this racial crisis and more time considering how to assist the people in those communities which are situated on the racial frontier." The statement added that scholars, journalists and urbanologists have devoted little attention to the white ethnic communities of the cities, despite the fact that many elderly white ethnics are living in abject poverty, that most working class families do not earn "middle class" incomes and their children must grapple with the same problems that have produced alienation among affluent college youth.

The problem of "middle America" does not mean that those of black America and its other minorities have been or should be removed to the back burner of social priorities. What is important is that the domestic crisis of the 70s has deflected attention from the issues most germane to the older white ethnic communities, and these are the planning and development programs which affect the future of their neighborhoods.

The myth of "middle America" was summed up by an AFL-CIO policy statement in 1969, which declared that "the truth is that the majority of people who work for a living are not a part of 'affluent' America." The median family made $8,632 in 1968—less than the "modest but adequate" standard defined by the government. In 1965 the average industrial worker with three dependents took home $88.06 a week and his after-tax pay in 1969 was $87.27 when price adjustments are taken into account.

"The anxious majority" was the description of the plight of blue collar workers in Chicago in a recent series in the Chicago *Daily News*. They capsuled the fears of a typical worker who "after 25 years of working toward a wage that he hoped would give him security and perhaps something to spare, finds that inflation keeps draining off the 'surplus' so that he not only can't send the kids to college, he can't even be sure of a comfortable old age."

The typical worker in the study was white, and his anxieties are largely in white and black: fear that when blacks move in his neighborhood, property values will dwindle; fear that even his job may be in jeopardy. Yet the irony embedded in the decline of the inner cities is that the white and black workers who seem headed toward confrontation may be approaching an unlikely point when both embattled sides become aware of their acute need for each other.

"The enemy is not the black man," said an Italian-American councilman from a large northern industrial city at the recent Urban Task Force conference. "It is the power structure that plays off one group against the other." Another added: "Nobody has done anything for the ethnics since Social Security. Yet they are being blamed for white racism, despite the fact that they are not the people in the executive suites who would not hire a single Jew or Negro for so long. The ethnics are the people whose jobs are threatened."

WHO SPEAKS FOR ETHNIC AMERICA?

BARBARA MIKULSKI

THE Ethnic American is forgotten and forlorn. He is infuriated at being used and abused by the media, government and business. Pejorative epithets such as "pigs" and "racists" or slick, patronizing labels like the "silent majority" or "hard hats" are graphic examples of the lack of respect, understanding and appreciation of him and his way of life.

FROM: *The New York Times* (September 28, 1970), p. 72. © 1970 by The New York Times Company. Reprinted by permission.

355

The Ethnic Americans are 40 million working class Americans who live primarily in 58 major industrial cities like Baltimore and Chicago. Our roots are in Central and Southern Europe. We have been in this country for one, two or three generations. We have made a maximum contribution to the U.S.A., yet received minimal recognition.

The ethnics came to America from the turn of the century through the twenties, until we were restricted by prejudicial immigration quotas—65,000 Anglo-Saxons to 300 Greeks. We came looking for political freedom and economic opportunity. Many fled from countries where there had been political, religious and cultural oppression for 1,000 years.

It was this working class which built the Great Cities— constructed the skyscrapers, operated the railroads, worked on the docks, factories, steel mills and in the mines. Though our labor was in demand, we were not accepted. Our names, language, food and cultural customs were the subject of ridicule. We were discriminated against by banks, institutions of higher learning and other organizations controlled by the Yankee Patricians. There were no protective mechanisms for safety, wages and tenure. We called ourselves Americans. We were called "wop," "polak" and "hunky."

For our own protection, we formed our own institutions and organizations and clung together in our new neighborhoods. We created communities like "Little Italy" and "Polish Hill." The ethnic parish church and the fraternal organizations like the Polish Women's Alliance and the Sons of Italy became the focal points of our culture.

These neighborhoods were genuine "urban villages." Warmth, charm and zesty communal spirit were their characteristics. People knew each other. This was true not only of relatives and friends but of the grocer, politician and priest. The people were proud, industrious and ambitious. All they wanted was a chance to "make it" in America.

Here we are in the 1970's, earning between $5,000–$10,000 per year. We are "near poor" economically. No one listens to our problems. The President's staff responds to our problems by patronizingly patting us on the head and putting pictures of construction workers on postage stamps. The media stereotypes us as gangsters or dumb clods in dirty sweat-shirts. The status of manual labor has been denigrated to the point where men are often embarrassed to say they are plumbers or tugboat operators. This robs men of the pride in their work and themselves.

The Ethnic American is losing ground economically. He is the victim of both inflation and anti-inflation measures. Though wages have increased by 20 per cent since the mid-sixties, true purchasing power has remained the same. He is hurt by layoffs due to cutbacks in production and construction. Tight money policies strangle him with high interest rates for installment buying and mortgages. He is the man who at 40 is told by the factory bosses that he is too old to be promoted. The old job is often threatened by automation. At the same time, his expenses are at their peak. He is paying on his home and car, probably trying to put at least one child through college.

In pursuing his dream of home ownership, he finds that it becomes a millstone rather than a milestone in his life. Since FHA loans are primarily restricted to "new" housing, he cannot buy a house in the old neighborhood. He has no silk stocking lawyers or fancy lobbyists getting him tax breaks.

He believes in the espoused norms of American manhood like "a son should take care of his mother" and "a father should give his children every opportunity." Yet he is torn between putting out $60 a month for his mother's arthritis medication or paying for his daughter's college tuition.

When the ethnic worker looks for some modest help, he is told that his income is too high. He's "too rich" to get help when his dad goes into a nursing home. Colleges make practically no effort to provide scholarships to kids named Colstiani, Slukowski or Klima.

The one place where he felt the master of his fate and had

357

status was in his own neighborhood. Now even that security is being threatened. He wants new schools for his children and recreation facilities for the entire family—not just the token wading pool for pre-schoolers or the occasional dance for teen-agers. He wants his street fixed and his garbage collected. He finds that the only thing being planned for his area are housing projects, expressways and fertilizer factories. When he goes to City Hall to make his problems known, he is either put off, put down or put out.

Liberals scapegoat us as racists. Yet there was no racial prejudice in our hearts when we came. There were very few black people in Poland or Lithuania. The elitists who now smuggly call us racists are the ones who taught us the meaning of the word: their bigotry extended to those of a different class or national origin.

Government is further polarizing people by the creation of myths that black needs are being met. Thus the ethnic worker is fooled into thinking that the blacks are getting everything.

Old prejudices and new fears are ignited. The two groups end up fighting each other for the same jobs and competing so that the new schools and recreation centers will be built in their respective communities. What results is angry confrontation for tokens, when there should be an alliance for a whole new Agenda for America. This Agenda would be created if black and white organized separately in their own communities for their own needs and came together to form an alliance based on mutual issues, interdependence and respect. This alliance would develop new strategies for community organization and political restructuring. From this, the new Agenda for America would be generated. It could include such items as "new towns in town," innovative concepts of work and creative structures for community control.

What is necessary is to get rid of the guilt of phony liberals, control by economic elitists and manipulation by selfish

politicians. Then, let us get on with creating the democratic
and pluralistic society that we say we are.

JEWS WITHOUT MONEY,
REVISITED

PAUL COWAN

THE poverty among the poor Jews who live on New York's
Lower East Side compares to poverty I've seen anywhere in
America—in Mississippi, the South Bronx, East Los Angeles.
Most people think of the Jewish immigration as the most
spectacularly successful one in American history, but the 50-
year journey from the shtetl to the Space Age left many cas-
ualties in its wake. An estimated 250,000 Jews in New York
City live below the poverty level of $3500; an estimated
150,000 more earn less than $4500 a year. Most of them are
over 65, many are Orthodox; but there are young people
among them, too, and Jews with all shades of religious belief.
They live all over New York City: in Far Rockaway, in
Coney Island, in Borough Park, and on the Upper West
Side. I interviewed scores who still live on the Lower East
Side.

There is a myth that the area, once the portal for the
large, energetic Eastern European Jewish immigration, has
"changed" completely: that blacks and Puerto Ricans dominate the neighborhood, while all the Jews who used to live
there have moved to Borough Park or Forest Hills or the
Upper West Side or Scarsdale. But a 1971 Human Resources
Administration report showed that 62 per cent of the neigh-

FROM: *The Village Voice* (September 1972), pp. 1–2. Reprinted by
permission of *The Village Voice*. Copyrighted by The Village Voice,
Inc., 1972.

359

borhood's population was white, 24 per cent was Puerto
Rican, and 14 per cent was black. About 10,000 "Jews without money," in a phrase Michael Gold's book made popular
nearly 50 years ago, still live there.

Traces of the earlier era remain. North of Delancey, Rivington Street and Orchard Street are still noisy, open-air markets, where Yiddish-speaking, yarmulke-wearing Jews invei-
gle virtually every passerby to purchase their cut-rate shoes
or pants, their briny pickles or strong-smelling fish. Only now
most of their customers are Puerto Ricans, not Jews from
Eastern Europe's shtetls, and most of the Jews who own the
small stores and the warehouses that line the quieter streets
near East Broadway have earned enough money to move outside the neighborhood. So the market is no longer an old
world bazaar, where lantsman haggled with lantsman in
terms that were familiar to everyone involved. And though
the relations between the shopkeepers and their customers
are usually quite friendly, there are occasional unsettling
signs of the tensions that plague the neighborhood. At lunch-
time one day a drunk black man walked down the street yell-
ing "Jew bastard" at merchant after merchant—an unusual
exception to a rule of civility, but one which echoes menac-
ingly in the memories of Jews who have endured pogroms or
concentration camps. In one warehouse, a city inspector
searched for the owner to tell him that his application for a
gun permit had been granted.

Walk into the courtyard of the city-owned Vladeck Houses,
near the Henry Street Settlement House, just a few blocks
from the corner of East Broadway and Rutgers which the
Daily Forward building, the Garden Cafeteria, and Seward
Park once made the hub of immigrant life. When the project
was built more than 30 years ago, the bulk of its population
was Jewish. Many of those people moved away. Now it
houses a majority of Puerto Ricans and blacks. But on a hot
summer day you can still see plenty of old Jews sunning
themselves on the benches of the noisy courtyard. For them,

the immigrant days are faint, irrelevant memories. Most of them would rather grieve than reminisce.

Many live on social security checks and small pensions often averaging less than $200 a month income. One reason they stay in the project is that the rents are so low—about $35 a month. They're too proud to supplement that income by applying for welfare. (Many of them still call welfare by its 1930s name, "relief," and complain that it subsidizes black and Puerto Rican crime.) They are afflicted with the diseases of the aged—diabetes, arthritis, Parkinson's disease. Many are widows or widowers, haunted by memories of dead relatives. And they are terrified of muggers and thieves.

They feel as if they've been abandoned by uptown liberal Jewish intellectuals, politicians, and philanthropists who, they think, care more about blacks and Puerto Ricans than about the nagging problems of the Jewish slums. And, worse than that, abandoned by their own children. Many successful young people who have escaped the neighborhood haven't sent their parents money or even mail in years. And many of those who still help out do so with visible annoyance. It is impossible to know the inner history of each family situation —whether a particular parent was unforgivably cruel to his offspring or whether a particular child is now unforgivably insensitive to his parent—but it's clear that now many old people on the Lower East Side feel a lasting bitterness toward assimilated, middle-class Jews—their children. Some were secretly happy about the problems that afflicted them in Forest Hills. "They've never helped us out," one old man in the Vladeck Projects told me. "Why should we care about them. They got what they deserved."

During my weeks on the Lower East Side I began to feel some ethnic loyalties I never knew I possessed. Yet I also realized that, in real life, I represented many of the things the people I met there were complaining about. I have always lived in an assimilated environment, I married a Gentile without feeling a trace of emotional conflict, I knew very lit-

361

tle about my religious heritage. During the past decade I've worked with blacks in the civil rights movement and Latins in the Peace Corps but, except for a six-month stay in Israel, I have never worked with or written about dispossessed Jews —or even realized that they existed in America.

I've always seen my politics as an outgrowth of the Jewish tradition that obliged one to work with the oppressed both because it was morally right and because the oppression of a group like the blacks could quickly spread out to include the Jews. These are still my deep commitments, of course, but as I grew to care about people on the Lower East Side I became tensely aware that many of them would regard my ideas and activities as a form of betrayal. And the more I learned about their problems the more unsettling that contradiction became.

Once the Lower East Side, with its polyglot population, seemed to symbolize the melting pot America might become. Now it is an ethnic tinderbox, where poor Jews and blacks and Puerto Ricans fight over issue after issue (where Chinese, Italians, and hippies are in the fray, too). Some fights arise out of government oversights, like the virtual exclusion of "Jews without money" from the war on poverty. Others arise out of hatreds, fears, and stereotypes that will take decades to resolve.

Most result from the fact that so very few of America's resources ever reach poor people that ethnic groups are forced to scratch and claw for every cent they can get. But only a relative handful of the people I interviewed for this series saw their problem that way. Most acted as if the issue was race, not class, and no argument could shake that conviction. There are some unifying forces on the Lower East Side, but the situation there still seems quite tense.

During the weeks I was there an election to the local poverty board was the most pressing neighborhood issue. Another month it might have been a fight over the Seward Park housing extension or over a local school board. The specifics might have varied greatly from issue to issue; the tensions were a constant. They were mostly between Jews and Latins, though many of the Jews I interviewed failed to distinguish between Latins and blacks.

APPENDIX IV

THE Blau-Duncan Study findings (*The American Occupational Structure*), based on the very first national sample of intragenerational mobility and upon which Marc Fried relies heavily, have been subject to a variety of contradictory interpretations. Blau and Duncan themselves, for example, interpret their correlations between the occupational status of the father and that of his son (0.50) as being significant. But Daniel Bell, on the other hand (*The Coming of the Post-Industrial Society*), does not, arguing, on the basis of these data, that a considerable degree of equality of opportunity does exist in the United States, that "the class structure has not become rigid."

And yet, correlations of this magnitude are rarely exceeded in social research, albeit because of the crudeness of the measurement techniques used and the many uncontrolled factors which affect a study.

The following extract from Bertram Gross and Stanley Moses, "Measuring the Real Work Force: 25 Million Unemployed," shows the complexity of such analyses, and suggests also the degree to which our analytic definitions have actually weighted findings in favor of optimistic interpretation.

MEASURING THE REAL
WORK FORCE:
25 MILLION UNEMPLOYED

BERTRAM GROSS
AND STANLEY MOSES

THE annual average rate of unemployment, as reported "officially" by the Department of Labor, was 5.9 percent during 1971. Based on the "official" civilian labor force, which was reported as 84.1 million, this percentage represented a total of 4.99 million persons who were unemployed.

As a result of the assiduous activity of the Department of Labor, the Bureau of the Census, and various other government agencies, we possess a great deal of information about the numbers and characteristics of the employed and unemployed. They have been studied and restudied and researched and analyzed according to the various sorts of attributes that distinguish people—sex, age, race, industry, occupation, and income among others—and presented to us in an impressive array of data and information. The most critical of all these indicators in terms of political interest and concern is the unemployment rate. Its rise or fall is taken as the major gauge of the extent to which the society is succeeding in meeting the needs and aspirations of people for work. And, indeed, the official rate is an important indicator of trends and developments regarding the economy, people, and jobs.

But it is far from being a complete and accurate picture of

FROM: *Social Policy*, Vol. 3, No. 3 (September/October 1972), pp. 5–10. Published by Social Policy Corporation, New York, New York 10010.

the real dimensions of unemployment in the United States. . . . The undercount stems from the very concept of officially defined unemployment, which includes only those actively seeking work. In contrast, the more logical, indeed the more human, definition of unemployment would be *all those who are not working and are able and willing to work for pay*. The following table on "Real Unemployment in the United States" presents some of our preliminary estimates of discounted and unrecorded unemployment.

TABLE 8

Real Unemployment in the United States, 1971
(Preliminary Estimates)

	MILLIONS
1. Official labor force (including Armed Forces)	85.8
2. Gainfully employed (including Armed Forces)	81.1
3. Official unemployment	
a. Numbers	4.7
b. As percentage of civilian labor force	5.7%
4. Unofficial unemployment	
I. Disclosed but set aside	
a. Underemployed	2.7
b. Job wanters	
1. Discouraged	.8
2. Encourageable	3.6
II. Hidden and ignored	
c. Unemployables	1.0
d. Housewives	5.0
e. Men (25–54)	.5
f. Older people (55 and over)	4.0
g. Students	3.0
h. Enrollees in manpower programs	.3
Subtotal (4)	20.9
5. Real labor force (1 plus 4, excluding underemployed)	104
6. Real unemployment	
a. Millions	25.6
b. As percentage of real labor force	24.6%

EXPLANATION OF TABLE

1. *Official labor force*—The Armed Forces are included in order to provide perspective on shifts from military to civilian employment. The institutional population, about two million, is excluded—a questionable omission considering the many very low paying jobs held by the resident population.[1]

2. *Gainfully employed*—Refers solely to jobs involving direct cash payment. It does not include the unpaid work performed by about 35.4 million persons, mostly women, who are not in the labor force and are engaged in "keeping house," or the millions more who hold paid jobs and also keep house.[2]

3. *Official unemployment*—Based upon official Department of Labor categories, which consider only those persons who do not have a job at the current time, but who are available for work and have conducted an active search for a job during the four-week period preceding the Current Population Survey.[3]

4. *Unofficial unemployment*—Refers to those people who are able and willing to work and would be seeking jobs, either full- or part-time, if suitable opportunities were available. Suitability is a complex matter involving the nature of the work, pay, status, working conditions, and opportunities for personal growth and advancement. Millions of people, especially older people and housewives, who would not be available for full-time jobs, would be very available and most eager for part-time employment. Another aspect of suitability relates to the provision of services that would facilitate job holding, such as adequate day-care arrangements.

In our consideration of unofficial unemployment, we build upon the knowledge and evidence provided by the Depart-

[1] *Statistical Abstract of the United States, 1971*, Table 327, p. 210.
[2] *Ibid.*
[3] *Ibid.*

ment of Labor—knowledge that has been "disclosed but set aside"—and supplement this with our own estimates of additional hidden and ignored unemployment. What follows is a discussion of each of these eight categories, along with an explanation of the basis for our estimates. We have not considered all of the people not in the labor force who might be likely to be unofficially unemployed. For example, young people not attending school who are also not in the labor force, disabled people not on public assistance who are not in the labor force, and so forth. There also exists overlap and double counting between some of the groups—for example, (b) job wanters, (c) unemployables, and (d) housewives. Nevertheless, we present these groups in the following manner because they represent a clear delineation of the non-labor force population according to the major activities pursued.

I. *Disclosed but set aside:*

a. *Underemployed*—The national figure of 2.7 million refers to the more limited underemployment of those who are working part-time and desire full-time jobs.[4] These people are included in official labor force data and are counted as employed. This figure, based on a quarterly survey by the Labor Department, does not include the many millions more who are underutilized in jobs below the level for which they are trained or capable. We are also not considering the concept of subemployment, which is a special form of labor force analysis applied to urban areas with high percentages of the poor and minority groups. Subemployment subsumes underemployment and also consists of unemployment, 50 percent of male non-labor force participants in this area, numbers of males not reflected in the Census undercount, and those earning substandard incomes. Recent studies indicate that the rate of subemployment in sixty poverty areas located in fifty-one cities is about 61 percent.

[4] *Manpower Report of the President,* 1972, Table 825, p. 190.

b. *Job wanters not in the labor force*—The national figure of 4.4 million appears in the *Manpower Report of the President 1972*.[5] This category has been applied by the Department of Labor since 1967 and has been part of research on "persons not in the labor force, by desire for jobs and reason for nonparticipation." The group was divided into those who stated they were not seeking employment because they "think they cannot get a job"—discouraged workers—and those who cited a variety of other reasons for not seeking work (school, home responsibility, ill health)—encourageable workers. We consider both the discouraged and encourageables as the groups most likely to seek jobs if suitable opportunities were available. Together with the underemployed they total 7.1 million people who are disclosed as a result of official surveys, but are set aside and not included in the statistics on official unemployment.

II. *Hidden and ignored unemployment*—This refers to the millions of other persons who have been excluded from the official figures on unemployment.

c. *Unemployables*—This refers to recipients of public assistance, most of whom have been classified as unemployable in order to meet legal eligibility requirements. Of course, we have always known that this was not a true description of the population. Many are now being compelled to admit the duplicity of our statistical categorization—both liberals and conservatives who cooperated in this fiction out of a marriage of political convenience. *Statistical Abstract of the United States*[6] reports 3.2 million adult recipients of ADC and general assistance. This figure does not include the old, blind, or permanently disabled, who number another 3.1 million. We are conservatively estimating that one million members of the former group would desire employment if suitable opportunities were presented.

---

[5] *Ibid.*, Table A-8, p. 167.
[6] *Statistical Abstract of the United States, 1971*, Table 463, p. 91.

d. *Housewives*—35.4 million persons were reported as not in the labor force and keeping house.[7] We conservatively estimate that about one in seven of this group would desire jobs if suitable employment were available. Labor force participation rates have been increasing for women at all ages. Of late the increase has been greatest for young women in their twenties. There exists some overlap between this group and the ADC mothers who are included under unemployables.

e. *Men* (25–54)—There are about 1.6 million men between the ages of twenty-five to fifty-four who do not participate in the labor force.[8] About 100,000 have already been referred to under the heading job wanters. We conservatively estimate that about one in three, .5 million, would enter the labor force if suitable opportunities were presented.

f. *Older people*—7.2 million persons between the ages of fifty-five to sixty-four were nonparticipants in the labor force in 1971, of whom 1.6 million were males. An additional 16.2 million aged sixty-five and over were nonparticipants.[9] The push out and drop out rates are higher among the fifty-five to sixty-four age group. Workers in this group are encouraged to retire early and are also discouraged from seeking employment when they lose their jobs. Enforced retirement and leisure serve the same function that schooling does for the young. We are making a *very* conservative estimate that about one in five of the fifty-five to sixty-four age group would seek a job if suitable opportunities were available, resulting in an increase of 1.5 million to real unemployment figures.

g. *Students*—9.2 million persons over the age of sixteen were reported as not in the labor force and enrolled in school.[10] We are estimating that about a third of this group

[7] *Ibid.*, Table 327, p. 210.
[8] *Manpower Report of the President, 1972.*
[9] *Ibid.*, Table A-7, p. 166.
[10] *Statistical Abstract of the United States, 1971*, Table 327, p. 210.

would desire a job if suitable opportunities were presented. The schooling system has been developed as an alternative to labor market participation for the young. This has resulted in higher participation rates for each age group, a lengthening of the educational careers of the young, and often undesired extension of adolescence. The latter especially results from insufficient job opportunities. Many of the young are marking time in school and would prefer a job.

h. *Enrollees in manpower programs*—About 500,000 were enrolled in these programs in 1971. This does not include the 700,000 who are involved in various aspects of the Neighborhood Youth Corps, many of whom are in school and therefore considered under the heading of students. We conservatively estimate that 60 percent of this group would prefer a suitable job over participation in a training program, resulting in an increase of .3 million to the real unemployment figures. Manpower programs represent a new system of schooling designed to make people employable. While it often may not accomplish that purpose, it certainly does achieve the goal of keeping people out of the labor market and official unemployment calculations by developing another schooling system.

5. *Real labor force*—Our concept of real labor force differs from the concept of work potential. The work potential of a society refers to the fact that all people are capable of performing some kind of work and could be mobilized to do so during periods of national crisis or emergency. Our estimates for real labor force and real unemployment extend traditional concepts and categories to include those groups who do not participate in the labor force because they have been pushed out, dropped out, or discouraged, and who would be most likely to seek work if suitable opportunities were presented.

6. *Real unemployment*—This is the total of those disclosed by official unemployment data plus those who have been disclosed but set aside and those who have been hidden and ignored. We have deliberately presented conservative esti-

mates; we haven't even projected a figure for older workers over sixty-five. We believe that our figures reflect a truer picture of the extent to which the current economic system has failed to generate an adequate number of jobs to meet the needs and desires of people.

APPENDIX V

Ethnic Groups and Social Status

THE following tables are illustrative of the difficulty in making uncontestable mobility assessments.

Progress is at once both relative and absolute; incomes can be seen to increase and, frequently, material possession can be seen to increase too—even among those parts of the population where it is clear that mobility has been a much more selective phenomenon than our conventional wisdom about immigrant success has claimed.

Tables 9, 10, and 11, compiled by Nathan Glazer and Daniel Moynihan from U.S. Census reports, show that by 1950 the vast majority of immigrants and their children living in the New York metropolitan area worked in low-status, unskilled employment.

Table 12, Andrew Greeley's compilation of data derived from a NORC survey and Current Population Reports Numbers 220 and 221 (1971), shows the very high proportion of the white-ethnic population earning below $10,000 per annum. Furthermore, it shows—surprisingly enough—the high percentage of such persons even among those groups with the highest evidence of $15,000-plus earnings; for example, Jews and Orientals.

Table 13, from S. M. Miller and Pamela Roby's *The Future of Inequality*, shows the severe inequality characterizing the

373

nationwide income distribution which income and status based on ethnic categories derive from.

TABLE 9

Occupations of Immigrants from Italy and Their Children, New York–Northeastern New Jersey Standard Metropolitan Area, 1950

	MALE (PER CENT)		FEMALE (PER CENT)	
	IMMI-GRANTS	CHILDREN OF IMMIGRANTS	IMMI-GRANTS	CHILDREN OF IMMIGRANTS
Professional, technical, and kindred	3	6	2	5
Managers, officials, and proprietors	13	10	4	2
Clerical, sales, and kindred	6	17	8	40
Craftsmen, foremen, and kindred	24	22	2	2
Operatives and kindred	24	29	77	44
Private household workers	—	—	1	—
Service workers, excluding private household workers	14	6	4	4
Laborers	14	9	—	—
Occupation not reported	1	1	1	1
Total employed, in thousands	197	370	52	177

Source: *United States Census of Population, 1950, Nativity and Parentage,* Table 22.

TABLE 10

*Occupations of Immigrants from the U.S.S.R. and Their
Children, New York–Northeastern New Jersey Standard
Metropolitan Area, 1950*

	MALE (PER CENT)		FEMALE (PER CENT)	
	IMMI-GRANTS	CHILDREN OF IMMIGRANTS	IMMI-GRANTS	CHILDREN OF IMMIGRANTS
Professional, technical, and kindred	9	19	8	16
Managers, officials, and proprietors	32	27	12	8
Clerical, sales, and kindred	14	28	28	63
Craftsmen, foremen, and kindred	16	10	2	1
Operatives and kindred	23	12	40	8
Private household workers	—	—	2	—
Service workers, excluding private household workers	4	3	6	3
Laborers	2	1	—	—
Occupation not reported	2	1	1	1
Total employed, in thousands	130	217	30	81

Source: *United States Census of Population, 1950, Nativity and Parentage,* Table 22.

TABLE 11

*Occupations of Immigrants from Ireland and Their Children,
New York–Northeastern New Jersey Standard
Metropolitan Area, 1950*

	MALE (PER CENT)		FEMALE (PER CENT)	
	IMMI-GRANTS	CHILDREN OF IMMIGRANTS	IMMI-GRANTS	CHILDREN OF IMMIGRANTS
Professional, technical, and kindred	3	10	9	15
Managers, officials, and proprietors	8	11	3	3
Clerical, sales, and kindred	13	26	16	58
Craftsmen, foremen, and kindred	20	18	1	2
Operatives and kindred	20	15	11	10
Private household workers	—	—	24.5	2
Service, excluding private household workers	23	14	34	9
Laborers	11	6	1	—
Occupation not reported	1	1	—	1
Total employed, in thousands	59	139	31	76

Source: *United States Census of Population, 1950, Nativity and Parentage,* Table 22.

TABLE 12

Family Income and Ethnic Identification
(Per Cent)

RELIGIO-ETHNIC GROUP	UNDER $4,000	$4,000– $9,999	$10,000– $14,999	$15,000 PLUS
Protestant				
British	20.0	47.7	21.0	11.4
German	20.6	51.9	18.7	8.7
Scandinavian	21.6	49.1	21.3	8.0
Irish	30.2	46.7	15.7	7.5
Other	28.2	47.2	16.0	8.6
Catholic				
Irish	11.9	51.0	21.5	15.7
German	12.7	52.5	22.5	12.3
Italian	20.6	50.9	18.7	9.8
Polish	19.4	49.6	25.6	5.4
Slavic	20.2	54.3	18.4	7.2
French	24.2	50.3	18.1	7.4
Spanish-Speaking	33.3	51.3	14.5	0.9
Other	20.1	49.7	20.4	9.9
Jews				
German	19.2	38.5	23.1	19.2
East European	9.5	38.8	19.0	32.7
Other	16.3	27.9	18.6	37.2
Blacks	47.5	40.5	8.1	3.9
Orientals	16.7	66.7	0.0	16.7
No Religion	22.0	37.9	20.9	19.1
Other Religion	30.1	40.6	16.8	12.6
Total	25.8	47.3	17.4	9.5

From: Andrew Greeley, "Ethnic Demographic Data" (1973), mimeographed.

TABLE 13

Distribution of Total Money Income Received by Each Fifth and the Top 5 Per Cent of Families and Unrelated Individuals, 1947 to 1967 (Total Money Income)

			FAMILY INCOME	(PERCENTAGES)			
YEAR	TOTAL	LOWEST FIFTH	SECOND FIFTH	MIDDLE FIFTH	FOURTH FIFTH	HIGHEST FIFTH	TOP 5
1967	100.0	5.4	12.2	17.5	23.7	41.2	15.3
1966	100.0	5.5	12.4	17.7	23.7	40.7	14.8
1965	100.0	5.3	12.1	17.7	23.7	41.3	15.8
1964	100.0	5.2	12.0	17.6	24.0	41.1	15.4
1963	100.0	5.1	12.1	17.6	23.6	41.6	15.8
1962	100.0	5.1	12.0	17.3	23.8	41.7	16.3
1961	100.0	4.8	11.7	17.4	23.6	42.5	17.2
1960	100.0	4.9	12.0	17.7	23.4	42.1	16.9
1959	100.0	5.1	12.1	17.8	23.6	41.4	16.3
1958	100.0	5.1	12.4	17.8	23.7	41.0	15.8
1957	100.0	5.0	12.6	18.1	23.7	40.5	15.8
1956	100.0	4.9	12.4	17.9	23.6	41.1	16.4
1955	100.0	4.8	12.2	17.7	23.4	41.8	16.8
1954	100.0	4.5	12.0	17.6	24.0	41.9	16.4
1953	100.0	4.7	12.4	17.8	24.0	41.0	15.8
1952	100.0	4.9	12.2	17.1	23.5	42.2	17.7
1951	100.0	4.9	12.5	17.6	23.3	41.8	16.9
1950	100.0	4.5	11.9	17.4	23.6	42.7	17.3
1949	100.0	4.5	11.9	17.3	23.5	42.8	16.9
1948	100.0	5.0	12.1	17.2	23.2	42.5	17.1
1947	100.0	5.1	11.8	16.7	23.2	43.3	17.5

TABLE 13 (*Continued*)

UNRELATED INDIVIDUAL INCOME (PERCENTAGES)

YEAR	TOTAL	LOWEST FIFTH	SECOND FIFTH	MIDDLE FIFTH	FOURTH FIFTH	HIGHEST FIFTH	TOP 5
1967	100.0	3.0	7.5	13.3	24.4	51.8	22.0
1966	100.0	2.8	7.5	13.2	23.8	52.7	22.5
1965	100.0	2.6	7.6	13.5	25.1	51.2	20.2
1964	100.0	2.6	7.0	12.9	24.3	53.2	22.5
1963	100.0	2.6	7.2	12.5	24.6	53.0	21.2
1962	100.0	3.3	7.3	12.5	24.1	52.8	21.3
1961	100.0	2.9	6.8	12.8	24.2	53.3	22.6
1960	100.0	3.0	7.0	13.3	25.7	51.0	20.3
1959	100.0	2.5	6.9	12.8	23.9	53.8	23.2
1958	100.0	2.6	7.0	13.0	24.9	52.5	21.4
1957	100.0	2.9	7.2	13.6	25.3	51.0	19.7
1956	100.0	2.9	6.9	13.7	25.3	51.3	20.4
1955	100.0	2.4	7.3	13.4	24.8	52.0	21.9
1954	100.0	2.5	7.2	12.7	24.5	53.0	22.8
1953	100.0	2.3	6.8	13.5	24.4	53.0	25.3
1952	100.0	2.5	7.5	14.7	25.4	50.0	20.8
1951	100.0	2.9	7.0	14.1	26.7	49.4	18.2
1950	100.0	3.1	6.9	13.1	26.6	50.3	19.3
1949	100.0	3.2	7.4	13.4	25.9	50.2	19.4
1948	100.0	3.3	7.5	13.4	24.9	50.9	20.6
1947	100.0	2.9	5.4	11.5	21.3	58.9	33.3

Source: U.S. Bureau of the Census, *Trends in the Income of Families and Persons in the United States: 1947–1964*, Technical Paper No. 17 by Mary F. Henson (Washington, D.C.: U.S. Government Printing Office, 1967), pp. 176–181; data for years 1965–1967 from U.S. Bureau of the Census, *Current Population Reports,* Series P-60, No. 59, April 18, 1969, Table 25, p. 24.

BIBLIOGRAPHY

BIBLIOGRAPHY*

PART I

BOOKS

Ander, O. F. (ed.). *In the Trek of the Immigrants*. Rock Island, Ill.: Augustana College Library, 1964.

Bailey, Harry A., and Katz, Ellis (ed.). *Ethnic Group Politics*. Columbus, Ohio: Charles Merrill, 1969.

Baroni, Geno C. (ed.). *All Men Are Brothers*. Washington, D.C.: U.S. Catholic Conference, 1970.

Bell, Daniel (ed.). *The Radical Right*. New York: Doubleday, 1964.

Bernard, William S. (ed.). *American Immigration Policy—A Reappraisal*. New York: Harper and Row, 1950.

Brody, David. *Steelworkers in America*. New York: Russell and Russell, 1970.

Commager, Henry Steele (ed.). *Immigration and American History*. Minneapolis: University of Minnesota Press, 1961.

Dahl, Robert A. *Who Governs?* New Haven: Yale University Press, 1961.

Eisenstadt, S. N. *The Absorption of Immigrants*. Glencoe, Ill.: Free Press, 1955.

Feinstein, Otto. *Ethnic Groups in the City*. Lexington, Mass.: Heath/Lexington Books, 1971.

Fellows, Donald K. *A Mosaic of America's Ethnic Minorities*. New York: Wiley, 1972.

Fishman, Joshua A. (ed.). *Language Loyalty in the United States*. London: Mouton, 1966.

Fuchs, Lawrence H. (ed.). *American Ethnic Politics*. New York: Harper and Row, 1968.

Gans, Herbert J. *The Urban Villagers*. Glencoe, Ill.: Free Press, 1962.

Glazer, Nathan, and Moynihan, Daniel P. *Beyond the Melting Pot*. Cambridge, Mass.: M.I.T. Press, 1963.

Gordon, Milton M. *Assimilation in American Life*. New York: Oxford University Press, 1964.

* This bibliography is divided into two parts. The first consists of general works in the field. The second consists of books and articles that deal with specific groups.

Greeley, Andrew M. *Why Can't They Be Like Us?* New York: Dutton, 1971.

Greer, Colin. *Cobweb Attitudes: Essays on American Education and Culture.* New York: Teachers College Press, Columbia University, 1970.

———. *The Great School Legend: A Revisionist Interpretation of American Public Education.* New York: Basic Books, 1972.

Handlin, Oscar. *Boston Immigrants, 1790–1865: A Study in Acculturation.* Cambridge, Mass.: Harvard University Press, 1959.

——— (ed.). *Children of the Uprooted.* New York: Braziller, 1966.

———. *Race and Nationality in American Life.* Boston: Little, Brown, 1957.

———. *The Uprooted.* New York: Grosset and Dunlap, 1951.

Hansen, Marcus L. *The Immigrant in American History.* Cambridge, Mass.: Harvard University Press, 1940.

Hawkins, Brett W., and Lorinskas, Robert A. (ed.). *The Ethnic Factor in American Politics.* Columbus, Ohio: Charles Merrill, 1970.

Herberg, Will. *Protestant-Catholic-Jew.* New York: Doubleday, 1955.

Herskovitz, Melville J. *Acculturation: The Study of Culture Contact.* Gloucester, Mass.: Peter Smith, 1941.

Higham, John. *Strangers in the Land: Patterns of American Nativism, 1860–1925.* New York: Atheneum, 1968.

Hourwich, Isaac. *Immigration and Labor.* New York: B. W. Huebsch, 1922.

Hutchinson, E. P. *Immigrants and Their Children, 1850–1950.* New York: Wiley, 1956.

Huthmacher, J. Joseph. *Massachusetts People and Politics, 1919–1933.* Cambridge, Mass.: Harvard University Press, 1959.

Kallen, Horace M. *Cultural Pluralism and the American Idea.* Philadelphia: University of Pennsylvania Press, 1956.

———. *Culture and Democracy in the United States.* New York: Boni and Liveright, 1922.

Kraus, Michael. *Immigration, the American Mosaic: From Pilgrims to Modern Refugees.* Princeton: Van Nostrand, 1966.

Lenski, Gerhard. *The Religious Factor: A Social Inquiry.* New York: Doubleday, 1961.

Levitan, Sar A. (ed.). *Blue Collar Workers.* New York: McGraw-Hill, 1971.

Lieberson, Stanley. *Ethnic Patterns in American Cities; A Comparative Study Using Data from Ten Urban Centers.* New York: Free Press, 1963.

Lonn, Ella. *Foreigners in the Confederacy.* Gloucester, Mass.: Peter Smith, 1965.

Lubell, Samuel. *The Future of American Politics.* 3d. ed. New York: Harper and Row, 1965.

Bibliography

Miller, S. M., and Roby, Pamela. *The Future of Inequality.* New York: Basic Books, 1970.

Moynihan, Daniel P. *On Understanding Poverty.* New York: Basic Books, 1967.

Novak, Michael. *The Rise of the Unmeltable Ethnics.* New York: Macmillan, 1972.

Park, Robert E. *The Immigrant Press and Its Control.* Westport: Greenwood, 1922.

Patterson, S. *Immigrants in Industry.* New York: Oxford University Press, 1968.

Phillips, Kevin P. *The Emerging Republican Majority.* New Rochelle, N.Y.: Arlington House, 1969.

Plumb, J. H. *In the Light of History.* Boston: Houghton-Mifflin, 1972.

Rose, Peter (ed.). *Nation of Nations: The Ethnic Experience and the Racial Crisis.* New York: Random House, 1972.

––––––. *They and We: Racial and Ethnic Relations in the United States.* New York: Random House, 1964.

Saveth, Edward. *American Historians and European Immigration.* New York: Columbia University Press, 1948.

Schoener, Allen. *Portals to America.* Minneapolis: University of Minnesota Press, 1967.

Schrag, Peter. *The Decline of the WASP.* New York: Simon and Schuster, 1971.

Segal, Bernard E. (ed.). *Racial and Ethnic Relations.* New York: Thomas Crowell, 1966.

Sennett, Richard. *The Uses of Disorder.* Cambridge, Mass.: Harvard University Press, 1970.

–––––– and Cobb, Jonathan. *The Hidden Injuries of Class.* New York: Knopf, 1972.

Shibutani, Tamotsu, and Kwan, Kian M. *Ethnic Stratification.* New York: Macmillan, 1965.

Simirenko, Alex. *Pilgrims, Colonists, and Frontiersmen.* New York: Free Press, 1964.

Solomon, Barbara. *Ancestors and Immigrants.* Cambridge, Mass.: Harvard University Press, 1956.

Steinfield, Melvin. *Cracks in the Melting Pot.* Beverly Hills: Glencoe Press, 1970.

Thomas, Brinley. *Migration and Economic Growth.* New York: Cambridge University Press, 1954.

Vander Zanden, James W. *American Minority Relations: The Sociology of Race and Ethnic Groups.* New York: Ronald Press, 1966.

Warner, W. Lloyd, and Srole, Leo. *The Social Systems of American Ethnic Groups.* New Haven: Yale University Press, 1945.

Wheeler, Thomas (ed.). *The Immigrant Experience: The Anguish of Becoming American.* New York: Penguin, 1971.

Wittke, Carl. *We Who Built America*. New York: Prentice-Hall, 1939.

Yinger, J. Milton. *A Minority Group in American Society*. New York: McGraw-Hill, 1965.

Zangwill, Israel. *The Melting Pot, a Play*. New York: Macmillan, 1923.

ARTICLES

Aronowitz, Stanley. "The Working Class: A Break with the Past," *Liberation* (August 1972).

Duncan, Otis Dudley, and Lieberson, Stanley. "Ethnic Segregation and Assimilation," *American Journal of Sociology* (January 1959).

"Ethnic Groups in American Life." Special Issue. *Daedalus* (Spring 1961).

Francis, E. K. "The Nature of the Ethnic Group," *American Journal of Sociology* (1945).

Glaser, Daniel. "Dynamics of Ethnic Identification," *American Sociological Review* (1958).

Glazer, Nathan. "Blacks and White Ethnics: The Difference, and the Political Difference It Makes," *Social Problems* (Spring 1971).

———. "Ethnic Groups in America," in Monroe Berger, Theodore Abel, and Charles H. Page (eds.), *Freedom and Control in Modern Society*. New York: Van Nostrand, 1954.

———. "The Street Gangs and Ethnic Enterprise," *Public Interest* (Summer 1972).

Gleason, Phillip. "The Melting-Pot: Symbol of Fusion or Confusion?" *American Quarterly* (Spring 1964).

Goering, John M. "The Emergence of Ethnic Interests," *Social Forces* (March 1971).

Greeley, Andrew M. "Ethnic Demographic Data," (1973) mimeographed.

Greene, Victor. "For God and Country," *Church History* (December 1966). .

Handlin, Oscar, *et al.* "Ethnic Groups in American Life," *Daedalus* (Spring 1961).

Jencks, Christopher, and Riesman, David. "On Class in America," *Public Interest* (Winter 1968).

Larsen, Karen. "Review of Oscar Handlin's *The Uprooted*," *American Historical Review* (April 1952).

Lerner, Michael. "Respectable Bigot," *American Scholar* (August 1969).

Levine, Irving, and Herman, Judith. "The Life of White Ethnics," *Dissent* (Winter 1972).

Lieberson, Stanley. "Suburbs and Ethnic Residential Patterns," *American Journal of Sociology* (May 1962).

Nam, Charles. "Nationality Groups and Social Stratification in America," *Social Forces* (May 1959).

Parenti, Michael. "Ethnic Politics and the Persistence of Ethnic Identification," *American Political Science Review* (September 1967).

Bibliography

Rosenthal, Eric. "Acculturation Without Assimilation," *American Journal of Sociology* (November 1960).

Spear, Allan. "Marcus Lee Hansen," *Wisconsin Magazine of History* (Summer 1961).

Vecoli, Rudolph J. "Ethnicity: The Neglected Dimension of American History." Paper presented to the Organization of American Historians, 1969.

Weber, Max. "The Ethnic Group," in Talcot Parsons (ed.), *Theories of Society*. Vol. 1. Glencoe, Ill.: Free Press, 1961.

PART II

BOOKS

Anderson, Charles H. *White Protestant Americans*. Englewood Cliffs, N.J.: Prentice-Hall, 1970.

Berthoff, Rowland. *British Immigrants in Industrial Society, America 1790–1950*. Cambridge, Mass.: Harvard University Press, 1953.

Birmingham, Stephen. *Our Crowd*. New York: Harper and Row, 1968.

Blassingame, John. *The Slave Community*. New York: Oxford University Press, 1972.

Blegen, T. C. *Norwegian Migration to America*. Northfield, Minn.: Norwegian-American Historical Foundation, 1940.

Boewe, Charles. *Prairie Albion: An English Settlement in Pioneer Illinois*. Carbondale, Ill.: Southern Illinois University Press, 1962.

Broehl, Wayne G., Jr. *The Molly Maguires*. Cambridge, Mass.: Harvard University Press, 1964.

Brotz, Howard. *Black Jews of Harlem*. New York: Schocken, 1970.

Cada, Joseph. *Czech-American Catholics, 1850–1920*. Lisle, Ill.: St. Procopius College, 1964.

Capek, Thomas. *The Czechs in America*. New York: Arno Press, 1969.

Chiu, Ping. *Chinese Labor in California, 1850–1880, an Economic Study*. Madison: University of Wisconsin, 1963.

Clark, Kenneth B. *Dark Ghetto*. New York: Harper and Row, 1965.

Cole, Donald B. *Immigrant City: Lawrence, Massachusetts, 1845–1921*. Chapel Hill: University of North Carolina Press, 1963.

Conway, Alan. *The Welsh in America: Letters from the Immigrants*. Minneapolis: University of Minnesota Press, 1961.

Dowie, J. Iverne. *The Swedish Immigrant Community*. Rock Island, Ill.: Augustana Historical Society, 1963.

Dvornik, Francis. *Czech Contributions to the Growth of the United States*. Chicago: Benedictine Abbey Press, 1961.

Finkelstein, Louis. *The Jews*. Philadelphia: Jewish Publication Society, 1949.

Frazier, E. Franklin. *The Negro Family in the U.S.* New York: Macmillan, 1957.

Glanz, Rudolph. *Jew and Irish.* New York: Waldon, 1966.

Gleason, Philip. *The Conservative Reformers: German-American Catholics and the Social Order.* Notre Dame, Ind.: University of Notre Dame Press, 1968.

Greeley, Andrew W. *That Most Distressful Nation: The American Irish.* New York: Quadrangle, 1972.

Greene, Victor R. *The Slavic Community on Strike.* Notre Dame, Ind.: University of Notre Dame Press, 1968.

Harlan, Louis R. *Booker T. Washington.* New York: Oxford University Press, 1972.

Haugen, Einar. *The Norwegian Language in America: A Study of Bilingual Behavior.* Philadelphia: University of Pennsylvania Press, 1953.

Hawgood, John A. *The Tragedy of German America.* New York: Putnam, 1940.

Herskovitz, Melville J. *The Myth of the Negro Past.* Boston: Beacon Press, 1958.

Hoglund, A. William. *Finnish Immigrants in America.* Madison: University of Wisconsin Press, 1960.

Hsu, Francis L. *Americans and Chinese: Purpose and Fulfillment.* New York: Natural History Press, 1970.

Huebener, Theodore. *The Germans in America.* Philadelphia: Chilton, 1962.

King, Irene M. *John O. Meusbach: German Colonizer in Texas.* Austin: University of Texas Press, 1967.

Kung, S. W. *Chinese in American Life: Some Aspects of Their History, Status, Problems, and Contributions.* Seattle: University of Washington Press, 1962.

Lee, Rose Hum. *The Chinese in the United States of America.* Cambridge: Oxford University Press, 1960.

Levine, Edward M. *The Irish and Irish Politicians.* Notre Dame, Ind.: University of Notre Dame Press, 1966.

Lewis, Oscar. *La Vida.* New York: Random House, 1965.

Leyburn, James. *The Scotch-Irish: A Social History.* Chapel Hill: University of North Carolina Press, 1962.

Light, Ivan H. *Ethnic Enterprise Among Chinese, Japanese, and Blacks.* Berkeley: University of California Press, 1973.

Lopreato, Joseph. *Italian Americans.* New York: Random House, 1970.

Morley, Charles (ed.). *Portrait of America: Letters of Henry Sienkiewicz.* New York: Columbia University Press, 1959.

Nelli, Humbert S. *The Italians in Chicago, 1880–1930.* New York: Oxford University Press, 1970.

Olson, N. W. (ed.). *A Pioneer in Northwest America, 1841–1858: The Memoirs of Gustav Unonius.* Minneapolis: University of Minnesota Press, 1960.

Bibliography

Peterson, William. *Japanese Americans*. New York: Random House, 1971.

Portal, Roger. *The Slavs*. New York: Harper and Row, 1969.

Powell, Summer Chilton. *Puritan Village: The Formation of a New England Town*. Middletown, Conn.: Wesleyan University Press, 1963.

Rischin, Moses. *The Promised City: New York's Jews, 1870–1914*. Cambridge, Mass.: Harvard University Press, 1962.

Saloutos, Theodore. *The Greeks in the United States*. New York: Teachers College Press, Columbia University, 1967.

Scheiner, Seth M. *Negro Mecca: A History of the Negro in New York City, 1865–1920*. New York: New York University Press, 1965.

Schreiber, William I. *Our Amish Neighbors*. Chicago: University of Chicago Press, 1962.

Schrier, Arnold. *Ireland and American Emigration*. Minneapolis: University of Minnesota Press, 1958.

Schulz, David. *Coming Up Black*. Englewood Cliffs, N.J.: Prentice-Hall, 1969.

Shepperson, Wilbur S. *Emigration and Disenchantment: Portraits of Englishmen Repatriated from the United States*. Norman: Oklahoma University Press, 1965.

Sklare, Marshall (ed.). *The Jews: Social Patterns of an American Group*. New York: Free Press, 1958.

Szczepanski, Jan. *Polish Society*. New York: Random House, 1970.

Thomas, William I., and Znaniecki, Florian. *The Polish Peasant in Europe and America*. Chicago: University of Chicago Press, 1918; New York: Knopf, 1928, Dover, 1958.

Tomasi, Silvano (ed.). *The Italian Experience in America*. Staten Island, N.Y.: Center for Migration Studies, 1970.

Walker, Mack. *Germany and the Emigration, 1816–1885*. Cambridge, Mass.: Harvard University Press, 1964.

Wittke, Carl. *Germans in America*. New York: Teachers College Press, 1967.

Wytrwal, Joseph A. *America's Polish Heritage: A Social History of the Poles in America*. Detroit: Endurance Press, 1961.

ARTICLES

Bøhn,Tora. "A Quest for Norwegian Folk Art in America," *Norwegian American Studies and Records* (1956).

Cowan, Paul. "Jews Without Money, Revisited," *The Village Voice* (September 1972).

Fenton, Edwin. "Italians in the Labor Movement," *Pennsylvania History* (April 1959).

Glazer, Nathan. "Negroes and Jews: The New Challenge to Pluralism," *Commentary* (December 1964).

Gorenstein, Arthur. "A Portrait of Ethnic Politics." American Jewish Historical Society Publication (April 1961).

Iwata, Masakazo. "The Japanese Immigrants in California Agriculture," *Agricultural History* (January 1962).

Meyer, Carl. "Lutheran Immigrant Churches Face the Frontier," *Church History* (December 1960).

Osofsky, Gilbert. "Hebrew Immigrants and Society." American Jewish Historical Society Publication (1960).

Price, George M. "The Russian Jews in America." American Jewish Historical Society Publication (1958).

Puzo, Mario. "Choosing a Dream," in Thomas Wheeler (ed.), *The Immigrant Experience*. New York: Penguin, 1971.

Rischin, Moses. "The Jewish Labor Movement in America: A Social Interpretation," *Labor History* (Fall 1963).

Saloutos, Theodore. "Exodus U.S.A.," in O. F. Ander (ed.), *In the Trek of the Immigrant*. Rock Island, Ill.: Augustana College Library, 1964.

Semmingen, I. "Norwegian Emigration in the Nineteenth Century," *The Scandinavian Economic History Review* (1960).

Spear, Allan. "Marcus Lee Hansen," *Wisconsin Magazine of History* (Summer 1961).

Vecoli, Rudolph J. "Contadini in Chicago: A Critique of *The Uprooted*," *Journal of American History* (December 1965).

Zatko, James J. "Slovaks in the U.S.A.," *Slovakia* (1966).

INDEX

Acculturation, 42, 46; of blacks, 335; and discrimination, 48, 50; of ethnic groups, 337; and immigration history of United States, 46, 48; and mobility, 48; and prejudice, 50; and spatial isolation and segregation, 48; and structural assimilation, 51

Adamic, Louis, 122–124

Addams, Jane, 16, 126, 221

A.F.L., 319 n., 320

A.F.L.-C.I.O., 354

Age, 209, 211

Ajisafe, A. K., 248

Amalgamated Clothing Workers, 319 n.

American character, 125, 127, 218

American Jewish Committee, 105–106

American Occupational Structure, The (Blau and Duncan), 364

American Railway Union (A.R.U.), 319

Amoral familism, 217, 226

Antin, Mary, 127

Archer, William, 205

Ardener, Shirley, 238

Assimilation: and acculturation, 42, 46, 48, 50, 51; agents of, 89–90; and Anglo-conformity, 25; attitude receptional, 42; behavior receptional, 42; civic, 42; complete form of, 40; cultural, 42, 46; and cultural pluralism, 25; and factories, 89–90; of foreign born, 9, 11, 12; identificational, 41, 42, 50; implications of, 75; major theories of, 25; marital, 42, 50; and melting

pot, 25; and mobility, 56, 59; nature of, 39; opportunity for, 65; and segregation, 63; structural, 41, 42, 50, 51; subprocesses of, 40, 41; and unions, 89–90; variables, 40, 42, 45

Austrian aliens: emigration after World War I, 154; emigration between 1908 and 1914, 137

Austro-Hungarian aliens, emigration of, 303

Baldwin, James, 95

Banton, Michael, 257

Bascom, W. R., 248, 249

Belgian immigrants, in textile mills, 168

Bell, Daniel, 313, 364

Belson, Frederick, 208

Bendix, Reinhard, 54

Beyond the Melting Pot (Glazer and Moynihan), 14

Black Hand, 222

Blacks: acculturation (cultural assimilation), 46, 48, 335; achievement rates, 66, 67; achievements since emancipation, 335; and American urbanization, 335; anti-Semitism, 95; as artisans, 197, 205, 211, 212; assimilation, 47, 60, 61, 65; as barbers, 199, 200, 202; in Britain, 252, 253; as carpenters, 200, 208; and caste, 91; as caterers, 199; and church, 214; and civil rights movement, 347, 351; as coachmen, 197, 199, 200; collaboration with other blocs of voters,

Index

school failure, 92, 93; as seamstresses, 197, 202; segregation of, 52–53, 61, 62, 338, 339, 351; self-help activities, 214; serial monogamy, 289; as servants, 198, 201, 202, 204, 206; and settlement workers, 28; in skilled trades, 198, 200, 203, 204, 207, 208, 209, 210, 211, 212; and slavery, 257, 335; and small businesses, 234, 235, 236, 237, 250, 251; social deprivations, 344; social mobility, 56, 60, 61, 62, 65; subordination, 338; in suburbs, 100; as successful businessmen, 237; support of immigration restriction proposals, 212; as teachers, 198; tokenism, 345; in trades, 202, 203, 204, 205, 206, 208, 209, 210; trade schools, 214; in transportation fields, 202, 203, 206, 210; truancy rates, 91; at turn of century, 84, 85, 93; unemployment, 213, 214, 344; unique educational problems, 92; unique position of, 334–335, 336; as unskilled workers (common laborers), 197, 200, 201, 203, 207, 212, 213, 344; and urban experience, 23; in urban ghettos, 8, 9; as waiters, 197, 199, 200, 201, 204, 205, 206, 208; West African, 239, 247; West Indian, 239, 249, 250, 251, 252, 253; and white liberalism, 97, 99, 101; women workers, 201, 204, 206, 207, 210, 212; Yoruba, 247
Blascoer, Frances, 91, 92
Blau, Peter M., 12, 54, 364
Bloch, H. D., 203
Bohemian immigrants and their descendents: attitudes toward, 264; as main competitors with blacks for jobs, 205
Boston's West End, 275–280

Brandt, Lillian, 87
Bridges, Harry, 99, 320
Brierley, Ben, 164
Brody, David, 316
Brogan, D. W., 125
Brotz, Howard, 107
Buckmaster, L. S., 320
Bulgarian immigrants and their descendents: emigration after World War I, 154; reasons for emigration, 141; in steel mills, 296, 304
Bulkley, William L., 85, 210
Bundy, William, 132
Bureau of the Census, 365

Campbell, Sir George, 199
Canadian immigrants and their descendents: and "immigrant problem," 175; settlements in U.S., 172–173, 174
Carey, James, 320
Carmichael, Stokeley, 25
Carnegie, Andrew, 127, 315, 316
Cather, Helen, 241, 242
Chicago *Daily News*, 354
Chinese immigrants and their descendents: in Boston, 279; *hui* (rotating credit associations), 239–243; mobility, 56; in New York City, 241, 242, 362; and rotating credit associations (*hui*), 239–243, 253, 254; in San Francisco, 241, 242; and small businesses, 236; *yueh-woey* custom, 242
C.I.O., 319
Civil rights movement, 98, 101, 347, 351
Clark, Helen, 241
Clark, Kenneth, 94, 95
Colored American Magazine, 211
Colored Mission, 201, 208, 209, 213
"Colored School Children" (Blascoer), 91

393

Immigrants (*continued*)
and urban ghettos, 8; and urban life, 301; and urban renewal, 266; in urban villages, 264, 266; view of America, 125; WASP cultural patterns as reference point, 43, 44; *see also* individual immigrant groups

Immigration: blacks' support of restriction on, 212; conservative influence of, 322; disorganizing effects of, 220; from 1820 to 1860, 73; government suppression of, 322, 323; and Great American Idea, 77; history of, 67–68; and humanitarianism, 82; and nationalism, 68, 69, 70, 75, 76, 80; and nativism, 51, 76, 77; open door on, 86; opponents of restrictions on, 77; prejudicial quotas, 356; and prosperity of American industry, 303; reasons for, 294–295, 314, 315, 321; restriction of, 75, 77, 125, 212; and schools, 87; unrestricted, 77; after World War I, 323

Integration, 34, 35; and blacks, 22–25, 31, 83; and educational needs of deprived children, 348; as elimination of differences, 341, 343; as false issue, 349; illogic of, 351; meanings of, 337; and racial balance, 334, 341, 346, 347, 348; ultimate model of, 345; versus desegregation, 341, 351

International Ladies Garment Workers, 319 n.

International Longshoreman's and Warehouseman's Union, 99

Interracial Council, 152

Irish and Irish Politicians, The (Levine), 178

Irish immigrants and their descendents: and alcoholism, 181; and antipathy toward blacks, 197–198; attitudes toward swarthier people, 126; and birth control, 183; "blue collar" status, 90; in Boston, 265, 275, 277, 279, 283; and Catholic church, 123, 180, 182, 183–186, 287; and community intactness, 19; comparative advancement of, 17; and desire to win, 180–181; displacing blacks in jobs, 198, 200, 201, 202; disproportionate power and influence in American Catholic church, 183–184; as domestics, 198, 200; domineering mothers, 182; as efficient employees, 138; emigration after World War I, 154; and ethnic consciousness, 13; in excavation and street work, 224; experiences of peasants, 335; family income, 377; family life and structure, 181, 182, 288; as foremen, 313–314, 316; immigration after Civil War, 51, 52; immigration in 1830s and 1840s, 162; immigration before 1861, 73, 74; immigration between 1875 and 1910, 53, 163; in Ireland, 288; matriarchal households and delinquency, 350; as miners, 170, 171, 318; mobility of, 13; and mother-son relationships, 287; occupational levels, 22; occupational status, 55, 57; occupations of, 17, 376; and paternal authority, 287; peer group society, 287; as policemen, 179; political activities of, 20; as political brokers, 126; and political system in Ireland, 179; politics of, 178–181; on railroads, 316; rapid rise in hierarchy of occupations, 317; relations with blacks, 96, 197–198; and religious "vocations,"

Index

291; persecution in Lithuania, 262; portrayal in early twentieth-century textbooks, 28; in poverty, 359–363; in printing trades, 194; rapid social mobility, 65; rate of progress, 344; reasons for immigration, 321; relations with blacks, 94–109; and religious laws concerning foods, 189; respect for clergy, 185; Russian, 17, 262, 344; self-hatred, 181; self-segregation, 63; shopkeepers, 291; skilled and semiskilled workmen, 192; and socialist movements, 326; so-social mobility, 56; in soda water business, 190; in steel mills, 297; stereotype of mother, 182; in union leadership, 319, 320; urban experience of, 21; vaudeville caricature of, 176; as victims of mob violence, 337
Johnson, James Weldon, 206
Jordon, Winthrop D., 258, 259
Jusserand, Jean A. J., 143, 145

Kallen, Horace, 26
King, Martin Luther, Jr., 346
Knight, O. A., 320
Kristol, Irving, 5
Ku Klux Klan, 337
Kulp, D. H., 239
Kurokawa, Minako, 246

Lansing, Robert, 143, 145
Laughing in the Jungle (Adamic), 123
Law and order, 131
Leong, Gor Yun, 243
Levi, Carlo, 217
Levine, Edwin, 178, 179, 180
Lewis, John L., 320
Lieberson, Stanley, 64
Lipset, S. M., 54
Lodge, Henry Cabot, 81

McDonald, J. S., 218
Magyar immigrants, in steel mills, 295
Malcolm X, 25
Manpower Report of the President 1972, 369
Marcuse, Herbert, 312
Markens, J., 189
Martin, Homer, 320
Marx, Karl, 261, 310, 313
Mason, George, 336
Matsui, Schichiro, 245
Maxwell, William Henry, 86, 87
Mayor's Unemployment Committee (New York City), 213
Melting pot, 25, 26, 44, 45, 65, 67, 75, 84, 86, 91, 122, 123, 129, 332
Mexican-Americans and their descendents: discrimination, 53; mobility achievements and assimilation, 59; segregation, 53; social mobility, 53
Mihailovitch, Lioubomir, 144, 145
Miller, Herbert A., 16
Miller, Kelly, 85
Miller, S. M., 373
Miller, Walter, 289
Miyamoto, S. F., 246
Mobility: and acculturation, 48; and assimilation, 59; difficulty in making assessments of, 373; economic, 4, 9, 17; educational, 65, 66; through ethnic identification, 30; and ethnicity, 22; and negative definition of self, 29; occupational, 54, 55, 58, 65, 66; opportunities for, 59; patterns, comparison of whites and nonwhites, 13; social, 9, 17, 56, 59, 61, 65, 321; and status incongruity, 270; upward, discontent caused by, 270
Money, Edward, 200
Morris, Charles, 209

Index

Index

Segregation (*continued*)
in North, 339; as response to
abolition of slavery, 338; as
response to dissolution of earlier
forms of stratification, 338; in
South, 338
Serbian immigrants and their descendents: inability to obtain
passports, 152; living quarters,
301; reasons for emigration, 141;
in steel mills, 295; during World
War I, 145
Serial monogamy, 289
Shannon, William, 19
Slater, Samuel, 161
Slavery: and abolitionists, 258,
259, 338; and attitude toward
poor laborers, 259, 260;
and blacks, 257, 335; and exploitation, 258, 260; and matrifocal families, 289, 290; and
poverty, 256, 257; and Quakers,
259; and racism, 255, 257, 258,
260, 261; roots in England, 256,
257; and Tudors, 256; white,
256
Slavic immigrants and their descendents: attitudes toward,
264; discharge by Pittsburgh
manufacturers in 1907, 138;
and ethnicity, 18; experience of,
123, 124; immigration in late
nineteenth century and early
twentieth century, 52; in mining, 171, 318; occupations of,
17; on railroads, 316; and religion, 123; salaries, 317; in steel
mills, 293, 304; unskilled workers, 315, 317
Slawson, John, 105
Slovak immigrants, in steel mills,
295
Social class, hidden injuries of,
268–274
Social mobility, 56, 65; and academic success, 17; and assimilation, 59; and cultural background, 17; and economic status,
17; of foreign born, 9; opportunity for, 65; persistence of,
17; from ranks of unskilled, 321;
and urban industrial societies,
61
Sons of Italy, 323, 356
Spanish aliens, emigration after
World War I, 150
Spanish-speaking immigrants and
their descendents, family in-
come of, 377
Status incongruity, 270
Steiner, Edward A., 139, 140
Structural pluralism, 27
Strutt, Jedediah, 259
Sung, Betty Lee, 242, 243
Syrian immigrants, in Boston, 279

Task Force on Urban Problems,
353
Textile Union, 319
Thernstrom, Stephan, 54, 61, 130,
131
Times, see *New York Times*
Tobin, Dan, 320
Tobin, James, 62
Tribune, see *New York Herald
Tribune*
Turkish aliens, emigration after
World War I, 154

Unemployment, 365–372; enrollees
in manpower programs, 371; hidden and ignored, 369–371;
housewives, 370; job wanters not
in the labor force, 369; men
(ages 25–54), 370; official, 366,
367; older people, 370; rate as
critical indication, 365; real, 371–
372; real labor force, 371; students, 370–371; and suitable
opportunities for employment,
367; undercount of, 366; and
underemployment, 368; unem-

404

Index

ployables, 369; unofficial, 366, 367; *see also* individual immigrant and ethnic groups
United Garment Workers, 319 n.
United Hebrew Charities, 191
United Mine Workers, 318
U.S. Catholic Bishops, 353
U.S. Department of Interior, 87
United Waiters' Mutual Beneficial Association, 199
Uprooted, The (Handlin), 7, 13, 31, 215, 219, 222, 331
Urban League, 92, 212, 213, 214
Urban villages, 264, 266, 276, 277, 356

Vecoli, Rudolph, 7, 16, 20

Wald, Lillian, 16
Washington, Booker T., 24, 25, 237
WASPs (White Anglo-Saxon Protestants), 29; cultural patterns as reference for immigrants, 43; and cultural pluralism, 133; different kinds of, 130; elements of culture, 126; and English conceptions, 132; and internalized order, 131, 132; and Irish immigrants, 183; lower-class, 130; newly rich, 133; northeastern establishment, 133; picture of, 33; and religion, 123; and stability, 131; and strict discipline, 131; traditions, 131, 132; upper class, 130, 131

Weber, Max, 40
Webster, D. Macon, 205
Wedgwood, Josiah, 259
Welsh immigrants and their descendents, 12; and "immigrant problem," 175; immigration from 1875 to 1910, 53; in mining, 170, 171, 316, 318; and native Americans, 176, 177; occupational status, 55; on railroads, 316; settlements in U.S., 173, 175; in textiles, 314, 316; in union leadership, 320
White, James C., 147
White Anglo-Saxon Protestants, *see* WASPs
White over Black (Jordon), 258
Wilson, James Q., 179
Wilson, Woodrow, 143
Working class, 283–287, 356; antagonisms within, 312; broadening of, 310; composition of, 310, 311; and education, 311; ethnic splits within, 313; fear of unemployment, 325; government suppression of, 322; homogeneous, 313; and immigrants, 313–326; incomes, 354; mobility within, 318; necessity for, 310; postwar, 327; and unions, 318–321, 324–325

Yugoslav aliens: emigration after World War I, 150, 153, 154; volunteers during World War I, 142, 144, 145, 146, 148

405